ALLYN & BACON
GUIDE TO WRITING

John D. Ramage
Arizona State University

John C. Bean
Seattle University

June Johnson
Seattle University

Third Custom Edition
University of Houston

Taken from:

Allyn & Bacon Guide to Writing, Fourth Edition
by John D. Ramage, John C. Bean, and June Johnson

PEARSON CUSTOM PUBLISHING
75 Arlington Street, Suite 300, Boston, MA 02116
A Pearson Education Company

Brief Contents

Detailed Contents

➤ **WRITING TO LEARN**

CHAPTER 18   Composing and Revising Closed-Form Prose   527

Posing Problems
The Demands of College Writing

It seems to me, then, that the way to help people become better writers is not to tell them that they must first learn the rules of grammar, that they must develop a four-part outline, that they must consult the experts and collect all the useful information. These things may have their place. But none of them is as crucial as having a good, interesting question.

—RODNEY KILCUP, *HISTORIAN*

Our purpose in this introductory chapter is to help you see writers as questioners and problem posers—a view of writing that we believe will lead to your greatest growth as a college-level thinker and writer. In particular, we want you to think of writers as people who pose interesting questions or problems and struggle to work out answers or responses to them. As we show in this chapter, writers pose two sorts of problems: *subject-matter problems* (for example, Should the homeless mentally ill be placed involuntarily in mental hospitals?) and *rhetorical problems* (for example, How much background about the homeless population does my audience need? What is their current attitude about mental institutions? What form and style should I use?).

We don't mean to make this focus on problems sound scary. Indeed, humans pose and solve problems all the time and often take great pleasure in doing so. Psychologists who study critical and creative thinking see problem solving as a productive and positive activity. According to one psychologist, "Critical thinkers are actively engaged with life. [. . .] They appreciate creativity, they are innovators, and they exude a sense that life is full of possibilities."* By focusing first on the kinds of problems that writers pose and struggle with, we hope to increase your own engagement and pleasure in becoming a writer.

In this chapter we introduce you to the following concepts and principles:

- Why a writing course is valuable, with special emphasis on the connection between writing and thinking

---

*Academic writers regularly document their sources. The standard method for documenting sources in student papers and in many professional scholarly articles is the MLA or the APA citation system explained in Chapter 22. In this text we have cited our sources in an "Acknowledgments" section. To find our source for this quotation (or for the quotation from Kilcup above), see the Acknowledgments at the end of the text.

- How writers pose subject-matter problems, in which they wrestle with the complexities of their topics
- How writers pose rhetorical problems, in which they must make decisions about content, organization, and style based on their purpose, audience, and genre
- How the rules of writing vary along a continuum from closed to open prose
- How to ask good subject-matter questions and show how they are problematic and significant

The chapter concludes with a brief writing assignment in which you can try your own hand at proposing a subject-matter question.

Why Take a Writing Course?

Before turning directly to the notion of writers as questioners and problem posers, let's ask why a writing course can be valuable for you.

For some people, being a writer is part of their identity, so much so that when asked, "What do you do?" they are apt to respond, "I'm a writer." Poets, novelists, scriptwriters, journalists, technical writers, grant writers, self-help book authors, and so on see themselves as writers the way other people see themselves as chefs, realtors, bankers, or musicians. But many people who don't think of themselves primarily as writers nevertheless *use* writing—often frequently—throughout their careers. They are engineers writing proposals or project reports; attorneys writing legal briefs; nurses writing patient assessments; business executives writing financial analyses or management reports; concerned citizens writing letters to the editor about public affairs; college professors writing articles for scholarly journals.

In our view, all these kinds of writing are valuable and qualify their authors as writers. If you already identify yourself as a writer, then you won't need much external motivation for improving your writing. But if you have little interest in writing for its own sake and aspire instead to become a nurse, an engineer, a business executive, a social worker, or a marine biologist, then you might question the benefits of taking a writing course.

What are these benefits? First of all, the skills you learn in this course will be directly transferable to your other college courses, where you will have to write papers in a wide variety of styles. Lower-division (general education or core) courses often focus on general academic writing, while upper-division courses in your major introduce you to the specialized writing and thinking of your chosen field. What college professors value are the kinds of questioning, analyzing, and arguing skills that this course will help you develop. You will emerge from this course as a better reader and thinker and a clearer and more persuasive writer, able to meet the demands of different academic writing situations.

Effective writing skills are also essential for most professional careers. To measure the importance of writing to career success, researchers Andrea Lunsford and Lisa Ede surveyed randomly selected members of such professional organizations as the American Consulting Engineers Counsel, the American Institute of Chemists, the American Psychological Association, and the International City

Management Association. They discovered that members of these organizations spend, on average, forty-four percent of their professional time writing, including (most commonly) letters, memos, short reports, instructional materials, and professional articles and essays.

Besides the pragmatic benefits of college and career success, learning to write well can bring you the personal pleasure of a richer mental life. As we show throughout this text, writing is closely allied to thinking and to the innate satisfaction you take in exercising your curiosity, creativity, and problem-solving ability. Writing connects you to others and helps you discover and express ideas that you would otherwise never think or say. Unlike speaking, writing gives you time to think deep and long about an idea. Because you can revise writing, it lets you pursue a problem in stages, with each new draft reflecting a deeper, clearer, or more complex level of thought. In other words, writing isn't just a way to express thought; it is a way to do the thinking itself. The act of writing stimulates, challenges, and stretches your mental powers and, when you do it well, is profoundly satisfying.

Subject Matter Problems: The Starting Point of Writing

Having made a connection between writing and thinking, we now move to the spirit of inquiry that drives the writing process. From your previous schooling, you are probably familiar with the term *thesis statement,* which is the main point a writer wants to make in an essay. However, you may not have thought much about the question that lies behind the thesis, which is the problem or issue that the writer is wrestling with. An essay's thesis statement is actually the writer's one-sentence summary answer to this question, and it is this question that has motivated the writer's thinking. Experienced writers immerse themselves in subject matter questions in pursuit of answers or solutions. They write to share their proposed solutions with readers who share their interests. As we will show in Chapter 2, introductions to academic essays typically begin with the question or problem that the writer plans to address. In this section we show you more fully the nature of subject matter questions that initiate the writing process.

Shared Problems Unite Writers and Readers

Everywhere we turn, we see writers and readers forming communities based on questions or problems of mutual interest. Perhaps nowhere are such communities more evident than in academe. Many college professors are engaged in research projects stimulated and driven by questions or problems. At a recent workshop for new faculty members, we asked participants to write a brief description of a question or problem that motivated them to write a seminar paper or article. Here are two examples of their responses.

A Biochemistry Professor During periods of starvation, the human body makes physiological adaptations to preserve essential protein mass. Unfortunately, these adaptations don't work well during long-term starvation. After the body depletes its carbohydrate storage, it must shift to depleting protein in order to produce glucose. Eventually, this loss of functional protein leads to metabolic dysfunction and death. Interestingly, several animal species are capable of surviving for extensive periods without food and water while conserving protein and maintaining glucose levels. How do the bodies of these animals accomplish this feat? I wanted to investigate the metabolic functioning of these animals, which might lead to insights into the human situation.

A Journalism Professor Several years ago, I knocked on the wooden front door of the home of an elderly woman in Tucson, Arizona. Tears of grief rolled down her cheeks as she opened the door. The tears turned to anger when I explained that I was a reporter and wished to talk with her about her son's death in jail. Her face hardened. "What right do you have coming here?" I recall her saying. "Why are you bothering me?" Those questions have haunted me throughout my journalism career. Do journalists have the right to intrude on a person's grief? Can they exercise it any time they want? What values do journalists use to decide when to intrude and violate someone's privacy?

Of course these are not new college students speaking about problems they posed; they are college professors recalling problems that fueled a piece of professional writing. We share these problems with you to persuade you that most college professors value question asking and want you to be caught up, as they are, in the spirit of inquiry.

As you progress through your college career, you will find yourself increasingly engaged with questions. All around college campuses you'll find clusters of professors and students asking questions about all manner of curious things—the reproductive cycles of worms and bugs, the surface structure of metals, the social significance of obscure poets, gender roles among the Kalahari Bushmen, the meaning of Balinese cockfighting, the effect of tax structure on economies, the rise of labor unions in agriculture, the role of prostitutes in medieval India, the properties of concrete, and almost anything else a human being might wonder about. A quick review of the magazine rack at any large supermarket reveals that similar communities have formed around everything from hot rods to model railroads, from computers to kayaks to cooking.

At the heart of all these communities of writers and readers is an interest in common questions and the hope for better or different answers. Writers write because they have something new or surprising or challenging to say in response to a question. Readers read because they share the writer's interest in the problem and want to deepen their understanding.

Posing a Problem: A Case Study of a Beginning College Writer

So far we have talked about how professional writers pose problems. In this section we show you how student writer Christopher Leigh posed a problem for an argumentative paper requiring research.

At the start of his process, Christopher was interested in the issue of school violence. Like many of his classmates, Christopher had been disturbed by the massacre at Columbine High School in Littleton, Colorado, in April 1999. When he discussed Columbine with his small group in his first-year composition course, he explained that these killings were especially unsettling for him because Columbine seemed like a safe, middle-class school with no previous record of violence. He wondered what would cause a normal-seeming group of kids to open fire on their classmates.

When he started doing research, he had formulated only a broad question: What can be done to prevent school violence? On his first trip to the library, however, he came across an article on psychological profiling. Here is what he wrote in his journal on that day:

> Today I came across an article in the *New York Times* that disturbed me. It was about psychological profiling, which means that they figure out psychological traits that are apt to indicate a person may become violent. Then they look for kids in the schools that fit those traits. After reading this article, I began to think about whether or not the use of profiles to identify potentially violent students is effective, and if it is somehow a violation of students' rights or privacy. Profiles that use signs such as "antisocial behavior" and "mood swings" may be problematic because almost any student would fit the profiles at some point. Think of all the bad, depressing days that teenagers have. And singling out a student because he or she fits the profile is never going to be able to predict for sure if that student will become violent. I know someone who was suspended for making a joke about a bomb, and even though it was a careless remark, she had no intention of doing harm. So profiling may victimize students who are not violent. Right now my feeling is that profiling in any form is wrong, but I need to learn more about how they are used and if they are effective. Also if they violate students' rights, and how other students feel about them.

After writing this journal entry, Christopher wrote out his new research question as follows: Is psychological profiling an effective way to help reduce school violence? When he discussed this question with his small group, his friends thought it was an interesting question worth researching. The group was divided about profiling. Some thought that schools should do everything they can to identify disturbed classmates and intervene with psychological counseling. Others thought profiling is a total violation of privacy. This division of opinion convinced Christopher that the question was a good one.

We will return to Christopher's story occasionally throughout this text. You can read his final paper in Chapter 22, pages 675–686, where Christopher argues against metal detectors in schools—a moderately changed focus from his initial interest in psychological profiling. You can also read his earlier exploratory paper (Ch. 8, pp. 197–202), which narrates the evolution of his thinking as he researched ways of preventing school violence.

Posing Your Own Subject-Matter Questions

Where do good questions come from and how can you learn to pose them? At the outset, we should say that the kinds of questions we discuss in this chapter may lead you toward new and unfamiliar ways of thinking. Beginning college students typically value questions that have right answers. Students ask their professors questions about a subject because they are puzzled by confusing parts of a text-book, a lecture, or an assigned reading. They hope their professors will explain the confusing material clearly. Their purpose in asking these questions is to eliminate misunderstandings, not to open up controversy and debate. Although basic comprehension questions are important, they are not the kinds of inquiry questions that initiate strong college-level writing and thinking.

The kinds of questions that stimulate the writing most valued in college are open-ended questions that focus on unknowns or invite multiple points of view rather than factual questions that have single right answers. These are what historian Rodney Kilcup refers to when he says that writers should begin with a "good, interesting question" (see the epigraph to this chapter, p. 5). For Kilcup, a good question sets the writer on the path of inquiry, critical thinking, analysis, and argument.

Later in your college career, many of the questions you pursue will come from your chosen major, particularly from controversies, uncertainties, and unknowns within the subject matter of that discipline. Nevertheless, you currently have many other areas of experience or knowledge that can lead to good, interesting questions. Consider, for example, the various communities to which you belong: your dorm or apartment complex; your campus; your city or region of the country; your job or volunteer work; your connection with any religious, sports, or activity group. Consider also your civic role as a citizen of a city, state, nation, and global community. If you read newspapers or magazines, watch television, listen to radio programs, or surf the Internet, you are exposed to problems that merit investigation and critical analysis. Many writers find that questions emerge when they perceive differences between their own views and those of others within a given community or when they discover confusions, gaps, and inconsistencies within information, ideas, or beliefs. Good questions can arise when you do any of the following:

 • Discover holes in your knowledge of something
- Note gaps or inconsistencies in the evidence for something, or realize that you and someone else are drawing different conclusions from the same set of facts
- Think about contradictions among different perspectives and different points of view
- Consider why you are dissatisfied with someone else's explanation of a phenomenon, analysis of an event, or solution to a problem
- Feel curious about the cause, consequence, purpose, function, or value of something
- Note discrepancies between the ideal and the real, between what someone values and what he or she does, between the current state of something and your desired state of something

Once you start practicing these ways of thinking, you will see yourself as a more powerful writer able to contribute your own views to a community of readers drawn into conversation by mutual interest in a problem.

Characteristics of Good Subject-Matter Questions

Questions that lead to good college-level writing generally exhibit three main qualities:

- *A good question is problematic.* By problematic, we mean that community members do not currently know the answer or agree on the answer. A question whose answer can be looked up in a reference book or solved by applying a mathematical formula is not problematic.
- *A good question is significant.* In addition, a good question should have something at stake. Writers need to answer their readers' "So what?" question by showing that a problem is worth pursuing. Why does the problem matter? Who are its stakeholders? How will a community gain by considering the writer's answer to the question?
- *A good question is interesting to the writer.* Finally, you as writer need to be genuinely engaged with this question; it has to be a real question for you, a problem in which you feel invested. You can infuse your writing with vitality only when you, the writer, are truly curious about a question or passionately concerned about it.

Our way of thinking about problems has been motivated by the South American educator Paulo Freire, who wanted his students (often poor, illiterate villagers) to become *problematizers* instead of memorizers. Freire opposed what he called "the banking method" of education, in which students deposited knowledge in their memory banks and then made withdrawals during exams. The banking method, Freire believed, left third world villagers passive and helpless to improve their situations in life. He wanted students to ask disturbing questions and then to act on their discoveries. When students are taught to read and write through the banking method, they learn the word *water* by repeating an irrelevant, self-evident sentence such as, "The water is in the well." With Freire's method of teaching literacy, students might learn the word *water* by asking, "Why is the water dirty and who is responsible?" Freire believed that good questions have stakes and that answering the questions can make a difference in the world.

For Writing and Discussion

Your task: Working in small groups or as a whole class, create a list of problematic, significant, and interesting questions about any topic area assigned by your instructor. In the following pages we provide a context for one possible subject: the problem of the world's growing desire for automobiles in the face of a declining supply of fossil fuels. If you choose this topic, derive your questions from your personal experiences with automobiles and your energy knowledge based on reading and observation. For further context, we provide an array of data for you to examine.

(continued)

The seven visual and verbal texts in this data set present a range of perspectives on energy usage and automobiles, yet these texts represent only a small sampling of the views currently being voiced. As you read through the passages and ponder the images and graphics in light of your own personal experiences, look for controversies, inconsistencies, and gaps in knowledge that can prompt you to articulate problems worth exploring.

Some examples of questions: The range of questions you can ask is very wide. You can ask questions based on your own personal experience and observations ("What can we do to make bike riding more popular?" or "How did Hummers or Dodge Ram pickups become prestigious urban vehicles?"), or you can ask questions spinning off the exhibits ("What will happen to our way of life if oil becomes unaffordable?" or "Should the government force people into smaller cars? If so, how?") When your class shares the questions you have produced, you will begin experiencing what it is like to be drawn into inquiry—to feel the pleasure and exhilaration of doing your own critical thinking in response to a problem.

Exhibit 1: The Hummer ad that appears on page 3 as the part opener image for Part One of this text.

Exhibit 2: Excerpt from news story on China

SHIFTING INTO HIGH GEAR

From a nation of bikes and donkey carts, China has shifted to a mobile population in just a generation. Automobile sales on the mainland are doubling almost every year, with all the car makers racing to China to cash in on the world's most revved-up auto market. . . .

China really has been a dream market for the world's auto makers, who have seen profits steadily decline due to gloomy economic conditions around the globe. Except in China.

In 2002, for instance, China sales soared 37 percent, even as overall sales across Europe tumbled seven percent. And, contrary to most of the mainland products, profit margins in China are sky-high, amongst the world's biggest margins.

No wonder all the world's auto makers are established on the mainland. Most arrived less than a decade ago. All are racing to keep apace of demand.
                    —Source: http://www.gluckman.com/ChinaCars.html

Exhibit 3: Excerpt from the Bush Administration's *National Energy Policy*

Estimates indicate that over the next 20 years, U.S. oil consumption will increase by 33 percent, natural gas consumption by well over 50 percent, and demand for electricity will rise by 45 percent. If America's energy production grows at the same rate as it did in the 1990s we will face an ever-increasing gap.

Increases on this scale will require preparation and action today. Yet America has not been bringing on line the necessary supplies and infrastructure. . . .

A primary goal of the National Energy Policy is to add supply from diverse sources. This means [increasing the domestic production of] oil, gas, and coal. It also means [increasing our use of] hydropower and nuclear power. And it means making greater use of non-hydro renewable sources now available.

Exhibit 4: Excerpt from "Greenpeace Responds to the Bush/Cheney National Energy Policy Task Force"

The Bush/Cheney Task Force's National Energy Policy leads the nation down the wrong road. Though the administration claims to have crafted a long-term solution, the shortsighted policy includes:

- No efforts to cut the nation's global warming pollution
- Massive electric power plant construction—1,300 new polluting fossil fuel and nuclear power plants are proposed
- New oil extraction in ecologically sensitive areas such as the Arctic National Wildlife Refuge and the Rocky Mountains
- More oil refineries, pipelines and electrical transmission lines
- Additional U.S. taxpayer subsidies for the fossil fuel and nuclear industries

And in an effort to hide their true agenda, the Administration proposes:

- Minor efforts toward saving energy through energy efficiency and renewable energy sources

—Source: http://archive.greenpeace.org/climate/climatecountdown/
documents/bushrealitycheck.pdf

Exhibit 5: News analysis excerpt

In interviews at the New York International Auto Show this month, top executives of General Motors and the Ford Motor company, both of which make and sell a lot of cars in Europe, reiterated their support for high gasoline taxes—as opposed to stricter fuel economy regulations.

"Anything that can align the individual customer's purchase decisions with society's goals [is] the way to go," Ford's chairman and chief executive, William Clay Ford, Jr., said, adding that his company has previously supported a 50-cent increase in gas taxes. . . .

Mr. Ford said the current regulatory system, which compels automakers to make cars and trucks that meet minimum standards for fuel efficiency, "puts the manufacturer in this tug of war that's unsustainable between what the customer wants and what society says it wants."

In other words, most customers want bigger and faster cars—actually, light-duty trucks like sport utility vehicles—not efficient ones.

—Danny Hakim, "A Fuel-Saving Proposal From Your Automaker: Tax the Gas"
The New York Times (18 April 2004): BU 5

Exhibit 6: From "The Energy Guy Website" (Ray Darby, PE)

Let's look at the case for oil, our most used fuel. Data from the *Energy Information Administration (EIA)* indicates about 981.4 billion barrels of *oil reserves remain* on the planet (it was 1,033 BB when I checked a year earlier?!?). Although this may sound like a lot, the world has consumed about 800 billion barrels of oil thus far. Half of the oil we've used so far has been consumed since 1970—a mere 28 years ago. In addition to the known (verified) oil reserves on the planet, there are an estimated 547 billion more barrels of "technically feasible" oil to recover. That leaves us with a total of 1,528 billion barrels.

(continued)

The world consumed about *75 billion barrels* of oil in 1999. In another 38 years from now, at a constant 2% rate of world oil consumption growth we will have used up virtually all of the remaining oil on the planet! . . . Unfortunately, the aforementioned "current rate of world oil consumption growth" is not likely to remain constant at 2%, but increase due to world economic development. For example, the annual *percent change in world oil consumption* (over the preceding year) was 0.8% in 1998, 1.7% in 1999, and 2.4% (estimated) for 2000 . . .

Are we going to run out of oil? No. It will get very expensive long before that! It's just a matter of time and circumstances, supply and demand. As demand continues to grow while reserves continue to decline, it's simply a matter of time before a permanent oil-price spiral begins. The graphic below illustrates how supply problems will begin to limit production. The area under the curve is the total amount of (known) oil remaining on the planet (the dotted line represents production if additional discoveries, which can be reasonably anticipated, are included). Note the peak is estimated to occur around 2010 (only eight short years away)!

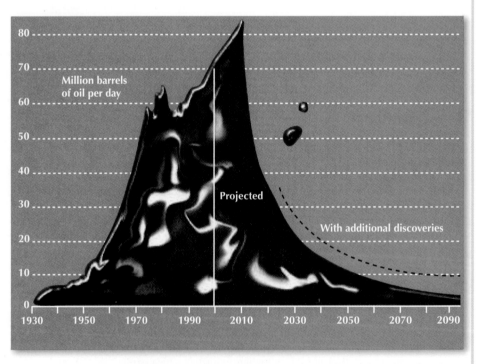

—Source: http://www.theenergyguy.com/IssuesSummary.html

Exhibit 7: Oil consumption table

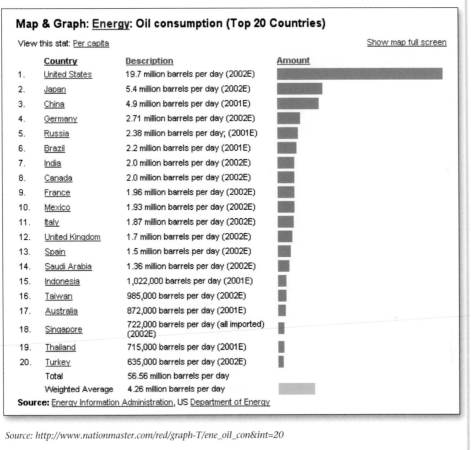

Source: http://www.nationmaster.com/red/graph-T/ene_oil_con&int=20

Rhetorical Problems: Reaching Readers Effectively

So far we have been focusing on subject-matter problems. In this section we shift our attention to rhetorical problems.

By rhetorical problems, we refer to a network of questions writers must ask about audience, purpose, and genre (a *genre* is a recurring type of writing with established conventions, such as an academic article, a personal essay, a newspaper feature story, a grant proposal, an article for *Seventeen* or *Rolling Stone*, a

Web page, and so forth). These questions often loom as large for writers as do the subject-matter problems that drive their writing in the first place. Suppose, for example, that you have asked the subject-matter question: To what extent will hydrogen cars be an effective solution to the problem of dwindling fossil fuels? Suppose further that your research casts doubt on hydrogen cars. Consider the number of rhetorical problems you must think about as you sit down to write a draft.

One of our students did a short research project on this question. You can read her paper in Chapter 9, pp. 233–235.

- Who are my readers? How much background do they need on hydrogen cell cars? Do I need to explain how hydrogen cells work?
- Are my readers already interested in the problem of dwindling supply of fossil fuels? Do they believe the world may soon run out of oil, or do they think the supply is endless? Do I need to hook them on this problem?
- Should I take a strong stand against hydrogen cars or just raise some doubts?
- How should I organize my essay to make it most effective?
- Should I write this paper as a formal college research paper or as a more popular magazine-style article?

Subject-matter problems and rhetorical problems are often so closely linked that writers can't address one without addressing the other. You would not even be able to decide on a title, for example, until you decided whether the paper should have an academic or a popular tone.

In Chapters 2 and 3 we discuss in more detail the kinds of rhetorical problems that writers must pose and solve. In this chapter we simply introduce you to one extended example of a rhetorical problem. From a student's point of view, we might call this "the problem of varying rules." From our perspective, we call it a problem of "genre"—or "what kind of prose does my audience expect me to write?"

An Example of a Rhetorical Problem: When to Choose Closed Versus Open Forms

In our experience, beginning college writers are often bothered by the ambiguity and slipperiness of rules governing writing. Many beginning writers wish that good writing followed consistent rules such as "Never use 'I' in a formal paper" or "Start every paragraph with a topic sentence." The problem is that different kinds of writing follow different rules, leaving the writer with rhetorical choices rather than with hard-and-fast formulas for success. To develop this point, we begin by asking you to consider a problem about how writing might be classified.

Read the following short pieces of nonfiction prose. The first is a letter to the editor written by a professional civil engineer in response to a newspaper editorial arguing for the development of wind-generated electricity. The second short piece is entitled "A Festival of Rain." It was written by the American poet and religious writer Thomas Merton, a Trappist monk. After reading the two samples carefully, proceed to the discussion questions that follow.

READINGS

David Rockwood
A Letter to the Editor

1   Your editorial on November 16, "Get Bullish on Wind Power," is based on fantasy rather than fact. There are several basic reasons why wind-generated power can in no way serve as a reasonable major alternative to other electrical energy supply alternatives for the Pacific Northwest power system.

2   First and foremost, wind power is unreliable. Electric power generation is evaluated not only on the amount of energy provided, but also on its ability to meet system peak load requirements on an hourly, daily, and weekly basis. In other words, an effective power system would have to provide enough electricity to meet peak demands in a situation when the wind energy would be unavailable—either in no wind situations or in severe blizzard conditions, which would shut down the wind generators. Because wind power cannot be relied on at times of peak needs, it would have to be backed up by other power generation resources at great expense and duplication of facilities.

3   Secondly, there are major unsolved problems involved in the design of wind generation facilities, particularly for those located in rugged mountain areas. Ice storms, in particular, can cause sudden dynamic problems for the rotating blades and mechanisms which could well result in breakdown or failure of the generators. Furthermore, the design of the facilities to meet the stresses imposed by high winds in these remote mountain regions, in the order of 125 miles per hour, would indeed escalate the costs.

4   Thirdly, the environmental impact of constructing wind generation facilities amounting to 28 percent of the region's electrical supply system (as proposed in your editorial) would be tremendous. The Northwest Electrical Power system presently has a capacity of about 37,000 megawatts of hydro power and 10,300 megawatts of thermal, for a total of about 48,000 megawatts. Meeting 28 percent of this capacity by wind power generators would, most optimistically, require about 13,400 wind towers, each with about 1,000 kilowatt (one megawatt) generating capacity. These towers, some 100 to 200 feet high, would have to be located in the mountains of Oregon and Washington. These would encompass hundreds of square miles of pristine mountain area, which, together with interconnecting transmission facilities, control works, and roads, would indeed have major adverse environmental impacts on the region.

5   There are many other lesser problems of control and maintenance of such a system. Let it be said that, from my experience and knowledge as a professional engineer, the use of wind power as a major resource in the Pacific Northwest power system is strictly a pipe dream.

Thomas Merton
A Festival of Rain

1   Let me say this before rain becomes a utility that they can plan and distribute for money. By "they" I mean the people who cannot understand that rain is a festival, who do not appreciate its gratuity, who think that what has no price has no value, that what cannot be sold is not real, so that the only way to make something *actual* is to place it on the market. The time will come when they will sell you even your rain. At the moment it is still free, and I am in it. I celebrate its gratuity and its meaninglessness.

2   The rain I am in is not like the rain of cities. It fills the woods with an immense and confused sound. It covers the flat roof of the cabin and its porch with insistent and controlled rhythms. And I listen, because it reminds me again and again that the whole world runs by rhythms I have not yet learned to recognize, rhythms that are not those of the engineer.

3   I came up here from the monastery last night, sloshing through the corn fields, said Vespers, and put some oatmeal on the Coleman stove for supper. . . . The night became very dark. The rain surrounded the whole cabin with its enormous virginal myth, a whole world of meaning, of secrecy, of silence, of rumor. Think of it: all that speech pouring down, selling nothing, judging nobody, drenching the thick mulch of dead leaves, soaking the trees, filling the gullies and crannies of the wood with water, washing out the places where men have stripped the hillside! What a thing it is to sit absolutely alone, in a forest, at night, cherished by this wonderful, unintelligible, perfectly innocent speech, the most comforting speech in the world, the talk that rain makes by itself all over the ridges, and the talk of the watercourses everywhere in the hollows!

4   Nobody started it, nobody is going to stop it. It will talk as long as it wants, this rain. As long as it talks I am going to listen.

5   But I am also going to sleep, because here in this wilderness I have learned how to sleep again. Here I am not alien. The trees I know, the night I know, the rain I know. I close my eyes and instantly sink into the whole rainy world of which I am a part, and the world goes on with me in it, for I am not alien to it.

For Writing and Discussion

Working in small groups or as a whole class, try to reach consensus on the following specific tasks:

1. What are the main differences between the two types of writing? If you are working in groups, help your recorder prepare a presentation describing the differences between Rockwood's writing and Merton's writing.
2. Create a metaphor, simile, or analogy that best sums up your feelings about the most important differences between Rockwood's and Merton's writing: "Rockwood's writing is like . . . , but Merton's writing is like. . . . "
3. Explain why your metaphors are apt. How do your metaphors help clarify or illuminate the differences between the two pieces of writing?

Now that you have done some thinking on your own about the differences between these two examples, turn to our brief analysis.

Distinctions between Closed and Open Forms of Writing

David Rockwood's letter and Thomas Merton's mini-essay are both examples of nonfiction prose. But as these examples illustrate, nonfiction prose can vary enormously in form and style. From the perspective of structure, we can place nonfiction prose along a continuum that goes from closed to open forms of writing (see Figure 1.1).

Of our two pieces of prose, Rockwood's letter illustrates tightly closed writing and falls at the far left end of the continuum. The elements that make this writing closed are the presence of an explicit thesis in the introduction (i.e., wind-generated power isn't a reasonable alternative energy source in the Pacific Northwest) and the

FIGURE 1.1 A Continuum of Essay Types: Closed to Open Forms

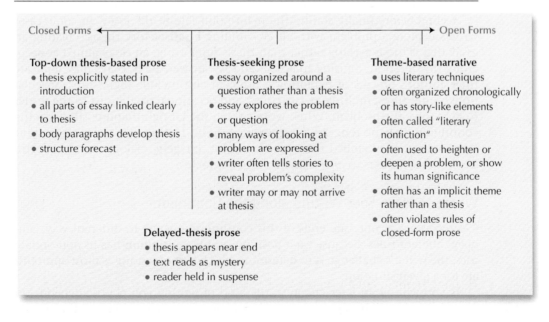

Closed Forms ←   → Open Forms

Top-down thesis-based prose
- thesis explicitly stated in introduction
- all parts of essay linked clearly to thesis
- body paragraphs develop thesis
- structure forecast

Thesis-seeking prose
- essay organized around a question rather than a thesis
- essay explores the problem or question
- many ways of looking at problem are expressed
- writer often tells stories to reveal problem's complexity
- writer may or may not arrive at thesis

Theme-based narrative
- uses literary techniques
- often organized chronologically or has story-like elements
- often called "literary nonfiction"
- often used to heighten or deepen a problem, or show its human significance
- often has an implicit theme rather than a thesis
- often violates rules of closed-form prose

Delayed-thesis prose
- thesis appears near end
- text reads as mystery
- reader held in suspense

writer's consistent development of that thesis throughout the body (i.e., "First and foremost, wind power is unreliable. . . . Secondly, there are major unsolved [design] problems. . . . Thirdly, . . . "). Once the thesis is stated, the reader knows the point of the essay and can predict its structure. The reader also knows that the writer's point won't change as the essay progresses. Because its structure is transparent and predictable, the success of closed-form prose rests entirely on its ideas, which must "surprise" readers by asserting something new, challenging, doubtful, or controversial. It aims to change readers' view of the subject through the power of reason, logic, and evidence. Closed-form prose is what most college professors write when doing their own scholarly research, and it is what they most often expect of their students. It is also the most common kind of writing in professional and business contexts.

Merton's "A Festival of Rain" falls toward the right end of the closed-to-open continuum. It resists reduction to a single, summarizable thesis. Although Merton praises rain, and clearly opposes the consumer culture that will try to "sell" you the rain, it is hard to pin down exactly what he means by "festival" or by rain's "gratuity and its meaninglessness." The main organizing principle of Merton's piece, like that of most open-form prose, is a story or narrative—in this case the story of Merton's leaving the monastery to sleep in the rain-drenched cabin. Rather than announce a thesis and support it with reasons and evidence, Merton lets his point emerge suggestively from his story and his language. Open-form essays still have a focus, but the focus is more like a theme in fiction than like a thesis in argument. Readers may argue over its meaning in the same way that they argue over the meaning of a film or poem or novel.

As you can see from the continuum in Figure 1.1, essays can fall anywhere along the scale. Not all thesis-with-support writing has to be top down, stating its thesis explicitly in the introduction. In some cases writers choose to delay the thesis, creating a more exploratory, open-ended, "let's think through this together" feeling before finally stating the main point late in the essay. In some cases writers explore a problem without *ever* finding a satisfactory thesis, creating an essay that is thesis seeking rather than thesis supporting, an essay aimed at deepening the question, refusing to accept an easy answer. Such essays may replicate their author's process of exploring a problem and include digressions, speculations, conjectures, multiple perspectives, and occasional invitations to the reader to help solve the problem. When writers reach the far right-hand position on the continuum, they no longer state an explicit thesis. Instead, like novelists or short story writers, they embed their points in plot, imagery, dialogue, and so forth, leaving their readers to *infer* a theme from the text.

Where to Place Your Writing along the Continuum

Clearly, essays at opposite ends of this continuum operate in different ways and obey different rules. Because each position on the continuum has its appropriate uses, the writer's challenge is to determine which sort of writing is most appropriate for a given situation.

As you will see in later chapters, the kind of writing you choose depends on your purpose, your intended audience, and your genre (you will recall that a *genre* is a recurring type of writing with established conventions). Thus, if you were writing an analytical paper for an academic audience, you would typically choose a closed-form structure, and your finished product would include elements such as the following:

- An explicit thesis in the introduction
- Forecasting of structure
- Cohesive and unified paragraphs with topic sentences
- Clear transitions between sentences and between parts
- No digressions

But if you were writing an autobiographical narrative about, say, what family means to you, you would probably move toward the open end of the continuum and violate one or more of these conventions (note how extensively Merton violates them). It's not that open-form prose doesn't have rules; it's that the rules are different, just as the rules for jazz are different from the rules for a classical sonata.

For another perspective on how rules vary, consider two frequently encountered high school writing assignments: the five-paragraph theme and the personal-experience narrative (for example, the infamous "What I Did Last Summer" essay). The five-paragraph theme is a by-the-numbers way to teach closed-form, thesis-with-support writing. It emphasizes logical development, unity, and coherence. The five-paragraph structure may emerge naturally if you are writing an argument based on three supporting reasons—an introductory paragraph, three body paragraphs (one for each reason), and a concluding paragraph. Rockwood's letter is a real-world example of a five-paragraph theme even though Rockwood certainly didn't have that format in mind when writing.

In contrast, the "What I Did Last Summer" assignment calls for a different sort of writing, probably an open-form, narrative structure closer to Merton's piece about the night in the rain. Whether the writer chooses a closed-form or an open-form approach depends on the intended audience of the piece and the writer's purpose.

For Writing and Discussion

Do you and your classmates most enjoy writing prose at the closed or more open end of the continuum? Prior to class discussion, work individually by recalling a favorite piece of writing that you have done in the past. Jot down a brief description of the kind of writing this was (a poem, a personal-experience essay, a research paper, a newspaper story, a persuasive argument). Then, working in small groups or as a whole class, report one at a time on your favorite piece of writing and speculate where it falls on the continuum from closed to open forms. Are you at your best in closed-form writing that calls for an explicit thesis statement and logical support? Or are you at your best in more open and personal forms?

Is there a wide range of preferences in your class? If so, how do you account for this variance? If not, how do you account for the narrow range?

Chapter Summary

This chapter introduced you to the notion of writers as questioners and problem posers who wrestle with both subject-matter and rhetorical problems. We have shown how writers start with questions or problems about their subject matter rather than with topic areas, and how they take their time resolving the uncertainties raised by such questions. We saw that writers must ask questions about their rhetorical situation and make decisions about content, form, and style based on their understanding of their purpose, their audience, and their genre. We described how the rules governing writing vary as the writer moves along the continuum from closed to open forms.

The next chapter looks closely at how writers pose problems, pursue them in depth, and then pose answers that bring something new, surprising, or challenging to readers.

BRIEF WRITING PROJECT

We close this chapter with two options for a brief writing project, each aimed at helping you appreciate the value of a "good, interesting question." The first option is the easier of the two and can be done informally. The second option is more formal and yet can be completed in one page.

Option 1: Think of a recent experience in your life that has generated questions for you—for example, reading a book or magazine, watching a film or TV show, participating in a class discussion, or observing an incident in the dorms. Briefly describe the experience and then, based on your ponderings, pose several questions arising from the experience that you think are problematic, significant, and interesting.

Option 2: Write a one-page (double-spaced) essay that poses a question about automobiles and fossil fuels (or some other topic provided by your instructor). Besides explaining your question and providing needed background information, you will need to help readers see (1) why the question is problematic— that is, why it is a genuine problem with no easy right answers—and (2) why the question is significant or worth pursuing—that is, what benefit will come from solving it. Your essay should not answer the question; your purpose is only to ask it.

The goal of these brief writing project options is to give you practice at posing problematic questions. As you will see in Chapter 2, the second option, which focuses on a single question, will give you practice at writing the question-posing part of a typical academic introduction.

Either of these options will anchor your questions in a specific experience, reading, or set of data. The best kinds of questions are neither so broad that they are virtually unanswerable nor so narrow that they have only one right answer. If you can imagine several different ways to answer the questions you ask, you are on the right track. What follows are student examples for each option.

READINGS

Our first reading, by student writer Noel Gaudette, responds to Option 1.

Noel Gaudette
Questions about Genetically Modified Foods

A few weeks ago I was eating breakfast while listening to the news on the radio. One report I heard was about the political and economic tension over shipping genetically modified (GM) food to African nations. One of the concerns of Africans was the long-term safety of GM products. They worried about the food disrupting the natural biological balance we maintain in our bodies from eating traditionally grown foods. While listening to this program, I peered at my food service breakfast of reconstituted eggs, uniform hash browns, perfect-looking sausages, and little cup of bright red ketchup. My orange juice tasted fresh squeezed and my coffee seemed very ordinary. Still, I started to wonder if my breakfast contained genetically modified foods. I began to think of these questions:

1. How do I know if I am eating a GM product? How should consumers be made aware that their food contains GM products? Are these labeled on cans and boxes? If not, should they be?
2. Are the African nations correct in their assumption that GM food is unsafe?
3. What testing has been done on these new GM foods and is it sufficient?
4. To what extent should we promote the development and consumption of GM foods?

Describes the specific experience that generated the questions

Shows how details of the experience caused writer to ponder questions

States specific questions or issues that the writer feels are both problematic and significant

Our second reading, by student writer Brittany Tinker, responds to Option 2.

Brittany Tinker
Can the World Sustain an American Standard of Living?

Yesterday's class discussion about the growing demand for automobiles in China combined with all the problems of smog and air pollution in Beijing raised lots of dilemmas for me. Because the United States and other developed nations are already using up vast quantities of the world's oil, adding oil demands from China and other developing nations will cause the world to deplete its oil even sooner. Moreover, third world development adds even

Hooks reader's interest and provides background

States the question

more to the air pollution and global warming caused by consumerism in the United States and other developed countries. So I wonder, what standard of living can the whole world sustain once third world countries expand their own economies?

Begins to show that the question is problematic by presenting one side of her dilemma

Part of me hopes that the poor people in second and third world countries can one day enjoy the standard of living that I have had. The disparity between first world and second or third world countries hit me when I visited Nicaragua. Most Nicaraguans live in small, one-room homes made from corrugated tin and cinder blocks. The plumbing is underdeveloped and the electricity is inconstant. Most Nicaraguan families do not have enough food to provide adequate nutrition. But through economic development, I hope that these people can have the comforts that I and many other fortunate Americans have such as hot water, lots of nutritious food, numerous bedrooms, at least one car in the family, paved sidewalks or driveways, and a backyard, swimming pool, or hot tub.

Shows the other side of her dilemma

But another part of me sees that my own standard of living may be what's at fault; maybe this model for the good life won't work anymore. If second and third world countries attain the standard of living that I have been lucky enough to have, then air pollution, destruction of forests, global warming, and harm to wildlife, as well as the depletion of oil reserves, will pose even greater risks for the world than they already do. A lot of my classmates seem confident that scientists will discover alternative energy sources and solutions to pollution and global warming so that the whole world can live in comfort. But this pessimistic side of me doesn't share their confidence. Maybe the solution is for Americans to greatly reduce their own consumption and to begin reducing the environmental damage they have already created.

Shows why question is significant

So I am left wondering, Can the world sustain for everybody the standard of living I have enjoyed? This question is significant because there is so much at stake. If our model for the happy life is to have all the American luxuries, then the development of the third world might mean a much speedier destruction of the planet. If we hope to preserve the planet while eliminating the poverty and misery of third world people, then maybe Americans have to develop a new model for happiness. Is it possible for developing countries to find a new path to economic prosperity that shows the developed world a new model of preserving the environment?

Showing Why Your Question Is Problematic and Significant (Option 2)

If you have been assigned the second option for your brief writing project, you will need to show why your question is both problematic and significant. (Doing so helps your readers understand the puzzling nature of your problem and motivates their interest in it.) Some strategies writers can use to show that a question is problematic and significant are given in the following charts.

Strategies for Showing That a Question Is Problematic

POSSIBLE STRATEGY	EXAMPLE
Show how your own (or previous researchers') attempts to solve the problem have failed.	If your problem were "How can our university encourage more students, faculty, and staff to carpool?" you could show how the university's previous attempts to encourage carpooling (reduced-rate parking, privileged parking spots) have failed.
Show different ways that people have attempted to answer the question (different theories or competing explanations) and indicate how no one answer is fully adequate.	If you were puzzled by why Europeans accept much higher fuel prices than Americans do, you could summarize several theories presented by your classmates and show why each one isn't fully convincing.
Show the alternative points of view on an issue.	If your problem were whether to save fossil fuels by building more nuclear power plants, you could summarize the main arguments for and against nuclear power.
Show why an expected or "easy" answer isn't satisfactory.	Suppose you asked, "What is the best alternative to using fossil fuels for generating electricity?" and one of your environmentalist friends says, "All we have to do is put our money into developing wind energy." You could problematize this easy answer by summarizing engineer David Rockwood's objections to the technical feasibility of wind power (see pp. 17–18).
Narrate your own attempts to think through the problem, revealing how none of your possible answers fully satisfied you.	You might use the strategy "Part of me thinks this . . . ; but another part of me thinks this . . . " or "I used to think this, but now I think . . . ." This is the strategy used by Brittany Tinker in the example essay.

Strategies for Showing That a Question Is Significant

POSSIBLE STRATEGY	EXAMPLE
Show how solving the problem will lead to practical, real-world benefits.	If we could figure out how to get people to buy fuel-efficient cars rather than SUVs, we could cut down substantially on fossil fuel use.
Show how solving a small knowledge problem will help us solve a larger, more important knowledge problem.	If we could better understand why Europeans are willing to live with high gasoline prices, we might better understand how cultural values influence consumer behavior.

Planning Your Essay

To help you develop a plan for your Option 2 brief essay, you can make an informal outline or flowchart in which you plan out each of the required parts. Here are some examples of student plans that led to successful question-posing essays on problems other than cars and fossil fuels.

EXAMPLE 1

I would like to question the ethics of interspecies transplants and show why it is not an easy question to answer.

Illustrate question with case of a man who had a transplant of a baboon heart.

View One: Interspecies transplants are unethical. It is unethical to "play God" by taking the organs of one species and placing them into another.

View Two: Interspecies transplants may save lives. Medical research done with the intention of improving human life is ethical.

This is a significant problem because it causes us to question the limits of medical research and to ask what it means to be human.

EXAMPLE 2

I am wondering whether Eminem's music ought to be censored in some way or at least kept out of the hands of children or unknowledgeable listeners.
Show how I am conflicted by all the different points of view:

- I agree that his lyrics are vile, misogynistic, homophobic, and obscene. Children should not be allowed to listen to his music.
- Yet I believe in free speech.
- Also rap is more complex than the general public realizes. Eminem's irony and complexity are often misunderstood. Therefore, serious listeners should have access to his music.
- Additionally, there may be some value just in expressing politically incorrect thoughts, but not if doing so just leads to more hatred.

Explain how I am left with a dilemma about whether or not to censor Eminem and if so, how.
This is an important question because it involves the larger question of individual freedom versus public good.

Exploring Problems, Making Claims

"In management, people don't merely 'write papers,' they solve problems," said [business professor Kimbrough Sherman]. . . . He explained that he wanted to construct situations where students would have to "wallow in complexity" and work their way out, as managers must.

—A. KIMBROUGH SHERMAN, *MANAGEMENT PROFESSOR*

In the previous chapter we introduced you to the role of the writer as a questioner and problem poser. In this chapter, we narrow our focus to thesis-governed writing—the kind of writing most frequently required in college courses and often required in civic and professional life. Thesis-governed writing requires a behind-the-scenes ability to think rigorously about a problem and then to make a claim* that summarizes your "best solution."

In Part Three of this text, "A Guide to Composing and Revising," we give you compositional advice on the actual drafting and revising of a thesis-governed essay. Our goal in this chapter is to stand back from the nuts and bolts of writing to give you some big-picture principles of thesis-governed prose. We believe these principles, which you can transfer across most of your college courses, can significantly improve your writing. Your payoff for reading this chapter will be a marked increase in your ability to write engaging and meaningful prose targeted to the audience of your choice. In particular, you will learn the following:

- How college professors value a kind of thinking that one professor calls "wallow[ing] in complexity"
- How each academic discipline is a field of inquiry and argument, not just a repository of facts and concepts to be learned
- How the thinking process of posing questions and proposing answers is reflected in the introductions of academic articles and how an effective question must engage the interests of your intended audience
- How your thesis statement should contain a surprising element aimed at changing your reader's view of your topic

*In this text we use the words *claim* and *thesis statement* interchangeably. As you move from course to course, instructors typically use one or the other of these terms. Other synonyms for thesis statement include *proposition, main point,* or *thesis sentence.*

- How thesis statements are supported by a network of points and particulars
- How you can deepen and complicate your thinking through "the believing and doubting game" (the brief writing project for this chapter)

What Does a Professor Want?

It is important to understand the kind of thinking most college professors want in student writing. Many beginning students imagine that professors want students primarily to comprehend course concepts as taught in textbooks and lectures and to show their understanding on exams. Such comprehension is important, but it is only a starting point. As management professor A. Kimbrough Sherman explains in the epigraph to this chapter, college instructors expect students to wrestle with problems by applying the concepts, data, and thought processes they learn in a course to new situations. As Sherman puts it, students must learn to "wallow in complexity and work their way out."

Learning to Wallow in Complexity

Wallowing in complexity is not what most first-year college students aspire to do. (Certainly that wasn't what we, the authors of this text, had uppermost in our minds when we sailed off to college!) New college students tend to shut down their creative thinking processes too quickly and head straight for closure to a problem. Harvard psychologist William Perry, who has studied the intellectual development of college students, found that few of them become skilled wallowers in complexity until late in their college careers. According to Perry, most students come to college as "dualists," believing that all questions have right or wrong answers, that professors know the right answers, and that the student's job is to learn them. Of course, these beliefs are partially correct. First-year students who hope to become second-year students must indeed understand and memorize mounds of facts, data, definitions, and basic concepts.

But true intellectual growth requires the kind of problematizing we discussed in Chapter 1. It requires students to *do* something with their new knowledge, to apply it to new situations, to conduct the kinds of inquiry, research, analysis, and argument pursued by experts in each discipline. Instead of confronting only questions that have right answers, students need to confront the kinds of open-ended problems we discussed in Chapter 1. Cognitive psychologists call such problems "ill-structured" because they seldom yield a single, correct answer and often require the thinker to operate in the absence of full and complete data.* Your college professors pursue ill-structured problems in their professional writing. The kinds of problems vary from discipline to discipline, but they all require

---

*In contrast, a "well-structured" problem eventually yields a correct answer. Math problems that can be solved by applying the right formulae and processes are well structured. That's why you can have the correct answers in the back of the book.

the writer to use reasons and evidence to support a tentative solution. Because your instructors want you to learn how to do the same kind of thinking, they often phrase essay exam questions or writing assignments as ill-structured problems. They are looking not for one right answer, but for well-supported arguments that acknowledge alternative views. A C paper and an A paper may have the same "answer" (identical thesis statements), but the C writer may have waded only ankle deep into the mud of complexity, whereas the A writer wallowed in it and worked a way out.

What skills are required for successful wallowing? Specialists in critical thinking have identified the following:

1. The ability to pose problematic questions
2. The ability to analyze a problem in all its dimensions—to define its key terms, determine its causes, understand its history, appreciate its human dimension and its connection to one's own personal experience, and appreciate what makes it problematic or complex
3. The ability (and doggedness) to find, gather, and interpret facts, data, and other information relevant to the problem (often involving library, Internet, or field research)
4. The ability to imagine alternative solutions to the problem, to see different ways in which the question might be answered and different perspectives for viewing it
5. The ability to analyze competing approaches and answers, to construct arguments for and against alternatives, and to choose the best solution in light of values, objectives, and other criteria that you determine and articulate
6. The ability to write an effective argument justifying your choice while acknowledging counterarguments

We discuss and develop these skills throughout this text.

In addition to these generic thinking abilities, critical thinking requires what psychologists call "domain-specific" skills. Each academic discipline has its own characteristic ways of approaching knowledge and its own specialized habits of mind. The questions asked by psychologists differ from those asked by historians or anthropologists; the evidence and assumptions used to support arguments in literary analysis differ from those in philosophy or sociology.

What all disciplines value, however, is the ability to manage complexity, and this skill marks the final stage of William Perry's developmental scheme. At an intermediate stage of development, after they have moved beyond dualism, students become what Perry calls "multiplists." At this stage students believe that since the experts disagree on many questions, all answers are equally valid. Professors want students merely to have an opinion and to state it strongly. A multiplist believes that a low grade on an essay indicates no more than that the teacher didn't like his or her opinion. Multiplists are often cynical about professors and grades; to them, college is a game of guessing what the teacher wants to hear. Students emerge into Perry's final stages—what he calls "relativism" and "commitment in relativism"— when they are able to take a position in the face of complexity and to justify that decision through reasons and evidence while weighing and acknowledging contrary reasons and counterevidence. Professor Sherman articulates what is expected at Perry's last stages—wading into the messiness of complexity and working your way back to solid ground.

Seeing Each Academic Discipline as a Field of Inquiry and Argument

When you study a new discipline, you must learn not only the knowledge that scholars in that discipline have acquired over the years, but also the processes they used to discover that knowledge. It is useful to think of each academic discipline as a network of conversations in which participants exchange information, respond to each other's questions, and express agreements and disagreements. The scholarly articles and books that many of your instructors write (or would write if they could find the time) are formal, permanent contributions to an ongoing discussion carried on in print in your college's or university's library. Each book or article represents a contribution to a conversation; each writer agreed with some of his or her predecessors and disagreed with others.

As each discipline evolves and changes, its central questions evolve also, creating a fascinating, dynamic conversation that defines the discipline. At any given moment, scholars are pursuing hundreds of cutting-edge questions in each discipline. Table 2.1 provides examples of questions that scholars have debated over the years as well as questions they are addressing today.

As you study a discipline, you are learning how to enter its network of conversations. To do so, you have to build up a base of knowledge about the discipline, learn its terminology, observe its conversations, read its major works, see how it asks questions, and learn its methods. To help you get a fuller sense of how written "conversation" works within a discipline, the rest of this chapter shows you how a typical academic writer poses a question and then presents and supports his or her proposed answer to the question.

Posing an Engaging Question

In Chapter 1, we said that a thesis statement is the writer's answer to a thesis question. But, as we have suggested, the kinds of questions that engage audiences vary from discipline to discipline or, in popular culture, from magazine to magazine. Let's suppose, for example, that you want to write an essay on rap music. How might your essay differ if you wanted to write it for different courses you might be taking or for different popular media? Here are some examples of rap questions that would interest different audiences:

- *Psychology course:* To what extent does rap music increase misogynistic or homophobic attitudes in listeners?
- *Sociology course:* Based on a random sampling of student interview subjects, how does the level of appreciation for rap music vary by ethnicity, class, age, and gender?

TABLE 2.1 Scholarly Questions in Different Disciplines

Field	Examples of Current Cutting-Edge Questions	Examples of Historical Controversies
Anatomy	What is the effect of a pregnant rat's alcohol ingestion on the development of fetal eye tissue?	In 1628, William Harvey produced a treatise arguing that the heart, through repeated contractions, caused blood to circulate through the body. His views were attacked by followers of the Greek physician Galen.
Literature	To what extent does the structure of a work of literature, for example Conrad's *Heart of Darkness,* reflect the class and gender bias of the author?	In the 1920s, a group of New Critics argued that the interpretation of a work of literature should be based on close examination of the work's imagery and form and that the intentions of the writer and the biases of the reader were not important. These views held sway in U.S. universities until the late 1960s, when they came increasingly under attack by deconstructionists and other postmoderns, who claimed that author intentions and reader's bias were important parts of the work's meaning.
Rhetoric/ Composition	How does hypertext structure and increased attention to visual images in Web-based writing affect the composing processes of writers?	Prior to the 1970s, college writing courses in the United States were typically organized around the rhetorical modes (description, narration, exemplification, comparison and contrast, and so forth). This approach was criticized by the expressivist school associated with the British composition researcher James Britton. Since the 1980s, composition scholars have proposed various alternative strategies for designing and sequencing assignments.
Psychology	What are the underlying causes of gender identification? To what extent are differences between male and female behavior explainable by nature (genetics, body chemistry) versus nurture (social learning)?	In the early 1900s under the influence of Sigmund Freud, psychoanalytic psychologists began explaining human behavior in terms of unconscious drives and mental processes that stemmed from repressed childhood experiences. Later, psychoanalysts were opposed by behaviorists, who rejected the notion of the unconscious and explained behavior as responses to environmental stimuli.

- *Rhetoric/composition course:* What images of rap artists, urban life, and women do the lyrics of rap songs portray?
- *Local newspaper:* Should Bill Cosby be criticized or applauded for attacking "obscene rap music" as an example of bad values that keep poor African-Americans impoverished?
- *Rolling Stone Magazine:* Was the murder of Biggie used to set up a civil war in hip-hop and the Black community?

In each of these cases, the writer understands how readers in a particular community pose questions. The first three examples show differences in the way that psychologists, sociologists, and rhetoric/composition scholars might ask questions about rap music. For newspaper readers, the Bill Cosby question would interest readers who followed the public reaction to Cosby's June 2004 speech to the NAACP in which he criticized young African-Americans for wearing sagging pants, speaking in street slang, and listening to rap. The question about the murder of Biggie actually appeared in the June 7, 2004, issue of *Rolling Stone Magazine*. In all these cases, the writer poses a subject-matter question that connects in some way to the intended readers' values, beliefs, or characteristic ways of thinking.

How a Prototypical Introduction Poses a Question and Proposes an Answer

To show you how academic writers typically begin by asking a question, we will illustrate with a "prototype" introduction from a scholarly journal. A *prototype* is the most typical or generic instance of a class and doesn't constitute a value judgment. For example, a prototype bird might be a robin or blackbird (rather than an ostrich, chicken, hummingbird, or pelican) because these birds seem to exhibit the most typical features of "birdiness." Likewise, a prototype dog would be a medium-sized mutt rather than a Great Dane or toy poodle. The article we have chosen for our illustration comes from a scholarly journal called the *Journal of Popular Culture*. Other articles in this same journal are on topics ranging from *Buffy the Vampire Slayer* to international transformations of Barbie dolls in India or Mexico. In the following introduction, note how the authors first present a question and then move, at the end of the introduction, to their thesis and the overview of their argument. Note also how the question-posing part of the introduction is similar to the question-posing essay one might write for the brief writing project (Option 2) in Chapter 1.

See student writer Brittany Tinker's problem-posing essay on pp. 23–24.

PIT BULL PANIC

Provides background showing dangerous reputation of pit bulls in the media

Parenthetical citation of sources

The news media has long been criticized for being sensationalist as well as biased. One ongoing story that the media has offered their audience is a melodrama regarding the American Pit Bull Terrier (hereafter referred to as "Pit Bull"). The Pit Bull has been portrayed in the past one and a half decades as ". . . the archetype of canine evil, predators of the defenseless. Unpredictable companions that kill and maim without discretion. Walking horror shows bred with an appetite for violence (sic)" (Verzemnieks B6). This news coverage has had profound effects. Pit Bull ownership brings with it consequences not associated with most acquisitions. "These days, buying a Pit Bull means buying into a controversy; Pit Bull owners had better not be afraid of public opinion" (B6). In some places, Pit Bull ownership is not even allowed; in fact, ownership is banned in 75 communities in the United States (Sanchez-Beswick 1). Many insurance companies refuse to insure homeowners with Pit Bulls (V. Richardson 189). A survey done by the American Society for the Prevention of Cruelty to Animals found that 30% of shelters that responded do not adopt out Pit Bulls. Most of these shelters have this policy due to community bans, but others choose not to (Schultz 36). Obviously these organizations feel that Pit Bulls are dangerous. They are, no doubt, in part influenced by media accounts. The general public also looks to the media for information to warn them of dangers that they need to avoid (De Becker 294–5). The extent to which the public has caught the wave of "Pit Bull panic" is the focus of a study that is presented in this paper.

Such a panic would be rational if, in fact, Pit Bulls were as dangerous as the media has portrayed. But is the media portrayal of Pit Bulls truly accurate? Advocates feel that Pit Bulls have been unfairly maligned by the media. As Hallum* makes painfully clear, there are always two sides to every story. Additional evidence that Pit Bulls have been unfairly demonized comes from the personal experience of the authors themselves. The authors have worked with dozens of Pit Bulls at a local animal shelter in southern New Jersey. The vast majority of these Pit Bulls have been stray dogs brought in by animal control officers from a neighborhood where residents use Pit Bulls as macho status symbols, over-breed them severely, and are alleged to hold at least occasional informal dog fights. These Pit Bulls do not belong to a special pampered minority who have been given a "genteel" upbringing. Yet, as a breed, they are consistently among the most people-friendly dogs in the shelter.

This paper examines the negative portrayal of the Pit Bull in the media. It offers a theory regarding why such a portrayal has come about. It then discusses the results of a study that examined three major issues regarding Pit Bulls: (1) people's perception of Pit Bulls; (2) attitudes towards legislation designed to place restrictions on Pit Bull ownership; and (3) whether certain variables affect these perceptions and attitudes. This research is important for several reasons. Although our primary purpose is not to prove the ultimate truth about Pit Bulls, we do offer an abundance of evidence to discredit the media's negative portrayals of Pit Bulls. Only by offering counter-evidence can we establish the existence of media bias on this topic. More importantly, we offer an innovative theory of media bias. This theory is not based on the political orientation of journalists. Indeed, many issues covered by the media can be biased for reasons other than political orientation. Furthermore, we examine, for our specific topic, whether the news media actually influences the attitudes of the people it is supposedly informing. Ultimately, media bias should only be worrisome if the public actually believes the misinformation it is exposed to.

—Judy Cohen and John Richardson

Presentation of question

Provides counterevidence that pit bulls are people friendly (shows why question is problematic)

Thesis sentences showing purpose of paper and forecasting main parts

Shows why question is significant

This introduction, like most introductions to academic articles, includes the following prototypical features:

- *Focus on a question or problem to be investigated.* In this case the question is stated explicitly: "But is the media portrayal of Pit Bulls truly accurate?" This direct question implies a further question: If the media portrayal of pit bulls is not accurate, then how do we account for the media bias? In many introductions, the question to be investigated is implied rather than stated directly.
- *An explanation of why the question is problematic.* To show that their question is problematic, Cohen and Richardson juxtapose two opposing views: the common media representation of pit bulls as dangerous, countered by their

For a detailed discussion of posing questions in closed-form introductions, see Chapter 18, "Composing and Revising Closed-Form Prose," pp. 542–546.

*Hallum is one of the "advocates" of pit bulls. He is identified in the bibliography at the end of the article as the author of a book entitled *Pit Bull Sting: The Other Side of the Story.*

own personal experience working in animal shelters and by a book by Hallum, a pit bull advocate, showing that pit bulls are "people friendly."

- *An explanation of why the question is significant.* To show the significance of their question, Cohen and Richardson see two benefits of their research and analysis: First, they hope to rectify public misunderstandings about pit bulls. Second, they hope to offer a new theory about the causes of media bias as a way of helping the public guard itself against misinformation. This explanation addresses the reader's "So what?" question.

For a detailed discussion of thesis statements, purpose statements, and blueprint statements, see Chapter 18, "Composing and Revising Closed-Form Prose," pp. 542–546.

- *The writer's tentative "answer" to this question (the essay's "thesis"), which brings something new to the audience.* In closed-form articles the thesis is usually stated explicitly at the end of the introduction. Although Cohen and Richardson do not condense their whole thesis into one sentence, such a thesis is clearly implied: The media have misrepresented pit bulls for reasons that we explain through our innovative theory of media bias.

- *[optional] A mapping statement forecasting the content and shape of the rest of the article ("First X is discussed, then Y, and finally Z").* Cohen and Richardson forecast the shape of their article by identifying its major parts Such forecasting is typical of longer articles, where readers appreciate a roadmap of what is coming. In shorter articles, writers typically omit forecasting or mapping statements.

We have used Cohen and Richardson's article to show how academic writers—in posing a problem and proposing an answer—join an ongoing conversation. The papers you will be asked to write in college will be much stronger if you create the same kind of introduction that poses a problem and then asserts a tentative, risky answer (your thesis), which you will support with reasons and evidence.

Seeking a Surprising Thesis

It is not enough to ask a good question. You also have to have a strong thesis. But what makes a thesis strong?

For one thing, a strong thesis usually contains an element of uncertainty, risk, or challenge. A strong thesis implies a naysayer who could disagree with you. According to composition theorist Peter Elbow, a thesis has "got to stick its neck out, not just hedge or wander. [It is] something that can be quarreled with." Elbow's sticking-its-neck-out metaphor is a good one, but we prefer to say that a strong thesis *surprises* the reader with a new, unexpected, different, or challenging view of the writer's topic. By surprise, we intend to connote, first of all, freshness or newness for the reader. Many kinds of closed-form prose don't have a sharply contestable thesis of the sticking-its-neck-out kind highlighted by Elbow. A geology report, for example, may provide readers with desired information about rock strata in an exposed cliff, or a Web page for diabetics may explain how to coordinate meals and insulin injections during a plane trip across time zones. In these cases, the information is surprising because it brings something new and significant to intended readers.

In other kinds of closed-form prose, especially academic or civic prose addressing a problematic question or a disputed issue, surprise requires an argumentative, risky, or contestable thesis. In these cases also, surprise is not inherent in the material but in the intended readers' reception; it comes from the writer's providing an adequate or appropriate response to the readers' presumed question or problem.

In this section, we present two ways of creating a surprising thesis: (1) trying to change your reader's view of your subject; and (2) giving your thesis tension.

Try to Change Your Reader's View of Your Subject

To change your reader's view of your subject, you must first imagine how the reader would view the subject *before* reading your essay. Then you can articulate how you aim to change that view. A useful exercise is to write out the "before" and "after" views of your imagined readers:

Before reading my essay, my readers think this way about my topic:

_____

After reading my essay, my readers will think this different way about my

topic: _____

You can change your reader's view of a subject in several ways.* First, you can enlarge it. Writing that enlarges a view is primarily informational; it provides new ideas and data to add to a reader's store of knowledge about the subject. For example, suppose you are interested in the problem of storing nuclear waste (a highly controversial issue in the United States) and decide to investigate how Japan stores radioactive waste from its nuclear power plants. You could report your findings on this problem in an informative research paper. (Before reading my paper, readers would be uncertain how Japan stores nuclear waste. After reading my paper, my readers would understand the Japanese methods, possibly helping us better understand our options in the United States.)

Second, you can clarify your reader's view of something that was previously fuzzy, tentative, or uncertain. Writing of this kind often explains, analyzes, or interprets. This is the kind of writing you do when analyzing a short story, a painting, an historical document, a set of economic data, or other puzzling phenomena or when speculating on the causes, consequences, purpose, or function of something. Suppose, for example, you are analyzing the persuasive strategies used in various perfume ads and are puzzled by an advertisement for Jennifer Lopez's "Still" perfume. Your paper tries to explain how the unusual name "Still" is essential for understanding the verbal and visual aspects of the ad. (Before reading my paper, my readers will be puzzled by what this ad is trying to do. After reading my paper, my readers will see how the words and images of this ad are connected to different meanings of the word "Still.")

*Our discussion of how writing changes a reader's view of the world is indebted to Richard Young, Alton Becker, and Kenneth Pike, *Rhetoric: Discovery and Change* (New York: Harcourt Brace & Company, 1971).

Another kind of change occurs when an essay actually restructures a reader's whole view of a subject. Such essays persuade readers to change their minds or make decisions. For example, the writers of "Pit Bull Panic," the introduction to which you have just read, want to restructure their readers' thinking about pit bulls. (Before reading our article, readers would think that pit bulls are vicious animals bred to maim and kill. After reading our article, readers will regard pit bulls as people-friendly animals demonized by the media.) Likewise, engineer David Rockwood, in his letter to the editor that we reprinted in Chapter 1 (pp. 17–18), wants to change readers' views about wind power. (Before reading my letter, readers would believe that wind-generated electricity can solve our energy crisis. After reading my letter, they will see that the hope for wind power is a pipe dream.)

Surprise then is the measure of change an essay brings about in a reader. Of course, to bring about such change requires more than just a surprising thesis; the essay itself must persuade the reader that the thesis is sound as well as novel. Later in this chapter, we talk about how writers support a thesis through a network of points and particulars.

Give Your Thesis Tension

Another element of a surprising thesis is tension. By *tension* we mean the reader's sensation of being pulled away from familiar ideas toward new, unfamiliar ones or being pulled in two or more directions by opposing ideas. One of the best ways to create tension in a thesis statement is to begin the statement with an *although* or *whereas* clause: "Whereas most people believe X, this paper asserts Y." The *whereas* or *although* clause summarizes the reader's "before" view of your topic or the counterclaim that your essay opposes; the main clause states the surprising view or position that your essay will support. You may choose to omit the *although* clause from your actual essay, but formulating it first will help you achieve focus and surprise in your thesis. The examples that follow illustrate the kinds of tension we have been discussing and show why tension is a key requirement for a good thesis.

Question	What effect has the cell phone had on our culture?
Thesis without Tension	The invention of the cell phone has brought many advantages to our culture.
Thesis with Tension	Although the cell phone has brought many advantages to our culture, it may also have contributed to an increase in risky behavior among boaters and hikers.
Question	Do reservations serve a useful role in contemporary Native American culture?
Thesis without Tension	Reservations have good points and bad points.
Thesis with Tension	Although my friend Wilson Real Bird believes that reservations are necessary for Native Americans to preserve their heritage, the continuation of reservations actually degrades Native American culture.

In the first example, the thesis without tension (cell phones have brought advantages to our culture) is a truism with which everyone would agree and hence lacks surprise. The thesis with tension places this truism (the reader's "before" view) in an *although* clause and goes on to make a surprising or contestable assertion. The idea that the cell phone contributes to risky behavior among outdoor enthusiasts alters our initial complacent view of the cell phone and gives us new ideas to think about.

In the second example, the thesis without tension may not at first seem tensionless because the writer sets up an opposition between good and bad points. But *almost anything* has good and bad points, so the opposition is not meaningful, and the thesis offers no element of surprise. Substitute virtually any other social institution (marriage, the postal service, the military, prisons), and the statement that it has good and bad points would be equally true. The thesis with tension, in contrast, is risky. It commits the reader to argue that reservations have degraded Native American culture and to oppose the counterthesis that reservations are needed to *preserve* Native American culture. The reader now feels genuine tension between two opposing views.

Tension, then, is a component of surprise. The writer's goal is to surprise the reader in some way, thereby bringing about some kind of change in the reader's view. Here are some specific strategies you can use to surprise a reader:

- Give the reader new information or clarify a confusing concept.
- Make problematic something that seems nonproblematic by showing paradoxes or contradictions within it, by juxtaposing two or more conflicting points of view about it, or by looking at it more deeply or complexly than expected.
- Identify an unexpected effect, implication, or significance of something.
- Show underlying differences between two concepts normally thought to be similar or underlying similarities between two concepts normally thought to be different.
- Show that a commonly accepted answer to a question isn't satisfactory or that a commonly rejected answer may be satisfactory.
- Oppose a commonly accepted viewpoint, support an unpopular viewpoint, or in some other way take an argumentative stance on an issue.
- Propose a new solution to a problem or an unexpected answer to a question.

For Writing and Discussion

It is difficult to create thesis statements on the spot because a writer's thesis grows out of an exploratory struggle with a problem. However, in response to a question one can often propose a possible claim and treat it hypothetically as a tentative thesis statement put on the table for testing. What follows are several problematic questions that we have used as examples in this and the previous chapter, along with some possible audiences that you might consider addressing. Working individually, spend ten minutes considering possible thesis statements

(continued)

that you might pose in response to one or more of these questions. (Remember that these are tentative thesis statements that you might abandon after doing research.) Be ready to explain why your tentative thesis brings something new, enlightening, challenging, or otherwise surprising to the specified readers. Then, working in small groups or as a whole class, share your possible thesis statements. Finally, choose one or two thesis statements that your small group or the whole class thinks are particularly effective and brainstorm the kinds of evidence that would be required to support the thesis.

1. To what extent should the public support genetically modified foods? (possible audiences: readers of health food magazines; general public concerned about food choices; investors in companies that produce genetically modified seeds)
2. Should people be encouraged to drive more fuel-efficient cars? If so, how? (possible audiences: SUV owners; conservative legislators generally in favor of free markets; investors in the automobile industry)
3. What social views—particularly of male success and of women or gays—are promoted by rap music? (possible audiences: consumers of rap music; parents concerned about their children's exposure to rap music; black parents who read about Bill Cosby's speech to the 2004 NAACP convention—see pp. 31–32).
4. Any questions that your class might have developed through discussing Chapter 1.

Here is an example:

Problematic question: What can cities do to prevent traffic congestion?

One possible thesis: Although many people think that building light rail systems won't get people out of their cars, new light rail systems in many cities have attracted new riders and alleviated traffic problems.

Intended audience: Residents of cities concerned about traffic congestion but skeptical about light rail

Kinds of evidence needed to support thesis: Examples of cities with successful light rail systems; evidence that many riders switched from driving cars; evidence that light rail alleviated traffic problems

Supporting Your Thesis with Points and Particulars

Of course, a surprising thesis is only one aspect of an effective essay. An essay must also persuade the reader that the thesis is believable as well as surprising. Although tabloid newspapers have shocking headlines "Britney Spears Videos Contain FBI Spy Secrets!"), skepticism quickly replaces surprise when you look inside and find the article's claims unsupported. A strong thesis, then, must both surprise the reader and be supported with convincing particulars.

In fact, the particulars are the flesh and muscle of writing and comprise most of the sentences. In closed-form prose, these particulars are connected clearly to points, and the points precede the particulars. In this section, we explain this principle more fully.

How Points Convert Information to Meaning

When particulars are clearly related to a point, the point gives meaning to the particulars, and the particulars give force and validity to the point. Particulars constitute the evidence, data, details, examples, and subarguments that develop a point and make it convincing. By themselves, particulars are simply information—mere data without meaning.

In the following example, you can see for yourself the difference between information and meaning. Here is a list of information:*

- In almost all species on earth, males are more aggressive than females.
- Male chimpanzees win dominance by brawling.
- To terrorize rival troops, they kill females and infants.
- The level of aggression among monkeys can be manipulated by adjusting their testosterone levels.
- Among humans, preliminary research suggests that male fetuses are more active in the uterus than female fetuses.
- Little boys play more aggressively than little girls despite parental efforts to teach gentleness to boys and aggression to girls.

To make meaning out of this list of information, the writer needs to state a point—the idea, generalization, or claim—that this information supports. Once the point is stated, a meaningful unit (point with particulars) springs into being:

> Aggression in human males may be a function of biology rather than culture. In almost all species on earth, males are more aggressive than females. Male chimpanzees win dominance by brawling; to terrorize rival troops, they kill females and infants. Researchers have shown that the level of aggression among monkeys can be manipulated by adjusting their testosterone levels. Among humans, preliminary research suggests that male fetuses are more active in the uterus than female fetuses. Also, little boys play more aggressively than little girls despite parental efforts to teach gentleness to boys and aggression to girls.

Point

Particulars

Once the writer states this point, readers familiar with the biology/culture debate about gender differences immediately feel its surprise and tension. This writer believes that biology determines gender identity more than does culture. The writer now uses the details as evidence to support a point.

To appreciate the reader's need for a logical connection between points and particulars, note how readers would get lost if, in the preceding example, the

---

*The data in this exercise are adapted from Deborah Blum, "The Gender Blur," *Utne Reader* Sept. 1998: 45–48.

writer included a particular that seemed unrelated to the point ("Males also tend to be taller and heavier than women"—a factual statement, but what does it have to do with aggression?) or if, without explanation, the writer added a particular that seemed to contradict the point ("Fathers play more roughly with baby boys than with baby girls"—another fact, but one that points to culture rather than biology as a determiner of aggression).

Obviously, reasonable people seek some kind of coordination between points and particulars, some sort of weaving back and forth between them. Writing teachers use a number of nearly synonymous terms for expressing this paired relationship: *points/particulars, generalizations/specifics, claims/evidence, ideas/details, interpretations/data, meaning/support.*

How Removing Particulars Creates a Summary

What we have shown, then, is that skilled writers weave back and forth between generalizations and specifics. The generalizations form a network of higher-level and lower-level points that develop the thesis; the particulars (specifics) support each of the points and subpoints in turn. In closed-form prose, the network of points is easily discernible because points are clearly highlighted with transitions, and main points are placed prominently at the heads of paragraphs. (In open-form prose, generalizations are often left unstated, creating gaps where the reader must actively fill in meaning.)

Being able to write summaries and abstracts of articles is an important academic skill. See Chapter 6 on strategies for writing summaries and strong responses, pp. 126–165.

If you remove most of the particulars from a closed-form essay, leaving only the network of points, you will have written a summary or abstract of the essay. As an example, reread the civil engineer's letter to the editor arguing against the feasibility of wind-generated power (pp. 17–18). The writer's argument can be summarized in a single sentence:

> Wind-generated power is not a reasonable alternative to other forms of power in the Pacific Northwest because wind power is unreliable, because there are major unsolved problems involved in the design of wind-generation facilities, and because the environmental impact of building thousands of wind towers would be enormous.

What we have done in this summary is remove the particulars, leaving only the high-level points that form the skeleton of the argument. The writer's thesis remains surprising and contains tension, but without the particulars the reader has no idea whether to believe the generalizations or not. The presence of the particulars is thus essential to the success of the argument.

For Writing and Discussion

Compare the civil engineer's original letter with the one-sentence summary just given and then note how the engineer uses specific details to support each point. How do these particulars differ from paragraph to paragraph? How are they chosen to support each point?

How to Use Points and Particulars When You Revise

The lesson to learn here is that in closed-form prose, writers regularly place a point sentence in front of detail sentences. When a writer begins with a point, readers interpret the ensuing particulars not as random data but rather as *evidence* in support of that point. The writer depends on the particulars to make the point credible and persuasive.

This insight may help you clarify two of the most common kinds of marginal comments that readers (or teachers) place on writers' early drafts. If your draft has a string of sentences giving data or information unconnected to any stated point, your reader is apt to write in the margin, "What's your point here?" or "Why are you telling me this information?" or "How does this information relate to your thesis?" Conversely, if your draft tries to make a point that isn't developed with particulars, your reader is apt to write marginal comments such as "Evidence?" or "Development?" or "Could you give an example?" or "More details needed."

Don't be put off by these requests; they are a gift. It is common in first drafts for main points to be unstated, buried, or otherwise disconnected from their details and for supporting information to be scattered confusingly throughout the draft or missing entirely. Having to write point sentences obliges you to wrestle with your intended meaning: Just what am I trying to say here? How can I nutshell that in a point? Likewise, having to support your points with particulars causes you to wrestle with the content and shape of your argument: What particulars will make this point convincing? What further research do I need to do to find these particulars? In Part Three of this text, which is devoted to advice about composing and revising, we show how the construction and location of point sentences are essential for reader clarity. Part Three also explains various composing and revising strategies that will help you create effective networks of points and particulars.

For more about the importance of points, see pp. 548–549, which discuss topic sentences in paragraphs.

Chapter Summary

In this chapter we looked at the kind of wallowing in complexity that professors expect from students and saw how academic writing is rooted in subject matter problems. We saw how a prototypical introduction for an academic essay poses a question, explains how the question is problematic and significant, and then states the writer's thesis. We explained how a strong thesis aims to change readers' view of a topic by bringing to the reader something new, surprising, or challenging. Finally we saw how a writer supports a thesis through a network of points and particulars.

BRIEF WRITING PROJECT

Throughout this chapter we have shown the close relationship between a thesis question and a thesis statement. We conclude this chapter with a powerful thinking exercise that will keep you from being satisfied with a thesis statement too

Strategies for doing exploratory writing, composing first drafts, revising, and editing are treated in detail in Part Three of this text, "A Guide to Composing and Revising."

soon. As we have explained, writing is an active process of problem solving involving periods of pondering, researching, note-taking, exploratory writing, talking with others, drafting, and revising. The following exercise, developed by writing theorist Peter Elbow, is called the "believing and doubting game." To play the game, you explore many sides of a problematic question by posing a possible answer and then systemically trying first to believe that answer and then to doubt it. The game, as you will see, stimulates your critical thinking, helping you resist early closure.

Playing the Believing and Doubting Game

Play the believing and doubting game with one of the assertions listed on pp. 44–46 (or another assertion provided by your instructor) by freewriting your believing and doubting responses. Spend fifteen minutes believing and then fifteen minutes doubting for a total of thirty minutes.

When you play the believing side of this game, you try to become sympathetic to an idea or point of view. You listen carefully to it, opening yourself to the possibility that it is true. You try to appreciate why the idea has force for so many people; you try to accept it by discovering as many reasons as you can for believing it. It is easy to play the believing game with ideas you already believe in, but the game becomes more difficult, sometimes even frightening and dangerous, when you try believing ideas that seem untrue or disturbing.

The doubting game is the opposite of the believing game. It calls for you to be judgmental and critical, to find fault with an idea rather than to accept it. When you doubt a new idea, you try your best to falsify it, to find counterexamples that disprove it, to find flaws in its logic. Again, it is easy to play the doubting game with ideas you don't like, but it, too, can be threatening when you try to doubt ideas that are dear to your heart or central to your own worldview.

READING

Here is how one student played the believing and doubting game with the following assertion from professional writer Paul Theroux that emphasizing sports is harmful to boys.

Just as high school basketball teaches you how to be a poor loser, the manly attitude towards sports seems to be little more than a recipe for creating bad marriages, social misfits, moral degenerates, sadists, latent rapists and just plain louts. I regard high school sports as a drug far worse than marijuana.

Believing and Doubting Paul Theroux's Negative View of Sports

Believe

1   Although I am a woman I have a hard time believing this because I was a high school basketball player and believe high school sports are *very* important. But here goes. I will try to believe this statement even though I hate it. Let's see. It would seem that I wouldn't have much first-hand experience with how society turns boys into men. I do see though that Theroux is right about some major problems. Through my observations, I've seen many young boys go through humiliating experiences with sports that have left them scarred. For example, a 7-year-old boy, Matt, isn't very athletic and when kids in our neighborhood choose teams, they usually choose girls before they choose Matt. I wonder if he sees himself as a sissy and what this does to him? I have also experienced some first-hand adverse effects of society's methods of turning boys into men. In our family, my dad spent much of his time playing football, basketball, and baseball with my brother. I've loved sports since I was very young so I was eager to play. In order to play with them, I had to play like a boy. Being told you threw or played like a girl was the worst possible insult you could receive. The phrase, "be tough" was something I heard repeatedly while I was growing up. Whenever I got hurt, my dad would say, "Be tough." It didn't matter how badly I was hurt, I always heard the same message. Today, I think, I have a very, very difficult time opening up and letting people get to know me, because for so long I was taught to keep everything inside. Maybe sports does have some bad effects.

Doubt

2   I am glad I get to doubt this too because I have been really mad at all the sports bashing that has been going on in class. I think much of what Theroux says is just a crock. I know that the statement "sports builds character" is a cliché, but I really believe it. It seems to me that the people who lash out at sports clichés are those who never experienced these aspects of athletics and therefore don't understand them. No one can tell me that sports didn't contribute to some of my best and most meaningful friendships and growing experiences. I am convinced that I am a better person because through sports I have had to deal with failure, defeat, frustration, sacrificing individual desires for the benefit of the team, and so on. After my last high school basketball game when after many years of mind games, of hating my coach one minute and the next having deep respect for him, of big games lost on my mistakes, of hours spent alone in the gym, of wondering if the end justifies the means, my coach put his arm around me and told me he was proud. Everything, all the pain, frustration, anxiety, fear, and sacrifice of the past years seemed so worthwhile. You might try to tell me that this story

is hackneyed and trite, but I won't listen because it is a part of me, and some thing you will never be able to damage or take away. I think athletes share a special bond. They know what it is like to go through the physical pain of practice time and again. They understand the wide variety of emotions felt (but rarely expressed). They also know what a big role the friendships of teammates and coaches play in an athlete's life.

We admire this writer a great deal—both for the passion with which she defends sports in her doubting section and for the courage of walking in a sports basher's shoes in the believing section. This exercise clearly engaged and stretched her thinking.

We invite you now to stretch your own thinking by playing the believing and doubting game with one of the following assertions. The first set of assertions focuses on the constellation of issues surrounding fossil fuels and energy that we introduced in Chapter 1. The last set gives you other options to explore.

Option 1: Energy Issues

For these energy issues, we have identified the source for each assertion to help you imagine yourself joining a public conversation of ideas already in print.

1. ". . . the car is the greatest modern symbol of American freedom." (John Bragg, "The American Dream: Why Environmentalists Attack the SUV," *Capitalism Magazine Online*)
2. ". . . most customers want bigger and faster cars—actually, light-duty trucks like sport utility vehicles—not efficient ones." ["A Fuel-Saving Proposal from Your Automaker: Tax the Gas," *New York Times* (April 18, 2004): BU 5]
3. "This country must immediately start phasing out its national dependence on fossil fuel [and] support policies to immediately reduce carbon emissions and greenhouse gases . . . ." ("Climate Justice: Indigenous Peoples, Global Warming and Climate Change," Indigenous Environmental Network www.ienearth.org)
4. "The best way to break the back of OPEC [Organization of Petroleum Exporting Countries] is to produce more oil here at home." [Stephen Moore, "Stick a Pump in It," *National Review Online* (May 10, 2004)]
5. "If Congress is serious about ensuring our national security, it should immediately pass legislation to raise fuel economy standards to 40 miles a gallon by 2012 and 55 by 2020." [Robert F. Kennedy, Jr., "Better Gas Mileage, Greater Security," *New York Times* (November 24, 2001)]
6. You can also play the believing and doubting game with advertisements or other visual texts. Consider using the Shell corporate ad (Figure 2.1) or the Adbusters' spoof ad (Figure 2.2) as visual commentary on the oil industry's approach to oil exploration. If you are responding to one of these visual texts, begin by stating the main point of the text in a one-sentence assertion. For example, "The Shell ad says that the oil industry, especially our company, will

FIGURE 2.1 Shell Corporate Ad

WHAT DO WE REALLY NEED IN TODAY'S ENERGY HUNGRY WORLD? MORE GARDENERS.

The Flower Gardens of the Gulf of Mexico. Home to some of the most spectacular banks of coral and sponges to be found in this part of the world.

In fact, this National Marine Sanctuary forms the most northerly reef on the U.S. continental shelf. Which is why, when Shell went looking for oil and natural gas in this region, we looked for help from Jim Ray—a marine biologist and Shell employee.

For some thirty years now, Jim and others just like him have been working to protect this magnificent area and other sensitive marine environments.

They're providing a habitat for all manner of marine life, so everyone from ecologists to schoolteachers has the opportunity to study this wonderful world firsthand.

Because at Shell, we focus on energy but that's not our only focus. To find out more, see the Shell Report at www.shell.com.

FIGURE 2.2 Adbusters' Spoof Ad

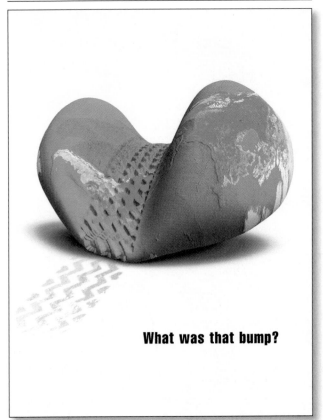

solve the problem of diminishing fossil fuel reserves by using our company's innovative thinking and technological expertise." Then play the believing and doubting game with the assertion.

Option 2: Other Issues

1. Grades are an effective means of motivating students to do their best work.
2. In recent years advertising has made enormous gains in portraying women as strong, independent, and intelligent.
3. To help fight terrorism and promote public safety, individuals should be willing to give up some of their rights.
4. It is often OK to tell a lie.
5. The United States should reinstate the draft.
6. Violent video games are harmful to young people.
7. NASCAR drivers are not real athletes.
8. It is rude to talk on a cell phone in a public place.
9. Hate speech should be forbidden on college campuses.

Thinking Rhetorically about Purpose, Audience, and Genre

It is amazing how much so-called writing problems clear up when the student really cares, when he is realistically put into the drama of somebody with something to say to somebody else.

—JAMES MOFFETT, *WRITING TEACHER AND THEORIST*

In Chapters 1 and 2 we introduced you to rhetorical thinking by showing you how experienced writers think about their audience and purpose as they wrestle with subject-matter questions. They must pose questions that matter to their intended readers and propose claims that bring those readers something new, surprising, or challenging. In all these cases, the writer's subject-matter considerations are influenced by rhetorical context.

In this chapter, we extend the idea of rhetorical thinking by probing three key variables in a writer's rhetorical context: purpose, audience, and genre. While thinking about subject matter, writers also think about rhetorical issues, posing questions about their purpose (What am I trying to accomplish in this paper?), their audience (What are my readers' values and assumptions? What do they already know and believe about my subject?), and genre (What kind of document am I writing? What are its requirements for structure, style, and document design?). We show how your answers to these questions influence many of the decisions you make as a writer. We end by explaining the generic rhetorical context assumed by most teachers for college papers across the disciplines.

In this chapter you will learn the following principles:

- How to think productively about your purpose, audience, and genre
- How to make decisions about structure and style based on your analysis of these elements
- How to adjust your writing on the scale of abstraction to fit your purpose, audience, and genre
- How to recognize and employ document design features appropriate for different genres
- How to understand the generic rhetorical context for most college papers

How Writers Think about Purpose

In this section, we want to help you think more productively about your purpose for writing, which can be examined from several different perspectives: your rhetorical aim, the motivating occasion that gets you going, and your desire to change your reader's view. All three perspectives will help you make your awareness of purpose work for you and increase your savvy as a writer. Let's look at each in turn.

Purpose as Rhetorical Aim

One powerful way to think about purpose is through the general concept of "rhetorical aim." In this text, we identify six different rhetorical aims of writing: to express, to explore, to inform, to analyze and synthesize, to persuade, and to give aesthetic pleasure. Thinking of each piece of writing in terms of one or more of these rhetorical aims can help you understand typical ways that your essay can be structured and developed and can help you clarify your relationship with your audience. The writing projects in Part Two of this text are based on these rhetorical aims.* Table 3.1 gives you an overview of each of the six rhetorical aims and sketches out how the subject matter differs from aim to aim, how the writer's task and relationship to readers differ according to aim, and how a chosen aim affects the writing's genre and its position on the spectrum from open to closed forms.

Purpose as a Response to a Motivating Occasion

Another important way to think about purpose is to think about each piece of writing as a response to a particular motivating occasion. Almost all writing is compelled by some sort of motivating occasion or exigency.† This exigency can be external (someone giving you a task and setting a deadline) or internal (your awareness of a problem stimulating your desire to bring about some change in people's views). Thus, when engineer David Rockwood read a newspaper editorial supporting wind-power projects, his own belief in the impracticality of wind power motivated him to write a letter to the editor in rebuttal (see pp. 17–18). But he also knew that he had to write the letter within one or two days or else it stood no chance of being published. His exigency thus included both internal and external factors.

---

*An additional aim, not quite parallel to these others, is sometimes called "writing-to-learn." When your purpose is writing-to-learn, your writing is aimed at helping you understand an important concept or learn a skill necessary for expert performance in a discipline. Teachers often design writing-to-learn assignments focusing on specific course learning goals. In Part Two of this text, the first two writing projects (for Chapters 5 and 6) are writing-to-learn pieces.

†An *exigency* is an urgent or pressing situation requiring immediate attention. Rhetoricians use the term to describe the event or occasion that causes a writer to begin writing.

TABLE 3.1 Purpose as Rhetorical Aim

Rhetorical Aim	Focus of Writing	What Writers Do	Relationship to Audience	Form and Genres
Express or share (Chapter 7)	Your own life, personal experiences that you want to make public, reflections	You express your feelings and thoughts (even venting); you write to move others.	You ask readers to see the world your way; you invite them to see connections between your life and theirs; you surprise readers with your experiential insights.	**Form:** Tends to have many open-form features **Sample genres:** Diary or journal; personal essay; literary nonfiction, perhaps using plot, character, image, and symbol
Explore or inquire (Chapter 8)	Subject-matter problems; a significant, problematic question; shows a writer seeking to understand these problems or questions	You ask questions, wade into complexity by posing or deepening a problem, raising new questions, considering alternative views, and showing the limitations of other answers and approaches.	You invite readers on your intellectual journey; you ask readers to think with you, to collaborate in discovering a new understanding of a subject.	**Form:** Follows open form in being narrative based; seeks a thesis rather than supporting one **Sample genres:** Freewriting; idea mapping; journals; notes; formal essays in narrative form dramatizing the writer's thinking about a question
Inform or explain (Chapter 9)	Subject matter on which you present new or needed information based on your own experience or research	You provide information your readers need or want, or you arouse curiosity and then present new, surprising information.	You, as knowledgeable teacher, surprise by enlarging readers' view of a subject; you expect readers to trust your authority and information.	**Form:** Usually has a closed-form structure but could be open form **Sample genres:** Encyclopedia, newspaper, and magazine articles; brochures; instruction booklets; sales reports; technical reports; informative Web sites
Analyze, synthesize, or interpret (Chapters 10–13)	Subject matter that is problematic and complex and that you can break down into parts and put together in new ways for greater understanding	Using critical thinking and possibly research, you examine parts and their relationships to each other and the whole; you put together ideas from your analyses into a new whole that represents your enlarged, enriched understanding of a subject or issue.	You challenge readers with a new, illuminating way of seeing, thinking about, or understanding your subject; readers may be skeptical, expecting you to support your thesis with good particulars.	**Form:** Typically has a closed-form structure; introduces a question or problem, sketches an answer, and develops this answer with good supporting points and particulars **Sample genres:** Scholarly articles and much other academic writing across the disciplines; critiques; public affairs magazine articles; newspaper feature articles

(continued)

TABLE 3.1 continued

Rhetorical Aim	Focus of Writing	What Writers Do	Relationship to Audience	Form and Genres
Persuade (Chapters 14–16)	Subject-matter questions that have multiple, controversial answers	You enter a controversy in hopes of persuading readers to accept your own views on a controversial issue; you surprise your readers with reasons and evidence to change their beliefs and actions.	You try to convince your readers, who are like jurors, of the soundness of your position; you must appeal to your readers' values and beliefs and anticipate the objections and alternative views of skeptical readers.	**Form:** Anywhere on the open-to-closed-form spectrum; could be a closed-form argument consisting of logical point-by-point reasons and evidence; could also be an open-form story or collage of emotionally charged scenes **Sample genres:** Letters to the editor; op-ed pieces; policy statements for public affairs magazines and advocacy Web sites; researched academic arguments
Entertain or give aesthetic pleasure (Chapter 19)	Language itself shaped to convey experience or emotion	You explore the properties of language, using words the way artists use clay and paint; you work with sounds, rhythms, and word images to make readers see and feel.	You seek to entice and move your readers— please, delight, thrill, or disturb them.	**Form:** Open form; literary nonfiction may combine a literary purpose with an expressive or explanatory purpose **Sample genres:** Literary nonfiction; poetry; all genres of fiction

You might think that school is the only place where people are compelled to write. However, some element of external compulsion is present in nearly every writing situation, although this external compulsion is almost never the sole motivation for writing. Consider a middle manager requested by the company vice president to write a report explaining why his division's profits are down. The manager is motivated by several factors: He wants to provide a sound analysis of why profits have declined; he wants to propose possible solutions that will remedy the situation; he wants to avoid looking personally responsible for the dip in profits; he wants to impress the vice president in the hope that she will promote him to upper management; and so on.

College students' motivations for writing can be equally complex: In part, you write to meet a deadline; in part, you write to please the teacher and get a good grade. But ideally you also write because you have become engaged with an intellectual problem and want to say something significant about it. Our point here is that your purposes for writing are always more complex than the simple desire to meet an assignment deadline.

Purpose as a Desire to Change Your Reader's View

Perhaps the most useful way to think about purpose is to focus on the change you want to bring about in your audience's view of the subject. When you are given a college writing assignment, this view of purpose engages you directly with the intellectual problem specified in the assignment. This view of purpose has already been introduced in Chapter 2, where we explained the importance of surprise as a measure of what is new or challenging in your essay. For most essays, you can write a one-sentence, nutshell statement about your purpose.

See Chapter 2, pp. 34–37, for an explanation of surprise in thesis statements.

My purpose is to give my readers a vivid picture of my difficult struggle with Graves' disease.

My purpose is to raise serious doubts about the value of the traditional grading system.

My purpose is to inform my readers about the surprising growth of the marijuana industry in the Midwestern farm states.

My purpose is to explain how Thoreau's view of nature differs in important ways from that of contemporary environmentalists.

My purpose is to persuade the general public that wind-generated electricity is not a practical energy alternative in the Pacific Northwest.

In closed-form academic articles, technical reports, and other business and professional pieces, writers often place explicit purpose statements in their introductions along with the thesis. In most other forms of writing, the writer uses a behind-the-scenes purpose statement to achieve focus and direction but seldom states the purpose explicitly. Writing an explicit purpose statement for a paper is a powerful way to nutshell the kind of change you want to bring about in your reader's view of the subject.

Chapter 18, pp. 545–546, shows you how purpose statements can be included in closed-form introductions.

For Writing and Discussion

This exercise will show you how the concept of "rhetorical aim" can help you generate ideas for an essay. As a class, choose one of the following topic areas or another provided by your instructor. Then imagine six different writing situations in which a hypothetical writer would compose an essay about the selected topic. Let each situation call for a different aim. How might a person write about the selected topic with an expressive aim? An exploratory aim? An informative aim? An analytic aim? A persuasive aim? A literary aim? How would each essay surprise its readers?

automobiles	animals	hospices or nursing homes
homelessness	music	dating or marriage
advertising	energy crisis	sports injuries

(continued)

Working on your own or in small groups, create six realistic scenarios, each of which calls for prose in a different category of aim. Then share your results as a whole class. Here are two examples based on the topic "hospices."

Expressive Aim	Working one summer as a volunteer in a hospice for dying cancer patients, you befriend a woman whose attitude toward death changes your life. You write an autobiographical essay about your experiences with this remarkable woman.
Analytic Aim	You are a hospice nurse working in a home care setting. You and your colleagues note that sometimes family members cannot adjust psychologically to the burden of living with a dying person. You decide to investigate this phenomenon. You interview "reluctant" family members in an attempt to understand the causes of their psychological discomfort so that you can provide better counseling services as a possible solution. You write a paper for a professional audience analyzing the results of your interviews.

How Writers Think about Audience

In our discussion of purpose, we already had a lot to say about audience. What you know about your readers—their familiarity with your subject matter, their reasons for reading, their closeness to you, their values and beliefs—affects most of the choices you make as a writer.

The value of moving from old information to new information is explained in Chapter 18, pp. 529–530 and 556–559.

In assessing your audience, you must first consider what, to them, is old information and what is new information. You'll ask questions like these: What in my essay will be familiar and what will be new, challenging, and surprising? How much background will my readers need? What can I assume they know and don't know? What is their current view of my topic that I am trying to change?

As you think about your readers' current views on your topic, you also need to think about their methods and reasons for reading. Imagine that you want to persuade your boss to reconfigure your office's computer network. You've discussed your ideas with her briefly, and she's asked you to write a formal proposal for the next technology meeting. Knowing of her harried environment—people waiting to see her, meetings to attend, e-mails piling up, memos and reports filling her inbox—you use a tightly closed structure for your proposal. Your document must be clear, concise, summarizable, and immediately comprehensible. The same reader in a different mood and setting may turn to a more leisurely kind of prose, say, an article in her favorite magazine or a new book on her favorite subject, where she might enjoy the subtlety and stylistic pleasures of open-form prose.

Now consider how a change in audience can affect the content of a piece. Suppose you want voters in your city to approve a bond issue to build a new baseball stadium. If most members of your audience are baseball fans, you can appeal to their love of the game, the pleasure of a new facility, and so forth. But non-baseball fans won't be moved by these arguments. To reach them, you must tie the new baseball stadium to their values. You can argue that a new stadium will bring new tax revenues to the city, clean up a run-down area, revitalize local businesses, or stimulate the tourist industry. Your purpose remains the same—to persuade taxpayers to fund the stadium—but the content of your argument changes if your audience changes.

In college, you often seem to be writing for an audience of one—your instructor. However, most instructors try to read as a representative of a broader audience. To help college writers imagine these readers, many instructors try to design writing assignments that provide a fuller sense of audience. They may ask you to write for the readers of a particular magazine or journal, or they may create case assignments with built-in audiences (for example, "You are an accountant in the firm of Numbers and Fudge; one day you receive a letter from . . ."). If your instructor does not specify an audience, you can generally assume the audience to be what we like to call "the generic academic audience"—student peers who have approximately the same level of knowledge and expertise in the field as you do, who are engaged by the question you address, and who want to read your writing and be surprised in some way.

Assessing Your Audience

In any writing situation, you can use the following questions to help you make decisions about content, form, and style:

QUESTIONS TO ASK ABOUT AUDIENCE

1. Who is going to read what I write? A specific individual? A specific group with special interests? Or a general readership with wide-ranging interests and backgrounds?
2. What relationship do I have to these readers? Do I and my readers have an informal, friendly relationship or a polite, formal one? Is my readers' expertise in my general subject area greater, less, or equal to mine?
3. How much do my readers already know about the specific problem I address? How much background will I have to provide?
4. How much interest do my readers bring to my topic? Do I need to hook readers with a vivid opening and use special techniques to maintain their interest throughout? Or are they interested enough in the problem I am examining that the subject matter itself will drive their reading? (In persuasive writing, particularly in writing that proposes a solution to a problem, you may need to shock your readers into awareness that the problem exists.)

   How to hook your readers' interest through an effective introduction is covered in Chapter 18, pp. 542–546.

5. What are my audience's values, beliefs, and assumptions in relation to my topic? If I am writing on a controversial issue, will my readers oppose my position, be neutral to it, or support it? To which of their values, beliefs, or assumptions can I appeal? Will my position unsettle or threaten my audience or stimulate a strong emotional response? (Because a concern for audience is particularly relevant to persuasive writing, we treat these questions in more depth in Chapters 14 through 16.)

Posing these questions will not lead to any formulaic solutions to your writing problems, but it can help you develop strategies that will appeal to your audience and enable you to achieve your purpose.

How Writers Think about Genre

The term *genre* refers to broad categories of writing that follow certain conventions of style, structure, approach to subject matter, and document design. Literary genres include the short story, the novel, the epic poem, the limerick, the sonnet, and so forth. Nonfiction prose has its own genres: the business memo, the technical manual, the scholarly article, the scientific report, the popular magazine article (each magazine, actually, has its own particular conventions), the Web page, the five-paragraph theme (a school genre), the newspaper editorial, the cover letter for a job application, the legal contract, the advertising brochure, and so forth.

The concept of genre creates strong reader expectations and places specific demands on writers. How you write any given letter, report, or article is influenced by the structure and style of hundreds of previous letters, reports, or articles written in the same genre. If you wanted to write for *Reader's Digest*, for example, you would have to use the conventions that appeal to its older, conservative readers: simple language, subjects with strong human interest, heavy reliance on anecdotal evidence in arguments, an upbeat and optimistic perspective, and an approach that reinforces the conservative *ethos* of individualism, self-discipline, and family. If you wanted to write for *Seventeen* or *Rolling Stone*, however, you would need to use quite different conventions.

To illustrate the relationship of a writer to a genre, we sometimes draw an analogy with clothing. Although most people have a variety of different types of clothing in their wardrobes, the genre of activity for which they are dressing (Saturday night movie date, job interview, wedding) severely constrains their choice and expression of individuality. A man dressing for a job interview might express his personality through choice of tie or quality and style of business suit; he probably wouldn't express it by wearing a Hawaiian shirt and sandals. Even when people deviate from a convention, they tend to do so in a conventional way. For example, teenagers who do not want to follow the genre of "teenager admired by adults" form their own genre of purple hair and pierced body parts. The concept of genre raises intriguing and sometimes unsettling questions about the relationship of the unique self to a social convention or tradition.

These same kinds of questions and constraints perplex writers. For example, academic writers usually follow the genre of the closed-form scholarly article. This highly functional form achieves maximum clarity for readers by orienting them quickly to the article's purpose, content, and structure. Readers expect this format, and writers have the greatest chance of being published if they meet these expectations. In some disciplines, however, scholars are beginning to publish more experimental, open-form articles. They may slowly alter the conventions of the scholarly article, just as fashion designers alter styles of dress.

For Writing and Discussion

1. On the previous page we offered you a brief description of the conventions governing *Reader's Digest* articles, which appeal mainly to older, conservative readers. For this exercise, prepare similar descriptions of the conventions that govern articles in several other magazines such as *Rolling Stone, Sports Illustrated, Cosmopolitan, Details, The New Yorker,* or *Psychology Today*. Each person should bring to class a copy of a magazine that he or she enjoys reading. The class should then divide into small groups according to similar interests. Your instructor may supply a few scholarly journals from different disciplines. In preparing a brief profile of your magazine, consider the following:

   - Scan the table of contents. What kinds of subjects or topics does the magazine cover?
   - Look at the average length of articles. How much depth and analysis are provided?
   - Consider the magazine's readership. Does the magazine appeal to particular political or social groups (liberal/conservative, male/female, young/old, white-collar/blue-collar, in-group/general readership)?
   - Look at the advertisements. What kinds of products are most heavily advertised in the magazine? Who is being targeted by these advertisements? What percentage of the magazine consists of advertisements?
   - Read representative pages, including the introductions, of some articles. Would you characterize the prose as difficult or easy? Intellectual or popular? Does the prose use the jargon, slang, or other language particular to a group? Are the paragraphs long or short? How are headings, inserts, visuals, and other page-formatting features used? Is the writing formal or informal?
   - Think about what advice you would give a person who wanted to write a freelance article for this magazine.

2. Imagine that someone interested in hospices (see the example in the For Writing and Discussion exercise on pp. 51–52) wanted to write an article about hospices for your chosen magazine. What approach would the writer have to take to have a hospice-related article published in your magazine? There may be no chance of this happening, but be creative. Here is an example:

   > Ordinarily *Sports Illustrated* would be an unlikely place for an article on hospices. However, *SI* might publish a piece about a dying athlete in a hospice setting. It might also publish a piece about sports memories of dying patients or about watching sports as therapy.

Rhetorical Context and Your Choices about Structure

So far in this chapter, we have examined purpose, audience, and genre as components of a writer's rhetorical context. In this section and the next, our goal is to help you appreciate how these variables influence a writer's choices regarding structure and style. Although there is no formula that allows you to determine an appropriate structure and style based on particular purposes, audiences, and genres, there are some rules of thumb that can help you make decisions. Let's look first at structure.

Because most academic, business, and professional writing uses a closed-form structure, we spend a significant portion of this text advising you how to write such prose. But open-form prose is equally valuable and is often more subtle, complex, and beautiful, so it is good to practice writing at different positions on the continuum. The following advice will help you decide when closed or open forms are more appropriate:

WHEN IS CLOSED-FORM PROSE MOST APPROPRIATE?

- When your focus is on the subject matter itself and your goal is to communicate efficiently to maximize clarity. In these cases, your aim is usually to inform, analyze, or persuade.
- When you imagine your audience as a busy or harried reader who needs to be able to read quickly and process ideas rapidly. Closed-form prose is easy to summarize; moreover, a reader can speed-read closed-form prose by scanning the introduction and then glancing at headings and the openings of paragraphs, where writers place key points.
- When the conventional genre for your context is closed-form writing and you choose to meet, rather than break, readers' expectations.
- When you encounter any rhetorical situation that asks you to assert and support a thesis in response to a problem or question.

WHEN IS A MORE OPEN FORM DESIRABLE?

- When you want to delay your thesis rather than announce it in the introduction (for example, to create suspense). A delayed-thesis structure is less combative and more friendly; it conveys an unfolding "let's think through this together" feeling.
- When your aim is expressive, exploratory, or literary. These aims tend to be served better through narrative rather than through thesis-with-support writing.
- When you imagine your audience reading primarily for enjoyment and pleasure. In this context you can often wed a literary purpose to another purpose.
- When the conventional genre calls for open-form writing—for example, autobiographical narratives, character sketches, or personal reflective pieces. Popular magazine articles often have a looser, more open structure than do scholarly articles or business reports.

- When you are writing about something that is too complex or messy to be captured in a fixed thesis statement, or when you feel constrained by the genre of thesis with support.

Rhetorical Context and Your Choices about Style

Writers need to make choices not only about structure but also about style. By *style*, we mean the choices you make about how to say something. Writers can say essentially the same thing in a multitude of ways, each placing the material in a slightly different light, subtly altering meaning, and slightly changing the effect on readers. In this section we illustrate more concretely the many stylistic options open to you and explain how you might go about making stylistic choices.

Factors That Affect Style

As we shall see, style is a complex composite of many factors. We can classify the hundreds of variables that affect style into four broad categories:

1. *Ways of shaping sentences:* long/short, simple/complex, many modifiers/few modifiers, normal word order/frequent inversions or interruptions, mostly main clauses/many embedded phrases and subordinate clauses
2. *Types of words:* abstract/concrete, formal/colloquial, unusual/ordinary, specialized/general, metaphoric/literal, scientific/literary
3. *The implied personality projected by the writer (often called* voice *or* persona*):* expert/layperson, scholar/student, outsider/insider, political liberal/conservative, neutral observer/active participant
4. *The writer's implied relationship to the reader and the subject matter (often called* tone*):* intimate/distant, personal/impersonal, angry/calm, browbeating/sharing, informative/entertaining, humorous/serious, ironic/literal, passionately involved/aloof

Recognizing Different Styles and Voices

When discussing style, rhetoricians often use related terms such as *voice* and *persona*. We can distinguish these terms by thinking of style as analyzable textual features on a page (length and complexity of sentences, level of abstraction, and so forth) and of voice or persona as the reader's impression of the writer projected from the page. Through your stylistic choices, you create an image of yourself in your readers' minds. This image can be cold or warm, insider or outsider, humorous or serious, detached or passionate, scholarly or hip, antagonistic or friendly, and so forth.

What style you adopt depends on your purpose, audience, and genre. Consider, for example, the following thought exercise: Suppose you are interested in the subject of flirting. (Perhaps you have asked a research question such as the following: How has concern about sexual harassment affected views on flirting in the workplace? Or, When is flirting psychologically and emotionally healthy?) You decide to do library research on flirting and are surprised by the different styles and genres you encounter. Here are the opening paragraphs of three different articles that discuss flirting—from a scholarly journal, from a fairly intellectual special interest magazine, and from a popular magazine devoted to women's dating and fashion. At the moment, we are considering only differences in the verbal styles of these articles. Later in this chapter, we reproduce the actual opening pages of two of these articles as they originally appeared in order to discuss document design.

SCHOLARLY JOURNAL

[*From* The Journal of Sex Research]

Sexual Messages: Comparing Findings from Three Studies

Sexual socialization is influenced by a wide range of sources, including parents, peers, and the mass media (Hyde & DeLameter, 1997). In trying to understand the process by which young people acquire their sexual beliefs, attitudes, and behaviors, the study of media provides information about potential socializing messages that are an important part of everyday life for children and adolescents (Greenberg, Brown, & Buerkel-Rothfuss, 1993). The significance of media content in this realm stems from a number of unique aspects surrounding its role in the lives of youth, including its early accessibility and its almost universal reach across the population.

Electronic media, and television in particular, provide a window to many parts of the world, such as sexually related behavior, that would otherwise be shielded from young audiences. Long before many parents begin to discuss sex with their children, answers to such questions as "When is it OK to have sex?" and "With whom does one have sexual relations?" are provided by messages delivered on television. These messages are hardly didactic, most often coming in the form of scripts and plots in fictional entertainment programs. Yet the fact that such programs do not intend to teach sexual socialization lessons hardly mitigates the potential influence of their portrayals.

—Dale Kunkel, Kirstie M. Cope, and Erica Biely

SPECIAL INTEREST MAGAZINE

[*From* Psychology Today]

The New Flirting Game

"It may be an ages-old, biologically-driven activity, but today it's also played with artful self-awareness and even conscious calculation" [opening lead in large, all-caps text].

To hear the evolutionary determinists tell it, we human beings flirt to propagate our genes and to display our genetic worth. Men are constitutionally predisposed to flirt with the healthiest, most fertile women, recognizable by their biologically correct waist-hip ratios. Women favor the guys with dominant demeanors, throbbing muscles and the most resources to invest in their offspring.

Looked at up close, human psychology is more diverse and perverse than the evolutionary determinists would have it. We flirt as thinking individuals in a particular culture at a particular time. Yes, we may express a repertoire of hardwired nonverbal expressions and behaviors—staring eyes, flashing brows, opened palms—that resemble those of other animals, but unlike other animals, we also flirt with conscious calculation. We have been known to practice our techniques in front of the mirror. In other words, flirting among human beings is culturally modulated as well as biologically driven, as much art as instinct.

—Deborah A. Lott

WOMEN'S DATING AND FASHION MAGAZINE

[*From* Cosmopolitan]

Flirting with Disaster

"I'd never be unfaithful, but . . ." [opening lead in very large type].

"You're in love and totally committed—or are you? You dirty danced with a cute guy at the office party, and make an effort to look sexy for the man in the coffee shop. Are you cheating without knowing it?" [second lead in large type]

I think I've been cheating on my partner. Let me explain. I went out clubbing recently with a really good friend, a guy I've known for years. We both love to dance. [. . .] [W]henever we get together, there comes a moment, late in the evening, when I look at him and feel myself beginning to melt. [. . .] This is not the way people who are "just friends" touch each other.

[. . .] So I suppose the question is, at what point does flirting stop being harmless fun and become an actual betrayal of your relationship?

—Lisa Sussman and Tracey Cox

For Writing and Discussion

Working in small groups or as a whole class, analyze the differences in the styles of these three samples.

1. How would you describe differences in the length and complexity of sentences, in the level of vocabulary, and in the degree of formality?
2. How do the differences in styles create different voices, personas, and tones?
3. Based on clues from style and genre, who is the intended audience of each piece? What is the writer's purpose? How does each writer hope to surprise the intended audience with something new, challenging, or valuable?
4. How are the differences in content and style influenced by differences in purpose, audience, and genre?

Rhetorical Context and Your Choices along the Scale of Abstraction

In Chapter 2, we explained how writers use particulars—examples, details, numerical data, and other kinds of evidence—to support their points. We said that strong writing weaves back and forth between points and particulars; points give meaning to particulars and particulars flesh out and develop points, making them credible and convincing. However, the distinction between points and particulars is a matter of context. The same sentence might serve as a point in one context and as a particular in another. What matters is the relative position of words and sentences along a scale of abstraction. As an illustration of such a scale, consider the following list of words descending from the abstract to the specific:

> Clothing→footwear→shoes→sandals→Birkenstocks→my old hippie Birkenstocks with salt stains

Where you pitch a piece of writing on this scale of abstraction helps determine its style, with high-on-the-scale writing creating an abstract or theoretical effect and low-on-the-scale writing creating a more vivid and concrete effect. In descriptive and narrative prose, writers often use sensory details that are very low on the scale of abstraction. Note how shifting down the scale improves the vividness of the following passage:

> Mid-scale The awkward, badly dressed professor stood at the front of the room.
> Low on the scale At the front of the room stood the professor, a tall, gawky man with inch-thick glasses, an enormous Adam's apple, an old brown-striped jacket, burgundy and gray plaid pants, a silky vest with what appeared to be "scenes from an aquarium" printed on it, and a tie with blue koalas.

The details in the more specific passage help you experience the writer's world. They don't just tell you that the professor was dressed weirdly; they *show* you.

In closed-form prose such specific sensory language is less common, so writers need to make choices about the level of specificity that will be most effective based on their purpose, audience, and genre. Note the differences along the level of abstraction in the following passages:

PASSAGE 1: FAIRLY HIGH ON SCALE OF ABSTRACTION

Point sentence

Particulars high on scale of abstraction

> Although lightning produces the most deaths and injuries of all weather-related accidents, the rate of danger varies considerably from state to state. Florida has twice as many deaths and injuries from lightning strikes as any other state. Hawaii and Alaska have the fewest.

—Passage from a general interest informative article on weather-related accidents

PASSAGE 2: LOWER ON SCALE OF ABSTRACTION

Point sentence

> Florida has twice as many deaths and injuries from lightning strikes as any other state, with many of these casualties occurring on the open spaces of golf courses.

Florida golfers should carefully note the signals of dangerous weather conditions such as darkening skies, a sudden drop in temperature, an increase in wind, flashes of light and claps of thunder, and the sensation of an electric charge on one's hair or body.

Particulars at midlevel on scale

In the event of an electric storm, golfers should run into a forest, get under a shelter, get into a car, or assume the safest body position. To avoid being the tallest object in an area, if caught in open areas, golfers should find a low spot, spread out, and crouch into a curled position with feet together to create minimal body contact with the ground.

Particulars at lower level on scale

—Passage from a safety article aimed at Florida golfers

Both of these passages are effective for their audience and purpose. Besides sensory details, writers can use other kinds of particulars that are low on the scale of abstraction such as quotations or statistics. Civil engineer David Rockwood uses low-on-the-scale numerical data about the size and number of wind towers to convince readers that wind generation of electricity entails environmental damage.

See Rockwood's letter to the editor, pp. 17–18.

Other kinds of closed-form writing, however, often remain high on the scale. Yet even the most theoretical kind of prose will move back and forth between several layers on the scale. Your rhetorical decisions about level of abstraction are important because too much high-on-the-scale writing can become dull for readers, while too much low-on-the-scale writing can seem overwhelming or pointless. Each of the assignment chapters in Part Two of this text gives advice on finding the right kinds and levels of particulars to support each essay.

For Writing and Discussion

The following exercise will help you appreciate how details can be chosen at different levels of abstraction to serve different purposes and audiences. Working in small groups or as a whole class, invent details at appropriate positions on the scale of abstraction for each of the following point sentences.

1. The big game was a major disappointment. You are writing an e-mail message to a friend who is a fan (of baseball, football, basketball, another sport) and missed the game; use midlevel details to explain what was disappointing.
2. Although the game stunk, there were some great moments. Switch to low-on-the-scale details to describe one of these "great moments."
3. Advertising in women's fashion magazines creates a distorted and unhealthy view of beauty. You are writing an analysis for a college course on popular culture; use high-to-midlevel details to give a one-paragraph overview of several ways these ads create an unhealthy view of beauty.
4. One recent ad, in particular, conveys an especially destructive message about beauty. Choose a particular ad and describe it with low-on-the-scale details
5. In United States politics, there are several key differences between Republicans and Democrats. As part of a service learning project, you are creating a page on "American Politics" for a Web site aimed at helping international students understand American culture. Imagine a two-columned bulleted list contrasting Republicans and Democrats and construct two or

(continued)

three of these bullets. Choose details at an appropriate level on the scale of abstraction.

6. One look at Pete's pickup, and you knew immediately he was an in-your-face Republican (Democrat). You are writing a feature story for your college newspaper about Pete, a person who has plastered his pickup with political signs, bumper stickers, and symbols. Choose details at an appropriate level on the scale of abstraction.

Rhetorical Context and your Choices about Document Design

When thinking about structure, style, and genre, writers also need to consider document design. Document design refers to the visual features of a text. The "look" of a document is closely bound to the rhetorical context, to the way writers seek to communicate with particular audiences for particular purposes, and to the audience's expectations for that genre of writing. In this section, we explain the main components of document design that you will encounter as a reader. In Chapter 18, Lesson 10, we explain some principles of document design that you can use as a writer for producing different kinds of texts.

Historically, the use of images to convey information is more important than we may realize. Alphabets, for example, derived from picture drawings, and in earlier centuries, when only a small portion of the population could read, images—such as on signs—were an important means of communication. Now in the twenty-first century, some cultural critics theorize that we are moving from a text-based culture to an image-based culture. These critics speculate that visual communication has become more important, partly because of the increased pace of life, the huge volume of information that bombards us daily, and the constantly improving technology for creating better and more varied electronic images. We rely more heavily on information transmitted visually, and we depend on receiving that information more quickly. Visual details become a shorthand code for conveying this information concisely, quickly, and vividly. The visual details of document design are part of a code for recognizing genres and part of audience expectations that writers must meet.

As a writer, you are often expected to produce manuscript (typed pages of text) rather than a publication-ready document. When your task is to produce manuscript, your concerns for document design usually focus on margins, font style and size, location of page numbers, and line spacing. As an academic writer, you generally produce manuscripts following the style guidelines of the Modern Language Association (MLA), the American Psychological Association (APA), or some other scholarly organization. In business and professional settings, you employ different kinds of manuscript conventions for writing letters, memoranda, or reports.

Chapter 22 explains MLA and APA conventions.

In contrast to manuscript, today's writers are sometimes asked to use desktop publishing software to produce camera-ready or Web-ready documents that have a professional visual appeal (such as a pamphlet or brochure, a Web page, a poster, a marketing proposal that incorporates visuals and graphics, or some other piece with a "professionally published" look). Occasionally in your manuscript documents, you may want to display ideas or information visually—for example, with graphs, tables, or images.

See Chapter 10 for suggestions about when and how to use graphics and tables.

Key Components of Document Design

The main components of document design are use of type, use of space and layout, use of color, and use of graphics or images.

Use of Type

Type comes in different typeface styles, or fonts, that are commonly grouped in three font families: serif fonts that have tiny extensions on the letters, which make them easier to read for long documents; sans serif fonts that lack these extensions on the letters and are good for labels, headings, and Web documents; and specialty fonts, often used for decorative effect, that include script fonts and special symbols. Common word processing programs usually give you a huge array of fonts. Some examples of different fonts are shown in the box on page 64.

Fonts also come in different sizes, measured in points (one point = 1/72 of an inch). Much type in printed texts is set in ten or twelve points. In addition, fonts can be formatted in different ways: boldface, italics, underlining, or shading.

Font style and size contribute to the readability and overall impression of a text. Scholarly publications use few, plain, and regular font styles that don't draw attention to the type. Their use of fonts seeks to keep the readers' focus on the content of the document, to convey a serious tone, and to maximize the readers' convenience in grappling with the ideas of the text. (Teachers regularly expect a conservative font such as CG Times, Times New Roman, or Courier New for academic papers. Were you to submit an academic paper in a specialty or scripted font, you'd make a "notice me" statement, analogous to wearing a lime green jumpsuit to a college reception.) In academic papers, boldface can be used for headings and italics for occasional emphasis, but otherwise design flourishes are seldom used.

Popular magazines, on the other hand, tend to use fonts playfully and artistically, using a variety of fonts and sizes to attract readers' attention initially and to make a document look pleasingly decorative on the page. Although the body text of articles is usually the same font throughout, the opening page often uses a variety of fonts and sizes, and font variations may occur throughout the text to highlight key ideas for readers who are reading casually or rapidly.

Examples of Font Styles

Font Style	Font Name	Example
Serif fonts	Times New Roman	Have a good day!
	Courier New	Have a good day!
Sans serif fonts	Arial	Have a good day!
	Century Gothic	Have a good day!
Specialty fonts	Monotype Corsiva	*Have a good day!*
	Symbol	Ηαϖε α γοοδ δαψ!

Use of Space and Layout of Documents

Layout refers to how the text is formatted on the page. Layout includes the following elements:

- The size of the page itself
- The proportion of text to white space
- The arrangement of text on the page (single or multiple columns, long or short paragraphs, spaces between paragraphs)
- The size of the margins
- The use of justification (alignment of text with the left margin or both margins)
- The placement of titles
- The use of headings and subheadings to signal main and subordinate ideas and main parts of the document
- The spacing before and after headings
- The use of numbered or bulleted lists
- The use of boxes to highlight ideas or break text into visual units

Academic and scholarly writing calls for simple, highly functional document layouts. Most scholarly journals use single or double columns of text that are justified at both margins to create a regular, even look. (In preparing an academic manuscript, however, justify only the left-hand margin, leaving the right margin ragged.) Layout—particularly the presentation of titles and headings and the formatting of notes and bibliographic data—is determined by the style of the individual journal, which treats all articles identically. The layout of scholarly documents strikes a balance between maximizing the amount of text that fits on a page and ensuring readability by using headings and providing adequate white space in the margins.

In contrast, popular magazines place text in multiple columns that are often varied and broken up by text in boxes or by text wrapped around photos or drawings. Readability is important, but so is visual appeal and entertainment: Readers must enjoy looking at the pages. Many popular magazines try to blur the distinction between content and advertising so that ads become part of the visual appeal. This is why, in fashion magazines, the table of contents is often buried a dozen or more pages into the magazine. The publisher wants to coax readers to look at the ads as they look for the contents. (In contrast, the table of contents for most academic journals is on the cover.)

Use of Color

Colors convey powerful messages and appeals, even affecting moods. While man-uscripts are printed entirely in black, published documents often use color to identify and set off main ideas or important information. Color-tinted boxes can indicate special features or allow magazines to print different but related articles on the same page.

Academic and scholarly articles and books use color minimally, if at all, relying instead on different font styles and sizes to make distinctions in content. Popular magazines, on the other hand, use colors playfully, artistically, decoratively, and strategically to enhance their appeal and, thus, their sales. Different colors of type may be used for different articles within one magazine or within articles them-selves. Some articles may be printed on colored paper to give variety to the whole magazine.

The rhetorical use of visuals is introduced in Chapter 4, pp. 85–87. More detailed discussion of tables and graphs is found in Chapter 10, pp. 261–265, and of drawings and photo-graphs throughout Chapter 11.

Use of Graphics or Images

Graphics include visual displays of information such as tables, line graphs, bar graphs, pie charts, maps, cartoons, illustrations, and photos.

As with the use of type, space, and color, the use of graphics indicates the focus, seriousness, function, and complexity of the writing. In scientific articles and books, many of the important findings of the articles may be displayed in complex, technical graphs and tables. Sources of information for these graphics are usually prominently stated, with key variables clearly labeled. In the humani-ties and social sciences, content-rich photos and drawings also tend to be vital parts of an article, even the subject of the analysis.

Popular magazines typically use simple numeric visuals (for example, a color-ful pie chart or a dramatic graph) combined with decorative use of images, espe-cially photos. If photos appear, it is worthwhile to consider how they are used. For example, do photos aim to look realistic and spontaneous like documentary photos of disaster scenes, sports moments, or people at work, or are they highly constructed, aesthetic photos? (Note that many political photos are meant to look spontaneous but are actually highly scripted—for example, a photograph of the president mending a fence with a horse nearby.) Are they concept (thematic) photos meant to illustrate an idea in an article (for example, a picture of a woman surrounded by images of pills, doctors, expensive medical equipment, and wran-gling employers and insurance agents, to illustrate an article on health care costs)? The use of photos and illustrations can provide important clues about a publication's angle of vision, philosophy, or political leaning. For example, the *Utne Reader* tends to use many colored drawings rather than photos to illustrate its articles. These funky drawings with muted colors suit the magazine's liberal, socially progressive, and activist angle of vision.

Understanding the political slant of magazines, newspapers, and Web sites is essential for researchers. See Chapter 21, pp. 628–631.

Examples of Different Document Designs

In our earlier discussion of style, we reprinted the opening paragraphs of three arti-cles on flirting. Figures 3.1 and 3.2 show the opening pages of two of these articles as they appeared in *The Journal of Sex Research* and *Psychology Today* (*Cosmopolitan*

FIGURE 3.1 Opening Page from Article in The *Journal of Sex Research*

Sexual Messages on Television: Comparing Findings From Three Studies

Dale Kunkel, Kirstie M. Cope, and Erica Biely

University of California Santa Barbara

Television portrayals may contribute to the sexual socialization of children and adolescents, and therefore it is important to examine the patterns of sexual content presented on television. This report presents a summary view across three related studies of sexual messages on television. The content examined ranges from programs most popular with adolescents to a comprehensive, composite week sample of shows aired across the full range of broadcast and cable channels. The results across the three studies identify a number of consistent patterns in television's treatment of sexual content. Talk about sex and sexual behaviors are both found frequently across the television landscape, although talk about sex is more common. Most sexual behaviors tend to be precursory in nature (such as physical flirting and kissing), although intercourse is depicted or strongly implied in roughly one of every eight shows on television. Perhaps most importantly, the studies find that TV rarely presents messages about the risks or responsibilities associated with sexual behavior.

Sexual socialization is influenced by a wide range of sources, including parents, peers, and the mass media (Hyde & DeLamater, 1997). In trying to understand the process by which young people acquire their sexual beliefs, attitudes, and behaviors, the study of media provides information about potential socializing messages that are an important part of everyday life for children and adolescents (Greenberg, Brown, & Buerkel-Rothfuss, 1993). The significance of media content in this realm stems from a number of unique aspects surrounding its role in the lives of youth, including its early accessibility and its almost universal reach across the population.

Electronic media, and television in particular, provide a window to many parts of the world, such as sexually-related behavior, that would otherwise be shielded from young audiences. Long before many parents begin to discuss sex with their children, answers to such questions as "When is it OK to have sex?" and "With whom does one have sexual relations?" are provided by messages delivered on television. These messages are hardly didactic, most often coming in the form of scripts and plots in fictional entertainment programs. Yet the fact that such programs do not intend to teach sexual socialization lessons hardly mitigates the potential influence of their portrayals.

While television is certainly not the only influence on sexual socialization, adolescents often report that they use portrayals in the media to learn sexual and romantic scripts and norms for sexual behavior (Brown, Childers, & Waszak, 1990). Indeed, four out of ten (40%) teens say they have gained ideas for how to talk to their boyfriend or girlfriend about sexual issues directly from media portrayals (Kaiser Family Foundation, 1998).

Just as it is well established that media exposure influences social behaviors such as aggression and social stereotyping, there is a growing body of evidence documenting the possible effects of sexual content on television (Huston, Wartella, & Donnerstein, 1998). For example, two studies have reported correlations between watching television programs high in sexual content and the early initiation of sexual intercourse by adolescents (Brown & Newcomer, 1991; Peterson, Moore, & Furstenberg, 1991), while another found heavy television viewing to be predictive of negative attitudes toward remaining a virgin (Courtright & Baran, 1980). An experiment by Bryant and Rockwell (1994) showed that teens who had just viewed television dramas laden with sexual content rated descriptions of casual sexual encounters less negatively than teens who had not viewed any sexual material.

Another important aspect of sexual socialization involves the development of knowledge about appropriate preventative behaviors to reduce the risk of infection from AIDS or other sexually-transmitted diseases. When teenagers begin to engage in sexual activity, they assume the risk of disease as well as the risk of unwanted pregnancy, and it appears that many lack adequate preparation to avoid such negative consequences.

Two Americans under the age of 20 become infected with HIV every hour (Office of National AIDS Policy, 1996). Almost one million teenagers become pregnant every year in the United States (Kirby, 1997). In the face of these sobering statistics, it is important to consider the extent to which media portrayals engage in or overlook concerns such as these, which are very serious issues in the lives of young people today.

In summary, media effects research clearly suggests that television portrayals contribute to sexual socialization.

The Family Hour Study was supported by the Henry J. Kaiser Family Foundation (Menlo Park, CA) and Children Now (Oakland, CA). The Teen Study was the Master's Thesis for Kirstie M. Cope. The V-Chip Study was supported by the Henry J. Kaiser Family Foundation. The authors wish to thank Carolyn Colvin, Ed Donnerstein, Wendy Jo Farinola, Ulla Foehr, Jim Potter, Vicky Rideout, and Emma Rollin, each of whom made significant contributions to one or more of the studies summarized here.

Address correspondence to Dr. Dale Kunkel, Department of Communication, University of California Santa Barbara, Santa Barbara, CA 93106: e-mail: kunkel@ahshaw.ucsb.edu.

FIGURE 3.2 Opening Page from Article in *Psychology Today*

THE NEW
Flirting Game

IT MAY BE AN AGES-OLD, BIOLOGICALLY-DRIVEN ACTIVITY, BUT TODAY IT'S ALSO PLAYED WITH ARTFUL SELF-AWARENESS AND EVEN CONSCIOUS CALCULATION.

By Deborah A. Lott

To hear the evolutionary determinists tell it, we human beings flirt to propagate our genes and to display our genetic worth. Men are constitutionally predisposed to flirt with the healthiest, most fertile women, recognizable by their biologically correct waist-hip ratios. Women favor the guys with dominant demeanors, throbbing muscles and the most resources to invest in them and their offspring.

Looked at up close, human psychology is more diverse and perverse than the evolutionary determinists would have it. We flirt as thinking individuals in a particular culture at a particular time. Yes, we may express a repertoire of hardwired non-verbal expressions and behaviors—staring eyes, flashing brows, opened palms—that resemble those of other animals, but unlike other animals, we also flirt with consciousness calculation. We have been known to practice our techniques in front of the mirror. In other words, flirting among human beings is culturally modulated as well as biologically driven, as much art as instinct.

In our culture today, it's clear that we do not always choose as the object of our desire those people the evolutionists might deem those most biologically desirable. After all, many young women today find the pale, androgynous, scarcely muscled yet emotionally expressive Leonardo DiCaprio more appealing than the burly Tarzans (Arnold Schwarzenegger, Bruce Willis, etc.) of action movies. Woody Allen may look nerdy but has had no trouble winning women—and that's not just because he has material resources, but because humor is also a precious cultural commodity. Though she has no breasts or hips to speak of, Ally McBeal still attracts because there's ample evidence of a quick and quirky mind.

In short, we flirt with the intent of assessing potential lifetime partners, we flirt to have easy, no-strings-attached sex, and we flirt when we are not looking for either. We flirt because, most simply, flirtation can be a liberating form of play, a game with suspense and ambiguities that brings joys of its own. As Philadelphia-based social psychologist Tim Perper says, "Some flirters appear to want to prolong the interaction because it's pleasurable and erotic in its own right, regardless of where it might lead."

Here are some of the ways the game is currently being played.

TAKING The Lead

When it comes to flirting today, women aren't waiting around for men to make the advances. They're taking the lead. Psychologist Monica Moore, Ph.D. of Webster University in St. Louis, Missouri, has spent more than 2000 hours observing women's flirting maneuvers in restaurants, singles bars and at parties. According to her findings, women give non-verbal cues that get a flirtation rolling fully two-thirds of the time. A man may think he's making the first move because he is the one to literally move from wherever he is to the woman's side, but usually he has been summoned.

By the standards set out by evolutionary psychologists, the women who attract the most

PHOTOGRAPHY BY FRANK VERONSKY

Psychology Today, November/December 1999

would not permit these images in its opening two-page spread to be reproduced for this textbook. However, we describe the opening pages in some detail in the For Writing and Discussion exercise below, discussion question 4).

For Writing and Discussion

Working individually or in small groups, analyze how content, style, genre, and document design are interrelated in these articles.

1. How does the document design of each article—its use of fonts, layout, color, and graphics—identify each piece as a scholarly article or an article in a popular magazine? From your own observation, what are typical differences in the document design features of an academic article and a popular magazine article? For example, how are fonts and color typically used in articles in women's and men's fashion magazines?

2. What makes the style and document design of each article appropriate for its intended audience and purpose?

3. What is the function of the abstract (article summary) at the beginning of the academic journal article? What is the function of the large-font "leads" at the beginning of popular articles?

4. Consider the photographs that accompany popular magazine articles. To illustrate the concept of flirting as potential cheating, the opening page (not shown) of the *Cosmopolitan* article, quoted on page 59, features a two-page spread showing a beautiful, young, mysterious woman in a low-cut dress that shows her glistening tan skin. She is looking seriously but coyly at the reader, and behind her are shadowy images of handsome men in loosely buttoned white shirts and sports coats. Think about the photograph in the *Psychology Today* article shown in Figure 3.2. Is it a realistic, candid "documentary" photo? Is it a scripted photo? Is it a concept photo aimed at illustrating the article's thesis or question? What aspects of the *Psychology Today* photo appeal to psychological themes and interests and make it appropriate for the content, audience, and genre of the article? How do you think photos accompanying *Cosmopolitan* articles differ from photos accompanying articles in *Psychology Today?*

5. When you download an article from an electronic database (unless it is in pdf format), you often lose visual cues about the article's genre such as document design, visuals, and so forth. Even when an article is in pdf format, you lose cues about its original print context—the kind of magazine or journal the article appeared in, the magazine's layout and advertisements, and its targeted audience. How do these visual cues in the original print version of an article provide important contextual information for reading the article and using it in your own research? Why do experienced researchers prefer the original print version of articles rather than downloaded articles whenever possible?

A Generic Rhetorical Context for College Writing

How can you transfer this chapter's discussion of rhetorical context, style, and document design to the writing assignments you typically receive in college? Our general advice is to pay attention to cues about purpose, audience, and genre in your instructors' assignments and, when in doubt, to ask your instructors questions about their expectations. Our specific advice is that you should assume a "default" or "generic" rhetorical context unless the assignment suggests something different.

What Do We Mean by a "Default" or "Generic" Rhetorical Context?

We have spent years studying the assignments of professors across the curriculum and have found that, unless they specify otherwise, instructors generally assume the following context:

- *Purpose.* Generally, instructors want you to write a closed-form, thesis-governed essay in response to a problem the instructor provides or to a problem that you must pose yourself. The most common rhetorical aims are informative, analysis/synthesis, or persuasion.
- *Audience.* Generally, instructors ask you to write to fellow classmates who share approximately the same level of expertise in a discipline as you do. Your goal is to say something new and challenging to this audience (but not necessarily to the instructor, who has a much higher level of expertise).
- *Genre.* Generally, instructors expect you to follow the manuscript requirements of the discipline, often MLA or APA style. Instructors vary considerably, however, in how much they care about exact formats.

Given this generic context, what is an appropriate writer's voice for college papers? For most college assignments, we recommend that students approximate their natural speaking voices to give their writing a conversational academic style. By "natural," we mean a voice that strives to be plain and clear while retaining the engaging quality of a person who is enthusiastic about the subject.

Of course, as you become an expert in a discipline, you often need to move toward a more scholarly voice. For example, the prose in an academic journal article can be extremely dense in its use of technical terms and complex sentence structure, but expert readers in that field understand and expect this voice. Students sometimes try to imitate a dense academic style before they have achieved the disciplinary expertise to make the style sound natural. The result can seem pretentiously stilted and phony. Writing with clarity and directness within your natural range will usually create a more effective and powerful voice.

Besides striving for a natural voice, you need to be aware of subtle features of your prose that project your image to readers. For example, in an academic article, the overt function of documentation and a bibliography is to enable other scholars to track down your cited sources. But a covert function is to create an air

See Chapter 22 for lessons on how to cite and document sources professionally.

of authority for you, the writer, to assure readers that you have done your professional work and are fully knowledgeable and informed. Judicious use of the discipline's specialized language and formatting can have a similar effect. Your image is also reflected in your manuscript's form, appearance, and editorial correctness. Sloppy or inappropriately formatted manuscripts, grammatical errors, misspelled words, and other problems send a signal to the reader that you are unprofessional.

Assignments That Specify Different Rhetorical Contexts

Although the majority of college writing assignments assume the generic rhetorical context we have just described, many ask students to write in different genres and styles. At our own universities, for example, some professors ask students to link their writing to service-learning projects by creating Web sites, pamphlets, brochures, proposals, or news stories related to the organizations they are serving. Others ask students to role-play characters in a case study—writing as a marketing manager to a corporate policy board or as a lobbyist to a legislator. Still others ask students to write short stories using course ideas and themes or to create imaginary dialogues between characters with different points of view on a course issue. When you get such assignments, enter into their spirit. You'll usually be rewarded for your creative ability to imagine different voices, genres, and styles.

Chapter Summary

In this chapter we have looked at how experienced writers think rhetorically about purpose, audience, and genre. We began by examining how writers think productively about each of these elements in their rhetorical context, and then we considered how variations in purpose, audience, and genre influence a writer's choices about structure, style, and document design. We concluded with a brief discussion of the generic rhetorical context assumed in most college writing assignments.

BRIEF WRITING PROJECT

This assignment asks you to try your hand at translating a piece of writing from one rhetorical context to another. As background, you need to know that each month's *Reader's Digest* includes a section called "News from the World of Medicine," which contains one or more mini-articles reporting on recent medical research. The writers of these pieces scan articles in medical journals, select items of potential interest to the general public, and translate them from a formal, scientific style into a popular style. Here is a typical example of a *Reader's Digest* mini-article:

COMPLETE ARTICLE FROM *READERS DIGEST*

"For Teeth, Say Cheese," Penny Parker

Cheese could be one secret of a healthy, cavity-free smile, according to a recent study by a professor of dentistry at the University of Alberta in Edmonton, Canada.

In the study, John Hargreaves found that eating a piece of hard cheese the size of a sugar cube at the end of a meal can retard tooth decay. The calcium and phosphate present in the cheese mix with saliva and linger on the surface of the teeth for up to two hours, providing protection against acid attacks from sweet food or drink.

Now compare this style with the formal scientific style in the following excerpts, the introduction and conclusion of an article published in the *New England Journal of Medicine*.

EXCERPT FROM SCIENTIFIC ARTICLE IN A MEDICAL JOURNAL

From *"Aspirin as an Antiplatelet Drug," Carlo Patrono*

Introduction: The past 10 years have witnessed major changes in our understanding of the pathophysiologic mechanisms underlying vascular occlusion and considerable progress in the clinical assessment of aspirin and other antiplatelet agents. The purpose of this review is to describe a rational basis for antithrombotic prophylaxis and treatment with aspirin. Basic information on the molecular mechanism of action of aspirin in inhibiting platelet function will be integrated with the appropriate clinical pharmacologic data and the results of randomized clinical trials. . . .

Conclusions: Aspirin reduces the incidence of occlusive cardiovascular events in patients at variable risk for these events. Progress in our understanding of the molecular mechanism of the action of aspirin, clarification of the clinical pharmacology of its effects on platelets, and clinical testing of its efficacy at low doses have contributed to a downward trend in its recommended daily dose. The present recommendation of a single loading dose of 200–300 mg followed by a daily dose of 75–100 mg is based on findings that this dose is as clinically efficacious as higher doses and is safer than higher doses. The satisfactory safety profile of low-dose aspirin has led to ongoing trials of the efficacy of a combination of aspirin and low-intensity oral anti-coagulants in high-risk patients. Finally, the efficacy of a cheap drug such as aspirin in preventing one fifth to one third of all important cardiovascular events should not discourage the pharmaceutical industry from attempting to develop more effective antithrombotic drugs, since a sizeable proportion of these events continue to occur despite currently available therapy.

Assume that you are a writer of mini-articles for the medical news section of *Reader's Digest*. Translate the findings reported in the article on aspirin into a *Reader's Digest* mini-article.

Although the style of the medical article may seem daunting at first, a little work with a good dictionary will help you decipher the whole passage. We've reproduced excerpts from the article's introduction and all of the final section labeled "Conclusions." These two sections provide all the information you need for your mini-article.

Thinking Rhetorically about How Messages Persuade

A way of seeing is also a way of not seeing.

—KENNETH BURKE, *RHETORICIAN*

Every time an Indian villager watches the community TV and sees an ad for soap or shampoo, what they notice are not the soap and shampoo but the lifestyle of the people using them, the kind of motorbikes they ride, their dress and their homes.

—NAYAN CHANDA, *INDIAN-BORN EDITOR OF YALEGLOBAL ONLINE MAGAZINE*

Throughout Part One, we have focused on writing as a rhetorical act. When writers think rhetorically, they are aware of writing to an audience for a purpose within a genre. We have explained how writers pose both subject-matter questions and rhetorical questions, which are closely interlinked: Subject-matter questions must engage their audience's interests, and proposed solutions to these questions must bring something new, surprising, or challenging to that audience.

In this final chapter of Part One, we hope to expand your understanding of a writer's choices by focusing on the particular ways that messages persuade. We will use the words *message* and *persuade* in the broadest sense to refer to the success or failure of any communication act, including nonverbal acts, such as one's choices about clothing or music. Throughout this chapter we will ask: What makes a given message successful or unsuccessful in achieving its intended effect? What choices can a person make to increase the effectiveness of a message? The payoffs for doing this kind of rhetorical thinking are wide-ranging. Not only will such thinking make you a more powerful communicator, but it will also help you be a better reader, observer, and listener. When you understand how messages achieve their effects, you will be better prepared to analyze and evaluate those messages and to make your own choices about whether to resist them or accede to them.

A classic illustration of rhetorical thinking is this little thought exercise:

THOUGHT EXERCISE ON RHETORICAL THINKING

Suppose you attended a fun party on Friday night. (You get to choose what constitutes "fun" for you.) Now imagine two people asking you what you did on Friday night. Person A is your best friend, who missed the party. Person B is your grand-mother. How would your descriptions of Friday night differ?

Clearly there isn't just one way to describe this party. Your description will be shaped by your purpose and by the values and concerns of your intended audience. Along the way, you will have to make rhetorical decisions such as the following:

- What kind of image of myself should I project? (For your friend you might construct yourself as a party animal; for Grandma you might construct yourself as a demure, soda-sipping observer of the party action.)
- What details should I include or leave out? (Does Grandma really need to know that the neighbors called the police?)
- How much emphasis do I give the party? (Your friend might want a complete description of every detail. Grandma might only want assurance that you are having some fun at college.)
- What words should I choose? (The colorful slang you use with your friend might not be appropriate for Grandma.)

You'll note that our comments about your rhetorical choices are shaped by common assumptions about friends and grandmothers. You might actually have a party-loving grandma and a geeky best friend, in which case Grandma might want the party details while your friend prefers talking about gigabytes or modern poetry. No matter the case, your rhetorical decisions are shaped by your particular knowledge of your audience and context.

What we hope to do in this chapter is extend your basic awareness of rhetorical thinking so that you can apply it to any communication act—from reading primary sources in a history class to analyzing the use of visual images in a Web site. Here is what you will learn in this chapter:

- How an introductory knowledge of rhetorical theory can extend your ability to think rhetorically
- How writers use appeals to *logos, ethos,* and *pathos* to increase the effectiveness of their texts
- How writers construct an "angle of vision" in a text, which you as a reader can learn to identify and analyze
- How you can apply the skills of rhetorical analysis to any cultural "text" such as photographs, clothing, tattoos, or other communicative acts
- How the ability to think rhetorically can deepen your skills as a reader and writer

A Brief Introduction to Rhetorical Theory

Rhetoric is the study of how human beings use language and other symbols to influence the attitudes, beliefs, and actions of others. The study of rhetoric can help people write, speak, read, and listen more effectively. At its deepest level, rhetoric aims to improve human communities by enabling people, through better cooperative dialogue, to find the best solutions to complex problems.

Rhetoric and Symbolic Action

One prominent twentieth-century rhetorician, Kenneth Burke, calls rhetoric "a symbolic means of inducing cooperation in beings that by nature respond to symbols." To understand what Burke means by responding to symbols, consider the difference in flirting behavior between peacocks and humans. When peacocks flirt, they spread their beautiful tails, do mating dances, and screech weirdly to attract females, but the whole process is governed by instinct. Peacocks don't have to choose among different symbolic actions such as buying an Armani tail versus buying a Wal-Mart tail or driving to the mating grounds in the right car. Unlike a peacock, a flirting human must make symbolic choices, all of which involve consequences. Consider how what you wear might contribute to the effectiveness of your flirting behavior (For males: Feedlot cap? Doo rag? Preppy sweater? Baggy, low-riding pants? For females: Skirt and stockings? Low-cut jeans, halter top, and belly ring? Gothic makeup, black dress, and open-fingered black gloves?). Each of these choices sends signals about the groups you identify with. Your choice of language (for example, big words versus street slang) or conversation topics (football versus art films) gives further hints of your identity and values. All these choices carry symbolic significance about the identity you wish to project to the world. Rhetoricians study, among other things, how these symbols are constructed within a given culture and how they operate to persuade audiences toward certain beliefs or actions.

For Writing and Discussion

Working in small groups or as a whole class, construct a flirting scenario for two or more of the following situations. For each case, indicate how you think the participants would be dressed. How would they talk? What accessories or other items (watches, jewelry, backpacks/briefcases, bicycles/skateboards/cars, and so forth) might be included in the scene? What might be a typical flirting "move"? You might want to write up your scenario as a short dramatic scene, indicating how the characters look and what the characters say and do.

- High school students in the parking lot after a football game
- Couple standing in line for tickets at a foreign art film festival
- New college students in a dorm cafeteria
- Upscale urban singles bar
- Typical gathering place at your college or university
- Other situation of your choice

Inducing Cooperation: Rhetoric as Inquiry and Persuasion

Another important part of Burke's definition of *rhetoric* is his emphasis on cooperation. The art of rhetoric—to the extent that it results in more productive human conversation—is a foundation of democracy, for it enables humans to settle their differences through dialogue rather than war. When the art of rhetoric works well, it induces cooperation among persons with divergent views, who, in conversation, move back and forth between the modes of inquiry and persuasion. Let us show you in more detail what we mean.

One of our two modes is *inquiry,* which we might define as the pursuit of the best solutions to complex problems. Imagine a conversation of several speakers, each with differing points of view on an important question. Here is how Kenneth Burke describes such a conversation when its participants are persons of good will guided by the skills of rhetoric:

> A rhetorician, I take it, is like one voice in a dialogue. Put several such voices together, with each voicing its own special assertion, let them act upon one another in cooperative competition, and you get a dialectic that, properly developed, can lead to the views transcending the limitations of each.

Burke's point here is that dialectic conversation can lead to the discovery of new and better ideas. Human beings engaged in exchange of reasoned arguments can discover better ways of seeing and hence better solutions to shared problems.

For the conversation to work, however, each participant must be willing to voice his or her own views. This requirement leads to the other mode in our schema: the mode of *persuasion.* Perhaps the most famous definition of rhetoric comes from the Greek philosopher Aristotle, who defined it as "the ability to see, in any particular case, all the available means of persuasion." An effective speaker's task, within Aristotle's view, is to try to persuade listeners to accept the speaker's views on a question of action or belief. If we imagine the interaction of several speakers, each proposing different answers to the question, and if we imagine all the speakers listening to each other respectfully and open-mindedly,* we can see how productive human conversation could emerge.

The conversation works to develop new and better answers because, as rhetoricians understand, *no one person's point of view can be the whole truth.* This is the fundamental insight of rhetoric—that there is always more than one way to tell the same story. (Recall our opening thought exercise in which you were asked to describe the same party to two different audiences.) Each participant's persuasive argument always, by necessity, reflects an emphasis on some facts and values and a corresponding de-emphasis on other facts and values. Each argument—including our own—has characteristic insights and blind spots. Thinking rhetorically thus encourages us to value a diversity of views—to be willing to assert and justi-

---

*For now we are imagining an ideal situation where responsible arguers listen respectfully to each other and are willing to revise their original views. Shortly we will discuss more typical real-world situations where vested interests and the drive for power create nonideal contexts.

fy our own views but also to listen critically and to shift our own point of view in light of other ways of seeing the world.

To see how inquiry and persuasion work together, consider what happens in an ideal class discussion. Suppose an instructor gives students an open-ended discussion question such as, "Why doesn't Hamlet rush to his revenge?" or "To what extent was Louis XIV a good king?" If no one proposes an answer, no conversation takes place: Students simply wait in embarrassed silence for the instructor to tell them what to think. If everyone simply asserts his or her own initial opinion, the conversation stops after each student speaks. Productive discussion occurs only if students are willing to support their views with reasonable arguments and only if these arguments differ in fundamental ways so that students begin seeing "all the available means of persuasion." Soon students begin shifting their initial views, influenced by others' arguments, and find new and better positions to which they can commit themselves. As can be seen in the following list, the rhetorician's view of a productive conversation matches the criteria for effective class discussions established by researchers who study critical thinking:

CRITERIA FOR AN EFFECTIVE CLASS DISCUSSION

Students challenge one another for reasons and examples.

Students offer counterexamples, counterinstances, and counterarguments.

Students piggyback on one another's comments.

Students identify the function of their comments (e.g., "I would like to comment on A, add to B, or disagree with C").

Students view themselves as scholars discussing worthwhile materials.

Students search for and present relationships between the subject under discussion and other relevant school subjects and outside experiences.

Students relate the specific subject under discussion to more general principles.

Students ask relevant and sequential questions.

Students don't take things for granted, but ask for justification.

Students ask for clarification (e.g., "What do you mean?").

—Source: Matthew Lipman, Paper Presented at Connecticut
Critical Thinking Conference, 1985.

For Writing and Discussion

Working in groups, construct your own view of what constitutes a good class discussion. To what extent does your vision of a good class discussion match the criteria listed by Matthew Lipman? What advice would you give teachers and fellow students for improving the effectiveness of class discussions?

Persuasion and Power

So far we have been discussing an ideal rhetorical situation where open-minded participants are committed to inquiry. This view is often too rosy. In many public and personal controversies, vested interests fuel the argument. Participants aren't interested in inquiry but in victory for their own claims. They look for evidence only to support their own views, they don't listen to alternative arguments, and they close themselves off from new ideas. In such an environment, a skeptic might regard rhetoric simply as the art of bombast and propaganda—the ability to create reasonable-sounding arguments that actually serve the private interests of the arguer.

The defense against abuses of rhetoric is faith in your own power to analyze and weigh persuasive messages. Rhetorical thinking helps you become aware of vested interests, private agendas, suppressed evidence, and various kinds of bias in texts and take these into account as you weigh alternative points of view. That a clinical trial showing the value of a new medication was funded by a drug company or that arguments in favor of nuclear power plants often come from the nuclear industry doesn't mean that you should dismiss these views. Rather, your obligation is to seek out alternative voices and bring these voices into the dialogue. Our hope is that this brief introduction to rhetorical theory will help you become a more responsible inquirer who *does* listen to contrary views and who therefore resists early closure (which means not making up your mind based on the first forceful argument you read). Such a thinker understands the responsibilities and pleasures of productive conversation.

The Appeals to *Logos*, *Ethos*, and *Pathos*

We have seen how rhetoric involves both inquiry and persuasion. We next consider how participants in a written or oral conversation can make their contributions as persuasive as possible in order to win people's consideration of their ideas. In this section we explain Aristotle's three "appeals" that writers and speakers can use to increase the effectiveness of their messages: the appeals to *logos*, *ethos*, and *pathos*. These appeals are particularly important in argument when one takes a directly persuasive aim. But all kinds of messages, including writing with an expressive, informative or analytic aim, can be strengthened by a conscious and competent use of these appeals.

A fuller discussion of the these classical appeals appears in Chapter 14, "Writing a Classical Argument," pp. 408–410.

Developing the habit of examining how these appeals are functioning in texts and being able to employ these appeals in your own writing will substantially enhance your ability to read and write rhetorically. Let's look briefly at each of these strategies:

- *Logos* is the appeal to reason. It refers to the quality of the message itself—to its internal consistency, to its clarity in asserting a thesis or point, and to the quality of reasons and evidence used to support the point.

- *Ethos* is the appeal to the character of the speaker/writer. It refers to the speaker/writer's trustworthiness and credibility. One can often increase the *ethos* of a message by being knowledgeable about the issue, by appearing thoughtful and fair, by listening well, and by being respectful of alternative points of view. A writer's accuracy and thoroughness in crediting sources and professionalism in caring about the format, grammar, and neat appearance of a document are part of the appeal to *ethos*.
- *Pathos* is the appeal to the sympathies, values, beliefs, and emotions of the audience. Appeals to *pathos* can be made in many ways. *Pathos* can often be enhanced through evocative visual images, frequently used in Web sites, posters, and magazine or newspaper articles. In written texts, the same effects can be created through vivid examples and details, through connotative language, and through empathy with the audience's beliefs and values.

To see how these three appeals are interrelated, you can visualize a triangle with points labeled *Message, Audience,* and *Writer* or *Speaker.* Rhetoricians study how effective communicators consider all three points of this *rhetorical triangle.* (See Figure 4.1.)

We encourage you to ask questions about the appeals to *logos, ethos,* and *pathos* every time you examine a text. For example, is the appeal to *logos* weakened by the writer's use of scanty and questionable evidence? Has the writer made a powerful appeal to *ethos* by documenting her sources and showing that she is an authority on the issue? Has the writer relied too heavily on appeals to *pathos* by

FIGURE 4.1 Rhetorical Triangle

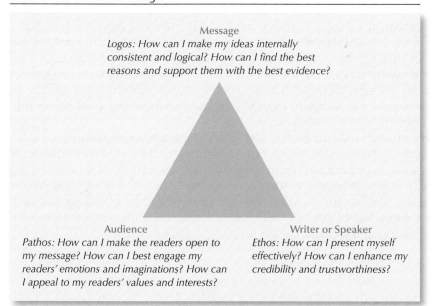

Message
Logos: How can I make my ideas internally consistent and logical? How can I find the best reasons and support them with the best evidence?

Audience
Pathos: How can I make the readers open to my message? How can I best engage my readers' emotions and imaginations? How can I appeal to my readers' values and interests?

Writer or Speaker
Ethos: How can I present myself effectively? How can I enhance my credibility and trustworthiness?

using numerous heart-wringing examples? Later chapters in this textbook will help you use these appeals well in your own writing as well as analyze these appeals in others' messages.

Angle of Vision

Another key insight of rhetoric, one that we mentioned at the beginning of this chapter, is the awareness that there is always more than one way to tell the same story and that no single way of telling it constitutes the whole truth. A writer's thesis necessarily commits a writer to a particular view of a subject that emphasizes some facts and values and de-emphasizes others. This particular point of view we call "angle of vision."

Recognizing the Angle of Vision in a Text

By saying that the writer writes from an "angle of vision," we mean that the writer cannot take a godlike stance that allows a universal, all-seeing, completely true, and whole way of knowing. Rather, the writer looks at the subject from a certain location, or, to use another metaphor, the writer wears a lens that colors or filters the topic in a certain way. The angle of vision, lens, or filter determines what part of a topic gets "seen" and what remains "unseen," what gets included or excluded from the writer's essay, what gets emphasized or de-emphasized, and so forth. It even determines what words get chosen out of an array of options— for example, whether you say "affirmative action" or "reverse discrimination," "terrorist" or "freedom fighter," "public servant" or "politician."

A good illustration of angle of vision is the political cartoon on stem cell research shown in Figure 4.2, which appeared in national newspapers in early summer 2001 when President Bush was contemplating his stance on federal funding for stem cell research. As the cartoon shows, nobody sees stem cells from a universal position. Each stakeholder has an angle of vision that emphasizes some aspects of stem cell research and de-emphasizes or censors other aspects. In the chart on page 81, we try to suggest how each of these angles of vision produces a different "picture" of the field.

In this cartoon, President Bush is cast as an inquirer trying to negotiate multiple perspectives. The cartoon treats Bush satirically—as if he were concerned only with the political implications of his decision. But if we think of him as seeking an ethically responsible stance, then his dilemma stands for all of us as writers confronting a problematic question. In such cases, we all have to forge our own individual stance and be ethically responsible for our decision, while acknowledging other stances and recognizing the limitations of our own.

FIGURE 4.2 Political Cartoon Illustrating Angle of Vision

Where do our stances come from? The stance we take on questions is partly influenced by our life experiences and knowledge, by our class and gender, by our ethnicity and sexual orientation, by our personal beliefs and values, and by our ongoing intentions and desires. But our stance can also be influenced by our rational and empathic capacity to escape from our own limitations and see the world from different perspectives, to imagine the world more fully. We have the power to take stances that are broader and more imaginative than our original limited vision, but we also never escape our own roots and situations in life.

The brief writing project at the end of this chapter will help you understand the concept of "angle of vision" more fully. Your instructor might also assign Chapter 5, which explores angle of vision in more depth.

The exercise on page 82 will help you understand the concept of "angle of vision" more fully.

Angle of Vision on Stem Cell Research

Angle of Vision	Words or Phrases Used to Refer to Stem Cells	Particulars that get "Seen" or Emphasized
Disease sufferer	Cluster of tiny cells that may help repair damaged tissues or grow new ones	The diseases that may be cured by stem cell research; the suffering of those afflicted; scientists as heroes; shelves of frozen stem cells; cells as objects that would just be thrown out if not used for research; emphasis on cures
Priest	Embryo as potential human life formed by union of sperm and egg	Moral consequences of treating human life as means rather than ends; scientists as Dr. Frankensteins; single embryo as potential baby
Scientist	Blastocysts, which are better suited for research than adult stem cells	Scientific questions that research would help solve; opportunities for grants and scholarly publication; emphasis on gradual progress rather than cures
Businessperson	New area for profitable investments	Potential wealth for company that develops new treatments for diseases or injuries
President Bush (at time of cartoon, Bush was uncertain of his stance)	Afraid to say "cluster of cells," "embryo," or "blastocyst" because each term has political consequences	Political consequences of each possible way to resolve the stem cell controversy; need to appease supporters from the Right without appearing callous to sufferers of diseases; need to woo Catholic vote

For Writing and Discussion

Background: Suppose that you are a management professor who is regularly asked to write letters of recommendation for former students. One day you receive a letter from a local bank requesting a confidential evaluation of a former student, one Uriah Rudy Riddle (U. R. Riddle), who has applied for a job as a management trainee. The bank wants your assessment of Riddle's intelligence, aptitude, dependability, and ability to work with people. You haven't seen U. R. for several years, but you remember him well. Here are the facts and impressions you recall about Riddle:

- Very temperamental student, seemed moody, something of a loner
- Long hair and very sloppy dress—seemed like a misplaced street person; often twitchy and hyperactive
- Absolutely brilliant mind; took lots of liberal arts courses and applied them to business
- Wrote a term paper relating different management styles to modern theories of psychology—the best undergraduate paper you ever received. You gave it an A+ and remember learning a lot from it yourself.
- Had a strong command of language—the paper was very well written
- Good at mathematics; could easily handle all the statistical aspects of the course
- Frequently missed class and once told you that your class was boring
- Didn't show up for the midterm. When he returned to class later, he said only that he had been out of town. You let him make up the midterm, and he got an A.
- Didn't participate in a group project required for your course. He said the other students in his group were idiots.
- You thought at the time that Riddle didn't have a chance of making it in the business world because he had no talent for getting along with people.
- Other professors held similar views of Riddle—brilliant, but rather strange and hard to like; an odd duck.

You are in a dilemma because you want to give Riddle a chance (he's still young and may have had a personality transformation of some sort), but you also don't want to damage your own professional reputation by falsifying your true impressions.

Individual task: Working individually for ten minutes or so, compose a brief letter of recommendation assessing Riddle; use details from the list to support your assessment. Role-play that you have decided to take a gamble with Riddle and give him a chance at this career. Write as strong a recommendation as possible while remaining honest. (To make this exercise more complex, your instructor might ask half the class to role-play a negative angle of vision in which you want to warn the bank against hiring Riddle without hiding his strengths or good points.)

Task for group or whole-class discussion: Working in small groups or as a whole class, share your letters. Pick out representative examples ranging from the most positive to the least positive and discuss how the letters achieve their different rhetorical effects. If your intent is to support Riddle, to what extent does honesty compel you to mention some or all of your negative memories? Is it possible to mention negative items without emphasizing them? How?

Analyzing Angle of Vision

Chapter 5, "Seeing Rhetorically," develops this connection between seeing and interpretation in more detail.

Just as there is more than one way to describe the party you went to on Friday night, there is more than one way to write a letter of recommendation for U. R. Riddle. The writer's angle of vision determines what is "seen" or "not seen" in a given piece of writing—what gets slanted in a positive or negative direction, what gets highlighted, what gets thrown into the shadows. As rhetorician Kenneth Burke claims, "A way of seeing is also a way of not seeing." Note how the writer controls what the reader "sees." As Riddle's professor, you might in your mind's eye see Riddle as long-haired and sloppy, but if you don't mention these details in your letter, they remain unseen to the reader. Note too that your own terms "long-haired and sloppy" interpret Riddle's appearance through the lens of your own characteristic way of seeing—a way that perhaps values business attire and clean-cut tidiness. Another observer might describe Riddle's appearance quite differently, thus seeing what you don't see.

In an effective piece of writing, the author's angle of vision often works so subtly that unsuspecting readers—unless they learn to think rhetorically—will be drawn into the writer's spell and believe that the writer's prose conveys the "whole picture" of its subject rather than a limited picture filtered through the screen of the writer's perspective. To understand more clearly how an angle of vision is constructed, you can analyze the language strategies at work. Some of these strategies—which writers employ consciously or unconsciously to achieve their intended effects—are as follows:

WAYS THAT WRITERS CONSTRUCT AN ANGLE OF VISION

- *Writers can state their meaning or intentions directly.* For example, your letter for U. R. Riddle might say, "Riddle would make an excellent bank manager" or "Riddle doesn't have the personality to be a bank manager."
- *Writers can select details that support their intended effect and omit those that don't.* If your intention is to support Riddle, you can include all the positive data about Riddle and omit the negative data (or vice versa if your letter opposes his candidacy). Instead of outright omission of data, you can de-emphasize some details while highlighting others.
- *Writers can choose words that frame the subject in a desired way or that have desired connotations.* For example, if you call Riddle "an independent thinker who doesn't follow the crowd," you frame him positively within a value system that favors individualism. If you call him "a loner who thinks egocentrically," you frame him negatively within a value system that favors consensus and social skills. Also, words can have connotations that serve to channel the reader's response in an intended direction. You thus could call Riddle either "forthright" or "rude" depending on your angle of vision.
- *Writers can use metaphors, similes, or analogies to create an intended effect.* For example, to suggest that Riddle has perhaps outgrown his earlier alienation from classmates, you might call him a "late-bloomer socially." But if you

see him out of place in a bank, you might say that Riddle's independent spirit would feel "caged in" by the routine of a banker's life.

- *Writers can vary sentence structure to emphasize or de-emphasize ideas and details.* Details can get emphasized or de-emphasized depending on where they appear in a sentence or paragraph. For example, material gets emphasized if it appears at the end of a long sentence, in a short sentence surrounded by long sentences, or in a main clause rather than a subordinate clause. Consider the difference between saying, "Although Riddle had problems relating to other students in my class, he is a brilliant thinker" versus "Although Riddle is a brilliant thinker, he had problems relating to other students in my class." The first sentence emphasizes his brilliance, the second his poor people skills.

The brief writing assignment at the end of this chapter will give you further practice in analyzing angle of vision.

Thinking Rhetorically about Any Cultural "Text"

To us, one of the most pleasurable aspects of rhetorical thinking is analyzing the rhetorical power of visual images or identifying rhetorical factors in people's choices about clothing, watches, cars, tattoos, and other consumer items.

Visual Rhetoric

Just as you can think rhetorically about texts, you can think rhetorically about photographs, drawings, paintings, statues, buildings, and other visual images. In Chapter 11, we deal extensively with visual rhetoric, explaining how color, perspective, cropping, camera angle, foreground/background, and other visual elements work together to create a persuasive effect. In this chapter, we intend only to introduce you to the concept of visual rhetoric and to suggest its importance. Consider, for example, the persuasive power of famous photographs from the war in Iraq. Early in the war, several widely publicized images, particularly the film footage of the toppling of the statue of Saddam Hussein and the "Mission Accomplished" photograph of President Bush wearing a pilot's flight suit on the deck of the aircraft carrier *Abraham Lincoln,* served to consolidate public support of the war. Later, certain images began eating away at public support. For example, an unauthorized picture of flag-draped coffins filling the freight deck of a military transport plane focused attention on those killed in the war. Particularly devastating for supporters of the war were the images of American prison guards sexually humiliating Iraqi prisoners in the Abu Ghraib prison. Images like these stick in viewers' memories long after specific texts are forgotten.

An illuminating example of the rhetorical power of paintings and photographs is evident in our cultural discussions of health care. In the early and middle

FIGURE 4.3 A Norman Rockwell Painting of a Family Doctor

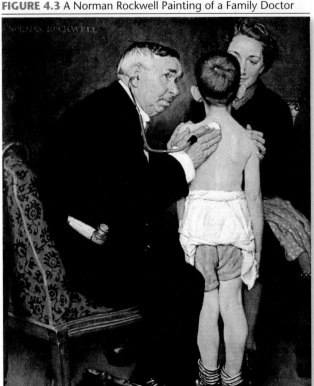

"Doc Melhorn and the Pearly Gates" by Norman Rockwell, inside illustration from
The Saturday Evening Post, December 24, 1938. Printed by permission of the Norman
Rockwell Family Agency. Copyright © 1938 the Norman Rockwell Family Entities.

decades of the twentieth century, a powerful concept of the "family doctor"
emerged. This "family doctor" was envisioned as a personal, caring individual—
usually a fatherly or grandfatherly male—with a stethoscope around his neck and
a little black bag for making house calls. This image was deeply embedded in the
American psyche through a series of paintings by Norman Rockwell, several of
which were reproduced on the cover of the influential *Saturday Evening Post* (see
Figure 4.3).

These paintings are now part of our cultural nostalgia for a simpler era and
help explain some of the cultural resistance in the United States to impersonal
HMOs, where medical decisions seem made by insurance bureaucrats. Yet, we also
want our doctors to be high-tech. In the last few decades, the image of doctors in
the popular imagination, especially furthered by advertising, has shifted away
from idealized Norman Rockwell scenes to images of highly specialized experts

FIGURE 4.4 A Modern High-Tech Image of a Doctor

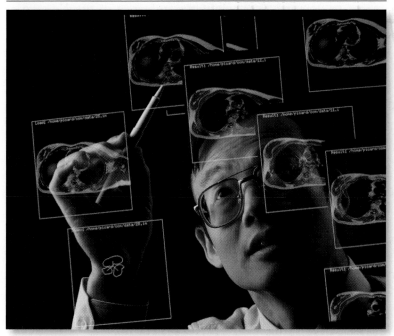

using the latest technological equipment. Figure 4.4 suggests the kinds of high-tech imagery that now characterizes popular media portrayal of doctors. However, in many current articles about health care in the United States, the Norman Rockwell paintings of the family doctor are still invoked to represent an older ideal about what people are looking for in their doctors.

The point we want to make in this brief introduction to visual rhetoric is that images make arguments. The Norman Rockwell painting and the high-tech photograph work rhetorically to influence an audience's view of what a doctor should be. The competing images of doctors serve the interests of different groups with different views about the role of medicine in our culture.

For Writing and Discussion

Working in small groups or as a whole class, explore your answers to the following questions:

1. How do the Norman Rockwell painting and the contemporary photograph work to create different images of doctors? What are the values conveyed by the Rockwell painting? What are the values conveyed by the photograph?

(continued)

2. Why is it in the interest of HMOs and insurance companies to portray high-tech images of doctors? How might the influence of the Norman Rockwell view of doctors serve the interests of alternative health care providers such as naturopathic physicians?

The Rhetoric of Clothing and Other Consumer Items

Not only do visual images have rhetorical power, but so also do many of our consumer choices. We choose our clothes, for example, not only to keep ourselves covered and warm but also to project our identification with certain social groups. For example, if you want to be identified as a skate-boarder, a preppy socialite, a gang member, a pickup-driving NASCAR fan, or a junior partner in a corporate law firm, you know how to select clothes and accessories that convey that identification. The way you dress communicates where you fit (or how you want to be perceived as fitting) within a class and social structure. For the most part, clothing codes are arbitrary, based on a system of differences. For example, there is no universal "truth" saying that long baggy basketball shorts are more attractive than short basketball shorts or that cargo pants are more beautiful than stirrup pants, even though one style may feel current and one out-of-date.

How do these symbolic codes get established? They can be set by fashion designers, by advertisers, or by trendy groups or individuals. The key to any new clothing code is to make it look different in some distinctive way from an earlier code or from a code of another group. Sometimes clothing codes develop to show rebellion against the values of parents or authority figures. At other times they develop to show new kinds of group identities.

Clothing codes are played on in conscious ways in fashion advertisements so that consumers become very aware of what identifications are signaled by different styles and brands. This aspect of consumer society is so ubiquitous that one of the marks of growing affluence in third-world countries is people's attention to the rhetoric of consumer goods. Consider the second epigraph to this chapter, which indicates that villagers in India watching TV ads notice not only the soap or shampoo but also the brands of motorbikes and the lifestyles of the people in the ads. Buying a certain kind of consumer good projects a certain kind of status or group or class identity. Our point, from a rhetorical perspective, is that in making a consumer choice, many people are concerned not only with the quality of the item itself but also with the symbolic messages that the item sends to different audiences. Note that the same item can send quite different messages to different groups: A Rolex watch might enhance one's credibility at a corporate board meeting while undercutting it at a barbecue for union workers. Or consider the clothing choices of preteen girls who want to dress like female pop rock stars. They often do so to fit in with their friends, perhaps unaware of the whole array of cultural messages that these clothes convey to other social groups.

For Writing and Discussion

Working in small groups or as a whole class, do a rhetorical analysis of the consumer items shown in Figures 4.5, 4.6, 4.7, and 4.8.

1. In each case, see if you can reach consensus on why persons might have chosen a particular way of dressing. How does the clothing style project a desire to identify with certain groups or to shock or reject certain groups? How do the clothing choices help establish and enhance the wearer's sense of identity?

2. When you and your friends make consumer purchases, to what extent are you swayed by the internal quality of the item (its materials and workmanship) versus the rhetorical messages it sends to an audience (its signals about social identity and standing)? (Note: Advertisers have long known that consumers, when queried, say: "I buy to please myself." However, advertisers' extensive psychological research suggests that consumers are intensely aware of audience: "I buy to maintain and project a certain way of being perceived by others.")

3. How does the rhetoric of clothing extend to other consumer items such as cars, vacations, recreational activities, home furnishings, music, and so forth?

FIGURE 4.5

FIGURE 4.6

(continued)

FIGURE 4.7

FIGURE 4.8

Chapter Summary

In this chapter we explained Kenneth Burke's definition of *rhetoric* as the use of language and other symbols to produce cooperation among humans. We saw how rhetoric operates under the modes of inquiry and persuasion and how, under ideal conditions, an exchange of different perspectives can lead reasonable people toward better solutions to problems. We also introduced the classical appeals of *logos, ethos,* and *pathos* as strategies for increasing the effectiveness of messages. Next we explained the concept of angle of vision. Any text necessarily looks at its subject from a perspective that emphasizes some details while minimizing others. We also showed you how to analyze angle of vision by considering the writer's word choices and the selection and arrangement of evidence. Finally, we explained how you can apply rhetorical thinking to visual images and to various kinds of consumer choices.

BRIEF WRITING PROJECT

Background and Readings

This brief writing project will give you practice at analyzing the angle of vision in different texts. This assignment focuses on two passages about nuclear power plants. Read the two passages; then we will describe your writing task.

The first passage is from the Bush administration's *National Energy Policy: Reliable, Affordable, and Environmentally Sound Energy for America's Future.* The document was written by an energy task force chaired by Vice President Dick Cheney. This passage is an overview paragraph on nuclear power from the opening chapter of the document; the last sentence of the passage is from a later section on recommendations for increasing energy supplies:

PASSAGE 1

Nuclear power plants serve millions of American homes and businesses, have a dependable record for safety and efficiency, and discharge no greenhouse gases into the atmosphere. As noted earlier, these facilities currently generate 20 percent of all electricity in America, and more than 40 percent of electricity generated in 10 states in the Northeast, South, and Midwest. Other nations, such as Japan and France, generate a much higher percentage of their electricity from nuclear power. Yet the number of nuclear plants in America is actually projected to decline in coming years, as old plants close and none are built to replace them. . . . [Later the Cheney document makes the following recommendation:] Provide for the safe expansion of nuclear energy by establishing a national repository for nuclear waste, and by streamlining licensing of nuclear power plants.

The second passage is from an op-ed piece by columnist Marianne Means, published on April 12, 2001, by Hearst Newspapers. It was entitled "Bush, Cheney Will Face Wall of Opposition If They Try to Resurrect Nuclear Power."

PASSAGE 2

Washington—Vice President Dick Cheney, head of the presidential task force studying our energy needs, favors building new nuclear power plants—and he's oddly casual about it.

The industry has been moribund in this country since the partial meltdown at Three Mile Island more than two decades ago set off fierce emotional resistance to an unreliable technology capable of accidentally spreading deadly radiation. No new plants have been ordered since then. Only 20 percent of our electricity is generated by nuclear power.

But President Bush has instructed Cheney to look into the prospect of resurrecting and developing nuclear power as a major part of a broad new energy policy. Cheney argues that modern, improved reactors operate safely, economically and efficiently. "It's one of the safest industries around," he says unequivocally.

There remains, however, a little problem of how to dispose of the plants' radioactive waste. Cheney concedes that issue is still unsolved. "If we're going to go forward with nuclear power, we need to find a way to resolve it," he said Sunday in an NBC "Meet the Press" interview.

No state wants to be the repository of the more than 40,000 tons of high-level nuclear waste currently accumulating at 103 commercial reactor sites around the country. This spent fuel is so deadly it can remain a potential threat to public health and safety for thousands of years. A leak could silently contaminate many miles of groundwater that millions of people depend on.

Your task: Contrast the differences in angle of vision in these two passages by analyzing how they create their different rhetorical effects. Consider factors such as overt statements of meaning, selection/omission of details, connotations of words and figures of speech, and sentence emphasis. To help guide your analysis, reread the section "Analyzing Angle of Vision" on pages 84–85. Your goal here is to explain to your readers how these two passages create different impressions of nuclear power.

Seeing Rhetorically
The Writer as Observer

About Seeing Rhetorically

Earlier in your school career, you may have been asked in an English class to write a description of a scene as if you were painting a picture of it in words. As you observed your scene carefully, trying to use sensory details to appeal to sight, sound, touch, smell, and even taste, you might have imagined that you were creating a true and objective description of your scene. But consider what happens to a description assignment if we give it a rhetorical twist. Suppose we asked you to write *two* descriptions of the same scene from two different perspectives or angles of vision (caused, say, by different moods or intentions) and then to analyze how the two descriptions differed. We could then ask you to reflect on the extent to which any description of a scene is objective as opposed to being shaped by the observer's intentions, experiences, beliefs, or moods.

Our goal in this chapter is to help you understand more fully the rhetorical concept of "angle of vision" which we introduced in Chapter 4. Learning to ask *why* a text includes certain details and not others and to ponder *how* a text creates its dominant impression will help you analyze any text more critically and understand the complex factors that shape what a writer sees.

Angle of vision is explained on pp. 80–85.

Your writing assignment for this chapter belongs to a category that we call "writing to learn." Many instructors from across the disciplines use writing-to-learn assignments intended to help students understand important disciplinary concepts. The assignment in this chapter, while teaching you about angle of vision, also shows you some of the subtle ways that language and perception are interconnected.

Exploring Rhetorical Observation

One of the intense national debates of the last five years has been whether the federal government should permit oil exploration in the Coastal Plain of the Arctic National Wildlife Refuge (ANWR). Arguments for and against drilling in the ANWR have regularly appeared in newspapers and magazines, and numerous advocacy groups have created Web sites to argue their cases. Nearly every argument contains descriptions of the ANWR that operate rhetorically to advance the writer's position. In the following exercise, we ask you to analyze the angle of vision of these verbal and visual depictions of the ANWR—that is, to analyze how these photographs and descriptions "see" the ANWR. We ask you to consider how different descriptions of the ANWR can be used to support different views of oil exploration. After examining the following data set of five verbal or visual texts, proceed to the questions under "Analyzing the Exhibits" (p. 101).

Exhibit 1: Web Page of the Arctic Power Advocacy Group

This text, with photograph labeled "Wildlife grow accustomed to oil operations at Prudhoe Bay" (Figure 5.1), is part of a pamphlet produced by Arctic Power, an advocacy group in favor of drilling for oil. We accessed this pamphlet through the organization's Web site.

FIGURE 5.1 Bears on Pipeline

Wildlife grow accustomed to oil operations at Prudhoe Bay.

ANWR has the nation's best potential for major additions to U.S. oil supplies

Most geologists think the Coastal Plain of the Artic National Wildlife Refuge has the best prospects for major additions to U.S. domestic oil supply. This is the part of ANWR set aside by Congress in 1980 for further study of its petroleum potential. There is a good chance that very large oil and gas fields, equal to the amount found at Prudhoe Bay further west, could be discovered in ANWR's coastal plain.

The Coastal Plain has very attractive geology and lies between areas of the Alaska North Slope and the Canadian Beaufort Sea where there have been major oil and gas discoveries. Oil and gas deposits have been discovered near ANWR's western border, and a recent oil discovery may result in the first pipeline built to the western boundary of the Coastal Plain.

Although the Coastal Plain was reserved for study of its oil potential, Congress must act to open it for oil and gas exploration. Alaskans and residents of the North Slope, including the Inupiat community of Kaktovik, within ANWR, widely support exploring the Coastal Plain.

Exhibit 2: Photograph from a Pro-Environment Newspaper Op Ed Piece
The photograph of the polar bears in Figure 5.2 accompanied a newspaper op-ed column entitled "Arctic Wildlife Refuge: Protect This Sacred Place."

FIGURE 5.2 Polar Bear with Cubs

Exhibit 3: Photograph Juxtaposing Alaskan Wildlife and Industry
This photograph, showing caribou crossing a road in front of a semi, typifies the Alaskan conflict over preserving nature versus the increasing presence of people and economic development (Figure 5.3).

FIGURE 5.3 Caribou and Truck

Exhibit 4: Photograph and Description on the Arctic Power Web Site
This photograph (Figure 5.4) and passage appeared on the Web site for Arctic Power, a pro-exploration advocacy group.

FIGURE 5.4 ANWR Coastal Plain

[The facts about ANWR] are not as pretty or as emotionally appealing [as the descriptions of ANWR by anti-exploration writers]. But they are important for anyone involved in the ANWR debate. On the coastal plain, the Arctic winter lasts for 9 months. It is dark continuously for 56 days in midwinter. Temperatures with the wind chill can reach −110 degrees F. It's not pristine. There are villages, roads, houses, schools, and military installations. It's not a unique Arctic ecosystem. The coastal plain is only a small fraction of the 88,000 square miles that make up the North Slope. The same tundra environment and wildlife can be found throughout the circumpolar Arctic regions. The 1002 Area [the legal term for the plot of coastal plain being contested] is flat. That's why they call it a plain. [. . .]

Some groups want to make the 1002 Area a wilderness. But a vote for wilderness is a vote against American jobs.

Exhibit 5: Excerpt from a Newspaper Feature Article
The following passage is the opening of a newspaper feature article in which freelance writer Randall Rubini describes his bicycle tour through the Prudhoe Bay Area of Alaska.

The temperature is 39 degrees. The going is slow but finally I am in motion. The bike churns through big rocks and thick gravel that occasionally suck the wheels to a dead halt.

Sixty miles to the east lies the Arctic National Wildlife Refuge, a place ARCO [a major oil-refining company] describes as "a bleak and forbidding land where temperatures plunge to more than 40 degrees below zero and the sun is not seen for nearly two months each year." To me the refuge is 19.5 million acres of unspoiled wilderness believed to contain crude oil and natural gas fields.

Prudhoe Bay production is on the decline, and oil corporations are salivating over the prospect of drilling on the 125-mile-long stretch of coastal plain within the refuge.

The area is a principal calving ground for the 180,000-member porcupine caribou herd that annually migrates to the windswept plain, seeking relief from insects.

The refuge also provides habitat for grizzlies, wolves, musk oxen, wolverines, and arctic foxes. Polar bears hunt over the ice and come ashore. Millions of waterfowl, seabirds, and shorebirds nest here.

Analyzing the Exhibits

Working in small groups or as a whole class, try to reach consensus answers to the following questions:

1. Which photographs do you think create visual claims opposing oil exploration in the ANWR? Which create visual claims supporting oil exploration? What is the verbal argument underlying each of these photos?
2. As we explained in Chapter 4, angle of vision focuses readers' attention on some details of a scene rather than on others; it accounts for what is "seen" and "not seen" by a given writer. What do the opponents of oil exploration tend to "see" and "not see" when they describe the ANWR? What do the proponents of oil exploration tend to "see" and "not see"?
3. When opponents of oil exploration mention oil companies or oil wells, they often try to plant a quick negative picture in the reader's mind. What rhetorical strategies, such as making direct statements and using highly connotative words, do the anti-exploration writers use to give a negative impression of oil companies?
4. In contrast, how do supporters of oil exploration try to create positive feelings about drilling in the ANWR?

WRITING PROJECT

Your writing project for this chapter is to write two descriptions and a self-reflection. The assignment has two parts.*

---

*For this assignment, we are indebted to two sources: (1) Richard Braddock, *A Little Casebook in the Rhetoric of Writing* (Englewood Cliffs, NJ: Prentice-Hall, 1971); and (2) Kenneth Dowst, "Kenneth Dowst's Assignment," *What Makes Writing Good?* eds. William E. Coles, Jr., and James Vopat (Lexington, MA: D.C. Heath, 1985), pp. 52–57.

Part A: Find an indoor or outdoor place where you can sit and observe for fifteen or twenty minutes in preparation for writing a focused description of the scene that will enable your readers to see what you see. Here is the catch: You are to write *two* descriptions of the scene. Your first description must convey a favorable impression of the scene, making it appear pleasing or attractive. The second description must convey a negative, or unfavorable, impression, making the scene appear unpleasant or unattractive. Both descriptions must contain only factual details and must describe exactly the same scene from the same location at the same time. It's not fair, in other words, to describe the scene in sunny weather and then in the rain or otherwise to alter factual details. Each description should be one paragraph long (approximately 125–175 words).

Part B: Self-reflection on What You Learned (300–400 words): Attach to your two descriptions a self-reflection about what you have learned from doing this assignment. This self-reflection should include your own rhetorical analysis of your two descriptions and explain some of the insights you have gained into the concepts of "angle of vision" and "seeing rhetorically."

Strategies for doing a rhetorical analysis were introduced in Chapter 4, pp. 84–85, and are explained further on pp. 105–108.

Part A of the assignment asks you to describe the same scene in two different ways, giving your first description a positive tone and the second description a negative one. You can choose from any number of scenes: the lobby of a dormitory or apartment building, a view from a park bench or a window, a favorite (or disliked) room, a scene at your workplace, a busy street, a local eating or drinking spot, whatever. A student example of two contrasting scenes written for this assignment is found on pp. 107–108. Part B of the assignment asks you to write a self-reflection in which you do a rhetorical analysis of your two descriptions and explore what you have learned from this exercise about seeing rhetorically. An excerpt from a student self-reflection, written for this assignment, is found on p. 114. Because this assignment results in a thought exercise rather than in a self-contained essay requiring an introduction, transitions between parts, and so forth, you can label your sections simply "Descriptions" and "Self-Reflection."

Understanding Observational Writing

In this section, we elaborate on the concept of angle of vision. We explore what factors influence angle of vision and show how a writer's angle of vision shapes the language he or she chooses, or, to put it inversely, how the chosen language both conveys and creates the angle of vision. We also examine the complex relationship between perception and belief by explaining how previous knowledge, cultural background, interests, and values influence perceptions.

Considering the Factors That Shape Perception

On the face of it, terms such as *observation, perception,* and *seeing* seem nonproblematic. Objects are objects, and the process of perceiving an object is immediate and automatic. However, perception is never a simple matter. Consider what we call "the expert-novice phenomenon": Experts on any given subject notice details about that subject that the novice overlooks. An experienced bird-watcher can distinguish dozens of kinds of swallows by subtle differences in size, markings, and behaviors, whereas a non-bird-watcher sees only a group of birds of similar size and shape. Similarly, people observing an unfamiliar game (for example, an American watching cricket or a Nigerian watching baseball) don't know what actions or events have meaning and, hence, don't know what to look for.

In addition to prior knowledge, cultural differences affect perception. An American watching two Japanese business executives greet each other might not know that they are participating in an elaborate cultural code of bowing, eye contact, speech patterns, and timing of movements that convey meanings about social status. An Ethiopian newly arrived in the United States and an American sitting in a doctor's office will see different things when the nurse points to one of them to come into the examination room: The American notices nothing remarkable about the scene; he or she may remember what the nurse was wearing or something about the wallpaper. The Ethiopian, on the other hand, is likely to remember the nurse's act of pointing, a gesture of rudeness used in Ethiopia only to beckon children or discipline dogs. Again, observers of the same scene see different things.

Your beliefs and values can also shape your perceptions, often creating blind spots. You might not notice data that conflict with your beliefs and values. Or you might perceive contradictory data at some level, but if they don't register in your mind as significant, you disregard them. Consider, for example, how advocates of gun control focus on a child's being accidentally killed because the child found a loaded firearm in Dad's sock drawer, while opponents of gun control focus on burglaries or rapes being averted because the home owner had a pistol by the bedside. The lesson here is that people note and remember whatever is consistent with their worldview much more readily than they note and remember inconsistencies. What you believe is what you see.

Another factor determining what you see is mood. We know that when people are upbeat they tend to see things through "rose-colored glasses"—a cliché with a built-in reference to angle of vision. When you are in a good mood, you see the flowers in a meadow. When you are depressed, you see the discarded wrappers from someone's pack of gum.

More direct and overt is the influence of rhetorical purpose. Consider again the case of the Arctic National Wildlife Refuge mentioned earlier in this chapter. In the passage by Randall Rubini (p. 100), the author juxtaposes his own view of the ANWR as an "unspoiled wilderness" against ARCO's view of the ANWR as a "bleak and forbidding land.' " Note how each way of seeing the ANWR serves the political purposes of the author. Opponents of oil exploration focus on the unspoiled beauty of the land, listing fondly the names of different kinds of animals that live there. What remains "unseen" in their descriptions are the native villages and military installations on the Coastal Plain and any references to economic issues, the U.S. need for domestic oil, or jobs. In contrast, supporters of oil exploration shift the focus from the caribou herds (their descriptions don't "see" the animals), to the bleak and frigid landscape and the native communities that would benefit from jobs.

This example suggests the ethical dimension of description. Rhetorical purpose entails responsibility. All observers must accept responsibility for what they see and for what they make others see because their descriptions can have real-world consequences—for example, no jobs for a group of people or potential harm to an animal species and an ecosystem. We should reiterate, however, that neither perspective on the ANWR is necessarily dishonest; each is true in a limited way. In any description, writers necessarily—whether consciously or unconsciously—include some details and exclude others. But the writer's intent is nevertheless to influence the reader's way of thinking about the described phenomenon, and ethical readers must be aware of what is happening. By noting what is *not there,* readers can identify a piece's angle of vision and analyze it. The reader can see the piece of writing not as the whole truth but as one person's perspective that can seem like the whole truth if one simply succumbs to the text's rhetorical power.

Finally, let's look at one more important factor that determines angle of vision—what we might call a writer's "guiding ideology" or "belief system." We touched on this point earlier when we showed how one's belief system can create blind spots. Let's examine this phenomenon in more depth by seeing how different beliefs about the role of women in primitive societies cause two anthropologists to describe a scene in different ways. What follows are excerpts from the works of two female anthropologists studying the role of women in the !Kung tribe* of the African Kalahari Desert (sometimes called the "Bushmen"). Anthropologists have long been interested in the !Kung because they still hunt and forage for food in the manner of their prehistoric ancestors.

Here is how anthropologist Lorna Marshal describes !Kung women's work:

MARSHAL'S DESCRIPTION

Women bring most of the daily food that sustains the life of the people, but the roots and berries that are the principal plant foods of the Nyae Nyae !Kung are apt to be tasteless, harsh and not very satisfying. People crave meat. Furthermore, there is only drudgery in digging roots, picking berries, and trudging back to the encampment with heavy loads and babies sagging in the pouches of the karosses: there is no splendid excitement and triumph in returning with vegetables.

—Lorna Marshal, *The !Kung of Nyae Nyae*

*The word *!Kung* is preceded by an exclamation point in scholarly work to indicate the unique clicking sound of the language.

And here is how a second anthropologist describes women's work:

DRAPER'S DESCRIPTION

A common sight in the late afternoon is clusters of children standing on the edge of camp, scanning the bush with shaded eyes to see if the returning women are visible. When the slow-moving file of women is finally discerned in the distance, the children leap and exclaim. As the women draw closer, the children speculate as to which figure is whose mother and what the women are carrying in the karosses. [. . .]

!Kung women impress one as a self-contained people with a high sense of self-esteem. There are exceptions—women who seem forlorn and weary—but for the most part, !Kung women are vivacious and self-confident. Small groups of women forage in the Kalahari at distances of eight to ten miles from home with no thought that they need the protection of the men or of the men's weapons should they encounter any of the several large predators that also inhabit the Kalahari.

—P. Draper, "!Kung Women: Contrasts in Sexual Egalitarianism
in Foraging and Sedentary Contexts"

As you can see, these two anthropologists "read" the !Kung society in remarkably different ways. Marshal's thesis is that !Kung women are a subservient class relegated to the heavy, dull, and largely thankless task of gathering vegetables. In contrast, Draper believes that women's work is more interesting and requires more skill than other anthropologists have realized. Her thesis is that there is an egalitarian relationship between men and women in the !Kung society.

The source of data for both anthropologists is careful observation of !Kung women's daily lives. But the anthropologists are clearly not seeing the same thing. When the !Kung women return from the bush at the end of the day, Marshal sees their heavy loads and babies sagging in their pouches, whereas Draper sees the excited children awaiting the women's return.

So which view is correct? That's a little like asking whether the ANWR is an "unspoiled wilderness" or a " 'bleak and forbidding land.' " If you believe that women play an important role in !Kung society, you "see" the children eagerly awaiting the women's return at the end of the day, and you note the women's courage in foraging for vegetables "eight to ten miles from home." If you believe that women are basically drudges in this culture, then you "see" the heavy loads and babies sagging in the pouches of the karosses. The details of the scene, in other words, are filtered through the observer's interpretive screen.

Conducting a Simple Rhetorical Analysis

Our discussion of two different views of the ANWR and two different views of the role of women in !Kung society shows how a seemingly objective description of a scene reflects a specific angle of vision that can be revealed through analysis. Rhetorically, a description subtly persuades the reader toward the author's angle of vision. This angle of vision isn't necessarily the author's "true self" speaking, for authors *create* an angle of vision through rhetorical choices they make while composing. We hope you will discover this insight for yourself while doing the assignment for this chapter.

In this section we describe five textual strategies writers often use (consciously or unconsciously) to create the persuasive effect of their texts. Each strategy creates textual differences that you can discuss in your rhetorical analysis.

For a more complete explanation of these five strategies, see Chapter 4's discussion of how an angle of vision is constructed on pp. 80–82.

Strategies for Creating a Persuasive Effect

Strategy 1: State your meaning or intended effect directly.

Example: The first anthropologist says that "there is only drudgery in digging roots" while the second anthropologist says, "!Kung women impress one as a self-contained people with a high sense of self-esteem." The first writer casts her view in negative terms while the second announces a more positive perspective.

Strategy 2: Select details that convey your intended effect and omit those that don't.

Example: The first anthropologist, Marshal, selects details about the tastelessness of the vegetables and the heaviness of the women's loads, creating an overall impression of women's work as thankless and exhausting. Draper, the second anthropologist, selects details about excitement of the children awaiting their mothers' return and the fearlessness of the mothers as they forage "eight to ten miles from home," creating an impression of self-reliant women performing an essential task.

Strategy 3: Choose words with connotations that convey your intended effect.

Example: Marshal chooses words connoting listlessness and fatigue such as *drudgery, trudging, heavy,* and *sagging.* Draper chooses words connoting energy: The children *scan* the bush, *leap and exclaim,* and *speculate,* while the women *forage.*

Strategy 4: Use figurative language (metaphors, similes, and analogies) that conveys your intended effect.

Example: Rubini writes that oil companies are "salivating" for new oil-drilling opportunities (p. 100). He equates oil companies with drooling dogs, giving readers an unpleasant vision of the oil companies' eagerness to get at the ANWR's oil reserves.

Strategy 5: Use sentence structure to emphasize and de-emphasize your ideas.

Example: Marshal uses sentence structure to create a negative impression of the !Kung women's plant-gathering role:

> Women bring most of the daily food that sustains the life of the people, but the roots and berries that are the principal plant foods of the Nyae Nyae !Kung are apt to be tasteless, harsh and not very satisfying. People crave meat.

The short sentence following the long sentence receives the most emphasis, giving readers the impression that meat is more important than the women's vegetables.

For Writing and Discussion

What follows is a student example of two contrasting descriptions written for the assignment in this chapter. Read the descriptions carefully. Working individually, analyze the descriptions rhetorically to explain how the writer has created contrasting impressions through overt statements of meaning, selection and omission of details, word choice, figurative language, and sentence structure. (You will do the same thing for your own two descriptions in Part B of the assignment.) Spend approximately ten minutes doing your own analysis of this example and taking notes. Then, working in small groups or as a whole class, share your analyses, trying to reach agreement on examples of how the writer has created different rhetorical effects by using the five strategies just explained.

Description 1: Positive Effect The high ceiling and plainness of this classroom on the second floor of the Administration Building make it airy, spacious, and functional. This classroom, which is neither dusty and old nor sterile and modern, has a well-used, comfortable feel like the jeans and favorite sweater you put on to go out for pizza with friends. Students around me, who are focused on the assignment, read the instructor's notes on the chalkboard, thumb through their texts, and jot down ideas in their notebooks spread out on the spacious two-person tables. In the back of the room, five students cluster around a table and talk softly and intently about the presentation they are getting ready to make to the class. Splashes of spring sunshine filtering through the blinds on the tall windows brighten the room with natural light, and a breeze pungent with the scent of newly mown grass wafts through the open ones, sweeps over the students writing at their desks, and passes out through the door to the hall. As I glance out the window, I see a view that contributes to the quiet harmony of the environment: bright pink and red rhododendron bushes and manicured beds of spring flowers ring the huge lawn where a few students are studying under the white-blossomed cherry trees.

Description 2: Negative Effect The high ceiling of this classroom on the second floor of the Administration Building cannot relieve the cramped, uncomfortable feeling of this space, which is filled with too many two-person tables, some of them crammed together at awkward angles. A third of the chalkboard is blocked from my view by the bulky television, VCR, and overhead projector that are stacked on cumbersome carts and wreathed in electrical cords. Students around me, working on the assignment, scrape their chairs on the bare linoleum floor as they try to see the chalkboard where some of the instructor's notes are blotted out by the shafts of sunlight piercing through a few bent slats in the blinds. In the back of the room, five students cluster around a table, trying to talk softly about their presentation, but their voices

(continued)

bounce off the bare floors. Baked by the sun, the classroom is so warm that the instructor has allowed us to open the windows, but the wailing sirens of ambulances racing to the various hospitals surrounding the campus distract us. The breeze, full of the smell of mown lawn, brings warm air from outside into this stuffy room. Several students besides me gaze longingly out the window at the bright pink and red rhododendrons in the garden and at the students reading comfortably in the shade under the white-blossomed cherry trees.

READINGS

The reading for this chapter consists of two eyewitness accounts of an event that occurred on the Congo River in Africa in 1877.* The first account is by the famous British explorer Henry Morton Stanley, who led an exploration party of Europeans into the African interior. The second account is by the African tribal chief Mojimba, as told orally to a Belgian missionary, Fr. Frassle, who recorded the story. The conflicting accounts suggest the complexity of what happens when different cultures meet for the first time.

Clash on the Congo: Two Eye Witness Accounts

Henry Morton Stanley's Account

1   We see a sight that sends the blood tingling through every nerve and fibre of the body . . . a flotilla of gigantic canoes bearing down upon us. A monster canoe leads the way . . . forty men on a side, their bodies bending and swaying in unison as with a swelling barbarous chorus they drive her down towards us . . . the warriors above the manned prow let fly their spears. . . . But every sound is soon lost in the ripping crackling musketry. . . . Our blood is up now. It is a murderous world, and we feel for the first time that we hate the filthy vulturous ghouls who inhabit it. . . . We pursue them . . . and continue the fight in the village streets with those who have landed, hunt them out into the woods, and there only sound the retreat, having returned the daring cannibals the compliment of a visit.

Mojimba's Account

2   When we heard that the man with the white flesh was journeying down the [Congo] we were open-mouthed with astonishment. . . . He will be one of our brothers who were drowned in the river. . . . We will prepare a feast, I

*These readings are taken from Donald C. Holsinger, "A Classroom Laboratory for Writing History," *Social Studies Review* 31.1 (1991): 59–64. The role-playing exercise following the readings is also adapted from this article.

ordered, we will go to meet our brother and escort him into the village with rejoicing! We donned our ceremonial garb. We assembled the great canoes. . . . We swept forward, my canoe leading, the others following, with songs of joy and with dancing, to meet the first white man our eyes had beheld, and to do him honor. But as we drew near his canoes there were loud reports, bang! bang! And fire-staves spat bits of iron at us. We were paralyzed with fright . . . they were the work of evil spirits! "War! That is war!" I yelled. . . . We fled into our village—they came after us. We fled into the forest and flung ourselves on the ground. When we returned that evening our eyes beheld fearful things: our brothers, dead, dying, bleeding, our village plundered and burned, and the water full of dead bodies. The robbers and murderers had disappeared.

Thinking Critically about the *Two Accounts*

Our purpose in presenting these two accounts is to raise the central problem examined in this chapter: the rhetorical nature of observation—that is, how observation is shaped by values, beliefs, knowledge, and purpose and therefore represents an angle of vision or one perspective.

1. How do the two accounts differ?

2. What is common to both accounts? Focusing on common elements, try to establish as many facts as you can about the encounter.

3. How does each observer create a persuasive effect by using one or more of the five strategies described on page 106 (overt statement of meaning, selection/omission of details, connotations of words, figurative language, ordering and shaping of sentences)?

4. What differences in assumptions, values, and knowledge shape these two interpretations of events?

5. As a class, try the following role-playing exercise:
   Background: You are a newspaper reporter who has a global reputation for objectivity, accuracy, and lack of bias. You write for a newspaper that has gained a similar reputation and prides itself on printing only the truth. Your editor has just handed you two eyewitness accounts of an incident that has recently occurred in central Africa. You are to transform the two accounts into a brief front-page article (between sixty and ninety words) informing your readers what happened. You face an immediate deadline and have no time to seek additional information.
   Task: Each class member should write a sixty- to ninety-word newspaper account of the event, striving for objectivity and lack of bias. Then share your accounts.

6. As a class, play the believing and doubting game with this assertion: "It is possible to create an objective and unbiased account of the Congo phenomenon."

Composing Your Essay

Since the assignment for this chapter has two parts—Part A, calling for two contrasting descriptions, and Part B, calling for a self-reflection—we address each part separately.

Exploring Rationales and Details for Your Two Descriptions

To get into the spirit of this unusual assignment, you need to create a personal rationale for why you are writing two opposing descriptions. Our students have been successful imagining any one of the following three rationales:

Rationales for Writing Opposing Descriptions
Different moods: One approach is to imagine observing your scene in different moods. How could I reflect a "happy" view of this scene? How could I reflect a "sad" view of this scene? Be sure, however, to focus entirely on a description of the scene, not on your mood itself. Let the mood determine your decisions about details and wording, but don't put yourself into the scene. The reader should infer the mood from the description.

Verbal game: Here you see yourself as a word wizard trying consciously to create two different rhetorical effects for readers. In this scenario, you don't worry how you feel about the scene but how you want your reader to feel. Your focus is on crafting the language to influence your audience in different ways.

Different rhetorical purposes: In this scenario, you imagine your description in service of some desired action. You might want authorities to improve an ugly, poorly designed space (for example, a poorly designed library reading room). Or you might want to commend someone for a particularly functional space (for example, a well-designed computer lab). In this scenario, you begin with a strongly held personal view of your chosen scene—something you want to commend or condemn. One of your descriptions, therefore, represents *the way you really feel*. Your next task is to see this same scene from an opposing perspective. To get beyond your current assessment of the scene—to recognize aspects of it that are inconsistent with your beliefs—you need to "defamiliarize" it, to make it strange. Artists sometimes try to disrupt their ordinary ways of seeing by drawing something upside down or by imagining the scene from the perspective of a loathsome character—whatever it takes to wipe away "the film of habit" from the object.

The student who wrote the example on pages 107–108 worked from this last rationale. She disliked one of her classrooms, which she found unpleasant and detrimental to learning. In choosing this place, she discovered that she valued college classrooms that were well equipped, comfortable, quiet, modernized, reasonably roomy, and unaffected by outside weather conditions. It was easy for her to write the negative description of this room, which used descriptive details showing how the scene violated all her criteria. However, she had trouble writing the positive description until she imagined being inside the head of someone totally different from herself.

Generating Details

Once you have chosen your scene, you need to compose descriptions that are rich in sensory detail. You might imagine yourself in descriptive partnership with a recently blinded friend in which you become your friend's eyes, while your friend—having a newly heightened sense of hearing, touch, and smell—can notice nonsight details that you might otherwise miss. In your writing, good description should be packed with sensory detail—sights, sounds, smells, textures, even on occasion tastes—all contributing to a dominant impression that gives the description focus.

After you have chosen a subject for your two descriptions, observe it intensely for fifteen or twenty minutes. One way to train yourself to notice sensory details is to create a two-column sensory chart. As you observe your scene, note details that appeal to each of the senses and then try describing them, first positively (left column) and then negatively (right column). One student, observing a scene in a local tavern, made these notes in her sensory chart:

Positive Description	Negative Description
Taste	**Taste**
salted and buttered popcorn	salty, greasy popcorn
frosty pitchers of beer	half-drunk pitchers of stale, warm beer
big bowls of salted-in-the-shell peanuts on the tables	mess of peanut shells and discarded pretzel wrappers on tables and floor
Sound	**Sound**
hum of students laughing and chatting	din of high-pitched giggles and various obnoxious frat guys shouting at each other
the jukebox playing oldies but goodies from the early Beatles	jukebox blaring out-of-date music

[She continued with the other senses of odor, touch, and sight]

Shaping and Drafting Your Two Descriptions

Once you have decided on your rationale for the two descriptions, observed your scene, and made your sensory chart, compose your two descriptions. You will need to decide on an ordering principle for your descriptions. It generally makes sense to begin with an overview of the scene to orient your reader.

From the park bench near 23rd and Maple, one can watch the people strolling by the duck pond.

By eight o'clock on any Friday night, Pagliacci's Pizzeria on Broadway becomes one of the city's most unusual gathering places.

Then you need a plan for arranging details. There are no hard-and-fast rules here, but there are some typical practices. You can arrange details in the following ways:

- By spatially scanning from left to right or from far to near
- By using the written equivalent of a movie zoom shot: begin with a broad overview of the scene, then move to close-up descriptions of specific details

Compose your pleasant description, selecting and focusing on details that convey a positive impression. Then compose your unpleasant description. Each description should comprise one fully developed paragraph (125–175 words).

Using *Show* Words Rather than *Tell* Words

In describing your scenes, use *show* words rather than *tell* words. *Tell* words interpret a scene without describing it. They name an interior, mental state, thus telling the reader what emotional reaction to draw from the scene.

TELL WORDS

There was a *pleasant* tree in the backyard.
There was an *unpleasant* tree in the backyard.

In contrast, *show* words describe a scene through sensory details appealing to sight, sound, smell, touch, and even taste. The description itself evokes the desired effect without requiring the writer to state it overtly.

SHOW WORDS

A *spreading elm* tree *bathed* the backyard with *shade.* [evokes positive feelings]
An *out-of-place elm, planted too close to the house, blocked our view* of the *mountains.* [evokes negative feelings]

The "scale of abstraction" is explained in Chapter 3, pp. 60–61.

Whereas *show* words are particulars that evoke the writer's meaning through sensory detail, *tell* words are abstractions that announce the writer's intention directly (strategy 1 on pp. 106). An occasional *tell* word can be useful, but *show* words operating at the bottom of the "scale of abstraction" are the flesh and muscle of descriptive prose.

Inexperienced writers often try to create contrasting impressions of a scene simply by switching *tell* words.

WEAK: OVERUSE OF *TELL* WORDS

The smiling merchants happily talked with customers trying to get them to buy their products. [positive purpose]
The annoying merchants kept hassling customers trying to convince them to buy their products. [negative purpose]

In this example, the negative words *annoying* and *hassling* and the positive words *smiling* and *happily* are *tell* words; they state the writer's contrasting intentions, but they don't describe the scene. Here is how the student writer revised these passages using *show* words.

STRONG: CONVERSION TO *SHOW* WORDS

One of the merchants, selling thick-wooled Peruvian sweaters, nodded approvingly as a woman tried on a richly textured blue cardigan in front of the mirror. [positive purpose]

One of the merchants, hawking those Peruvian sweaters that you find in every open-air market, tried to convince a middle-aged woman that the lumpy, oversized cardigan she was trying on looked stylish. [negative purpose]

Here are some more examples taken from students' drafts before and after revision:

Draft with *Tell* Words	Revision with *Show* Words
Children laugh and point animatedly at all the surroundings.	Across the way, a small boy taps his friend's shoulder and points at a circus clown.
The wonderful smell of food cooking on the barbecue fills my nose.	The tantalizing smell of grilled hamburgers and buttered corn on the cob wafts from the barbecue area of the park, where men in their cookout aprons wield forks and spatulas and drink Budweisers.
The paintings on the wall are confusing, dark, abstract, demented, and convey feelings of unhappiness and suffering.	The paintings on the wall, viewed through the smoke-filled room, seem confusing and abstract—the work of a demented artist on a bad trip. Splotches of black paint are splattered over a greenish-yellow background like bugs on vomit.

Revising Your Two Descriptions

The following checklist of revision questions will help you improve your first draft:

1. *How can I make my two descriptions more parallel—that is, more clearly about the same place at the same time?* The rules for the assignment ask you to use only factual details observable in the same scene at the same time. It violates the spirit of the assignment to have one scene at a winning basketball game and the other at a losing game. Your readers' sense of pleasure in comparing your two descriptions will be enhanced if many of the same details appear in both descriptions.

2. *Where can I replace* tell *words with* show *words?* Inexperienced writers tend to rely on *tell* words rather than give the reader sensory details and visual impressions. Find words that deliver prepackaged ideas to the reader (*pleasant, happy, depressing, annoying, pretty,* and so forth) and rewrite those sentences by actually describing what you see, hear, smell, touch, and taste. Pay particular attention to this advice if you are choosing "different moods" as your rationale for two descriptions.

3. *How can I make the angle of vision in each description clearer? How can I clarify my focus on a dominant impression?* Where could you use words with vividly appropriate connotations? Where could you substitute specific words for general ones? For example, consider synonyms for the generic word *shoe.* Most people wear shoes, but only certain people wear spiked heels or riding boots. Among words for kinds of sandals, *Birkenstocks* carries a different connotation from *Tevas* or *strappy espadrilles with faux-metallic finish.* Search your draft for places where you could substitute more colorful or precise words for generic words to convey your dominant impression more effectively.

Generating and Exploring Ideas for Your Self-Reflection

Writing self-reflections constitutes a powerful learning strategy. See Chapter 25 on the practice and value of self-reflective writing.

Part B of this Writing Project asks you to write a self-reflection about what you have learned. Your reflection should begin with a rhetorical analysis of your two descriptions in which you explain how you created your positive versus negative effects. Focus on how you used the strategies introduced in Chapter 4 (pages 84–85) and summarized in the chart "Strategies for Creating a Persuasive Effect" on page 106. In the rest of your self-reflection, explore what you have learned from reading this chapter and doing this exercise. You are invited to consider questions like these:

- What rationale or scenario did you use for explaining to yourself why one might write opposing descriptions (different moods? verbal game? different rhetorical purposes? something else?) Which description was easier for you to write and why?
- What new insights did you come away with? Specifically, what have you learned about the concept "angle of vision" and about ways writers can influence readers? What, if anything, was disturbing or challenging about the concepts developed in this chapter?
- Throughout this text we urge you to read rhetorically, that is, to be aware of how a text is constructed to influence readers. How has this chapter advanced your ability to read rhetorically?

To illustrate self-reflection, we reproduce here a portion of the self-reflection written by the student who wrote the two descriptions on pages 107–108.

SELECTIONS FROM A STUDENT'S SELF-REFLECTION

In writing the two descriptions, I used most of the strategies for creating rhetorical effects discussed in the text. In deliberately changing my angle of vision from positive to negative, I realized how much the connotation of individual words can convey particular ideas to readers. For example, in the positive description to get across the idea of a comfortably studious environment, I used words such as "airy," "spacious," "focused," and "quiet harmony." But in my negative description, I wanted readers to feel the unpleasantness of this room so I used words like "cramped," "crammed," "blocked," and "bulky." I also created different effects by including or excluding certain details. For example, in the positive description, I mentioned the "splashes of sunshine" coming through the window, but in the negative description

I mentioned the wailing sirens of ambulances. [She continues with this rhetorical analysis, explaining and illustrating the other strategies she used.]

I learned a lot from doing this assignment. In writing my two descriptions, I found it helpful both to imagine different moods and different rhetorical purposes. It was easy for me to write the negative view of my classroom because I often get irritated with the problems in this room—the discomfort, inconvenience, and noise. It was much harder to write the positive view. In fact, I couldn't do so until I imagined looking at the room from someone else's perspective. To do so, I imagined that a fellow student was interviewing me on the question, How could the classroom facilities on our campus be improved? I role-played telling this person what I really like in a classroom and then tried to give these features to the room.

What amazed me is that both of my descriptions are factually true but create totally different effects that depend on the observer's perspective. Writing my two descriptions made me think about how much power writers have to influence readers' thinking. . . .

[In the rest of her self-reflection, she explains further what she learned from this assignment and also notes how she has begun to notice similar rhetorical strategies being used in some of her recent reading.]

GUIDELINES FOR PEER REVIEWS

Instructions for peer reviews are provided in Chapter 17 (pp. 519–520).

For the Writer

Prepare two or three questions you would like your peer reviewer to address while responding to your draft. The questions can focus on some aspect of your draft that you are uncertain about, on one or more sections where you particularly seek help or advice, on some feature that you particularly like about your draft, or on some part you especially wrestled with. Write out your questions and give them to your peer reviewer along with your draft.

For the Reviewer

To write a peer review for a classmate, use your own paper, numbering your responses to correspond to the question numbers. At the head of your paper, place the author's name and your own name, as shown.

Author's Name: _____

Peer Reviewer's Name: _____

I. Read the draft at a normal reading speed from beginning to end. As you read, do the following:
   A. Place a wavy line in the margin next to any passages that you find confusing, that contain something that doesn't seem to fit, or that otherwise slow down your reading.
   B. Place a "Good!" in the margin next to any passages where you think the writing is particularly strong or interesting.

II. Read the draft again slowly and answer the following questions by writing brief explanations of your answers:
   A. The two descriptions
      1. How could the two descriptions be made more parallel or more detailed and vivid? How might the writer sharpen or clarify the angle of vision in each description?
      2. Where could the writer replace *tell* words with *show* words? How could the writer use *show* words more effectively? How could the writer include more sensory details appealing to more of the senses?
      3. If the writer has used only one or two of the strategies for creating contrast (direct statement of meaning, selection of details, word choice, figurative language, sentence structure), how might he or she use other strategies?
   B. Self-reflection
      1. How might the writer improve the effectiveness of the rhetorical analysis? How many strategies does the writer include? Where might the writer use more or better examples to illustrate the chosen strategies? What might the writer add or clarify?
      2. What does the writer say he or she has learned from doing this assignment? How could the writer's insights be expanded, explained more clearly, or developed more thoroughly?
III. Rhetorical considerations
   A. *Purpose, audience,* and *genre:* How do differences in organization and style in Parts A and B reveal the writer's awareness of differences in purpose, audience, and genre?
   B. *Logos, ethos,* and *pathos:* How might the writer improve the ideas in this draft, particularly in Part B? What image of the writer emerges in Parts A and B? How might the writer improve this image? How effectively does the writer appeal to the readers' feelings, emotions, and desires?
IV. If the writer has prepared questions for you, respond to his or her inquiries.
V. Sum up what you see as the chief strengths and problem areas of this draft.
   A. Strengths
   B. Problem areas
VI. Read the draft one more time. Place a check mark in the margin wherever you notice problems in grammar, spelling, or mechanics (one check mark per problem).

Reading Rhetorically
The Writer as Strong Reader

About Reading Rhetorically

Many new college students are surprised by the amount, range, and difficulty of reading they have to do in college. Every day they are challenged by reading assignments ranging from scholarly articles and textbooks on complex subject matter to primary sources such as Plato's dialogues or Darwin's *Voyage of the Beagle*.

The goal of this chapter is to help you become a more powerful reader of academic texts, prepared to take part in the conversations of the disciplines you study. To this end, we explain two kinds of thinking and writing essential to your college reading:

- Your ability to listen carefully to a text, to recognize its parts and their functions, and to summarize its ideas
- Your ability to formulate strong responses to texts by interacting with them, either by agreeing with, interrogating, or actively opposing them

To interact strongly with texts, you must learn how to read them both with and against the grain. When you read *with the grain* of a text, you see the world through its author's perspective, open yourself to the author's argument, apply the text's insights to new contexts, and connect its ideas to your own experiences and personal knowledge. When you read *against the grain* of a text, you resist it by questioning its points, raising doubts, analyzing the limits of its perspective, or even refuting its argument. We say that readers who respond strongly to texts in this manner read *rhetorically*; that is, they are aware of the effect a text is intended to have on them, and they critically consider that effect, entering into or challenging the text's intentions.

Exploring Rhetorical Reading

As an introduction to rhetorical reading, we would like you to read Dr. Andrés Martin's "On Teenagers and Tattoos," which appeared in the *Journal of the American Academy of Child and Adolescent Psychiatry*, a scholarly publication. Before reading the article, complete the following opinion survey. Answer each question using a 1–5 scale, with 1 meaning "strongly agree" and 5 meaning "strongly disagree."

1. For teenagers, getting a tattoo is like following any other fad such as wearing the currently popular kind of shoe or hairstyle.
2. Teenagers get tattoos primarily as a form of asserting independence from parents and other adults.
3. Teenagers get tattoos on the spur of the moment and usually don't consider the irreversibility of marking their skin.
4. Teenagers who get tattoos are expressing deep psychological needs.
5. A psychiatry journal can provide useful insights into teen choices to tattoo their bodies.

When you have finished rating your degree of agreement with these statements, read Martin's article, using whatever note-taking, underlining, or highlighting strategies you normally use when reading for a class. When you have finished reading, complete the exercises that follow.

READING

Andrés Martin, M.D.
On Teenagers and Tattoos

The skeleton dimensions I shall now proceed to set down are copied verbatim from my right arm, where I had them tattooed: as in my wild wanderings at that period, there was no other secure way of preserving such valuable statistics.

—Melville/*Moby Dick CII*

1   Tattoos and piercings have become a part of our everyday landscape. They are ubiquitous, having entered the circles of glamour and the mainstream of fashion, and they have even become an increasingly common feature of our urban youth. Legislation in most states restricts professional tattooing to adults older than 18 years of age, so "high end" tattooing is rare in children and adolescents, but such tattoos are occasionally seen in older teenagers. Piercings, by comparison, as well as self-made or "jailhouse" type tattoos, are not at all rare among adolescents or even among schoolage children. Like hairdo, makeup, or baggy jeans, tattoos and piercings can be subject to fad influence or peer pressure in an effort toward group affiliation. As with any other fashion statement, they can be construed as bodily aids in the inner struggle toward identity consolidation, serving as adjuncts to the defining and sculpting of the self by means of external manipulations. But unlike most other body decorations, tattoos and piercings are set apart by their irreversible and permanent nature, a quality at the core of their magnetic appeal to adolescents.

2   Adolescents and their parents are often at odds over the acquisition of bodily decorations. For the adolescent, piercings or tattoos may be seen as personal and beautifying statements, while parents may construe them as oppositional and enraging affronts to their authority. Distinguishing bodily adornment from self-mutilation may indeed prove challenging, particularly when a family is in disagreement over a teenager's motivations and a clinician is summoned as the final arbiter. At such times it may be most important to realize jointly that the skin can all too readily become but another battleground for the tensions of the age, arguments having less to do with tattoos and piercings than with core issues such as separation from the family matrix. Exploring the motivations and significance underlying tattoos (Grumet, 1983) and piercings can go a long way toward resolving such differences and can become a novel and additional way of getting to know teenagers. An interested and nonjudgmental appreciation of teenagers' surface presentations may become a way of making contact not only in their terms but on their turfs: quite literally on the territory of their skins.

3   The following three sections exemplify some of the complex psychological underpinnings of youth tattooing.

Identity and the Adolescent's Body

4   Tattoos and piercing can offer a concrete and readily available solution for many of the identity crises and conflicts normative to adolescent development. In using such decorations, and by marking out their bodily territories, adolescents can support their efforts at autonomy, privacy, and insulation. Seeking individuation, tattooed adolescents can become unambiguously demarcated from others and singled out as unique. The intense and often disturbing reactions that are mobilized in viewers can help to effectively keep them at bay, becoming tantamount to the proverbial "Keep Out" sign hanging from a teenager's door.

5   Alternatively, [when teenagers feel] prey to a rapidly evolving body over which they have no say, self-made and openly visible decorations may restore adolescents' sense of normalcy and control, a way of turning a passive experience into an active identity. By indelibly marking their bodies, adolescents can strive to reclaim their bearings within an environment experienced as alien, estranged, or suffocating or to lay claim over their evolving and increasingly unrecognizable bodies. In either case, the net outcome can be a resolution to unwelcome impositions: external, familial, or societal in one case; internal and hormonal in the other. In the words of a 16-year-old girl with several facial piercings, and who could have been referring to her body just as well as to the position within her family, "If I don't fit in, it is because *I* say so."

Incorporation and Ownership

6   Imagery of a religious, deathly, or skeletal nature, the likenesses of fierce animals or imagined creatures, and the simple inscription of names are some of the time-tested favorite contents for tattoos. In all instances, marks

become not only memorials or recipients for clearly held persons or concepts; they strive for incorporation, with images and abstract symbols gaining substance on becoming a permanent part of the individual's skin. Thickly embedded in personally meaningful representations and object relations, tattoos can become not only the ongoing memento of a relationship, but at times even the only evidence that there ever was such a bond. They can quite literally become the relationship itself. The turbulence and impulsivity of early attachments and infatuations may become grounded, effectively bridging oblivion through the visible reality of tattoos.

7   *Case Vignette.* A, a 13-year-old boy, proudly showed me his tattooed deltoid. The coarsely depicted roll of the dice marked the day and month of his birth. Rather disappointed, he then uncovered an immaculate back, going on to draw for me the great "piece" he envisioned for it. A menacing figure held a hand of cards: two aces, two eights, and a card with two sets of dates. A's father had belonged to "Dead Man's Hand," a motorcycle gang named after the set of cards (aces and eights) that the legendary Wild Bill Hickock had held in the 1890s when shot dead over a poker table in Deadwood, South Dakota. A had only the vaguest memory of and sketchiest information about his father, but he knew he had died in a motorcycle accident: the fifth card marked the dates of his birth and death.

8   The case vignette also serves to illustrate how tattoos are often the culmination of a long process of imagination, fantasy, and planning that can start at an early age. Limited markings, or relatively reversible ones such as piercings, can at a later time scaffold toward the more radical commitment of a permanent tattoo.

The Quest for Permanence

9   The popularity of the anchor as a tattoo motif may historically have had to do less with guild identification among sailors than with an intense longing for rootedness and stability. In a similar vein, the recent increase in the popularity and acceptance of tattoos may be understood as an antidote or counterpoint to our urban and nomadic lifestyles. Within an increasingly mobile society, in which relationships are so often transient—as attested by the frequencies of divorce, abandonment, foster placement, and repeated moves, for example—tattoos can be a readily available source of grounding. Tattoos, unlike many relationships, can promise permanence and stability. A sense of constancy can be derived from unchanging marks that can be carried along no matter what the physical, temporal, or geographical vicissitudes at hand. Tattoos stay, while all else may change.

10   *Case Vignette.* A proud father at 17, B had had the smiling face of his 3-month-old baby girl tattooed on his chest. As we talked at a tattoo convention, he proudly introduced her to me, explaining how he would "always know how beautiful she is today" when years from then he saw her semblance etched on himself.

11   The quest for permanence may at other times prove misleading and offer premature closure to unresolved conflicts. At a time of normative uncertain-

ties, adolescents may maladaptively and all too readily commit to a tattoo and its indefinite presence. A wish to hold on to a current certainty may lead the adolescent to lay down in ink what is valued and cherished one day but may not necessarily be in the future. The frequency of self-made tattoos among hospitalized, incarcerated, or gang-affiliated youths suggests such motivations: a sense of stability may be a particularly dire need under temporary, turbulent, or volatile conditions. In addition, through their designs teenagers may assert a sense of bonding and allegiance to a group larger than themselves. Tattoos may attest to powerful experiences, such as adolescence itself, lived and even survived together. As with *Moby Dick's* protagonist Ishmael, they may bear witness to the "valuable statistics" of one's "wild wandering(s)": those of adolescent exhilaration and excitement on the one hand; of growing pains, shared misfortune, or even incarceration on the other.

12   Adolescents' bodily decorations, at times radical and dramatic in their presentation, can be seen in terms of figuration rather than disfigurement, of the natural body being through them transformed into a personalized body (Brain, 1979). They can often be understood as self-constructive and adorning efforts, rather than prematurely subsumed as mutilatory and destructive acts. If we bear all of this in mind, we may not only arrive at a position to pass more reasoned clinical judgment, but become sensitized through our patients' skins to another level of their internal reality.

References

Brain, R. (1979). *The Decorated Body*. New York: Harper & Row.

Grumet, G. W. (1983). Psychodynamic implications of tattoos. *Am J Orthopsychiatry*, 53:482–492.

Thinking Critically about "On Teenagers and Tattoos"

1. Summarize in one or two sentences Martin's main points.

2. Freewrite a response to this question: In what way has Martin's article caused me to reconsider my answers to the opinion survey?

3. Working in small groups or as a whole class, compare the note-taking strategies you used while reading this piece. (a) How many people wrote marginal notes? How many underlined or highlighted? (b) Compare the contents of these notes. Did people highlight the same passage or different passages? (c) Individually, look at your annotations and highlights and try to decide why you wrote or marked what you did. Share your reasons for making these annotations. The goal of this exercise is to make you more aware of your thinking processes as you read.

4. Working as a whole class or in small groups, share your responses to the questionnaire and to the postreading questions. To what extent did this article

change people's thinking about the reasons teenagers choose to tattoo their bodies? What were the most insightful points in this article?

5. Assume that you are looking for substantial, detailed information about teenagers and tattooing. What parts of this article leave you with unanswered questions? Where is more explanation needed?

WRITING PROJECT

Write a "summary/strong response" essay that includes: (a) a summary (approximately 150–250 words) of a reading specified by your instructor and (b) a strong response to that reading in which you speak back to that reading from your own critical thinking, personal experience, and values. As you formulate your own response, consider both the author's rhetorical strategies and the author's ideas. Think of your response as your analysis of how the text tries to influence its readers rhetorically and how your wrestling with the text has expanded and deepened your thinking about its ideas.

The skills this assignment develops are crucial for academic writers. You will learn how to summarize an article (or book), including how to quote brief passages, how to use attributive tags to cue your reader that you are reporting someone else's ideas rather than your own, and how to cite the article using (in this case) the Modern Language Association (MLA) documentation system. Because writing summaries and producing strong responses are important writing-to-learn skills, you will draw on them any time you are asked to speak back to or critique a text. These skills are also needed for writing exploratory essays, analysis and synthesis essays, researched arguments, and any other scholarly work that uses sources. In learning how to summarize a text and interact with it in writing, you are learning how to contribute your own ideas to a conversation. Weak readers passively report what other people have said. Strong readers see themselves as contributors to the conversation, capable of analyzing and evaluating texts, speaking back to other authors, and thinking actively for themselves.

Understanding Rhetorical Reading

In this section we explain why college-level reading is often difficult for new students and offer suggestions for improving your reading process based on the reading strategies of experts. We then show you the importance of reading a text both with the grain and against the grain—skills you need to summarize a text and respond to it strongly.

What Makes College-Level Reading Difficult?

The difficulty of college-level reading stems in part from the complexity of the subject matter. Whatever the subject—from international monetary policies to the intricacies of photosynthesis—you have to wrestle with new and complex materials that might perplex anyone. But in addition to the daunting subject matter, several other factors contribute to the difficulty of college-level reading:

- *Vocabulary.* Many college-level readings—especially primary sources—contain unfamiliar technical language that may be specific to an academic discipline: for example, the terms *identity consolidation, normative, individuation,* and *object relations* in the Martin text or words like *existentialism* and *Neoplatonic* in a philosophy textbook. In academia, words often carry specialized meanings that evoke a whole history of conversation and debate that may be inaccessible, even through a specialized dictionary. You will not fully understand them until you are initiated into the disciplinary conversations that gave rise to them.
- *Unfamiliar rhetorical context.* As we explained in Part One, writers write to an audience for a purpose arising from some motivating occasion. Knowing an author's purpose, occasion, and audience will often clarify confusing parts of a text. For example, you can understand the Martin article more easily if you know that its author, writing in a scientific journal, is offering advice to psychiatrists about how to counsel tattooed teens and their families. A text's internal clues can sometimes help you fill in the rhetorical context, but often you may need to do outside research.
- *Unfamiliar genre.* In your college reading, you will encounter a range of genres such as textbooks, trade books, scholarly articles, scientific reports, historical documents, newspaper articles, op-ed pieces, and so forth. Each of these makes different demands on readers and requires a different reading strategy.
- *Lack of background knowledge.* Writers necessarily make assumptions about what their readers already know. Your understanding of Martin, for example, would be more complete if you had a background in adolescent psychology and psychiatric therapy.

For Writing and Discussion

The importance of background knowledge can be easily demonstrated any time you dip into past issues of a newsmagazine or try to read articles about an unfamiliar culture. Consider the following passage from a 1986 *Newsweek* article. How much background knowledge do you need before you can fully comprehend this passage? What cultural knowledge about the United States would a student from Ethiopia or Indonesia need?

(continued)

Throughout the NATO countries last week, there were second thoughts about the prospect of a nuclear-free world. For 40 years nuclear weapons have been the backbone of the West's defense. For almost as long American presidents have ritually affirmed their desire to see the world rid of them. Then, suddenly, Ronald Reagan and Mikhail Gorbachev came close to actually doing it. Let's abolish all nuclear ballistic missiles in the next 10 years, Reagan said. Why not all nuclear weapons, countered Gorbachev. OK, the president responded, like a man agreeing to throw in the washer-dryer along with the house.

What if the deal had gone through? On the one hand, Gorbachev would have returned to Moscow a hero. There is a belief in the United States that the Soviets need nuclear arms because nuclear weapons are what make them a superpower. But according to Marxist-Leninist doctrine, capitalism's nuclear capability (unforeseen by Marx and Lenin) is the only thing that can prevent the inevitable triumph of communism. Therefore, an end to nuclear arms would put the engine of history back on its track.

On the other hand, Europeans fear, a nonnuclear United States would be tempted to retreat into neo-isolationism.

—*Robert B. Cullen, "Dangers of Disarming,"* Newsweek

Working in small groups or as a class, identify words and passages in this text that depend on background information or knowledge of culture for complete comprehension.

Using the Reading Strategies of Experts

In Chapter 17, we describe the differences between the writing processes of experts and those of beginning college writers. There are parallel differences between the reading processes of experienced and inexperienced readers, especially when they encounter complex materials. In this section we describe some expert reading strategies that you can begin applying to your reading of any kind of college-level material.

Reconstruct the Text's Rhetorical Context
Before and as you read a text, ask questions about the author's audience, purpose, genre, and motivating occasion. Any piece of writing makes more sense if you think of its author as a real person writing for some real purpose in a real historical context.

If you read an article that has been anthologized (as in the readings in this textbook), note any information you are given about the author, publication data, and genre. Try to reconstruct the author's original motivation for writing. How have audience, purpose, and genre shaped this text?

Make Marginal Notes as You Read
Expert readers seldom use highlighters, which encourage passive, inefficient reading; instead, they make extensive marginal notes as they read. Advice on writing marginal notes is given throughout this chapter.

Get in the Dictionary Habit

When you can't tell a word's meaning from context, get in the habit of looking it up. One strategy is to make small check marks next to words you're unsure of; then look them up after you're done so as not to break your concentration.

Vary Your Reading Speed to Match Your Reading Goals

Unlike novices, experienced readers vary their reading speeds and strategies according to their goals. In other words, experienced readers know when to slow down or speed up. Robert Sternberg, a cognitive psychologist, discovered that novice readers tend to read everything at about the same pace, no matter what their purpose. In contrast, experienced readers vary their reading speed significantly depending on whether they are scanning for a piece of information, skimming for main ideas, reading deliberately for complete comprehension, or reading slowly for detailed analysis. Knowing when to speed up or slow down—especially if you are doing a research project and trying to cover lots of ground—can make your reading more efficient.

If a Text Is Complex, Read in a "Multidraft" Way

It may be comforting for you to know that expert readers struggle with difficult texts the same way you do. Often, experienced readers reread a text two or three times, treating their first readings like first drafts. They hold confusing passages in mental suspension, hoping that later parts of the essay will clarify earlier parts. The ironic point here is that sometimes you have to speed up to slow down. If you are lost in a passage, try skimming ahead rapidly, looking at the opening sentences of paragraphs and at any passages that sum up the writer's argument or that help clarify the argument's structure. Pay particular attention to the conclusion, which often ties the whole argument together. This rapid "first-draft reading" helps you see the text's main points and overall structure, thus providing a background for a second reading. The passage that puzzled you the first time might now be clearer.

Reading With the Grain and Against the Grain

The reading and thinking strategies that we have just described enable skilled readers to interact strongly with texts. Your purpose in using these strategies is to read texts both with the grain and against the grain, a way of reading that is analogous to the believing and doubting game we introduced in Chapter 2. This concept is so important that we have chosen to highlight it separately here.

For an explanation of the believing and doubting game, see pp. 42–46.

When you read with the grain of a text, you practice what psychologist Carl Rogers calls "empathic listening," in which you try to see the world through the author's eyes, role-playing as much as possible the author's intended readers by adopting their beliefs and values and acquiring their background knowledge. Reading with the grain is the main strategy you use when you summarize a text, but it comes into play also when you develop a strong response. When making with-the-grain points, you support the author's thesis with your own arguments and examples, or apply or extend the author's argument in new ways.

When you read against the grain of a text, you challenge, question, resist, and perhaps even rebut the author's ideas. You are a resistant reader who asks unanticipated questions, pushes back, and reads the text in ways unforeseen by the author. Reading against the grain is a key part of creating a strong response. When you make against-the-grain points, you challenge the author's reasoning, sources, examples, or choice of language. You generate counterexamples, present alternative lines of reasoning, deny the writer's values, or raise points that the writer has overlooked or specific data that the writer has omitted.

Strong readers develop their ability to read in both ways—with the grain and against the grain. Throughout the rest of this chapter, we show you different ways to practice and apply these strategies.

Understanding Summary Writing

In this section we explain techniques for writing an effective summary of a text. Summary writing fosters a close encounter between you and the text and demonstrates your understanding of it. When you write a summary, you practice reading with the grain of a text. You "listen" actively to the text's author, showing that you understand the author's point of view by restating his or her argument as completely and fairly as possible. Summary writing is an essential academic skill, regularly used in research writing of any kind, where you often present condensed views of other writers' arguments, either as support for your own view or as alternative views that you must analyze or respond to.

Reading for Structure and Content

In writing a summary, you must focus on both its structure and its content. In the following steps, we recommend a process that will help you condense a text's ideas into an accurate summary. As you become a more experienced reader and writer, you'll follow these steps without thinking about them.

Step 1:   The first time through, read the text fairly quickly for general meaning. If you get confused, keep going; later parts of the text might clarify earlier parts.

Step 2:   Reread the text carefully. As you read, write gist statements in the margins for each paragraph. A *gist statement* is a brief indication of the paragraph's function or purpose in the text or a brief summary of the paragraph's content. Sometimes it is helpful to think of these two kinds of gist statements as "what it does" statements and "what it says" statements.* A "what it does" statement specifies the paragraph's function—for example, "summarizes an opposing view," "introduces

---

*For our treatment of "what it does" and "what it says" statements, we are indebted to Kenneth A. Bruffee, *A Short Course in Writing*, 2nd ed. (Cambridge, MA: Winthrop, 1980).

another reason," "presents a supporting example," "provides statistical data in support of a point," and so on. A "what it says" statement captures the main idea of a paragraph by summarizing the paragraph's content. The "what it says" statement is the paragraph's main point, in contrast to its supporting ideas and examples. Sometimes an explicit topic sentence makes the main point easy to find, but often you have to extract the main point by shrinking an argument down to its essence. In some cases, you may be uncertain about the main point. If so, select the point that you think a majority of readers would agree is the main one.

When you first practice detailed readings of a text, you might find it helpful to write complete *does* and *says* statements on a separate sheet of paper rather than in the margins until you develop the internal habit of appreciating both the function and content of parts of an essay. Here are *does* and *says* statements for selected paragraphs of Andrés Martin's essay on teenage tattooing:

Paragraph 1: *Does:* Introduces the subject and sets up the argument. *Says:* The current popularity of tattoos and piercings is partly explained as an aid toward finding an identity, but the core of their appeal is their irreversible permanence.

Paragraph 2: *Does:* Narrows the focus and presents the thesis. *Says:* To counsel families in disagreement over tattoos, psychiatrists should exhibit a nonjudgmental appreciation of teen tattoos and use them to understand teenagers better.

Paragraph 4: *Does:* Discusses the first complex motivation behind youth tattooing. *Says:* Teens use tattoos to handle identity crises and to establish their uniqueness from others.

Paragraph 5: *Does:* Elaborates on the first motivation, the identity issue. *Says:* Tattoos provide teens with a sense of control over their changing bodies and over an environment perceived as adverse and domineering.

Paragraph 11: *Does:* Complicates the view of teens' use of tattoos to find permanence and belonging. *Says:* Although tattoos may unrealistically promise the resolution to larger conflicts, they may at least record the triumphs and miseries of adolescent turbulence, including gang and prison experience.

Paragraph 12: *Does:* Sums up the perspective and advice of the article. *Says:* Psychiatrists should regard adolescent tattoos positively as adornment and self-expression and employ tattoos to help understand teens' identities and sense of reality.

You may occasionally have difficulty writing a *says* statement for a paragraph because you may have trouble deciding what the main idea is, especially if the paragraph doesn't begin with a closed-form topic sentence. One way to respond to this problem is to formulate the question that you think the paragraph answers. If you think of chunks of the text as answers to a logical progression of questions, you can often follow the main ideas more easily. Rather than writing *says* statements in the margins, therefore, some readers prefer writing *says* questions. *Says* questions for the Martin text may include the following: What is the most constructive approach clinicians can take to teen tattooing when these tattoos have become the focus of family conflict? What psychological needs and problems are teenagers acting out through their tattoos? Why does the permanence of tattoos appeal to young people?

No matter which method you use—*says* statements or *says* questions—writing gist statements in the margins is far more effective than underlining or highlighting in helping you recall the text's structure and argument.

Step 3:   After you have analyzed the article paragraph by paragraph, try locating the article's main divisions or parts. In longer closed-form articles, writers often forecast the shape of their essays in their introductions or use their conclusions to sum up main points. Although Martin's article is short, it uses both a forecasting statement and subheads to direct readers through its main points. The article is divided into several main chunks as follows:

- Introductory paragraphs, which establish the problem to be addressed and narrow the focus to a clinical perspective (paragraphs 1–2)
- A one-sentence organizing and predicting statement (paragraph 3)
- A section explaining how tattoos may help adolescents establish a unique identity (paragraphs 4–5)
- A section explaining how tattoos help teens incorporate onto their bodies a symbolic ownership of something important to them (paragraphs 6–8)
- A section explaining how tattoos represent and satisfy teens' search for permanence (paragraphs 9–11)
- A conclusion that states the thesis explicitly and sums up Martin's advice to fellow psychiatrists (paragraph 12)

Outlines and tree diagrams are discussed in Chapter 18, pp. 538–540.

Instead of listing the sections, you might prefer to make an outline or tree diagram of the article showing its main parts.

The same basic procedures can work for summarizing a book, but you will need to modify them to fit a much longer text. For instance, you might write "what it does" and "what it says" statements for chapters or parts of a book. In summarizing a book, you might pay special attention to the introduction and conclusion of the book. In the introduction, usually authors state their motivation for writing the book and often put forth their thesis and the subtheses that the subsequent chapters of the book develop and explain. Chapter titles and chapter introductions often restate the author's subtheses and can help you identify main ideas to include in a book summary.

Producing the Summary

Once you have written gist statements or questions in the margins and clarified the text's structure by creating an outline or diagram, you are ready to write a summary. Typically, summaries range from 100 to 250 words, but sometimes writers compose summaries as short as one sentence. The order and proportions of your summary can usually follow the order and proportions of the text. However, if the original article has a delayed thesis or other characteristics of open-form writing, you can rearrange the order and begin with the thesis. With prose that has many open-form features, you may also have to infer points that are more implied than expressed.

A summary of another author's writing—when it is incorporated into your own essay—makes particular demands on you, the writer. Most of all, writing a summary challenges you to convey the main ideas of a text—ideas that are often complex—in as few and as clear words as you can. We tell our students that writing a summary is like having a word budget: you have only so many words (say, a 250- or 100-word limit), and you have to spend them wisely. In addition, a successful summary should do all of the following:

CRITERIA FOR AN EFFECTIVE SUMMARY

- Represent the original article accurately and fairly.
- Be direct and concise, using words economically.
- Remain objective and neutral, not revealing your own ideas on the subject but, rather, only the original author's points.
- Give the original article balanced and proportional coverage.
- Use your own words to express the original author's ideas.
- Keep your reader informed through attributive tags (such as *according to Martin* or *Martin argues that*) that you are expressing someone else's ideas, not your own.
- Possibly include quotations for a few key terms or ideas from the original, but quote sparingly.
- Be a unified, coherent piece of writing in its own right.
- Be properly cited and documented so that the reader can find the original text.

Some of these criteria for a successful summary are challenging to meet. For instance, to avoid interjecting your own opinions, note whether the verbs in your attributive tags reflect a bias. Consider the difference between *Smith argues* and *Smith rants* or between *Brown asserts* and *Brown leaps to the conclusion*. In each pair, the second verb, by moving beyond neutrality, reveals your own judgment of the author's ideas.

When you incorporate a summary into your own writing, it is particularly important to distinguish between the author's ideas and your own—hence the importance of frequent attributive tags, which tell the reader that these ideas belong to Smith or Jones or Brown rather than to you. If you choose to copy any of the author's words directly from the text, you need to use quotation marks and cite the quotation using an appropriate documentation system.

The following example, which summarizes Martin's article on teenagers and tattoos, uses the MLA documentation system.

Chapter 22 provides additional instruction on summarizing, paraphrasing, and quoting sources. It also explains how to work sources smoothly into your own writing and avoid plagiarism.

Summary of Martin Article

In "On Teenagers and Tattoos," published in the <u>Journal of the American Academy of Child and Adolescent Psychiatry</u>, Dr. Andrés Martin advises fellow psychiatrists to think of teenage tattooing not as a fad or as a form of self-mutilation but as an opportunity for clinicians to understand teenagers better. <u>Martin examines</u> three different reasons that teenagers get tattoos. <u>First,</u> <u>he argues</u> that tattoos help teenagers establish unique identities

Identification of the article, journal, and author

Thesis of article

— *Attributive tag*

— *Transition*

— *Attributive tag*

Transition and attributive tag

by giving them a sense of control over their evolving bodies and over an environment perceived as adverse and domineering. Second, he believes that a tattooed image often symbolizes the teen's

Transition and attributive tag

relationship to a significant concept or person, making the relationship more visible and real. Finally, says Martin, because

Inclusion of short quotation from article. MLA documentation style; number in parentheses indicates page number of original article where quotation is found

teens are disturbed by modern society's mobility and fragmentation and because they have an "intense longing for rootedness and stability" (120), the irreversible nature of tattoos may give them a sense of permanence. Martin concludes that tattoos can be a

Attributive tag

meaningful record of survived teen experiences. He encourages

Attributive tag

therapists to regard teen tattoos as "self-constructive and

Another short quotation

adorning efforts," rather than as "mutilatory and destructive

Brackets indicate that the writer changed the material inside the brackets to fit the grammar and context of the writer's own sentence

acts" (121) and suggests that tattoos can help therapists understand "another level of [teenagers'] internal reality" (121). [195 words]

Works Cited

Martin article cited completely using MLA documentation form; in a formal paper, the "works cited" list begins on a new page

Martin, Andrés. "On Teenagers and Tattoos." Journal of the
    American Academy of Child and Adolescent Psychiatry 36 (1997):
    860-61. Rpt. in The Allyn & Bacon Guide to Writing. John D.
    Ramage, John C. Bean, and June Johnson. 4th ed. New York:
    Longman, 2006. 118-121.

For Writing and Discussion

Imagine that the context of a research paper you are writing calls for a shorter summary of the Martin article than the one presented here (which is approximately 195 words, including attributive tags). To practice distilling the main ideas of an article to produce summaries of different lengths, first write a 100-word summary of "On Teenagers and Tattoos." Then reduce your summary further to 50 words. Discuss the principles you followed in deciding what to eliminate or how to restructure sentences to convey the most information in the fewest number of words.

Understanding Strong Response Writing

We have said that summary writing is an essential academic skill. Equally important is strong response writing in which you join the text's conversation and speak back to it. If a strong reading means to engage a text actively, both assenting to an author's ideas and questioning them, what exactly do you write about when you compose a strong response? To appreciate our answer to this question, you need to know the various ways that strong responses are assigned across the curriculum.

Kinds of Strong Responses

A strong response is one of the most common writing assignments you will encounter in college courses. However, teachers vary in what they mean by a "strong response," and they often use different terms for the same basic kind of assignment. Our conversations with instructors from across the disciplines suggest that there are three common kinds of strong response assignments:

- *Analysis or critique assignment.* Here your job is to analyze and critique the assigned reading. You discuss how a text is constructed, what rhetorical strategies it employs, and how effectively its argument is supported. Suppose, for example, that you are asked to critique an article, appearing in a conservative business journal, that advocates oil exploration in the Arctic National Wildlife Refuge (ANWR). For this kind of strong response, you'd be expected to analyze the article's rhetorical strategies (for example, How is it shaped to appeal to a conservative, business-oriented audience? How has the writer's angle of vision filtered the evidence for its arguments?) and evaluate its argument (for example, What are the underlying assumptions and beliefs on which the argument is based? Is the logic sound? Is the evidence accurate and up-to-date?). When you analyze and critique a reading, you focus on the text itself, giving it the same close attention that an art critic gives a painting, a football coach gives a game film, or a biologist gives a cell formation. This close attention can be with the grain, noting the effectiveness of the text's rhetorical strategies, or against the grain, discussing what is ineffective or problematic about these strategies. Or an analysis might point out both the strengths of and the problems with a text's rhetorical strategies.
- *"Your own views" assignment.* Here the instructor expects you to present your own views on the reading's topic or issue—for example, to give your own views on oil exploration in the ANWR, to support or challenge the writer's views, to raise new questions, and otherwise to add your voice to the ANWR conversation. This kind of strong response invites you to read both with and against the grain. A with-the-grain reading supports all or some of the article's arguments but supplies additional reasons or new evidence,

directs the argument to a different audience, extends the argument to a different context, or otherwise adds your own support to the writer's views. An against-the-grain reading attempts to challenge all or part of the writer's argument, to raise doubts in the audience, to show flaws in the writer's reasoning, and to support your own views as they arise from your personal experience, observation, other reading, and wrestling with the author's ideas.

- *A blended assignment that mixes both kinds of responses.* Here the instructor expects you to respond in both ways—to analyze and critique the article but also to engage the writer's ideas by developing your own views on the topic. As a writer, you can emphasize what is most important to you, but the paper should contain elements of analysis and critique as well as your own views on the issue. The assignment for this chapter calls for this kind of blended strong response, but your instructor can specify what kind of emphasis he or she desires.

Instructors also vary in their preferences for the tone and structure of strong response essays. Some instructors prefer the term *reflection paper* rather than *strong response*—a term that invites you to write a personal response with an open-form structure and an expressive or exploratory purpose. In a reflection paper, the instructor is particularly interested in how the reading has affected you personally—what memories it has triggered, what personal experiences it relates to, what values and beliefs it has challenged, and so forth. Other instructors prefer closed-form strong responses with an explicit thesis statement, an analytical or persuasive purpose, and a more academic tone.

The assignment in this chapter calls for a closed-form strong response with a clear thesis statement. Your instructor, however, may modify the assignment to fit the goals of his or her course or the curriculum at your university.

Student Example of a Summary/Strong Response Essay

Before giving you some tips on how to discover ideas for your strong response, we show you an example of a student essay for this chapter: a summary/strong response essay. Note that the essay begins by identifying the question under discussion: Why do teenagers get tattoos? It then summarizes the article by Andrés Martin.* Immediately following the summary, the student writer states his thesis, followed by the strong response, which contains both rhetorical points and points about the causes of teenage tattooing.

WHY DO TEENAGERS GET TATTOOS? A RESPONSE TO ANDRÉS MARTIN

Sean Barry (student)

Introduces topic and sets context

My sister has one. My brother has one. I have one. Just take a stroll downtown and you will see how commonplace it is for someone to be decorated with tattoos and hung with piercings. In fact, hundreds of teenagers, every day, allow themselves

---

*In this essay the student writer uses a shortened version of his 195-word summary that was used as an illustration on pages 129–130.

to be etched upon or poked into. What's the cause of this phenomenon? Why do so many teenagers get tattoos?

Dr. Andrés Martin has answered this question from a psychiatrist's perspective in his article "On Teenagers and Tattoos," published in the Journal of the American Academy of Child and Adolescent Psychiatry. Martin advises fellow psychiatrists to think of teenage tattooing as a constructive opportunity for clinicians to understand teenagers better. Martin examines three different reasons that teenagers get tattoos. First, he argues that tattoos help teenagers establish unique identities by giving them a sense of control over their evolving bodies and over an environment perceived as adverse and domineering. Second, he believes that a tattooed image often symbolizes the teen's relationship to a significant concept or person, making the relationship more visible and real. Finally, says Martin, because teens are disturbed by modern society's mobility and fragmentation and because they have an "intense longing for rootedness and stability" (120), the irreversible nature of tattoos may give them a sense of permanence. Martin concludes that tattoos can be a meaningful record of survived teen experiences. *[margin note: Summary of Martin's article]* Although Martin's analysis has relevance and some strengths, I think he overgeneralizes and over-romanticizes teenage tattooing, leading him to overlook other causes of teenage tattooing such as commercialization and teenagers' desire to identify with a peer group as well as achieve an individual identity. *[margin note: Thesis statement]*

Some of Martin's points seem relevant and realistic and match my own experiences. I agree that teenagers sometimes use tattoos to establish their own identities. When my brother, sister, and I all got our tattoos, we were partly asserting our own independence from our parents. Martin's point about the symbolic significance of a tattoo image also connects with my experiences. A Hawaiian guy in my dorm has a fish tattooed on his back, which he says represents his love of the ocean and the spiritual experience he has when he scuba dives. *[margin note: With-the-grain point in support of Martin's ideas]*

Martin, speaking as a psychiatrist to other psychiatrists, also provides psychological insights into the topic of teen tattooing even though this psychological perspective brings some limitations, too. In this scholarly article, Martin's purpose is to persuade fellow psychiatrists to think of adolescent tattooing in positive rather than judgmental terms. Rather than condemn teens for getting tattoos, he argues that discussion of the tattoos can provide useful insights into the needs and behavior of troubled teens (especially males). But this perspective is also a limitation because the teenagers he sees are mostly youths in psychiatric counseling, particularly teens struggling with the absence of or violent loss of a parent and those who have experience with gangs and prison-terms. This perspective leads him to overgeneralize. As a psychological study of a specific group of troubled teens, the article is informative. However, it does not apply as well to most teenagers who are getting tattoos today. *[margin note: Rhetorical point about Martin's audience, purpose, and genre that has both with-the-grain and against-the-grain elements]*

Besides overgeneralizing, Martin also seems to romanticize teenage tattooing. Why else would a supposedly scientific article begin and end with quotations from Moby Dick? Martin seems to imply a similarity between today's teenagers and the sailor hero Ishmael who wandered the seas looking for personal identity. In quoting Moby Dick, Martin seems to value tattooing as a suitable way for teenagers to record their experiences. Every tattoo, for Martin, has deep significance. Thus, Martin casts tattooed teens as romantic outcasts, loners, and adventurers like Ishmael. *[margin note: Against-the-grain rhetorical point: Barry analyzes use of quotations from Moby Dick]*

In contrast to Martin, I believe that teens are influenced by the commercial nature of tattooing, which has become big business aimed at their age group. Every movie or television star or beauty queen who sports a tattoo sends the commercial message that tattoos are cool: "A tattoo will help you be successful, sexy, handsome, or attractive like us." Tattoo parlors are no longer dark dives in seedy, dangerous parts of cities, but *[margin note: Transition to writer's own analysis]* *[margin note: Against-the-grain point: writer's alternative theory]* appear in lively commercial districts; in fact, there are several down the street from the university. Teenagers now buy tattoos the way they buy other consumer items.

Against-the-grain point: writer's second theory

Furthermore, Martin doesn't explore teenagers' desire not only for individuality but also for peer group acceptance. Tattooing is the "in" thing to do. Tattooing used to be defiant and daring, but now it is popular and more acceptable among teens. I even know a group of sorority women who went together to get tattoos on their ankles. As tattooing has become more mainstreamed, rebels/trendsetters have turned to newer and more outrageous practices, such as branding and extreme piercings. Meanwhile, tattoos bring middle-of-the-road teens the best of both worlds: a way to show their individuality and simultaneously to be accepted by peers.

Conclusion and summary

In sum, Martin's research is important because it examines psychological responses to teen's inner conflicts. It offers partial explanations for teens' attraction to tattoos and promotes a positive, noncritical attitude toward tattooing. But I think the article is limited by its overgeneralizations based on the psychiatric focus, by its tendency to romanticize tattooing, by its lack of recognition of the commercialization of tattooing, and by its underemphasis on group belonging and peer pressure. Teen tattooing is more complex than even Martin makes it.

Works Cited

Complete citation of article in MLA format

Martin, Andrés. "On Teenagers and Tattoos." Journal of the American Academy of Child and Adolescent Psychiatry 36 (1997): 860–61. Rpt. in The Allyn & Bacon Guide to Writing. John D. Ramage, John C. Bean, and June Johnson. 4th ed. New York: Longman, 2006. 118–121.

In the student example just shown, Sean Barry illustrates a blended strong response that intermixes rhetorical analysis of the article with his own views on tattooing. He analyzes Martin's article rhetorically by pointing out some of the limitations of a psychiatric angle of vision and by showing the values implications of Martin's references to *Moby Dick*. He adds his own ideas to the conversation by supporting two of Martin's points using his own personal examples. But he also reads Martin against the grain by arguing that Martin, perhaps influenced by his romantic view of tattoos, fails to appreciate the impact on teenagers of the commercialization of tattooing and the importance of peer group acceptance. Clearly, Sean Barry illustrates what we mean by a strong reader. In the next section on question-asking strategies, we help you begin developing the same skills.

Questions for Analyzing and Critiquing a Text

Now that you have read a sample student essay, let's consider questions you can ask to generate ideas for your own strong response. This section focuses on analyzing and critiquing a text and also offers ideas that can help you analyze texts that are partly or largely visual texts. The next section focuses on exploring your own views of the text's subject matter.

The concept of "angle of vision" is explained in Chapter 4, pp. 80–85. See also Chapter 5 where the concept is developed in more detail.

You may find that analyzing and critiquing a text represents a new kind of critical thinking challenge. At this stage in your academic career, we aren't expecting you to be an expert at this kind of thinking. Rather, the strong response assignment will help you begin learning this skill—to see how texts work, how they are written from an angle of vision, how they may reinforce or clash with your own views, and so forth.

A strong response focused on the rhetorical features of a text looks at how the text is constructed to achieve its writer's purpose. Here are sample questions you can ask to help you analyze and critique a text. (We have illustrated them with examples from a variety of texts read by our own students in recent years.) Of course, you don't have to address all these questions in your strong response. Your goal is to find a few of these questions that particularly illuminate the text you are critiquing.

Sample Questions for Analyzing and Critiquing

Questions about purpose and audience.   What is the author's purpose and audience in this text? How clearly does this text convey its purpose and reach its audience?

WHAT TO WRITE ABOUT
Explain your author's purpose and intended audience and show how the author appeals to that audience. Explain how choice of language and use of examples appeal to the values and beliefs of the intended audience. In critiquing the text, you might show how the article is effective for the intended audience but has gaping holes for those who don't share these values and beliefs.

HYPOTHETICAL EXAMPLE
In "Why Johnny Can't Read, but Yoshio Can," Richard Lynn, writing for the conservative magazine the *National Review*, tries to persuade readers that the United States should adopt Japanese methods of education. He appeals to a conservative audience by using evidence and examples that support conservative beliefs favoring competition, discipline, and high academic achievement.

Questions about the text's genre.   How has the genre of the text influenced the author's style, structure, and use of evidence? How might this genre be effective for certain audiences but not for others?

WHAT TO WRITE ABOUT
Show how certain features of the text can be explained by the genre of the work. Show how this genre contributes to the effectiveness of the piece for certain audiences but also has limitations.

HYPOTHETICAL EXAMPLE
Naomi Wolf's essay "The Beauty Myth" is actually the introduction to her book *The Beauty Myth*. Therefore, it presents her major thesis and subtheses for the whole book and only begins to provide supporting evidence for these points. This lack of development might make some readers question or reject her argument.

Questions about the author's style.   How do the author's language choices contribute to the overall impact of the text?

WHAT TO WRITE ABOUT
Discuss examples of images, figures of speech, and connotations of words that draw the reader into the writer's perspective and support the writer's points. In your critique, show how language choices can be effective for some audiences but not for others.

HYPOTHETICAL EXAMPLE
In his chapter "Where I Lived, and What I Lived For" from his book *Walden*, Henry David Thoreau describes his closeness to nature in vivid poetic language. His celebration of the beauty and wonder of nature makes readers reevaluate their indifference or utilitarian attitudes toward nature. Scientific readers might be put off, however, by his romanticism.

(continued)

Sample Questions for Analyzing and Critiquing *continued*

Questions about the appeal to *logos*, the logic of the argument. Does the argument seem reasonable? Do the points all relate to the thesis? Are the points well supported? Are there any obvious flaws or fallacies in the argument?

WHAT TO WRITE ABOUT	HYPOTHETICAL EXAMPLE
Describe the argument's logical structure and analyze whether it is reasonable and well supported. Also point out places where the argument is weak or fallacious.	Lynn attributes the success of Japanese students to three main causes: (1) High competition, (2) a national curriculum, and (3) strong cultural incentives to excel in school. These points are well supported with evidence. But his argument that this system should be adopted in the United States is flawed because he doesn't see the dangers in the Japanese system or appreciate the cultural differences between the two countries.

Questions about the author's use of evidence. Does the evidence come from reputable sources? Is it relevant to the points it supports? Is it appropriately up-to-date? Is it sufficiently broad and representative?

WHAT TO WRITE ABOUT	HYPOTHETICAL EXAMPLE
Describe the sources of evidence in an argument and determine their reliability. Pay particular attention to limitations or narrowness in these data. Point out whether the information is up-to-date, relevant, and compelling. Point out whether the author actually provides data for the argument.	In his book *The McDonaldization of Society*, sociologist George Ritzer elaborates on his thesis that the fast-food industry has come to dominate all of American society. Some readers might say that Ritzer pushes his provocative thesis too far. His discussion of health care, education, and reproductive technology is brief, general, and not developed with specific data.

Questions about the appeal to *ethos* and the credibility of the author. How does the author try to persuade readers that he or she is knowledgeable and reliable? Is the author successful in appearing credible and trustworthy?

WHAT TO WRITE ABOUT	HYPOTHETICAL EXAMPLE
Discuss features of the text that increase the reader's confidence in the author's knowledge and trustworthiness or that help the intended audience "identify" with the writer. Point out problems with the author's reliability, responsible use of sources, and fair treatment of alternative views.	In her article "The Gender Blur" in the liberal magazine *Utne Reader*, Deborah Blum establishes credibility by citing numerous scientific studies showing that she has researched the issue carefully. She also tells personal anecdotes about her liberal views, establishing credibility with liberal audiences.

Questions about the appeal to *pathos*.   How does the author appeal to the readers' emotions, sympathies, and values? Do these appeals to *pathos* enhance the rhetorical power of the text?

WHAT TO WRITE ABOUT
Explain how the author uses description, vivid examples, short narratives or scenarios, figurative language, or moving quotations to tap the emotions and sympathies of the audience and appeal to readers' values and beliefs. Explain whether these appeals to *pathos* are controlled and fitting or excessive and heavy-handed.

HYPOTHETICAL EXAMPLE
Compassionate Living, a brochure by the advocacy organization People for the Ethical Treatment of Animals (PETA), disturbs readers with vivid descriptions of animal suffering; however, these descriptions are so extreme in their appeals to *pathos* that they may offend readers who love animals and therefore lose their support.

Questions about the author's angle of vision.   What does the text reveal about the author's values and beliefs? What is excluded from the author's text? What other perspectives could a writer take on this topic?

WHAT TO WRITE ABOUT
Analyze the author's angle of vision or interpretive filter. Show what the text emphasizes and what it leaves out. Show how this angle of vision is related to certain key values or beliefs.

HYPOTHETICAL EXAMPLE
Dr. Andrés Martin, a psychiatrist, takes a clinical perspective on tattooed adolescents. He writes for fellow psychiatrists, and he uses his teen patients as the subject of his analysis. He does not consider more typical tattooed teenagers who do not need psychiatric therapy. If he had interviewed a wider range of teenagers, he might have reached different conclusions.

Questions for Analyzing and Critiquing a Visual-Verbal Text

In our increasingly visual world, many genres of texts—advocacy sites on the Web, public affairs advocacy ads, advertisements, posters for political and environmental campaigns, brochures, and leaflets—combine verbal and visual elements. As we discuss in Chapter 4, visual images such as photographs, drawings, and paintings can also be read rhetorically, and indeed may do much of the rhetorical work of a visual-verbal text.

Visual-verbal texts are often rhetorically complex and very interesting to examine and critique. A strong response to a visual-verbal text might examine how well the text connects with the intended audience, carries out its purposes, and fulfills readers' expectations for its genre. In critiquing a visual-verbal text, you might consider how well the words and images collaborate to strengthen the appeal to *logos*. For example, does this combination convey the main point clearly? The features of document design—use of type, layout, color, and images or graphics discussed in Chapter 3—are also extremely important in visual-verbal texts. Images can make powerful appeals to *pathos*, persuading through their appeal to readers' emotions, values, and beliefs. Many visual-verbal texts can also be discussed in terms of their appeal to *ethos* by focusing on how reliable and credible the creator of the text appears to be. Furthermore, these texts often reveal their angle of vision in interesting ways through the dominant impressions they convey and the ideas they ignore or exclude.

In Chapter 11, we explain visual rhetoric in more detail, especially such features as the composition of images, camera angle, and use of color.

In a summary strong response essay on a visual-verbal text, the summary would capture for readers the main points of the piece and would briefly describe the text's visual features. For a strong response, most of the questions that you would ask of a verbal text could apply to a visual-verbal text; however, here are some questions that might be particularly relevant to a text with visual elements.

Sample Questions for Analyzing and Critiquing Visual-Verbal Texts

Questions about use of type, layout, color, and image. Which of these design features is important in this text? How are these features used? How are they effective?

WHAT TO WRITE ABOUT
Explain what is distinctive about any or several of these visual features. Explain how these features work for the intended audience and contribute to the author's purpose. In critiquing the text, you might discuss how the visual features work to change the audience's views. You might comment on the problems or strengths of these features.

HYPOTHETICAL EXAMPLE
A poster on nicotine addiction by Project ALERT, a drug prevention program for middle schools, uses colors to make the poster stick in viewers' minds and create an alarmist tone. The use of unpleasant greens, oranges, and golds with the word "ADDICTING" in white overprinting gives a strong, memorable impression of illness and danger.

Questions about the relationship between image and verbal text and the appeals to *logos* and *pathos*. How much rhetorical work do the visual images perform in this text? How do the images and words work together in this text? Are words more important than images?

WHAT TO WRITE ABOUT
Explain whether words comment on the images or images illustrate the words. Discuss whether the words are labels and slogans connected to the images or presentations of the author's main points. Explain how the image or images in this piece convey the main point and affect the emotions and sympathies of the audience. Discuss whether the use of image is appropriate and effective or unnecessary, unfitting, or overdone.

HYPOTHETICAL EXAMPLE
In the Project ALERT poster on nicotine addiction, the cartoon imaginatively illustrates the concept of addiction and does all the persuasive work of the poster. All the features of this image—the cartoon figure, the burning ramp the figure is running on, and the unreachable package of cigarettes dangling from a stick—convey the poster's idea of addiction as frustration, desperation, and insatiability. The image works equally on the viewers' emotions, evoking a sense of danger.

Sample Questions for Analyzing and Critiquing Visual-Verbal Texts *continued*

Questions about the author's angle of vision and contribution to the social conversation.   How is an angle of vision constructed in this text? Does the text make a useful contribution to a discussion of this issue?

WHAT TO WRITE ABOUT
Explain how the author's angle of vision shapes and filters the message of the text. Discuss what is included in and excluded from the text. Discuss whether the angle of vision limits the appeal of the text.

HYPOTHETICAL EXAMPLE
The brochure *Compassionate Living*, by People for the Ethical Treatment of Animals (PETA), poses and responds to eighteen questions about humans' treatment of animals. While the brochure provides clear, vivid answers to the questions and the photos illustrate these points, readers sense that the brochure emphasizes and amasses incidents of cruelty and excludes all other perspectives.

Questions for Developing Your Own Views about the Text's Subject Matter

As you are analyzing and critiquing a text, you also want to imagine how you might speak back to the text's ideas. Look for ways to join the text's conversation using your own critical thinking, personal experience, observations, reading, and knowledge.

In responding to a text's ideas, you will most likely include both with- and against-the-grain points. Strong readers know how to build on a text's ideas and extend them to other contexts. They are also open to challenging or disturbing ideas and try to use them constructively rather than simply dismiss them. Strong readers, in other words, try to believe new ideas as well as doubt them. In speaking back to a text's ideas in your strong response, you will have to decide how affirming of or resistant to those ideas you want to be.

Here are questions you can use to help you generate ideas:

Sample Questions for Generating Your Own Views on the Topic

Question: Which of the author's points do you agree with?

WHAT TO WRITE ABOUT
Build on or extend the author's points with supporting evidence from personal experience or knowledge (with the grain).

HYPOTHETICAL EXAMPLE
Build on Dr. Andrés Martin's ideas by discussing examples of acquaintances who have marked significant moments in their lives (graduation, career changes, divorces) by getting tattoos.

(continued)

Sample Questions for Generating Your Own Views on the Topic *continued*

Question: What new insights has the text given you?

WHAT TO WRITE ABOUT
Illustrate your insights with examples (with the grain).

HYPOTHETICAL EXAMPLE
Explore Martin's idea that some teens use tattoos as a form of bonding by discussing the phenomenon of women in college sororities getting tattoos together.

Question: Which of the author's points do you disagree with?

WHAT TO WRITE ABOUT
Provide your own counterpoints and counterexamples (against the grain).

HYPOTHETICAL EXAMPLE
Challenge Martin's views by showing that tattooing has become a commonplace mainstream, middle-class phenomenon among teens.

Question: What gaps or omissions do you see in the text? What has the author overlooked?

WHAT TO WRITE ABOUT
Point out gaps. Supply your own theory for why these gaps exist. Explain the value of your own perspective, which includes what the author has excluded or overlooked (against the grain).

HYPOTHETICAL EXAMPLE
Point out that Martin's views leave out the role that parents play in teens' decisions to get tattoos. Explain how rebellion has influenced some of your friends.

Question: What questions or problems does the text raise for you? How has it troubled you or expanded your views?

WHAT TO WRITE ABOUT
Show how the text causes you to question your own values, assumptions, and beliefs; show also how you question the author's beliefs and values (with the grain and against the grain).

HYPOTHETICAL EXAMPLE
Martin's highly sympathetic attitude toward tattoos portrays body modification as positive, creative, and psychologically constructive, yet he glosses over health risks and long-term costs.

Question: In what contexts can you see the usefulness of the text? What applications can you envision for it?

WHAT TO WRITE ABOUT
Explore the applicability and consequences of the text or explore its limitations (with the grain or against the grain).

HYPOTHETICAL EXAMPLE
Martin's theory that troubled teens are seeking control over their bodies and their identities through getting tattoos is one important voice in the social conversation about tattoos. However, he doesn't explore why tattooing and piercing have become so popular in the last ten years. The relationship between fads and fashions and deeper psychological factors could lead to further research.

Rereading Strategies to Stimulate Thinking for a Strong Response

Earlier in the chapter, we presented general strategies to help you become an experienced reader. Now we turn to specific rereading strategies that will stimulate ideas for your strong response. Reread your assigned text, and as you do so, try the following strategies.

Step Up Your Marginal Note Taking, Making With-the-Grain and Against-the-Grain Comments

Writing a strong response requires a deep engagement with texts, calling on all your ability to read with the grain and against the grain. As you reread your text, make copious marginal notes looking for both with-the-grain and against-the-grain responses. Figure 6.1 shows Sean Barry's marginal comments on the opening page of Martin's article. Observe how the notes incorporate with-the-grain and against-the-grain responses and show the reader truly talking back to and interacting with the text.

Identify Hot Spots in the Text

Most texts will create "hot spots" for you (each reader's hot spots are apt to be different). By "hot spot" we mean a quotation or passage that you especially notice because you agree or disagree with it or because it triggers memories or other associations. Perhaps the hot spot strikes you as particularly thought provoking. Perhaps it raises a problem or is confusing yet suggestive. Mark all hot spots with marginal notes. After you've finished reading, find these hot spots and freewrite your responses to them in a reading journal.

Write Questions Triggered by the Text

Almost any text triggers questions as you read. A good way to begin formulating a strong response is simply to write out several questions that the text caused you to think about. Then explore your responses to those questions through freewriting. Sometimes the freewrite will trigger more questions.

Articulate Your Difference from the Intended Audience

In some cases you can read strongly by articulating how you differ from the text's intended audience. As we showed in Chapter 3, experienced writers try to imagine their audience. They ask: What are my audience's values? How interested in and knowledgeable about my topic is my audience? Eventually, the author makes decisions about audience—in effect "creates" the audience—so that the text reveals both an image of the author and of its intended reader.

See pp. 52–54 for a discussion of audience analysis.

Your own experiences, arising from your gender, class, ethnicity, sexual orientation, political and religious beliefs, interests, values, and so forth, may cause

FIGURE 6.1 Student Marginal Notes on Martin's Text

Andrés Martin, M.D.
on Teenagers and Tattoos

The skeleton dimensions I shall now proceed to set down are copied verbatim from my right arm, where I had them tattooed: as in my wild wanderings at that period, there was no other secure way of preserving such valuable statistics.

—Melville/ Moby Dick CII

Tattoos and piercings have become a part of our everyday landscape. They are ubiquitous, having entered the circles of glamour and the mainstream of fashion, and they have even become an increasingly common feature of our urban youth. Legislation in most states restricts professional tattooing to adults older than 18 years of age, so "high end" tattooing is rare in children and adolescents, but such tattoos are occasionally seen in older teenagers. Piercings, by comparison, as well as self-made or "jailhouse" type tattoos, are not at all rare among adolescents or even among schoolage children. Like hairdo, makeup, or baggy jeans, tattoos and piercings can be subject to fad influence or peer pressure in an effort toward group affiliation. As with any other fashion statement, they can be construed as bodily aids in the inner struggle toward identity consolidation, serving as adjuncts to the defining and sculpting of the self by means of external manipulations. But unlike most other body decorations, tattoos and piercings are set apart by their irreversible and permanent nature, a quality at the core of their magnetic appeal to adolescents.

Adolescents and their parents are often at odds over the acquisition of bodily decorations. For the adolescent, piercings or tattoos may be seen as personal and beautifying statements, while parents may construe them as oppositional and enraging affronts to their authority. Distinguishing bodily adornment from self-mutilation may indeed prove challenging, particularly when a family is in disagreement over a teenager's motivations and a clinician is summoned as the final arbiter. At such times it may be most important to realize jointly that the skin can all too readily become but another battleground for the tensions of the age, arguments having less to do with tattoos and piercings than with core issues such as separation from the family matrix. Exploring the motivations and significance underlying tattoos (Grumet, 1983) and piercings can go a long way toward resolving such differences and can become a novel and additional way of getting to know teenagers. An interested and nonjudgmental appreciation of teenagers' surface presentations may become a way of making contact not only in their terms but on their turfs: quite literally on the territory of their skins.

The following three sections exemplify some of the complex psychological underpinnings of youth tattooing.

1

2

3

Marginal notes (left):

Quotation from a novel?

Larger tattooing scene?

I like the phrase "the defining and sculpting of the self"—sounds creative, like art

Which teenagers? All teenagers?

Good open-minded, practical approach to teen tattoos

Marginal notes (right):

A strange beginning for a scientific article

What do 19th-century sailors have to do with 21st century teens?

Idea here: the body as a concrete record of experience?

This idea is surprising and interesting. It merits lots of discussion.

These terms show the main opposing views on tattoos.

Is he speaking only to psychiatrists? Does this clinical perspective have other applications?

I like Martin's focus on complexity

you to feel estranged from the author's imagined audience. If the text seems written for straight people and you are gay, or for Christians and you are a Muslim or an atheist, or for environmentalists and you grew up in a small logging community, you may well resist the text. Sometimes your sense of exclusion from the intended audience makes it difficult to read a text at all. For example, a female student of our acquaintance once brought a class to a standstill by slamming the course anthology on her desk and exclaiming, "How can you people stand reading this patriarchal garbage!" She had become so irritated by the authors' assumption that all readers shared their male-oriented values that she could no longer bear to read the selections.

When you differ significantly from the text's assumed audience, you can often use this difference to question the author's underlying assumptions, values, and beliefs.

For Writing and Discussion

What follows is a short passage by writer Annie Dillard in response to a question about how she chooses to spend her time. This passage often evokes heated responses from our students.

> I don't do housework. Life is too short. . . . I let almost all my indoor plants die from neglect while I was writing the book. There are all kinds of ways to live. You can take your choice. You can keep a tidy house, and when St. Peter asks you what you did with your life, you can say, "I kept a tidy house, I made my own cheese balls."

Individual task: Read the passage and then briefly freewrite your reaction to it.

Group task: Working in groups or as a whole class, develop answers to the following questions:

1. What values does Dillard assume her audience holds?
2. What kinds of readers are apt to feel excluded from that audience?
3. If you are not part of the intended audience for this passage, what in the text evokes resistance?

Articulate Your Own Purpose for Reading

You may sometimes read a text against the grain if your purposes for reading differ from what the author imagined. Normally you read a text because you share the author's interest in a question and want to know the author's answer. In other words, you usually read to join the author's conversation. But suppose that you wish to review the writings of nineteenth-century scientists to figure out what they assumed about nature (or women, or God, or race, or capitalism). Or suppose that you examine a politician's metaphors to see what they reveal about his or her values, or analyze *National Geographic* for evidence of political bias. In these cases, you will be reading against the grain of the text. In a sense, you would be blindsiding the authors—while they are talking about topic X, you are observing them for topic Y. This method of resistant reading is very common in academia.

READINGS

For this chapter, we offer readings on two major controversial issues: the health and social issue of smoking and the environmental, social, and economic issue of dams. The readings on smoking include two articles, a set of posters from an antismoking campaign, and a mock advertisement. The readings about dams include an article and the home page of an advocacy Web site. Some of the readings for this chapter are closed form; however, the others resist easy classification in that they include many features of open-form prose: lots of narrative elements and occasional implicit—rather than explicitly stated—points. The advocacy Web site home page and the posters have distinctive features of visual texts. Each reading in this chapter will prompt your personal and intellectual grappling with the author's ideas and beliefs as well as attract your attention to the author's rhetorical strategies.

You can use these readings in various ways. Your instructor may choose one of these pieces as the subject of your assignment for this chapter. You can also use the readings to build your knowledge base on these issues. Representing a few of the many voices in these public controversies, these verbal and visual-verbal texts help form a rhetorical context for each other. We think you will find them useful in illuminating the rhetorical strategies and angle of vision of the text that you are analyzing. Because your task is to summarize your assigned piece and respond strongly to it, we omit the questions for analysis that typically accompany readings elsewhere in this text.

The first reading, by writer and journalist Florence King, first appeared in 1990 in the *National Review*, a news commentary magazine with a conservative readership.

Florence King
I'd Rather Smoke than Kiss

1   I am a woman of 54 who started smoking at the late age of 26. I had no reason to start earlier; smoking as a gesture of teenage rebellion would have been pointless in my family. My mother started at 12. At first her preferred brands were the Fatimas and Sweet Caporals that were all the rage during World War I. Later she switched to Lucky Strike Greens and smoked four packs a day.

2   She made no effort to cut down while she was pregnant with me, but I was not a low-birth-weight baby. The Angel of Death saw the nicotine stains on our door and passed over. I weighed nine pounds. My smoke-filled childhood was remarkably healthy and safe except for the time Mama set fire to my Easter basket. That was all right, however, because I was not the Easter-basket type.

3   I probably wouldn't have started smoking if I had not been a writer. One day in the drugstore I happened to see a display of Du Maurier English cigarettes in pretty red boxes with a tray that slid out like a little drawer. I thought the boxes would be ideal for keeping my paperclips in, so I bought two.

4   When I got home, I emptied out the cigarettes and replaced them with paperclips, putting the loose cigarettes in the desk drawer where the loose paperclips had been scattered. Now the cigarettes were scattered. One day, spurred by two of my best traits, neatness and thrift, I decided that the cigarettes were messing up the desk and going to waste, so I tried one.

5   It never would have happened if I had been able to offer the Du Mauriers to a lover who smoked, but I didn't get an addicted one until after I had become addicted myself. When he entered my life it was the beginning of a uniquely pleasurable footnote to sex, the post-coital cigarette.

6   Today when I see the truculent, joyless faces of anti-tobacco Puritans, I remember those easy-going smoking sessions with that man: the click of the lighter, the brief orange glow in the darkness, the ashtray between us— spilling sometimes because we laughed so much together that the bed shook.

7   A cigarette ad I remember from my childhood said: "One of life's great pleasures is smoking. Camels give you all of the excitement of choice tobaccos. Is enjoyment good for you? You just bet it is." My sentiments exactly. I believe life should be savored rather than lengthened, and I am ready to fight the misanthropes among us who are trying to make me switch.

8   A *misanthrope* is someone who hates people. Hatred of smokers is the most popular form of closet misanthropy in America today. Smokists don't hate the sin, they hate the sinner, and they don't care who knows it.

9   Their campaign never would have succeeded so well if the alleged dangers of smoking had remained a problem for smokers alone. We simply would have been allowed to invoke the Right to Die, always a favorite with democratic lovers of mankind, and that would have been that. To put a real damper on smoking and making it stick, the right of others not to die had to be invoked somehow so "passive smoking" was invented.

10   The name was a stroke of genius. Just about everybody in America is passive. Passive Americans have been taking it on the chin for years, but the concept of passive smoking offered them a chance to hate in the land of compulsory love, a chance to dish it out for a change with no fear of being called a bigot. The right of self-defense, long since gone up in smoke, was back.

Smokers on the Run

11   The big, brave Passive Americans responded with a vengeance. They began shouting at smokers in restaurants. They shuddered and grimaced and said "Ugh!" as they waved away the impure air. They put up little signs in their cars and homes: at first they said, "Thank You for Not Smoking," but now they feature a cigarette in a circle slashed with a red diagonal. Smokists even issue conditional invitations. I know—I got one. The woman said, "I'd love to have you to dinner, but I don't allow smoking in my home. Do you think you could refrain for a couple of hours?" I said, "Go—yourself," and she told everybody I was the rudest person she had ever met.

12   Smokists practice a sadistic brutality that would have done Vlad the Impaler proud. *Washington Times* columnist and smoker Jeremiah O'Leary was the target of two incredibly baleful letters to the editor after he defended the habit. The first letter said, "Smoke yourself to death, but please don't smoke me to death," but it was only a foretaste of the letter that followed:

> Jeremiah O'Leary's March 1 column, "Perilous persuaders . . . tenacious zealots," is a typical statement of a drug addict trying to defend his vice.
> To a cigarette smoker, all the world is an ashtray. A person who would never throw a candy wrapper or soda can will drop a lit cigarette without a thought.
> Mr. O'Leary is mistaken that nonsmokers are concerned about the damage smokers are inflicting on themselves. What arrogance! We care about living in a pleasant environment without the stench of tobacco smoke or the litter of smokers' trash.
> If Mr. O'Leary wants to kill himself, that is his choice. I ask only that he do so without imposing his drug or discarded filth on me. *It would be nice if he would die in such a way that would not increase my health-insurance rates* [my italics].

13   The expendability of smokers has also aroused the tender concern of the Federal Government. I was taking my first drag of the morning when I opened the *Washington Post* and found myself starting at this headline: NOT SMOKING COULD BE HAZARDOUS TO PENSION SYSTEM. MEDICARE, SOCIAL SECURITY MAY BE PINCHED IF ANTI-TOBACCO CAMPAIGN SUCCEEDS, REPORT SAYS.

14   The article explained that since smokers die younger than non-smokers, the Social Security we don't live to collect is put to good use, because we subsidize the pensions of our fellow citizens like a good American should. However, this convenient arrangement could end, for if too many smokers heed the Surgeon General's warnings and stop smoking, they will live too long and break the budget.

15   That, of course, is not how the government economists phrased it. They said:

> The implications of our results are that smokers "save" the Social Security system hundreds of billions of dollars. Certainly this does not mean that decreased smoking

would not be socially beneficial. In fact, it is probably one of the most cost-effective ways of increasing average longevity. It does indicate, however, that if people alter their behavior in a manner which extends life expectancy, then this must be recognized by our national retirement program.

16   At this point the reporter steps in with the soothing reminder that "the war on tobacco is more appropriately cast as a public-health crusade than as an attempt to save money." But then we hear from Health Policy Center economist Gio Gori, who says: "Prevention of disease is obviously something we should strive for. But it's not going to be cheap. We will have to pay for those who survive."

17   Something darkling crawls out of that last sentence. The whole article has a die-damn-you undertow that would make an honest misanthrope wonder if perhaps a cure for cancer was discovered years ago, but due to cost-effectiveness considerations . . .

18   But honest misanthropes are at a premium that no amount of Raleigh coupons can buy. Instead we have tinpot Torquemadas like Ahron Leichtman, president of Citizens against Tobacco Smoke, who announced after the airline smoking bans: "CATS will next launch its smoke-free airports project, which is the second phase of our smoke-free skies campaign." Representative Richard J. Durbin (D., Ill.) promised the next target will be "other forms of public transportation such as Amtrak, the inter-city bus system, and commuter lines that receive federal funding." His colleague, Senator Frank Lautenberg (D., N.J.), confessed, "We *are* gloating a little bit," and Fran Du Melle of the Coalition on Smoking OR Health, gave an ominous hint of things to come when she heralded the airline ban as "only one encouraging step on the road to a smoke-free society."

Health Nazis

19   These remarks manifest a sly, cowardly form of misanthropy that the Germans call *Schadenfreude*: pleasure in the unhappiness of others. It has always been the chief subconscious motivation of Puritans, but the smokists harbor several other subconscious motivations that are too egregious to bear close examination—which is precisely what I will now conduct.

20   Study their agitprop and you will find the same theme of pitiless revulsion running through nearly all of their so-called public-service ads. One of the earliest showed Brooke Shields toweling her wet hair and saying disgustedly, "I hate it when somebody smokes after I've just washed my hair. Yuk!" Another proclaimed, "Kissing a smoker is like licking an ashtray." The latest, a California radio spot, asks: "Why sell cigarettes? Why not just sell phlegm and cut out the middle man?"

21   Fear of being physically disgusting and smelling bad is the American's worst nightmare, which is why bathsoap commercials never include the controlled-force shower nozzles recommended by environmentalists in *their* public-service ads. The showering American uses oceans of hot water to get "ZESTfully clean" in a sudsy deluge that is often followed by a deodorant commercial.

22   "Raise your hand, raise your hand, raise your hand if you're SURE!"
During this jingle we see an ecstatically happy assortment of people from all
walks of life and representing every conceivable national origin, all obedi-
ently raising their hands, until the ad climaxes with a shot of the Statue of
Liberty raising hers.

The New Greenhorns

23   The Statue of Liberty has become a symbol of immigration, the first
aspect of American life the huddled masses experienced. The second was
being called a "dirty little" something-or-other as soon as they got off the
boat. Deodorant companies see the wisdom in reminding their descendants
of the dirty-little period. You can sell a lot of deodorant that way. Ethnics
get the point directly; WASPs get it by default in the subliminal reminder
that, historically speaking, there is no such thing as a dirty little WASP.

24   Smokers have become the new greenhorns in the land of sweetness and
health, scapegoats for a quintessentially American need, rooted in our
fabled Great Diversity, to identify and punish the undesirables among us.
Ethnic tobacco haters can get even for past slurs on their fastidiousness by
refusing to inhale around dirty little smokers; WASP tobacco haters can once
again savor the joys of being the "real Americans" by hurling with impunity
the same dirty little insults their ancestors hurled with impunity.

25   The tobacco pogrom serves additionally as the basis for a class war in a
nation afraid to mention the word "class" aloud. Hating smokers is an excellent way to hate the white working class without going on record as hating
the white working class.

26   The anti-smoking campaign has enjoyed thumping success among the
"data-receptive," a lovely euphemism describing the privilege of spending
four years sitting in a classroom. The ubiquitous statistic that college gradu-
ates are two-and-a-half times as likely to be non-smokers as those who never
went beyond high school is balm to the data-receptive, many of whom are
only a generation or two removed from the lunch-bucket that smokers represent. Haunted by a fear of falling back down the ladder, and half-believing
that they deserve to, they soothe their anxiety by kicking a smoker as the
proverbial hen-pecked husband soothed his by kicking the dog.

27   The earnest shock that greeted the RJR Reynolds Uptown marketing
scheme aimed at blacks cramped the vituperative style of the data-receptive.
Looking down on blacks as smokers might be interpreted as looking down
on blacks as blacks, so they settled for aping the compassionate concern
they picked up from the media.

28   They got their sadism-receptive bona fides back when the same company
announced plans to target Dakota cigarettes at a fearsome group called "virile females."

29   When I first saw the headline I thought surely they meant me: what other woman writer is sent off to a book-and-author luncheon with the warning, "Watch your language and don't wear your Baltimore Orioles warm-up jacket." But they didn't. Virile females are "Caucasian females, 18 to 24, with no education beyond high school and entry-level service or factory jobs."

30   Commentators could barely hide their smirks as they listed the tractor pulls, motorcycle races, and macho-man contests that comprise the leisure activities of the target group. Crocodile tears flowed copiously. "It's blue-collar people without enough education to understand what is happening to them," mourned Virginia Ernster of the University of California School of Medicine. "It's pathetic that these companies would work so hard to get these women who may not feel much control over their lives." George Will, winner of the metaphor-man contest, wrote: "They use sophisticated marketing like a sniper's rifle, drawing beads on the most vulnerable, manipulable Americans." (I would walk a mile to see Virginia Ernster riding on the back of George Will's motorcycle.)

31   Hating smokers is also a guiltless way for a youth-worshipping country to hate old people, as well as those who are merely over the hill—especially middle-aged women. Smokers predominate in both groups because we saw Bette Davis's movies the same year they were released. Now we catch *Dark Victory* whenever it comes on television just for the pleasure of watching the scene in the staff lounge at the hospital when Dr. George Brent and all the other doctors light up.

32   Smoking is the only thing that the politically correct can't blame on white males. Red men started it, but the cowardly cossacks of the anti-tobacco crusade don't dare say so because it would be too close for comfort. They see no difference between tobacco and hard drugs like cocaine and crack because they don't wish to see any. Never mind that you will never be mugged by someone needing a cigarette; hatred of smokers is the conformist's substitute for the hatred that dare not speak its name. Condemning "substance abuse" out of hand, without picking and choosing or practicing discrimination, produces lofty sensations of democratic purity in those who keep moving farther and farther out in the suburbs to get away from . . . smokers.

The second reading is a peer-reviewed research article first published in 2004 in the *American Journal of Public Health*. Its author, Lyndon Haviland, is the chief operating officer of the American Legacy Foundation, an organization devoted to the reduction of tobacco use, especially by teens. As you read this text, you might consider how Haviland's treatment of the social stigma of smoking and the issue of class differ from Florence King's view of these points. How do you think that the date of publication of these articles might affect their positions on smoking?

A Silence That Kills

Lyndon Haviland

1   Tobacco-related disease kills 178,000 women each year in the United States,[1] yet a search for the public discourse on this fact reveals a profound silence. As a nation, we have failed to mount and support an organized public response to the ongoing public health tragedy of tobacco use. The public health community must find a way to give voice to the thousands of families who will experience the premature loss of a loved one because of tobacco use. In creative new ways, we must engage a broad range of partners, both public and private, and help them raise their voices to demand comprehensive action.

2   Although many of us are activists and many are working to counteract tobacco's harm, the public remains largely silent, its lack of outrage evident in the daily news, in the public debate on smoking bans, and in the lack of pressure on our government to protect workers, families, and children. There is so little public demand for action. We must find ways to spark a national movement to demand the funding and implementation of comprehensive tobacco control programs. We must overcome apathy and public silence. Tobacco control advocates must learn from the AIDS activists that silence equals a continuing saga of disease, suffering, and death.

3   How can we as public health practitioners change this silence into a public demand for comprehensive tobacco control that includes prevention, cessation, and regulation? How can we join together to give voice to the women and men who die each year in America of tobacco-related diseases? How can we prevent the needless suffering of families across the nation that results from tobacco use?

The Facts

4   As public health practitioners, we begin planning tobacco prevention and control programs with a review of the inarguable facts. Tobacco remains the leading cause of preventable death in the United States, killing more people each year than AIDS, suicide, murder, car accidents, and drugs combined.[2] It is the only product that when used as directed kills approximately one third of its users.[3] Indeed, the facts are hard to believe—for example, passive smoking (exposure to environmental tobacco smoke) kills 53,000 people each year in the United States and puts thousands more at risk.[4] The World Bank predicts that by 2030, tobacco-related illnesses will cause 10 million deaths per year, more than any other cause,[5] yet the recently passed Framework Convention on Tobacco Control negotiated among 193 countries has been signed by 76 participants and ratified by only 3 (Matt Barry, Campaign for Tobacco-Free Kids, oral communication, November 5, 2003).

5   Given the facts about the harmfulness of tobacco, why is public silence so deafening? Why does the tobacco control community confront apathy,

silence, and seemingly insurmountable barriers when implementing scientifically sound programs designed to prevent or reduce tobacco use in the United States? Nicotine is highly addictive, yet the marketing, production, and sale of products that contain nicotine are not regulated by the Food and Drug Administration.

The Shape of Our Epidemic

6   Lung cancer is the leading cause of cancer death among men and women,[2] and the majority of its victims die within one year of diagnosis.[6] Although it has been debated by the tobacco industry for decades, the scientific evidence of tobacco's impact on health is clear and well accepted. Tobacco use is implicated in a wide range of medical conditions, both adult and pediatric, including cardiovascular diseases, pulmonary conditions, a multitude of cancers, and reproductive health outcomes.[7] Perhaps the sheer magnitude of the diverse negative health consequences precludes a targeted demand for action.

7   An additional reason for the silence is the shape and the face of the current epidemic of tobacco use in the United States. Tobacco is not an equal opportunity killer. It is the poorest and least educated Americans who smoke at the highest rates[8] and who bear a disproportionate burden of death and disease as a result of their tobacco use.[9] There is evidence that sexual minorities smoke at much higher rates than the national average, but because there are no national data for this population, the full extent of the problem—and thus the means to address it—remains unclear.[10] And while racial and ethnic minorities smoke at lower rates than White Americans, tobacco takes a dramatic toll on their communities because they have poorer access to medical care.[11]

8   To find our voice as a movement, we must confront the social and class dimensions of tobacco use. A national movement to eradicate tobacco use must encourage participation at all levels and within all communities. A successful movement must have diversity in its leadership and must manifest a commitment to identify, train, and support the diverse communities most affected by tobacco use. Diverse leadership, vision, and voice will help us win the fight against disparities in access to prevention and cessation messages as well as access to the health care services necessary to treat tobacco-related illnesses.

Smoking as a Stigmatized Behavior

9   To change the social norms around tobacco use and to build a tobacco-free world, we must recognize that tobacco use in the United States is increasingly stigmatized. As local and statewide policies are enacted that restrict the use of tobacco products in public places, smokers can be seen enclosed in small glass smoking rooms in airports or huddled outside restaurants, bars, and office buildings. They are becoming a visible and stigmatized minority. To be successful, we must add the voice of smokers to our movement and support all Americans with evidence-based cessation services.

10   The debate about tobacco use is often clouded by discourse about smoking as a personal choice or a question of civil liberties. Public debate on smoking restrictions can devolve into a discussion of paternalism and prohibition. The debate often lacks a rigorous discussion of the power of nicotine addiction and the role of the tobacco industry in supporting the concept of smoking as an "adult choice." Insufficient attention is paid to the insidious work of the tobacco industry in marketing tobacco in minority communities and to the industry's philanthropic support of leadership organizations, unions, and community-based organizations.[12]

Silence in the Government

11   Although the facts speak for themselves, the governmental response to this epidemic of death and suffering is not on a par with the impact of tobacco use on American health, either on the prevention or the treatment side. Where is the concerted effort of government commensurate with the death, disability, and suffering that tobacco causes?

12   Every US surgeon general since 1964 has known about the death and suffering linked to tobacco use, and today the government is still documenting the mortality and morbidity linked to tobacco use but not supporting comprehensive plans for its eradication. On average, 1200 people are dying each day in America as a result of tobacco use.[1] The US Public Health Service knows how to prevent these deaths,[13, 14] yet the political will to act remains absent. The government has supported the development of comprehensive plans for tobacco use prevention and control and it has supported the development of a scientific basis for action, yet collective action and a collective voice calling for sweeping change are missing.

Public Health

13   Public health must take a leadership role and demand that the health care system and public policy protect Americans from the consequences of tobacco use. We know what to do to prevent tobacco-related deaths, but we have failed to demand systemic change from our government and from our colleagues in the health care field. We have let our voices be silenced. We must speak out to prevent needless suffering. Studies have demonstrated that health care providers fail to assess patients' smoking status and advise them to quit, yet a brief intervention by a doctor is one of the most effective methods of increasing use of cessation services.[15]

14   We, the public health community, must find our voice on this issue. We must confront the social inequities of tobacco use and its burden of death and disease. We must communicate a sense of urgency and engage all Americans in the battle against tobacco use. We must demand action and we must demand scientifically sound programs and policies that will help us build a world where young people reject tobacco and where anyone who does use tobacco can quit. Our future depends on it.

References

1. Centers for Disease Control and Prevention. Annual smoking-attributable mortality, years of potential life lost, and economic costs—United States, 1995–1999. *MMWR Morb Mortal Wkly Rep.* 2002; 51:300–303.

2. Arias E, Anderson RN, Kung HC, Murphy SL, Kochanek KD. Deaths: final data for 2001. *Natl Vital Stat Rep.* 2003; 52:1–115.

3. Centers for Disease Control and Prevention. Projected smoking-related deaths among youth. *MMWR Morb Mortal Wkly Rep.* 1996; 45:971–974.

4. Glantz SA, Parmley WW. Passive smoking and heart disease: mechanisms and risk. *JAMA.* 1995; 273:1047–1053.

5. *Curbing the Epidemic: Governments and the Economics of Tobacco Control.* Washington, DC: World Bank; 1999.

6. American Cancer Society. *What are the key statistics for lung cancer?* Available at: http://www.cancer.org/docroot/CRI/CRL2_3x.asp?mav=cridg&dt=26. Accessed December 17, 2003.

7. *Reducing the Health Consequences of Smoking: 25 Years of Progress: A Report of the Surgeon General.* Atlanta, Ga: Centers for Disease Control and Prevention; 1989.

8. Centers for Disease Control and Prevention. Cigarette smoking among adults—United States, 2000. *MMWR Morb Mortal Wkly Rep.* 2002; 51:642–645.

9. Northridge MK, Morabia A, Ganz ML, et al. Contribution of smoking to excess mortality in Harlem. *Am J Epidemial.* 1998; 147:250–258.

10. Ryan H, Wortley PM, Easton A, Pederson L, Greenwood G. Smoking among lesbians, gays, and bisexuals: a review of the literature. *Am J Prev Med.* 2001; 21:142–149.

11. Bach PB, Cramer LD, Warren JL, Begg CB. Racial differences in the treatment of early-stage lung cancer. *N Engl J Med.* 1999; 341:1198–1205.

12. Siegel M. *Tobacco industry sponsorship in the United States, 1995–1999.* Available at: http://dcc2.bumc.bu.edu/tobacco. Accessed December 17, 2003.

13. *Best Practices for Comprehensive Tobacco Control Programs.* Atlanta, Ga: National Center for Chronic Disease Prevention and Health Promotion, Office on Smoking and Health; August 1999. Available at: http://www.cdc.gov/tobacco/bestprac.htm. Accessed December 17, 2003.

14. Task Force on Community Preventive Services. Recommendations regarding interventions to reduce tobacco use and exposure to environmental tobacco smoke. *Am J Prev Med.* 2001; 20(suppl 2):10–15.

15. The Tobacco Use and Dependence Clinical Practice Guideline Panel, Staff, and Consortium Representatives. A clinical practice guideline for treating tobacco use and dependence: a US Public Health Service report. *JAMA.* 2000; 283:3244–3254.

The next reading is a set of four posters created by Gasp Consultancy, Ltd., a British consulting firm that "specializes in marketing, publicising, and organising tobacco control and stop smoking projects and events" (www.gasp.org.uk/). As you examine these posters, you might think about how Gasp's approach to quitting smoking differs from other stop-smoking and anti-smoking campaigns you have seen.

Step one

Step out to stop smoking

- Set a quit date
- Retrace your steps and learn from past quit attempts
- Rid your everyday environment of tobacco and tobacco smoke
- Stop smoking completely - not a single puff!

© GASP · Tel 0117 942 5185 · www.gasp.org.uk

steps to stopping smoking

Reasons to stop smoking:

- Live longer and be healthier
- Lower the chances of cancer, heart attack or stroke
- Family and friends will be healthier
- Babies and children are not exposed to smoke
- More money to spend or save
- Free from nicotine addiction

© GASP · Tel 0117 942 5185 · www.gasp.org.uk

Step three

Learn new steps to help you to stop

Step into a new way of living and
change your routines.

Develop the **D** steps:
- Do things differently
- Drink plenty of water
- Distract yourself
- Do something you enjoy each day
- Deep breathe

© GASP Tel: 0117 942 5180 www.gasp.org.uk

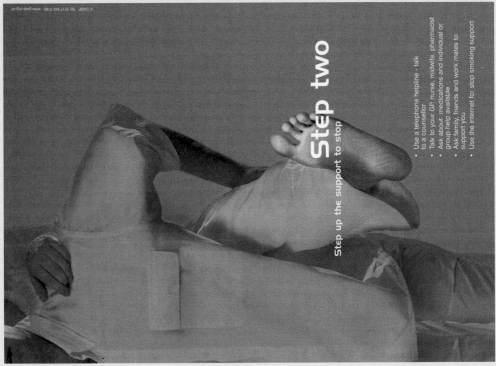

Step two

Step up the support to stop

- Use a telephone helpline - talk to a counsellor
- Talk to your GP, nurse, midwife, pharmacist
- Ask about medications and individual or group help available
- Ask family, friends and work mates to support you
- Use the internet for stop smoking support

© GASP Tel: 0117 942 5180 www.gasp.org.uk

155

Our last text in this group is a spoof advertisement, "Welcome to Malboro Country," that appears on the Web site for Adbusters.org. Adbusters is a media foundation with a global network that sponsors a Web site and a magazine dedicated to this purpose: "We want folks to get mad about corporate disinformation, injustices in the global economy, and any industry that pollutes our physical and mental commons" (http://adbusters.org/information/guidelines/). As you think about this ad, you might recall the hallmark features of Marlboro ads. What images have made those ads famous?

Our first reading on dams, by prolific environmental writer Edward Abbey, first appeared in 1971 in *Beyond the Wall: Essays from the Outside*. His view of Lake Powell, the reservoir formed on the border of Utah and Arizona by the damming of Glen Canyon, has helped stimulate a growing anti-dam movement among environmentalists.

Edward Abbey
The Damnation of a Canyon

1   There was a time when, in my search for essences, I concluded that the canyonland country has no heart. I was wrong. The canyonlands did have a heart, a living heart, and that heart was Glen Canyon and the golden, flowing Colorado River.

2   In the summer of 1959 a friend and I made a float trip in little rubber rafts down through the length of Glen Canyon, starting at Hite and getting off the river near Gunsight Butte—The Crossing of the Fathers. In this voyage of some 150 miles and ten days our only motive power, and all that we needed, was the current of the Colorado River.

3   In the summer and fall of 1967 I worked as a seasonal park ranger at the new Glen Canyon National Recreation Area. During my five-month tour of duty I worked at the main marina and headquarters area called Wahweap, at Bullfrog Basin toward the upper end of the reservoir, and finally at Lee's Ferry downriver from Glen Canyon Dam. In a number of powerboat tours I was privileged to see almost all of our nation's newest, biggest and most impressive "recreational facility."

4   Having thus seen Glen Canyon both before and after what we may fairly call its damnation, I feel that I am in a position to evaluate the transformation of the region caused by construction of the dam. I have had the unique opportunity to observe firsthand some of the differences between the environment of a free river and a powerplant reservoir.

5   One should admit at the outset to a certain bias. Indeed I am a "butterfly chaser, googly eyed bleeding heart and wild conservative." I take a dim view of dams; I find it hard to learn to love cement; I am poorly impressed by concrete aggregates and statistics in the cubic tons. But in this weakness I am not alone, for I belong to that ever-growing number of Americans, probably a good majority now, who have become aware that a fully industrialized, thoroughly urbanized, elegantly computerized social system is not suitable for human habitation. Great for machines, yes: But unfit for people.

6   Lake Powell, formed by Glen Canyon Dam, is not a lake. It is a reservoir, with a constantly fluctuating water level—more like a bathtub that is never drained than a true lake. As at Hoover (or Boulder) Dam, the sole practical function of this impounded water is to drive the turbines that generate electricity in the powerhouse at the base of the dam. Recreational benefits were

of secondary importance in the minds of those who conceived and built this dam. As a result the volume of water in the reservoir is continually being increased or decreased according to the requirements of the Basin States Compact and the power-grid system of which Glen Canyon Dam is a component.

7   The rising and falling water level entails various consequences. One of the most obvious, well known to all who have seen Lake Mead, is the "bathtub ring" left on the canyon walls after each drawdown of water, or what rangers at Glen Canyon call the Bathtub Foundation. This phenomenon is perhaps of no more than aesthetic importance; yet it is sufficient to dispel any illusion one might have, in contemplating the scene, that you are looking upon a natural lake.

8   The utter barrenness of the reservoir shoreline recalls by contrast the aspect of things before the dam, when Glen Canyon formed the course of the untamed Colorado. Then we had a wild and flowing river lined by boulder-strewn shores, sandy beaches, thickets of tamarisk and willow, and glades of cottonwoods.

9   The thickets teemed with songbirds: vireos, warblers, mockingbirds and thrushes. On the open beaches were killdeer, sandpipers, herons, ibises, egrets. Living in grottoes in the canyon walls were swallows, swifts, hawks, wrens, and owls. Beaver were common if not abundant: not an evening would pass, in drifting down the river, that we did not see them or at least hear the whack of their flat tails on the water. Above the river shores were the great recessed alcoves where water seeped from the sandstone, nourishing the semi-tropical hanging gardens of orchid, ivy and columbine, with their associated swarms of insects and birdlife.

10   Up most of the side canyon, before damnation, there were springs, sometimes flowing streams, waterfalls and plunge pools—the kind of marvels you can now find only in such small scale remnants of Glen Canyon as the Escalante area. In the rich flora of these laterals the larger mammals—mule deer, coyote, bobcat, ring-tailed cat, gray fox, kit fox, skunk, badger, and others—found a home. When the river was dammed almost all of these things were lost. Crowded out—or drowned and buried under mud.

11   The difference between the present reservoir, with its silent sterile shores and debris choked side canyons, and the original Glen Canyon, is the difference between death and life. Glen Canyon was alive. Lake Powell is a graveyard.

12   For those who may think I exaggerate the contrast between the former river canyon and the present man-made impoundment, I suggest a trip on Lake Powell followed immediately by another boat trip on the river below the dam. Take a boat from Lee's Ferry up the river to within sight of the dam, then shut off the motor and allow yourself the rare delight of a quiet, effortless drifting down the stream. In that twelve-mile stretch of living green, singing birds, flowing water and untarnished canyon walls—sights and sounds a million years older and infinitely lovelier than the roar of

motorboats—you will rediscover a small and imperfect sampling of the kind of experience that was taken away from everybody when the oligarchs and politicians condemned our river for purposes of their own.

13   Lake Powell, though not a lake, may well be as its defenders assert the most beautiful reservoir in the world. Certainly it has a photogenic backdrop of buttes and mesas projecting above the expansive surface of stagnant waters where the speedboats, houseboats and cabin cruisers play. But it is no longer a wilderness. It is no longer a place of natural life. It is no longer Glen Canyon.

14   The defenders of the dam argue that the recreational benefits available on the surface of the reservoir outweigh the loss of Indian ruins, historical sites, wildlife and wilderness adventure. Relying on the familiar quantitative logic of business and bureaucracy, they assert that whereas only a few thousand citizens even ventured down the river through Glen Canyon, now millions can—or will—enjoy the motorized boating and hatchery fishing available on the reservoir. They will also argue that the rising waters behind the dam have made such places as Rainbow Bridge accessible by power-boat. Formerly you could get there only by walking (six miles).

15   This argument appeals to the wheelchair ethos of the wealthy, upper-middle-class American slob. If Rainbow Bridge is worth seeing at all, then by God it should be easily, readily, immediately available to everybody with the money to buy a big powerboat. Why should a trip to such a place be the privilege only of those who are willing to walk six miles? Or if Pikes Peak is worth getting to, then why not build a highway to the top of it so that anyone can get there? Anytime? Without effort? Or as my old man would say, "By Christ, one man's just as good as another—if not a damn sight better."

16   It is quite true that the flooding of Glen Canyon has opened up to the motorboat explorer parts of side canyons that formerly could be reached only by people able to walk. But the sum total of terrain visible to the eye and touchable by hand and foot has been greatly diminished, not increased. Because of the dam the river is gone, the inner canyon is gone, the best parts of the numerous side canyons are gone—all hidden beneath hundreds of feet of polluted water, accumulating silt, and mounting tons of trash. This portion of Glen Canyon—and who can estimate how many cubic miles were lost?—*is no longer accessible to anybody*. (Except scuba divers.) And this, do not forget, was the most valuable part of Glen Canyon, richest in scenery, archaeology, history, flora, and fauna.

17   Not only has the heart of Glen Canyon been buried, but many of the side canyons above the fluctuating waterline are now rendered more difficult, not easier, to get into. This is because the debris brought down into them by desert storms, no longer carried away by the river, must unavoidably build up in the area where flood meets reservoir. Narrow Canyon, for example, at the head of the impounded waters, is already beginning to silt up and to amass huge quantities of driftwood, some of it floating on the surface, some of it half afloat beneath the surface. Anyone who has tried to

pilot a motorboat through a raft of half-sunken logs and bloated dead cows will have his own thoughts on the accessibility of these waters.

18   Second, the question of costs. It is often stated that the dam and its reservoir have opened up to the many what was formerly restricted to the few, implying in this case that what was once expensive has now been made cheap. Exactly the opposite is true.

19   Before the dam, a float trip down the river through Glen Canyon would cost you a minimum of seven days' time, well within anyone's vacation allotment and a capital outlay of about forty dollars—the prevailing price of a two-man rubber boat with oars, available at any army-navy surplus store. A life jacket might be useful but not required, for there were no dangerous rapids in the 150 miles of Glen Canyon. As the name implies, this stretch of the river was in fact so easy and gentle that the trip could be and was made by all sorts of amateurs: by Boy Scouts, Camp Fire Girls, stenographers, schoolteachers, students, little old ladies in inner tubes. Guides, professional boatmen, giant pontoons, outboard motors, radios, rescue equipment were not needed. The Glen Canyon float trip was an adventure anyone could enjoy, on his own, for a cost less than that of spending two days and nights in a Page motel. Even food was there, in the water: the channel catfish were easier to catch and a lot better eating than the striped bass and rainbow trout dumped by the ton into the reservoir these days. And one other thing: at the end of the float trip you still owned your boat, usable for many more such casual and carefree expeditions.

20   What is the situation now? Float trips are no longer possible. The only way left for the exploration of the reservoir and what remains of Glen Canyon demands the use of a powerboat. Here you have three options: (1) buy your own boat and engine, the necessary auxiliary equipment, the fuel to keep it moving, the parts and repairs to keep it running, the permits and licenses required for legal operation, the trailer to transport it; (2) rent a boat; or (3) go on a commercial excursion boat, packed in with other sightseers, following a preplanned itinerary. This kind of play is only for the affluent.

21   The inescapable conclusion is that no matter how one attempts to calculate the cost in dollars and cents, a float trip down Glen Canyon was much cheaper than a powerboat tour of the reservoir. Being less expensive, as well as safer and easier, the float trip was an adventure open to far more people than will ever be able to afford motorboat excursions in the area now.

22   All of the foregoing would be nothing but a futile exercise in nostalgia (so much water over the dam) if I had nothing constructive and concrete to offer. But I do. As alternate methods of power generation are developed, such as solar, and as the nation establishes a way of life adapted to actual resources and basic needs, so that the demand for electrical power begins to diminish, we can shut down the Glen Canyon power plant, open the diversion tunnels, and drain the reservoir.

23   This will no doubt expose a dreary and hideous scene: immense mud flats and whole plateaus of sodden garbage strewn with dead trees, sunken boats,

the skeletons of long-forgotten, decomposing water-skiers. But to those who find the prospect too appalling, I say give nature a little time. In five years, at most in ten, the sun and wind and storms will cleanse and sterilize the repellent mess. The inevitable floods will soon remove all that does not belong within the canyons. Fresh green willow, box elder and redbud will reappear; and the ancient drowned cottonwoods (noble monuments to themselves) will be replaced by young of their own kind. With the renewal of plant life will come the insects, the birds, the lizards and snakes, the mammals. Within a generation—thirty years—I predict the river and canyons will bear a decent resemblance to their former selves. Within the lifetime of our children Glen Canyon and the living river, heart of the canyonlands, will be restored to us. The wilderness will again belong to God, the people and the wild things that call it home.

Our second reading on dams is the homepage from the Web site of the advocacy organization Friends of Lake Powell (www.lakepowell.org). On its "mission link," this organization states that one of its goals is "To create awareness of and maintain the social, recreational, environmental and economic benefits of Lake Powell, Glen Canyon Dam and Glen Canyon National Recreation Area." You may want to explore some of the other links on this site, particularly its "25 Good Reasons Not to Drain Lake Powell," "Fact Sheet: Lake Powell & Glen Canyon Dam," and "Lake Powell, Habitat for Wildlife." As you browse this site, consider how the photographs and use of color contribute to the rhetorical effect. What appeals to *logos, ethos*, and *pathos* does this site make?

Composing Your Summary/Strong Response Essay

Generating and Exploring Ideas for Your Summary

After you have selected the piece you will use for this assignment, your first task is to read it carefully to get as accurate an understanding of the article as you can. Remember that summarizing is the most basic and preliminary form of reading with the grain of a text.

1. The first time through, read the piece for general meaning. Follow the argument's flow without judgment or criticism, trying to see the world as the author sees it.
2. Reread the piece slowly, paragraph by paragraph, writing "what it does" or "what it says" gist statements in the margins for each paragraph or writing out the question that you think each paragraph answers. We recommend that you supplement these marginal notations by writing out a complete paragraph-by-paragraph *does/says* analysis modeled after our example on page 127.
3. After you've analyzed the piece paragraph by paragraph, locate the argument's main divisions or parts and create an outline or tree diagram of the main points.

If you need to summarize a visual-verbal text such as a poster, advertisement, public affairs advocacy ad, Web page, or brochure, you can adapt the same processes you use for a verbal text piece to this kind of text. Of course, your summary will be longer for more complex texts such as Web pages and brochures than for posters. Examine the parts and record what each part contributes to the whole piece (similar to "what it does" statements). Basically, you are describing each part of the text. Imagine that you are describing the visual elements for someone who hasn't seen the document. For example, here is a brief summary of a brochure from People for the Ethical Treatment of Animals (PETA):

> The PETA brochure, *Compassionate Living*, consists of five pages. The front of the brochure states the title and shows inviting pictures of animals. The next ten panels of the brochure present questions the organization thinks its audience might ask such as, "What's wrong with animal experimentation?" and provides answers and photos of animal cruelty illustrating the answers. The final panel of the brochure describes PETA and has a membership and donation form. Its main argument is that . . . [here you would summarize the main ideas from the panels]

Shaping, Drafting, and Revising Your Summary

Once you have analyzed the article carefully paragraph by paragraph and understand its structure, you are ready to write a draft. If the piece you are summarizing is closed form, you can generally follow the order of the original article, keeping the proportions of the summary roughly equivalent to the proportions of the article. Begin the essay by identifying the question or problem that the reading addresses. Then state the article's purpose or thesis and summarize its argument point by point. If the article has a delayed thesis or some features of open-form prose, then you may have to rearrange the original order to create a clear structure for readers. For a summary of a visual-verbal text, blend your comments about the visual and verbal elements into a paragraph that enables readers to visualize the images, comprehend its parts, and understand the main points of its message.

Count the number of words in your first draft to see whether you are in the 150–250 word range specified by the assignment. When you revise your summary, follow the criteria presented on page 129. Also use the Guidelines for Peer Reviews (pp. 165–166) as a checklist for revision.

Generating and Exploring Ideas for Your Strong Response

After you have written your summary, which demonstrates your full understanding of the text, you are ready to write your strong response. Use the questions and specific reading strategies discussed on pages 134–140 to help you generate ideas. The following questions put this advice into a quick checklist. Look for the questions that most stimulate your thinking and try freewriting your responses.

- Who is the text's intended audience? How is the author trying to change that audience's view of his or her topic? What rhetorical strategies intended to influence the audience most stand out?
- How do I differ from the intended audience? How are my purposes for reading different from what the author imagined?
- How have the author's rhetorical strategies affected me?
- How have the author's ideas affected me? How have they extended or complicated my own thinking? What do I agree with? What can I support?
- How can I question the author's data, evidence, and supporting arguments? If I am not persuaded by the author's ideas and evidence, why not? What is missing? What can be called into question?
- What is excluded from the author's text? What do these exclusions tell me about the author's value system or angle of vision?
- How can I question the author's values, beliefs, and assumptions? Conversely, how does the text cause me to question my own values, beliefs, and assumptions?
- How has the author changed my view of the topic? What do I have to give up or lose in order to change my view? What do I gain?
- How can I use the author's ideas for my own purposes? What new insights have I gained? What new ways of thinking can I apply to another context?

Writing a Thesis for a Strong Response Essay

See Chapter 2, pp. 34–38 for a discussion of surprising thesis statements.

A thesis for a strong response essay should map out for readers the points that you want to develop and discuss. These points should be risky and contestable; your thesis should surprise your readers with something new or challenging. Your thesis might focus entirely on with-the-grain points or entirely on against-the-grain points, but most likely it will include some of both. Avoid tensionless thesis statements such as "This article has both good and bad points."

Here are some thesis statements that students have written for strong responses in our classes. Note that each thesis includes at least one point about the rhetorical strategies of the text.

EXAMPLES OF SUMMARY/STRONG RESPONSE THESIS STATEMENTS

- In "The Beauty Myth," Naomi Wolf makes a very good case for her idea that the beauty myth prevents women from ever feeling that they are good enough; however, Wolf's argument is geared too much toward feminists to be persuasive for a general audience, and she neglects to acknowledge the strong social pressures that I and other men feel to live up to male standards of physical perfection.
- Although Naomi Wolf in "The Beauty Myth" uses rhetorical strategies persuasively to argue that the beauty industry oppresses women, I think that she overlooks women's individual resistance and responsibility.
- Although the images and figures of speech that Thoreau uses in his chapter "Where I Lived, and What I Lived For" from *Walden* wonderfully support his argument that nature has valuable spiritually renewing powers, I disagree with his antitechnology stance and with his extreme emphasis on isolation as a means to self-discovery.
- In "Where I Lived, and What I Lived For" from *Walden*, Thoreau's argument that society is missing spiritual reality through its preoccupation with details and its frantic pace is convincing, especially to twenty-first century audiences; however, Thoreau weakens his message by criticizing his readers and by completely dismissing technological advances.
- Although the brochure *Compassionate Living* by People for the Ethical Treatment of Animals (PETA) uses the design features of layout, color, and image powerfully, its extreme examples, its quick dismissal of alternative views, and its failure to document the sources of its information weaken its appeal to *ethos* and its overall persuasiveness.

Revising Your Strong Response

In revising your strong response, you will find that peer reviews are especially helpful, both in generating ideas and in locating places that need expansion and development. As you revise, think about how well you have incorporated ideas from your initial explorations and how you can make your essay clearer and more meaningful to readers.

GUIDELINES FOR PEER REVIEWS

Instructions for peer reviews are provided in Chapter 17 (pp. 519–520).

For the Writer

Prepare two or three questions you would like your peer reviewer to address while responding to your draft. The questions can focus on some aspect of your draft that you are uncertain about, on one or more sections where you particularly seek help or advice, on some feature that you particularly like about your draft, or on some part you especially wrestled with. Write out your questions and give them to your peer reviewer along with your draft.

For the Reviewer

I. Read the draft at normal reading speed from beginning to end. As you read, do the following:
  A. Place a wavy line in the margin next to any passages where you get confused or find something that doesn't seem to fit or otherwise slowed down your reading.
  B. Place a "Good!" in the margin next to any passages where you think the writing is particularly strong or interesting.
II. Read the draft again slowly and answer the following questions by writing brief explanations of your answers.
  A. The summary
    1. How could the summary be more comprehensive, balanced, and accurate?
    2. Where could it be more fair and neutral?
    3. How could it use attributive tags more effectively?
    4. How could it include and cite quotations more effectively?
    5. What would make the summary read more smoothly?
  B. The strong response
    1. How could the writer's thesis statement be clearer in setting up several focused points about the text's rhetorical strategies and ideas?
    2. How could the body of the strong response follow the thesis more closely?
    3. How could the rhetorical points and "your own views" points engage more specifically and deeply with the text?
    4. Where do you as a reader need more clarification or support for the writer's rhetorical points and subject-matter points?
    5. How could the strong response be improved by adding points, developing points, or making points in a different way?
III. Rhetorical considerations
  A. *Purpose, audience,* and *genre*: This draft should fit the genre of academic writing. Its purpose is to summarize and critique a reading for an audience

interested in the reading's subject matter. How well does the draft fit the genre of academic writing? How effectively does it meet its purpose for its intended audience? How could the writer be more effective in communicating his or her critique and response to the intended readers?

B. *Logos, ethos,* and *pathos*: How convincing or effective is the logical or conceptual aspect of this draft? How has the writer shown his or her knowledgeable and responsible treatment of the reading? How has the writer connected with the values and sympathies of the intended readers? How could the writer improve these dimensions of the draft?

IV. If the writer has prepared questions for you, respond to his or her inquiries.

V. Sum up what you see as the chief strengths and problem areas of this draft.
    A. Strengths
    B. Problem areas

VI. Finally, read the draft one more time. This time place a check mark in the margin next to any places where you noticed problems in grammar, spelling, or mechanics. (One check mark per problem.)

Writing an Autobiographical Narrative

About Autobiographical Narrative

This chapter focuses on the rhetorical aim we have called "writing to express or share." This chapter's assignment asks you to write an autobiographical narrative about something significant in your own life. But rather than state the significance up front in a thesis, you let it unfold in storylike fashion. This narrative structure places autobiographical writing at the open end of the closed-to-open-form continuum, making it more like literary nonfiction than a traditional academic essay. Consequently, we advise you to consult Chapter 19, which discusses the features of open-form prose, prior to writing your assignment for this chapter. The student essays in this chapter, as well as "Berkeley Blues" in Chapter 19 (pp. 574–576), were written for an assignment like the one in this chapter.

See our explanation of rhetorical aims in Table 3.1, pp. 49–50.

The closed-to-open continuum is shown in Figure 1.1, page 19.

Don't let the term *literary* scare you. It simply refers to basic techniques such as dialogue, specific language, and scene-by-scene construction that you use when sharing stories, telling jokes, or recounting experiences to friends. These are the most natural and universal of techniques, the ones that peoples of all cultures have traditionally used to pass on their collective wisdom in myths, legends, and religious narratives.

Although most academic writing is closed form, it sometimes takes an open-form structure, especially when the writer tells the story of an intellectual discovery or narrates his or her wrestling with a problem. Some of the most profound and influential science writing for general audiences—for example, the work of Loren Eiseley, Jay Gould, Rachel Carson, and others—is narrative based. Additionally, many kinds of academic prose have sections of narrative writing. Autobiographical writing can explore, deepen, and complicate our perception of the world.

In addition to telling stories to convey the complexity and significance of phenomena, we use them to reveal ourselves. In this regard, autobiographical writing, like certain forms of conversation, fills a very basic need in our daily lives—the need for intimacy or nontrivial human contact. One of the best measures we have of our closeness to other human beings is our willingness or reluctance to share with them our significant life stories, the ones that reveal our aspirations or humiliations.

We also use others' stories, particularly during adolescence, to monitor our own growth. Many of us once read (and still read) the stories of such people as

Anne Frank, Maya Angelou, Helen Keller, Malcolm X, and Laura Ingalls Wilder in search of attitudes and behaviors to emulate. Reading their stories becomes a way of critiquing and understanding our own stories.

At this point, you might be thinking that your own life lacks the high drama needed for autobiographical prose. Perhaps you're thinking that unless you've dated a movie star, won an X-Game skateboard competition, starred on a reality TV show, or convinced a venture capitalist to fund your dot-com startup company devoted to Pez dispensers, you haven't done anything significant to write about. In this chapter we try to give you another view of significance—one that gets at the heart of what it means to write a story.

To our way of thinking, significance is not a quality somewhere out there in the events of your life: It's in the sensibility that you bring to those events and the way you write about them. When you mistakenly equate significance with singularity (it never happened to anyone else) or its public importance (what happened here made history), you misunderstand the power of a good writer to render any sort of event significant.

Many of the events your audience will find most interesting are those ordinary occurrences that happen to everyone. All of us have experienced a first day at a new school or job, a rival or sibling who seemed to best us at every turn, or a conflict with a parent, lover, spouse, or employer. But everyone enjoys hearing good writers describe their unique methods of coping with and understanding these universal situations. It is precisely because readers have experienced these things that they can project themselves easily into the writer's world. This chapter shows you how to write an autobiographical story by finding a significant moment in your life and writing about it compellingly using literary techniques.

Exploring Autobiographical Narrative

One of the premises of this book is that good writing is rooted in the writer's perception of a problem. Problems are at the center not only of thesis-based writing but also of narrative writing. In effective narration, the problem usually takes the form of a *contrary*, two or more things in opposition—ideas, characters, expectations, forces, worldviews, or whatever. Three kinds of contraries that frequently form the plots of autobiographical narratives are the following:

1. *Old self versus new self.* The writer perceives changes in himself or herself as a result of some transforming moment or event.
2. *Old view of person X versus new view of person X.* The writer's perception of a person (favorite uncle, friend, childhood hero) changes as a result of some revealing moment; the change in the narrator's perception of person X also indicates growth in self-perception.
3. *Old values versus new values that threaten, challenge, or otherwise disrupt the old values.* The writer confronts an outsider who challenges

his or her worldview, or the writer undergoes a crisis that creates a conflict in values.

Prior to class discussion, freewrite for ten minutes about episodes in your own life that fit one or more of these typical plots. Then, working in small groups or as a whole class, share your discoveries. Your goal is to begin seeing that each person's life is a rich source of stories.

For the moment think of *significant* not as "unusual" or "exciting" but as "revealing" or "conveying an unexpected meaning or insight." Thought of in this way, a significant moment in a story might be a gesture, a remark, a smile, a way of walking or tying a shoe, the wearing of a certain piece of clothing, or the carrying of a certain object in a purse or pocket. Invent a short scene in which a gesture, smile, or brief action reverses one character's feelings about, or understanding of, another character.

1. You think that Maria has led a sheltered life until _____.
2. You think Pete is a gruff, intimidating thug until _____.
3. Marco (Julia) seemed the perfect date until _____.

In each case, think of specific details about one revealing moment that reverse your understanding. Here is an example of a scene:

> My dad seemed unforgivingly angry at me until he suddenly smiled, turned my baseball cap backward on my head, and held up his open palm for a high five. "Girl, if you don't change your ways, you're going to be as big a high school screw-up as your old man was."

WRITING PROJECT

Write a narrative essay about something significant in your life using the literary strategies of plot, character, and setting. Develop your story through the use of contraries, creating tension that moves the story forward and gives it significance. You can discuss the significance of your story explicitly, perhaps as a revelation, or you can imply it (we discuss and illustrate each of these strategies later in this chapter). Use specific details and develop contraries that create tension.

This assignment calls for a *story*. In Chapter 19, we argue that a narrative qualifies as a story only when it depicts a series of connected events that create for the reader a sense of tension or conflict that is resolved through a new understanding or change in status. Your goal for this assignment is to write a story about your life that fulfills these criteria. The rest of this chapter will help you every step of the way.

Pp. 578–582 explain the criteria for a "story."

Understanding Autobiographical Writing

Autobiographical writing may include descriptions of places and people and depictions of events that are more entertaining than enlightening. However, the spine of most autobiographical writing is a key moment or event, or a series of key moments or events, that shapes or reveals the author's emerging character or growth in understanding.

Autobiographical Tension: The Opposition of Contraries

Key events in autobiography are characterized by a contrariety of opposing values or points of view. These oppositions are typically embodied in conflicts between characters or in divided feelings within the narrator. The contrariety in a story can often be summed up in statements such as these:

> My best friend from the eighth grade was suddenly an embarrassment in high school.
>
> My parents thought I was too young to drive to the movies when in fact I was ready to ride off with Iggy's Motorcycle Maniacs.
>
> My husband thought I was mad about his being late for dinner when in fact I was mad about things he had never understood.

Consider differences between "Berkeley Blues" (pp. 574–576) and "The Stolen Watch" (pp. 576–578).

An autobiographical piece without tension is like an academic piece without a problem or a surprising thesis. No writing is more tedious than a pointless "So what?" narrative that rambles on without tension. (You can read such a narrative in our discussion of the difference between a "story" and an "*and then* chronology" in Chapter 19. It is a good example of what *not* to do for this assignment.)

Like the risky thesis statement in closed-form writing, contrariety creates purpose and focus for open-form writing. It functions as an organizing principle, helping the writer determine what to include or omit. It also sets a direction for the writer. When a story is tightly wound and all the details contribute to the story line, the tension moves the plot forward as a mainspring moves the hands of a watch. The tension is typically resolved when the narrator experiences a moment of recognition or insight, vanquishes or is vanquished by a foe, or changes status.

Using the Elements of Literary Narrative to Generate Ideas

The basic elements of a literary narrative that work together to create a story are plot, character, setting, and theme. In this section we show how you can use each of these elements to help think of ideas for your autobiographical story.

Plot

By *plot* we mean the basic action of the story, including the selection and sequencing of scenes and events. Often stories don't open with the earliest chronological moment; they may start *in medias res* ("in the middle of things") at a moment of crisis and then flash backward to fill in earlier details that explain the origins of the crisis. What you choose to include in your story and where you place it are concerns of plot. The amount of detail you choose to devote to each scene is also a function of plot. How a writer varies the amount of detail in each scene is referred to as a plot's *pacing.*

Plots typically unfold in the following stages: (a) an arresting opening scene; (b) the introduction of characters and the filling in of background; (c) the building of tension or conflict through oppositions embedded in a series of events or scenes; (d) the climax or pivotal moment when the tension or conflict comes to a head; and (e) reflection on the events of the plot and their meaning.

To help you recognize story-worthy events in your own life, consider the following list of pivotal moments that have figured in numerous autobiographical narratives:

Possible Focuses for Autobiographical Narratives

Moments of enlightenment or coming to knowledge: understanding a complex idea for the first time, recognizing what is meant by love or jealousy or justice, mastering a complex skill, seeing some truth about yourself or your family that you previously hadn't seen

Passages from one realm to the next: from innocence to experience, from outsider to insider or vice versa, from child to adult, from novice to expert, from what you once were to what you now are

Confrontation with the unknown: with people or situations that challenged or threatened your old identity and values

Moments of crisis or critical choice: moments that tested your mettle or your system of values.

Major choices: about the company you keep (friends, love interests, cliques, larger social groups) and the effects of those choices on your integrity and the persona you project to the world

Problems with people: problems maintaining relationships without compromising your own growth or denying your own needs

Problems accepting limitations and necessities: confronting the loss of dreams, the death of intimates, the failure to live up to ideals, or the difficulty of living with a chronic illness or disability

Contrasts between common wisdom and your own unique knowledge or experience: doing what people said couldn't be done, failing at something others said was easy, finding value in something rejected by society, finding bad consequences of something widely valued

For Writing and Discussion

Prior to class, use one or more of the above pivotal-moment categories as an aid to brainstorm ideas for your own autobiographical essay. Then choose one of your ideas to use for your plot, and freewrite possible answers to the following questions:

1. How might you begin your story?
2. What events and scenes might you include in your story?
3. How might you arrange them?
4. What would be the climax of your story (the pivotal moment or scene)?
5. What insights or meaning might you want your story to suggest?

Then share your ideas and explorations with classmates. Help each other explore possibilities for good autobiographical stories. Of course, you are not yet committed to any pivotal moment or plot.

Character

Which characters from your life will you choose to include in your autobiography? The answer to that question depends on the nature of the tension that moves your story forward. Characters who contribute significantly to that tension or who represent some aspect of that tension with special clarity belong in your story. Whatever the source of tension in a story, a writer typically chooses characters who exemplify the narrator's fears and desires or who forward or frustrate the narrator's growth in a significant way.

Sometimes writers develop characters not through description and sensory detail but through dialogue. Particularly if a story involves conflict between people, dialogue is a powerful means of letting the reader experience that conflict directly. The following piece of dialogue, taken from African-American writer Richard Wright's classic autobiography *Black Boy*, demonstrates how a skilled writer can let dialogue tell the story, without resorting to analysis and abstraction. In the following scene, young Wright approaches a librarian in an attempt to get a book by Baltimore author and journalist H. L. Mencken from a whites-only public library. He has forged a note and borrowed a library card from a sympathetic white coworker and is pretending to borrow the book in his coworker's name.

> "What do you want, boy?"
> As though I did not possess the power of speech, I stepped forward and simply handed her the forged note, not parting my lips.
> "What books by Mencken does he want?" she asked.
> "I don't know ma'am," I said avoiding her eyes.
> "Who gave you this card?"
> "Mr. Falk," I said.
> "Where is he?"
> "He's at work, at the M— Optical Company," I said. "I've been in here for him before."

"I remember," the woman said. "But he never wrote notes like this."

Oh, God, she's suspicious. Perhaps she would not let me have the books? If she had turned her back at that moment, I would have ducked out the door and never gone back. Then I thought of a bold idea.

"You can call him up, ma'am," I said, my heart pounding.

"You're not using these books are you?" she asked pointedly.

"Oh no ma'am. I can't read."

"I don't know what he wants by Mencken," she said under her breath.

I knew I had won; she was thinking of other things and the race question had gone out of her mind.

—Richard Wright, *Black Boy*

It's one thing to hear *about* racial prejudice and discrimination; it's another thing to *hear* it directly through dialogue such as this. In just one hundred or so words of conversation, Wright communicates the anguish and humiliation of being a "black boy" in the United States in the 1920s.

Another way to develop a character is to present a sequence of moments or scenes that reveal a variety of behaviors and moods. Imagine taking ten photographs of your character to represent his or her complexity and variety and then arranging them in a collage. Your narrative can create a similar collage using verbal descriptions. Sheila Madden uses this strategy in "Letting Go of Bart," a story in the Readings section of this chapter, pages 184–186.

For Writing and Discussion

If you currently have ideas for the story you plan to write, consider now the characters who will be in it. If you haven't yet settled on a story idea, think of memorable people in your life. Explore questions such as these: Why are these characters significant to you? What role did they play in forwarding or frustrating your progress? Given that role, which of their traits, mannerisms, modes of dress, and actions might you include in your account? Could you develop your character through dialogue? Through a collage of representative scenes? After you have considered these questions privately, share your responses to them either as a whole class or in groups. Help each other think of details to make your characters vivid and memorable.

Setting

Elements of setting are selected as characters are selected, according to how much they help readers understand the conflict or tension that drives the story. When you write about yourself, what you notice in the external world often reflects your inner world. In some moods you are apt to notice the expansive lawn, beautiful flowers, and swimming ducks in the city park; in other moods you might note the litter of paper cups, the blight on the roses, and the scum on the duck pond. The setting typically relates thematically to the other elements of a story.

In "Berkeley Blues" (pp. 574–576), for example, the author contrasts the swimming pools and sunsets of his hometown to the grit and darkness of inner-city Berkeley. The contrast in settings mirrors the contrast in the worldviews of the high school debaters and the homeless person who confronts them.

For Writing and Discussion

In writing an autobiographical narrative, one of your challenges is to use words to capture scenes so vividly that readers can see in their own minds what you are describing and can share your experience vicariously. The four photos in Figures 7.1–7.4 present four memorable scenes: a wooded stream, a busy city plaza, a steep mountain trail, and an amusement ride at a fair. For this exercise, you can either use a scene in one of these photos or move directly to a scene from your own life that might become part of your own narrative.

Your goal in this exercise is to freewrite a vivid description of a scene and to explore how the scene may be used in your own narrative. If you use one of the scenes in the photos, freewrite a description of this place, imagining that you are there. Describe the scene fully. Alternatively, use the vividness of one of these scenes to help you picture and describe a possible setting of your own to include in your narrative. What do you see? Hear? Smell? Once you have described your scene, explore how this setting might be important to your story in terms of plot, character, or theme. Can you image a second, contrasting scene that reflects the contraries or oppositions in your story? Can you imagine one of these scenes associated with one of your characters? What does the scene reveal about your character's desires, hopes, fears, or predicament? What does the scene suggest about the ideas or themes in your story?

Then, share your descriptive freewrites with classmates, discussing how your settings might be used in your autobiographical narrative.

FIGURE 7.1 A Wooded Stream

FIGURE 7.2 Busy City Plaza

FIGURE 7.3 Steep Mountain Trail

FIGURE 7.4 Amusement Ride at a Fair

Theme

The word *theme* is difficult to define. Themes, like thesis statements, organize the other elements of the essay. But a theme is seldom stated explicitly and is never proved with reasons and factual evidence. Readers ponder—even argue about—themes, and often different readers are affected very differently by the same theme. Some literary critics view theme as simply a different way of thinking about plot. To use a phrase from critic Northrop Frye, a plot is "what happened" in a story, whereas the theme is "what happens" over and over again in this story and others like it. To illustrate this distinction, we summarize student writer Patrick José's autobiographical narrative "No Cats in America?", one of the essays in the Readings section of this chapter, from a plot perspective and from a theme perspective:

José's essay is on pp. 178–180.

    Plot Perspective It's the story of a Filipino boy who emigrates with his family from the Philippines to the United States when he is in the eighth grade. On the first day of school, he is humiliated when classmates snicker at the lunch his mother packed for him. Feeling more and more alienated each day, he eventually proclaims, "I hate being Filipino!"

    Theme Perspective It's the story of how personal identity is threatened when people are suddenly removed from their own cultures and immersed into new ones that don't understand or respect difference. The story reveals the psychic damage of cultural dislocation.

As you can see, the thematic summary goes beyond the events of the story to point toward the larger significance of those events. Although you may choose not to state your theme directly for your readers, you need to understand that theme to organize your story. This understanding usually precedes and guides your decisions about what events and characters to include, what details and dialogue to use, and what elements of setting to describe. But sometimes you need to reverse the process and start out with events and characters that, for whatever reason, force themselves on you, and then figure out your theme after you've written for a while. In other words, theme may be something you discover as you write.

For Writing and Discussion

Using the ideas you have brainstormed from previous exercises in this chapter, choose two possible ideas for an autobiographical narrative you might write. For each, freewrite your response to this question: What is the significance of this story for me? (Why did I choose this story? Why is it important to me? Why do I want to tell it? What am I trying to show my readers?)

In class, share your freewrites. All the exercises in this section are designed to generate discussion about the elements of autobiographical narrative and to encourage topic exploration.

READINGS

Now that we have examined some of the key elements of autobiographical writing, let's look at some particular examples.

The first reading is by Kris Saknussemm, an American fiction writer whose short stories have appeared in such publications as *The Boston Review, New Letters, The Antioch Review,* and *ZYZZYVA.* He is the author of an avant-garde novel to be published in 2005. This selection is taken from his autobiographical work in progress.

Kris Saknussemm
Phantom Limb Pain

1   When I was 13 my sole purpose was to shed my baby fat and become the star halfback on our football team. That meant beating out Miller King, the best athlete at my school. He was my neighbor and that mythic kid we all know—the one who's forever better than us—the person we want to be.

2   Football practice started in September and all summer long I worked out. I ordered a set of barbells that came with complimentary brochures with titles like "How to Develop a He-Man Voice." Every morning before sunrise I lumbered around our neighborhood wearing ankle weights loaded with sand. I taught myself how to do Marine push-ups and carried my football everywhere so I'd learn not to fumble. But that wasn't enough. I performed a ceremony. During a full moon, I burned my favorite NFL trading cards and an Aurora model of the great quarterback Johnny Unitas in the walnut orchard behind our house, where Miller and I'd gotten into a fight when we were seven and I'd burst into tears before he even hit me.

3   Two days after my ceremony, Miller snuck out on his older brother's
Suzuki and was struck by a car. He lost his right arm, just below the elbow. I
went to see him the day after football practice started—after he'd come back
from the hospital. He looked pale and surprised, but he didn't cry. It was
hard to look at the stump of limb where his arm had been, so I kept glancing around his room. We only lived about 200 feet away, and yet I'd never
been inside his house before. It had never occurred to me that he would also
have on his wall a poster of Raquel Welch from One Million Years B.C.

4   I went on to break all his records that year. Miller watched the home
games from the bench, wearing his jersey with the sleeve pinned shut. We
went 10-1 and I was named MVP, but I was haunted by crazy dreams in
which I was somehow responsible for the accident—that I'd found the man-
gled limb when it could've been sewn back on—and kept it in an aquarium
full of vodka under my bed.

5   One afternoon several months later, toward the end of basketball season,
I was crossing the field to go home and I saw Miller stuck going over the
Cyclone fence—which wasn't hard to climb if you had both arms. I guess
he'd gotten tired of walking around and hoped no one was looking. Or
maybe it was a matter of pride. I'm sure I was the last person in the world he
wanted to see—to have to accept assistance from. But even that challenge
he accepted. I helped ease him down the fence, one diamond-shaped hole
at a time. When we were finally safe on the other side, he said to me, "You
know, I didn't tell you this during the season, but you did all right. Thanks
for filling in for me."

6   We walked home together, not saying much. But together. Back to our
houses 200 feet apart. His words freed me from my bad dreams. I thought to
myself, how many things I hadn't told him. How even without an arm he
was more of a leader. Damaged but not diminished, he was still ahead of
me. I was right to have admired him. I grew bigger and a little more real
from that day on.

Thinking Critically about "Phantom Limb Pain"

Perhaps the first thing the reader realizes about Saknussemm's narrative is that
the climactic event—one boy helping another climb down a Cyclone fence—is a
small action; however, it has big psychological and emotional meaning for the
narrator. The events leading to this moment have prepared us to understand the
writer's revelation of his new relationship to his rival. Saknussemm's last paragraph comments on the preceding narrative, making connections and pulling out
threads of meaning.

1. Saknussemm chooses to leave a lot unsaid, depending on his readers to fill in
   the gaps. Why do you suppose that he had never been inside Miller King's

house before? Why does he feel "somehow responsible for the accident"? What details does Saknussemm use to sketch in Miller's admirable traits?

See Chapter 19, pp. 582–584, for a discussion of concrete language including revelatory words and memory-soaked words. See Chapter 5, pp. 112–113, for a discussion of *show* words and *tell* words.

2. What examples can you find in this narrative of revelatory words, memory-soaked words, and other concrete words low on the ladder of abstraction? Where does Saknussemm use words that *show* what is happening in the narrative instead of simply telling readers?

3. In closed-form prose, writers seldom use sentence fragments. In open-form prose, however, writers frequently use fragments for special effects. Note the two fragments in Saknussemm's final paragraph: "But together. Back to our houses 200 feet apart." Why does Saknussemm use these fragments? What is their rhetorical effect?

4. Part of Saknussemm's style in this narrative is to use understatement and minimalistic language while also using words that resonate with multiple meanings. For example, he lets readers imagine what Miller would look like trying to climb the Cyclone fence with one arm. However, some phrases and words are figurative and symbolic. What does Saknussemm mean by the phrases "grew bigger" and "a little more real" in his final sentence? How do the ideas of size and of reality versus illusion play a role in this narrative and relate to the theme?

For a different approach to narrative, consider student writer Patrick José's "No Cats in America?" Unlike Saknussemm's narrative, José's includes plentiful description. Note also how José creates tension through contrasts in his narrative: between an ideal image of America and a factual image, between life in the Philippines and life in California.

Patrick José (student)
No Cats in America?

1   "There are no cats in America." I remember growing up watching *An American Tail* with my sisters and cousins. Ever since I first saw that movie, I had always wanted to move to America. That one song, "There Are No Cats in America," in which the Mousekewitz family is singing with other immigrating mice, had the most profound effect on me. These were Russian mice going to America to find a better life—a life without cats. At first, I thought America really had no cats. Later, I learned that they meant that America was without any problems at all. I was taught about the American Dream with its promise of happiness and equality. If you wanted a better life, then you better pack up all your belongings and move to America.

2   However, I loved living in the Philippines. My family used to throw the best parties in Angeles City. For a great party, you need some delicious food.

Of course there would be lechon, adobo, pancit, sinigang, lumpia, and rice. We eat rice for breakfast, lunch, and dinner, and rice even makes some of the best desserts. (My mom's bibingka and puto are perfect!) And you mustn't forget the drinks. San Miguel and Coke are usually sufficient. But we also had homemade mango juice and coconut milk. And a party wouldn't be a party without entertainment, right? So in one room, we had the gambling room. It's usually outside the house. Everybody would be smoking and drinking while playing mahjong. And sometimes, others would play pepito or pusoy dos. Music and dancing is always a must. And when there are firecrackers, better watch out because the children would go crazy with them.

3   Then one day, a mixed feeling came over me. My dad told us that he had gotten a job . . . in California. In the span of two months, we had moved to America, found a small apartment, and located a small private Catholic school for the kids. We did not know many people in California that first summer. We only had ourselves to depend on. We would go on car trips, go to the beach, cook, play games. In August, I thought we were living the American Dream.

4   But at the end of summer, school began. I was in the eighth grade. I had my book bag on one shoulder, stuffed with notebooks, folder paper, calculators, a ruler, a pencil box, and my lunch. I still can remember what I had for lunch on the first day of school—rice and tilapia and, in a small container, a mixture of vinegar, tomatoes, and bagoong. My mom placed everything in a big Tupperware box, knowing I eat a lot.

5   When I walked into the classroom, everyone became quiet and looked at me. I was the only Filipino in that room. Everyone was white. We began the day by introducing ourselves. When it got to my turn, I was really nervous. English was one of the courses that I took in the Philippines, and I thought I was pretty proficient at it. But when I first opened my mouth, everyone began to laugh. The teacher told everyone to hush. I sat down, smiling faintly not understanding what was so funny. I knew English, and yet I was laughed at. But it had nothing to do with the language. It was my accent.

6   Some students tried to be nice, especially during lunch. But it didn't last long. I was so hungry for my lunch. I followed a group of students to the cafeteria and sat down at an empty table. Some girls joined me. I didn't really talk to them, but they asked if they could join me. As I opened my Tupperware, I saw their heads turn away. They didn't like the smell of fish and bagoong. The girls left and moved to another table of girls. From the corner of my eye I saw them looking and laughing at me. I tried to ignore it, concentrating on eating my lunch as I heard them laugh. In the Philippines, the only way to eat fish and rice is with your hands. But that was in the Philippines. My manners were primitive here in America. I was embarrassed at the smell, was embarrassed at the way I ate, was embarrassed to be me.

7   When I got home, I lied to my parents. I told them school was great and that I was excited to go back. But deep down, I wanted to go back to the Philippines. When lunch came the next day, I was hungry. In my hand was

my lunch. Five feet away was the trash. I stood up, taking my lunch in my hands. Slowly, I walked my way towards the trashcan, opened the lid, and watched as my lunch filled the trashcan. Again, I told my parents I enjoyed school.

8   When my grades began to suffer, the teacher called my parents and scheduled an appointment. The next day, my parents came to the classroom, and when they started talking to the teacher I heard laughter in the background. It humiliated me to have my classmates hear my parents talk.

9   That night, my parents and I had a private discussion. They asked why I lied to them. I told them everything, including my humiliation. They told me not to worry about it, but I pleaded for us to return to the Philippines. My parents said no. "Living here will provide a better future for you and your sisters," they said. Then the unexpected came. I didn't know what I was thinking. I yelled to them with so much anger, "I hate being Filipino!" Silence filled the room. Teardrops rolled down my cheeks. My parents were shocked, and so was I.

10   I went to my room and cried. I didn't mean what I said. But I was tired of the humiliation. Lying on my bed, with my eyes closed, my mind began to wander. I found myself in the boat with the Mousekewitz family singing, "There are no cats in America." If only they knew how wrong they were.

Thinking Critically about "No Cats in America?"

Unlike Saknussemm, who comments explicitly on the significance of his experience, Patrick José lets the reader infer his essay's significance from the details of the narrative and from their connection to the framing story of the fictional mice and cats.

1. How do the settings help you understand José's theme at different points in the story?

2. What would you say is the story's climax or pivotal moment?

3. José's title, first paragraph, and last paragraph are about a children's movie that features the Mousekewitz's song proclaiming that there are no cats in America. How does the "no cats" image function as both part of the underlying tension of this narrative and as a symbolic vehicle for conveying the theme of José's essay? What is the insight that José has achieved at the end?

4. During a rough draft workshop, José asked his peer reviewers whether he should retain his description of parties in the Philippines, which he thought was perhaps unconnected to the rest of the story. His classmates urged him to keep those details. Do you agree with their advice? Why?

5. For Filipinos and Filipinas, the specific names of foods and party games would be rich examples of memory-soaked words. For other readers, however,

See Chapter 19, p. 584, for a discussion of the power of memory-soaked words.

these names are foreign and strange. Do you agree with José's decision to use these specific ethnic names? Why?

For Writing and Discussion

Imagine a memorable party scene from your own life and experiences. It could be a family party, a neighborhood party, or a party from high school, college, or work. What specific words, revelatory words, and memory-soaked words will most likely make this party come to life in your readers' imagination? What details about food and drink, the activities of the partygoers, clothing and mannerisms, the party's setting (furniture, pictures on the walls, arrangement of rooms), and so on will trigger associations and memories for your readers? List these details and then share them with your classmates.

The next example was written in a first-year composition course by a student writer who wishes to remain anonymous.

Masks

1   Her soft, blond hair was in piggytails, as usual, with ringlets that bounced whenever she turned her head. As if they were springs, they could stretch, then shrink, then bounce, excited by the merest movement of her head. Never was there a hair that wasn't enclosed in those glossy balls which always matched her dress. I knew the only reason she turned her head was so they'd bounce. Because it was cute. Today, she wore a pink dress with frills and lace and impeccably white tights. Her feet, which swayed back and forth underneath her chair, were pampered with shiny, black shoes without a single scuff. She was very wise, sophisticated beyond her kindergarten years.

2   I gazed at her and then looked down at my clothes. My green and red plaid pants and my yellow shirt with tiny, blue stars showed the day's wear between breakfast, lunch, and recess. Showing through the toe of my tenny runners was my red sock.

3   At paint time, I closely followed behind her, making sure I painted at the easel next to hers. She painted a big, white house with a white picket fence and a family: Mom, Dad, and Daughter. I painted my mom, my brother, and myself. I, then, painted the sky, but blue streaks ran down our faces, then our bodies, ruining the picture.

4   The next day, I wore my hair in piggytails. I had done it all by myself, which was obvious due to my craftsmanship. She pointed and giggled at me when I walked by. I also wore a dress that day but I didn't have any pretty

white tights. The boys all gathered underneath me when I went on the monkeybars to peak at my underwear to chant, "I see London, I see France, I see Tiffy's underpants."

5   When the day was done, she ran to the arms of her mother that enveloped her in a loving and nurturing hug. She showed her mother her painting, which had a big, red star on it.

6   "We'll have to put this up on the refrigerator with all of your others," her mother said. I had thrown my painting away. I looked once more at the two of them as they walked hand in hand towards their big, white house with a white picket fence. I trudged to my babysitter's house. I wouldn't see my mother until six o'clock. She had no time for me, for my paintings, for my piggytails. She was too busy working to have enough money to feed my brother and me.

7   Digging absently through books and folders, I secretly stole a glance at her, three lockers down. Today she wore her Calvins and sported a brand new pair of Nikes. As always, at the cutting edge of fashion. If I wanted Nikes, I could pay for them myself, or so said my mother. In the meantime, I had to suffer with my cheap, treadless Scats. As I searched for a pen, her giggle caught my attention. Three of her friends had flocked around her locker. I continued searching for a pen but to no avail. I thought of approaching and borrowing one but I was fearful that they would make fun of me.

8   "Jim and Brad called me last night and both of them asked me to go to the show. Which one should I pick?" she asked. My mom wouldn't let me go out on dates until I was a sophomore in high school. We were only in seventh grade and she was always going out with guys. Not that it mattered that I couldn't date, yet. Nobody had ever asked me out.

9   "My hair turned out so yucky today. Ick," she commented. She bent down to grab a book and light danced among the gentle waves of her flowing, blond mane. Her radiant brown eyes and adorable smile captivated all who saw her. Once captured, however, none was allowed past the mask she'd so artfully constructed to lure them to her. We were all so close to her, so far away. She was so elusive, like a beautiful perfume you smell but can't name, like the whisper that wakes you from a dream and turns out to belong to the dream.

10   As she walked into the library, I heard a voice whisper, "There she is. God, she's beautiful." She was wearing her brown and gold cheerleader outfit. Her pleated skirt bounced off her thighs as she strutted by. Her name, "Kathy," was written on her sweater next to her heart and by it hung a corsage. As she rounded the corner, she flicked her long, blond curls and pivoted, sending a ripple through the pleats of the skirt. She held her head up high, befitting one of her social standing: top of the high school food chain. She casually searched the length of the library for friends. When she reached the end of the room, she carefully reexamined every table, this time less casually.

Her smile shaded into a pout. She furrowed her face, knitting her eyebrows together, and saddening her eyes. People stared at her until she panicked.

11   She was bolting toward the door when she spotted me. She paused and approached my table. Putting on her biggest smile, she said, "Oh hi! Can I sit by you?" Thrilled at the possibility of at last befriending her, I was only too happy to have her sit with me. As she sat down, she again scanned the expanse of the library.

12   "So, who does the varsity basketball team play tonight?" I asked.

13   "Great Falls Central," she replied. "Make sure you're there! . . . How's the Algebra assignment today?!"

14   "Oh, it's okay. Not too tough," I said.

15   "John always does my assignments for me. I just hate Algebra. It's so hard."

16   We stood up in silence, suddenly painfully aware of our differences. She glanced in the reflection of the window behind us, checked her hair, then again scanned the room.

17   "There's Shelly! Well, I'll see you later," she said.

18   She rose from the table and fled to her more acceptable friend.

19   The next day, she walked down the hall surrounded by a platoon of friends. As we passed, I called out "Hi!" but she turned away as if she didn't know me, as if I didn't exist.

20   I, then, realized her cheerleader outfit, her golden locks, her smile were all a mask. Take them away and nothing but air would remain. Her friends and their adoration were her identity. Without them she was alone and vulnerable. I was the powerful one. I was independent.

Thinking Critically about "Masks"

1. What are the main contrarieties in this piece?

2. Where does the writer's description of the setting help to portray the characters?

3. This piece focuses on the narrator's movement toward a significant recognition. What is it she recognizes? If you were a peer reviewer for this writer, would you recommend eliminating the last paragraph, expanding it, or leaving it as it is? Why?

4. In Chapter 19, we quote writer John McPhee's advice to prefer specific words over abstract ones—brand names, for example, rather than generic names. This student writer follows this advice throughout her essay. Where does she use details and specific words with particular effectiveness?

The discussion of concrete language in Chapter 19 is on pp. 582–584.

The final example uses a collage technique. Here the emphasis is so much on the character Bart that the narrator seems relatively unimportant, and you may wonder whether this piece is biography (the story of Bart) or autobiography (the story of the narrator). We include "Letting Go of Bart" in the category of autobiographical narrative because the way in which the writer, Sheila Madden, tells the story reveals her own growth in understanding, her own deepening of character.

Sheila Madden
Letting Go of Bart

1   Bart lies stiffly in bed, toes pointed downward like a dancer's, but Bart is far from dancing. When he tries to shift position, his limbs obey spasmodically because his nervous system has been whipsawed by the medications he has been taking for years to control the various manifestations of AIDS.

2   He is wearing diapers now, for incontinence—the ultimate indignity. An oxygen tube is hooked into his nose, morphine drips into his arm; his speech is slurred.

3   But Bart is not confused. He is intensely irritable and has been the terror of his nurses. Though he has a great self-deprecating grin, I haven't seen it for weeks.

4   I can't say a proper goodbye because he is never alone. I would like to pray silently by his bedside, meditating; but even if I could, he would barely tolerate it. Bart has no god.

5   I remember the day a tall, good-looking young man popped into the open door of the downstairs apartment I was fixing up in my San Francisco home. That late afternoon, I was tiredly putting the last coat of paint on the walls with the help of a couple of friends. Bart had seen the for-rent sign in the window and just walked in. Within moments he had all three of us laughing uproariously as he put a deposit in my hand. I had asked the angels for help in finding a decent renter; the angels had responded. Bart and I would get on famously.

6   For one thing, Bart managed to fix or overlook the unfinished bits in the apartment. He and his father built a fine, much-needed deck on the back garden, charging me only for the lumber. He made the small apartment look spacious, arranging the furniture skillfully, backlighting the sofas. And he was prompt with the rent.

7   However, Bart was far more than a satisfactory renter. He was a fine singer and a member of the symphony chorus. When he practiced, his rich baritone would sail up the stairs, smoothing the airways, never ruffling them.

8   He asked permission to put a piano in his apartment, and I agreed nervously. Because he was a beginner on the instrument, I feared endless, fumbling scales disturbing my peace. It never happened. He played softly, sensitively, and always at reasonable hours.

9   I attended some of his concerts and met his friends. At times we joined forces at parties upstairs or downstairs, but somehow we never got in each other's hair.

10   He was a skillful ballroom dancer. Once he agreed to stand in as partner for my visiting sister when we attended a Friday dance at the Embarcadero Plaza—although the prospect could not have thrilled him.

11   Another time I disabled my tape deck by spraying it with WD-40 and ran downstairs for help. Bart came up immediately, scolding me roundly for putting oil on such a machine. Then he spent the better part of an hour wrapping matchsticks in cotton batting (for lack of a better tool), degreasing the heads with rubbing alcohol, and putting all to rights.

12   Bart had family problems; I had them. We commiserated. Bart was an ally, a compatriot, a brother.

13   I suspected Bart was gay; but we never talked about it, although he knew I was working in the AIDS fields as a counselor and that it was a nonissue with me.

14   Then one day he got a bad flu, which turned into a deep, wracking cough that did not go away. I worried about it, having heard such coughs in the AIDS patients I dealt with daily. I encouraged him to see a doctor, and he did, making light of his visit.

15   Finally the cough receded, but psychically so did Bart. I saw him hardly at all for the next three months. When I did, he seemed somber and abstracted.

16   However, my life was hectic at the time. I didn't pay attention, assuming his problem was job dissatisfaction; I knew his boss was a constant thorn in his side. One day he told me that he was changing jobs and moving to Napa, an hour's drive away. I rejoiced for him and cried for myself. I would miss Bart.

17   Our lives separated. Napa might as well have been the moon. Over a two-year period we talked once or twice on the phone, and I met him once for dinner in the city.

18   Then one night my doorbell rang unexpectedly, and Bart came in to tell me of his recovery from a recent bout of pneumocystis pneumonia. "I'm out of the closet, willy-nilly," he said.

19   I was stunned. I had put him in the "safe" category, stuffing my fears about the telltale cough. It must have been then that he learned his diagnosis. For the next 24 hours I cried off and on, inconsolably, for Bart and probably for all the others I had seen die.

20   Now he is at the end, an end so fierce there is nothing to do but pray it will come quickly. Bart is courageous, his anger masking fear. He has thus far refused to let the morphine dull his consciousness. His eyes, hawklike, monitor all that is going on around him. Angels, who once brought him, take him home.

Thinking Critically about "Letting Go of Bart"

1. Madden uses a series of scenes to create her portrait of Bart. Briefly list each of these scenes identifying its setting and events. How do these scenes function to reveal Bart's character? In other words, what does the reader learn through each scene?

2. How and how much does Madden as the narrator reveal about her own character? To what extent could you call this essay an "autobiographical narrative"?

3. How does Madden's collage technique create tension and resolution?

For Writing and Discussion

To generate more ideas for an autobiographical narrative, each class member should do the following exercise independently and then share the results with the rest of the class:

1. Have you ever had a moment of revelation when you suddenly realized that your own view of something (a person, a place, the world) was wrong, narrow, or distorted, as did Kris Saknussemm? If you have, freewrite about this experience.

2. Have you ever been suddenly whisked from a familiar to an unfamiliar setting and made to feel like an outsider, alienated and alone, as did Patrick José in "No Cats in America?" If so, freewrite about this experience.

3. Have you ever changed your view of a person in a way analogous to the narrator's reassessment of the cheerleader in "Masks"? If so, freewrite about this character. What details reveal this person before and after your moment of reassessment?

4. Have you ever known a person whose presence in your life made an important difference to you, as did Bart to Sheila Madden? If you have, freewrite about this character, imagining a series of scenes that might create a collage effect.

Composing Your Essay

In deciding what to write about, keep in mind the basic requirement for a good story: It must portray a sequence of connected events driven forward by some tension or conflict that results in a recognition or new understanding. Not every memorable event in your life will lend itself to this sort of structure. The most common failing in faulty narratives is that the meaning of the event is clearer to the narrator than to the audience. "You had to be there," the writer comments, when a story just doesn't have the expected impact on an audience.

But it's the storyteller's job to *put the reader there* by providing enough detail and context for the reader to *see* why the event is significant. If an event didn't lead to any significant insight, understanding, knowledge, change, or other kind of difference in your life, and if you really had to be there to appreciate its significance, then it's a poor candidate for an autobiographical narrative.

Generating and Exploring Ideas

Choosing a Plot

For some of you, identifying a plot—a significant moment or insight arising out of contrariety—will present little problem; perhaps you have already settled on an idea you generated in one of the class discussion exercises earlier in this chapter. However, if you are still searching for a plot idea, you may find the following list helpful:

- A time when you took some sort of test that conferred new status on you (Red Cross lifesaving exam, driver's test, SAT, important school or work-related test, entrance exam, team tryout). If you failed, what did you learn from it or how did it shape you? If you succeeded, did the new status turn out to be as important as you expected it would be?
- A situation in which your normal assumptions about life were challenged (an encounter with a foreign culture, a time when a person you'd stereotyped surprised you).
- A time when you left your family for an extended period or forever (going to college, getting married, entering the military, leaving one parent for another after their divorce).
- A time that plunged you into a crisis (being the first person to discover a car crash, seeing a robbery in progress, being thrown in with people who are repugnant to you, facing an emergency).
- A situation in which you didn't fit or didn't fulfill others' expectations of you, or a situation in which you were acknowledged as a leader or exceeded others' expectations of you (call to jury duty, assignment to a new committee, being placed in charge of an unfamiliar project).
- A time when you overcame your fears to do something for the first time (first date, first public presentation, first challenge in a new setting).
- A situation in which you learned how to get along amicably with another human being, or a failed relationship that taught you something about life (your first extended romantic relationship; your relationship with a difficult sibling, relative, teacher, or boss; getting a divorce).
- A time when a person who mattered to you (parent, spouse, romantic interest, authority figure) rejected you or let you down, or a time when you rejected or let down someone who cared for you.
- A time when you made a sacrifice on behalf of someone else, or someone else made a sacrifice in your name (taking in a foster child, helping a homeless person, caring for a sick person).

- A time when you were irresponsible or violated a principle or law and thereby caused others pain (you shoplifted or drank when underage and were caught, you failed to look after someone entrusted to your care).
- A time when you were criticized unjustly or given a punishment you didn't deserve (you were accused of plagiarizing a paper that you'd written, you were blamed unjustly for a problem at work).
- A time when you were forced to accept defeat or death or the loss of a dream or otherwise learned to live with reduced expectations.
- A time when you experienced great joy (having a baby, getting your dream job) or lived out a fantasy.

Thickening the Plot

Once you've identified an event about which you'd like to write, you need to develop ways to show readers what makes that event particularly story worthy. In thinking about the event, consider the following questions:

- What makes the event so memorable? What particulars or physical details come most readily to mind when you think back on the event?
- What are the major contrarieties that gave the event tension? Did it raise a conflict between two or more people? Between their worldviews? Between before and after versions of yourself?
- How can you make the contrarieties memorable and vivid to the reader?
- What scenes can you create? What words could your characters exchange? Is there a moment of insight, recognition, or resolution that would give your plot a climax?
- What is the significance of the story? How does it touch on larger human issues and concerns? What makes it something your reader will relate to? What is its theme?

Shaping and Drafting

When stuck, writers often work their way into a narrative by describing in detail a vividly recalled scene, person, or object. This inductive approach is common with many creative processes. You may or may not include all the descriptive material in your final draft, but in the act of writing exhaustively about this one element, the rest of the story may begin to unfold for you, and forgotten items and incidents may resurface. In the course of describing scenes and characters, you will probably also begin reflecting on the significance of what you are saying. Try freewriting answers to such questions as "Why is this important?" and "What am I trying to do here?" Then continue with your rough draft.

Revising

Once you've written a draft, you need to get down to the real work of writing— rewriting. Revisit your prose critically, with an eye toward helping your reader share your experience and recognize its significance. Chapter 19, as well as the following guidelines for peer reviews, will be of particular help during revision.

GUIDELINES FOR PEER REVIEWS

Instructions for peer reviews are provided in Chapter 17 (pp. 519–520).

For the Writer

Prepare two or three questions you would like your peer reviewer to address while responding to your draft. The questions can focus on some aspect of your draft that you are uncertain about, on one or more sections where you particularly seek help or advice, or on some feature that you particularly like about your draft, or on some part you especially wrestled with. Write out your questions and give them to your peer reviewer along with your draft.

For the Reviewer

I. Read the draft at normal reading speed from beginning to end. As you read, do the following:
   A. Place a wavy line in the margin next to any passages that you find confusing, that contain something that doesn't seem to fit, or that otherwise slow down your reading.
   B. Place a "Good!" in the margin next to any passages where you think the writing is particularly strong or interesting.
II. Read the draft again slowly and answer the following questions by writing down brief explanations of your answers.
   A. Plot: What are the contrarieties, tensions, or conflicts in this story?
      1. How might the writer heighten or clarify the tension in the story?
      2. How might the writer improve the structure or pacing of scenes and the connection between these events? If you were to expand or reduce the treatment given to any events, which would you change and why?
      3. How could the writer use chronological order, flashbacks, or flash-forwards more effectively?
   B. Characters: How might the writer make the characters and their functions more vivid and compelling?
      1. Where might the writer provide more information about a character or describe the character more fully?
      2. Where might the writer use dialogue more effectively to reveal character?
   C. Setting: How might the writer use setting more effectively to create contrasts or convey thematic significance? Where might the writer add or revise details about setting?
   D. Theme: What do you see as the *So what?* or significance of this story?
      1. What insight or revelation do you get from this story?
      2. How could the story's thematic significance be made more memorable, powerful, or surprising? Should the writer comment more explicitly on the meaning or significance of the story or leave more for you to grasp on your own?
   E. Title and opening paragraphs: How could the writer improve the title? How could the opening paragraphs be made more effective to hook the readers' interest and prepare them for the story to follow?

    F. Language and details: Where do you find examples of specific language, including memory-soaked or revelatory words? Where and how could the writer use specific language more effectively?

III. Rhetorical considerations

    A. *Purpose, audience,* and *genre*: Where does this draft do a good job of fulfilling its expressive purpose, reaching its intended audience, and meeting the audience's expectations for autobiographical narratives? How could the writer improve in these areas?

    B. *Logos, ethos,* and *pathos*: How effective is the conceptual part of this draft and the logic of its structure? Where could the writer improve this content? What image of the writer comes through in this narrative? How could this image be made more effective? How does the writer appeal to the audience's emotions, interests, and values?

IV. If the writer has prepared questions for you, respond to his or her inquiries.

V. Briefly summarize in a list what you see as the chief strengths and problem areas in the draft.

    A. Strengths

    B. Problem areas

VI. Read the draft one more time. Place a check mark in the margin wherever you notice problems in grammar, spelling, or mechanics (one check mark per problem).

Analyzing Images

About Analyzing Images

This chapter asks you to analyze images in order to understand their persuasive power—a skill often called "visual literacy." By *visual literacy,* we mean your awareness of the importance of visual communication and your ability to interpret or make meaning out of images and graphics (photos, pictures, illustrations, icons, charts, graphs, and other visual displays of data). In this chapter, we seek to enhance your visual literacy by focusing on the way that images influence our conceptual and emotional understanding of a phenomenon and the way that they validate, reveal, and construct the world.

This chapter is the second of four assignment chapters on writing to analyze and synthesize. As you may recall from Chapter 3, when you write to analyze and synthesize, you apply your own critical thinking to a puzzling object or to puzzling data and offer your own new ideas to a conversation. Your goal is to raise interesting questions about the object or data being analyzed—questions that perhaps your reader hasn't thought to ask—and then to provide tentative answers to those questions, supported by points and particulars derived from your own close examination of the object or data. The word *analysis* derives from a Greek word meaning "to dissolve, loosen, undo." Metaphorically, analysis means to divide or dissolve the whole into its constituent parts, to examine these parts carefully, to look at the relationships among them, and then to use this understanding of the parts to better understand the whole—how it functions, what it means. Synonyms for writing to analyze might be *writing to interpret, clarify,* or *explain.* In this chapter, the objects being analyzed are photographs or other images as they appear in a rhetorical context—for example, as part of a news story, a television documentary, a public relations brochure, or an advertisement.

See Table 3.1, pp. 49–50 for an explanation of the aims of writing.

To appreciate the cultural importance of images, consider how British cultural critic John Berger, in his book *About Looking,* sketches the pervasive use of photographs shortly after the invention of the camera.

> The camera was invented by Fox Talbot in 1839. Within a mere 30 years of its invention as a gadget for an elite, photography was being used for police filing, war reporting, military reconnaissance, pornography, encyclopedic documentation, family albums, postcards, anthropological records (often, as with the Indians in the United States, accompanied by genocide), sentimental moralizing, inquisitive probing (the wrongly named "candid camera"), aesthetic effects, news reporting and formal portraiture. The speed with which the possible uses of photography were seized upon is surely an indication of photography's profound, central applicability to industrial capitalism.

One of photography's purposes—as Berger hints—is to create images that "have designs on" us, that urge us to believe ideas, buy things, go places, or otherwise alter our views or behaviors. Information brochures use carefully selected photographs to enhance a product's image (consider how the photographs in your college's catalog or view book have been selected); news photographs editorialize their content (during the Vietnam War a newspaper photograph of a naked Vietnamese child running screaming toward the photographer while a napalm bomb explodes behind her turned many Americans against the war; and recently, the images of weeping Iraqi mothers and houses reduced to rubble shown in newspapers, and documentary films have raised questions about U.S. tactics in Iraq); social issue posters urge us to protest capital punishment or contribute money to save the salmon or sponsor a child in a third world country; and advertisements urge us not only to buy a certain product but to be a certain kind of person with certain values.

Visual literacy is so important in our world that we have already introduced it elsewhere in this text. In Chapter 4, we showed how stakeholders in the current controversy over medical care enlist competing images of doctors such as Norman Rockwell's image of the family doctor who makes house calls versus images of physicians in lab coats surrounded by high technology equipment. In Chapter 5, we showed how specially selected photographs of the Arctic National Wildlife Refuge (ANWR) could be used to advance arguments for or against opening the ANWR to oil exploration (pp. 98–100). And for the Part Openers in this text, we have chosen examples of striking visual texts that grew out of particular rhetorical contexts and were created to have a specific rhetorical effect.

For the images in this chapter, we have selected those directly related to Berger's assertion that photographs often have a "profound, central applicability to industrial capitalism." We look specifically at how photographs and other images are used in "corporate image" advertisements and in product advertisements. We focus on advertisements because they are a wonderful source of images for analysis and because they raise important questions about how our own lives intersect with the processes of a free market economy. In addition to enhancing your visual literacy, studying advertising has other values as well. We suggest four benefits you will gain from your study of advertisements:

- You will appreciate more fully the fun, pleasure, and creativity of advertisements.
- You will become a more savvy consumer, better able to critique ads and make wise buying decisions.
- You will learn rhetorical strategies that you can use in your own career and civic life. (Your understanding of the relationship between words and images in advertising can be readily transferred to other rhetorical settings—for example, when you design a brochure or Web site or write any kind of document that incorporates images and depends on document design.)
- You will become a more perceptive cultural critic who understands how ads both convey and help construct our cultural values, our self-image, our sense of what is normal or ideal, and our ideas about gender, race, and class. A study of advertisements can raise viewers' consciousness to counter prejudice, injustice, and discrimination.

Exploring Image Analysis

To introduce you to the concept of image analysis, we provide two exercises to stimulate your thinking and discussion.

Task 1: Working on your own, freewrite your responses to the following questions:

1. Can you recall a time when a magazine or TV advertisement directly influenced you to buy a product? Describe the occasion and try to recall the specifics of how the ad influenced you.
2. Have the images in a magazine or TV advertisement ever caused you to desire a certain experience or style of life? For example, an ad might not have influenced you to buy a particular product, but it may have sparked a desire to ride a horse through a pounding surf, have a romantic encounter in a European café, or live in a certain kind of house or apartment. To what extent have the images of advertising shaped any of your values, longings, or desires?

In small groups or as a whole class, share your freewrites. From the ensuing discussion, create a list of specific ways in which magazine or TV advertisements have been successful in persuading members of your class to buy a product or to desire certain experiences or lifestyles.

Task 2: For further exploration, we invite you to imagine that you are an advertising consultant hired by the United States Army. Your mission is to create an advertisement recruiting women. Working in small groups, brainstorm ideas for the design of an advertisement that would cause women to consider enlisting in the Army. What photograph or drawing might be placed on your ad? What would the words say? Each group should propose one or two possible design ideas and explain why you think they might appeal to women.

Then look closely at an actual advertisement designed for this purpose. (See the Part Opener on page 95.) As a class, analyze this advertisement by responding to the following questions:

1. To what extent do you think this is an effective ad? Why or why not?
2. Why do you think the ad designers aimed the ad at fathers as well as daughters instead of directly at women? Why did the ad designers write the verbal part of the ad focusing on respect, honor, and courage rather than, say, on adventure or career?
3. Try playing the "what if they changed . . . ?" game. Try looking at specific details of the ad and asking how the effect of the ad would be different if the ad designers had made slight changes. For example:
   a. What if the girl in the picture were blonde rather than brunette? (Why did the ad designers decide against a blonde?)
   b. What if her hair style, makeup, or clothing were different in some way?
   c. What if the father were dressed differently—say wearing a suit—or had a different physical appearance—say the rugged, handsome type? Why is he wearing a plaid flannel shirt? Why is he clean-shaven rather than bearded?

How would the impact be different if the father and daughter were black or Asian rather than white?

    d. Why did they frame the father and daughter in a window and pose them as they did with the daughter in front looking out the window instead of toward her father? How would the impact be different if the father and daughter were walking in the woods, sitting beside a tennis court, or going for a drive?

    e. What if they had used a mother and daughter instead of a father and daughter?

4. Finally, why or why not do you think questions like these are worth asking? Do you think ad designers make choices as consciously and purposefully as we have suggested?

WRITING PROJECT

Choose two print advertisements—or use the two sport-utility ads shown in the For Writing and Discussion exercise on pages 301–302—that sell the same kind of product but appeal to different audiences (for example, a car advertisement aimed at men and one aimed at women; a cigarette ad aimed at upper-middle-class consumers and one aimed at working-class consumers; a clothing ad from *The New Yorker* and one from *Rolling Stone*). Describe the ads in detail so that an audience can easily visualize them without actually seeing them. Analyze the advertisements and explain how each appeals to its target audience. To what values does each ad appeal? How is each ad constructed to appeal to those values? In addition to analyzing the rhetorical appeals made by each ad, you may also wish to evaluate or criticize the ads, commenting on the images of our culture that they convey.

This writing assignment asks you to analyze how advertisers use words and images together to appeal to different audiences. By comparing ads for the same product targeted at different demographic groups, you learn how every aspect of an ad is chosen for an audience-specific rhetorical effect. You will discover, for example, that advertisers often vary their ads for female versus male audiences and that certain products or services are targeted at a specific socioeconomic class. Similarly, advertisers often vary their appeals to reach African-American, Hispanic, or Asian markets. This assignment asks you to explain how these appeals are targeted and created.

    As a variation of this assignment, your instructor might ask you to analyze two photographs of a politician from magazines with different political biases; two news photographs from articles addressing the same story from different angles of vision; the images on the home pages of two Web sites presenting different perspectives on heated topics such as global warming, medical research using animals, and environmental protection; or two advocacy ads for corporations or political causes that represent opposing views. Although these images, articles, and Web sites are not selling you a product per se, they are "selling" you a viewpoint on an issue, and thus this chapter's explanations of how to analyze camera techniques and the use of details, props, and the posing of human figures in photographs can also be applied to visual images other than commercial advertisements.

Understanding Image Analysis

Before we turn directly to advertising, let's look at some strategies you can use to analyze any image intended to have a specific rhetorical effect.

How Images Create a Rhetorical Effect

An image can be said to have a rhetorical effect whenever it moves us emotionally or intellectually. We might identify with the image or be repelled by it; the image might evoke our sympathies, trigger our fears, or call forth a web of interconnected ideas, memories, and associations. When the image is a photograph, its rhetorical effect derives from both the camera techniques that produced it and the composition of the image itself. Let's look at each in turn.

Analyzing Camera Techniques

The rhetorical effect of a photographic image often derives from skillful use of the camera and from the way the film is developed or the digital image is manipulated.* To analyze a photograph, begin by considering the photographer's choices about the camera's relationship to the subject:

- *Distance of camera from subject:* Note whether the photograph is a close-up, medium shot, or long shot. Close-ups tend to increase the intensity of the photograph and suggest the importance of the subject; long shots tend to blend the subject into the environment.
- *Orientation of the image and camera angle:* Note whether the camera is positioned in front of or behind the subject; note also whether the camera is positioned below the subject, looking up (a low-angle shot), or above the subject, looking down (a high-angle shot). Front-view shots tend to emphasize the persons being photographed; rear-view shots often emphasize the scene or setting. A low-angle camera tends to grant superiority, status, and power to the subject, while a high-angle camera can comically reduce the subject to childlike status. A level angle tends to imply equality.
- *Eye gaze:* Note which persons in the photograph, if any, gaze directly at the camera or look away. Looking directly at the camera implies power; looking away can imply deference or shyness.

*Our ideas in this section are indebted to Paul Messaris, *Visual Persuasion: The Role of Images in Advertising* (Thousand Oaks, CA: Sage, 1997).

- *Point of view:* Note whether the photographer strives for an "objective effect," in which the camera stands outside the scene and observes it, or a "subjective effect," in which the camera seems to be the eyes of someone inside the scene. Subjective shots tend to involve the viewer as an actor in the scene.

In addition, photographers often use other highly artistic film or digital techniques: making parts of an image crisp and in focus and others slightly blurred; using camera filters for special effects; distorting or merging images (a city that blends into a desert; a woman who blends into a tree); and creating visual parodies (a Greek statue wearing jeans).

There are also various ways that a photographic image can be manipulated or falsified. Be aware of the following devices used to create visual deception: staging images (scenes that appear to be documentaries but are really staged); altering images (for example, airbrushing, reshaping body parts, or constructing a composite image such as putting the head of one person on the body of another); selecting images or parts of images (such as cropping photographs so that only parts of the body or only parts of a scene are shown); and mislabeling (putting a caption on a photograph that misrepresents what it actually is).

For Writing and Discussion

Look at three photographic images of bears: Figure 5.1 (Chapter 5, p. 98), Figure 5.2 (Chapter 5, p. 99), and the Nikon camera advertisement (p.299). Then, working in small groups or as a whole class, analyze the camera techniques of each photograph, and explain how these techniques are rhetorically effective for the purpose of the message to which each is attached.

Analyzing the Compositional Features of the Image
In addition to analyzing camera and film or digital techniques, you need to analyze the compositional features of the photograph's subject. When photographs are used in ads, every detail down to the props in the photograph or the placement of a model's hands are consciously chosen.

1. *Examine the settings, furnishings, and props.*
   a. List all furnishings and props. If the photograph pictures a room, look carefully at such details as the kind and color of the rug; the subject matter of the paintings on the walls; furniture styles; objects on tables; and the general arrangement of the room. (Is it neat and tidy, or does it have a lived-in look? Is it formal or casual?) If the photograph is outdoors, observe the exact features of the landscape. (Why a mountain rather than a meadow? Why a robin rather than a crow or pigeon?)
   b. What social meanings are attached to the objects you listed? In a den, for example, duck decoys and fishing rods create a different emotional effect than computers and fax machines do. The choice of a breed of dog can signal differences in values, social class, or lifestyle—a Labrador retriever ver-

FIGURE 11.1 Nikon Ad

The camera for those who look at this picture and think, "Gosh, how'd they open up the shadows without blowing out the highlights?"

When staring into the mouth of a 10 ft. grizzly bear, you tend to think about life. Limbs. And how handy legs are. Not the fill-flash ratio needed to expose teeth about to rip your leg off.

Nikon created the N90 specifically for complicated situations like this. When you have no time to think. A brown bear on brown earth, about to mangle a brown shoe. So instead of overexposing this picture like other cameras might, the N90™ works for

you, properly analyzing the situation and delivering an accurate exposure.

Here's how it does it. The 3D Matrix Meter divides the scene into eight segments. It measures the brightness in each one of the segments and then compares them for contrast. D-type lenses incorporate the subject's distance which allows the N90 to calculate the proper ambient light exposure.

The SB-25 Speedlight fires a rapid series of imperceptible pre-flashes to

determine the bear's reflectance. And then provides the precise amount of fill-flash needed to lighten the bear's dark brown fur, without overexposing his slightly yellow teeth.

The N90 can give you near-perfect exposures when other cameras would be fooled. Or, for that matter, eaten.

Professionals trust the N90. So you can too. Because it works just as well on children eating ice cream as it does on bears eating people.

The N90 System

Nikon
We take the world's
greatest pictures.

See the Nikon N90 at authorized dealers where you see this symbol. Nikon Data Link System available Winter '93. For more on our MasterCard, call 1-800-NIKON-35.

sus a groomed poodle; an English sheepdog versus a generic mutt. Even choice of flowers can have symbolic significance: A single rose connotes romance or elegance, a bouquet of daisies suggests freshness, and a hanging fuchsia suggests earthy naturalness.

2. ***Consider the characters, roles, and actions.***

a. Create the story behind the image. Who are these people in the photograph? Why are they here? What are they doing? In advertisements, models can be either *instrumental,* in which case they are acting out real-life roles, or *decorative,* in which case they are eye candy. A female model working on a car engine in grungy mechanics clothes would be instrumental; a female model in a bikini draped over the hood would be decorative.

b. Note every detail about how models are posed, clothed, and accessorized. Note facial expressions, eye contact, gestures, activities, posed relationships among actors and among actors and objects, and relative sizes. (Who is looking at whom? Who is above or below whom? Who or what is in the foreground or background?) Pay special attention to hairstyles because popular culture endows hair with great significance.

c. Ask what social roles are being played and what values appealed to. Are the gender roles traditional or nontraditional? Are the relationships romantic, erotic, friendly, formal, uncertain? What are the power relationships among characters?

3. *Analyze the rhetorical context of the image.*

a. Images are always encountered in a rhetorical context: They accompany a news story, are part of a poster or Web site, or are used in an advertisement. Consider how the image functions within that context and how it contributes to the rhetorical effect of the whole to which it is a part.

b. In advertisements, consider carefully the relationship between the image and the words in the copy. The words in advertisements are chosen with the same care as the details in the image. Pay special attention to the document design of the copy, the style of the language, and the connotations, double entendres, and puns. Also note the kind of product information that is included or excluded from the ad.

See Chapter 3, pp. 62–68, for a discussion of document design.

For Writing and Discussion

This exercise asks you to consider both the camera and film techniques and the compositional features of two Jeep advertisements. Figure 11.2 shows an ad for Jeep Grand Cherokee that appeared in the March 2004 edition of *Brio,* an upscale, elegant, glamorous Japanese magazine. Figure 11.3 shows an ad for the Jeep Wrangler from the May 2004 edition of *Spin,* an American magazine about the contemporary rock music scene. An examination of these ads will help you see how an automobile company with a global reputation targets very different audiences through different publications.

Working individually or in groups, study these ads and answer the following questions:

1. Analysis of the composition of the ads

a. Describe the Jeep Grand Cherokee ad. In the full-size version of this ad, two shadowy figures are visible—the driver and the woman looking down on the Jeep from the lighted window high up in the building. How would you describe the building and the strange effect with water on the right side of the picture? Is the water coming from a fountain, or is the effect the result of composite trick photography? Then describe the Jeep Wrangler ad. Describe the setting and note the contents of the hiker's "backpack."

FIGURE 11.2 Jeep Grand Cherokee Ad

b. How is each ad composed? Note how the vehicle is positioned with regard to the viewer; also note the vehicle's size in relation to the setting. What is the relative importance of image versus verbal text in these ads?

(continued)

FIGURE 11.3 Jeep Wrangler Ad

c. What story does each ad tell? What roles do persons and vehicle play in each story? (In the Japanese ad, the words in the upper left part of the ad can be translated as "Always have adventure in your heart. Jeep Grand Cherokee.")

2. Analysis of the appeal of the ads
   a. To what values does each ad appeal?
   b. What connections do you see between the images and appeals of the ads and the nationality, age, class, and economic status of the audiences? How do these ads illustrate the concept of targeting different audiences?
   c. How do the features of each ad create their appeals? How would you explain the function of the setting in the Grand Cherokee ad, particularly the blended effect of an elegant building in a courtyard and an apparent waterfall? What effect is created by the woman looking down on the driver from a lighted window? Why is she behind the waterfall? Why is it a night scene rather than a day scene? In the Jeep Wrangler ad, why did the ad designers opt for humor? Why do they have the hiker carrying all the "stuff" rather than showing it packed in the Wrangler? Why is the setting a dry desert rather than a mountaintop or beach?
3. Sport-utility vehicles are at the center of the public controversy over global warming, pollution of the environment, and the growing shortage of fossil fuel. Critics of SUVs commonly point out two ironies: (1) these vehicles, which are designed to take people out into nature, are contributing disproportionately to the destruction of nature; and (2) these all-terrain vehicles are often used in urban driving that does not call for the size, power, or features of SUVs. How do these ads work to deflect these criticisms and "hide" these ironies?

How to Analyze an Advertisement

It is now time to examine advertising in more detail. In the previous section, we said that you should always analyze images within their specific rhetorical context. To analyze ads, you need to understand the context in which advertisers work—their specific goals and strategies.

Understanding an Advertiser's Goals and Strategies

Although some advertisements are primarily informational—explaining why the company believes its product is superior—most advertisements involve parity products such as soft drinks, deodorants, breakfast cereals, toothpaste, and jeans. (*Parity* products are products that are roughly equal in quality to their competitors and so can't be promoted through any rational or scientific proof of superiority.)

Advertisements for parity products usually use psychological and motivational strategies to associate a product with a target audience's (often subconscious) dreams, hopes, fears, desires, and wishes, suggesting that the product will magically dispel these fears and anxieties or magically deliver on values, desires, and dreams. Using sophisticated research techniques, advertisers study how people's fears, dreams, and values differ according to their ethnicity, gender, educational level, socioeconomic class, age, and so forth; this research allows advertisers to tailor their appeals precisely to the target audience.

Furthermore, advertisers often focus on long-range advertising campaigns rather than on just a single ad. Their goal is not simply to sell a product but to build brand loyalty or a relationship with consumers that will be long lasting. (Think of how the brand Marlboro has a different image from the brand Winston, or how Calvin Klein's "heroin chic" of the late 1990s differed from Tommy Hilfiger's "American freedom" image.) Advertisers try to convert a brand name from a label on a can or on the inside of a sweater to a field of qualities, values, and imagery that lives inside the heads of its targeted consumers. An ad campaign, therefore, uses subtle repetition of themes through a variety of individual ads aimed at building up a psychological link between the product and the consumer. Advertisers don't just want you to buy Nikes rather than Reeboks, but also to see yourself as a Nike kind of person who attributes part of your identity to Nikes. Some ad campaigns have been brilliant at turning whole segments of a population into loyal devotees of a brand. Among the most famous campaigns are the Volkswagen ads of the 1950s and early 1960s, the long-lived Marlboro cowboy ads, the independent female theme of Virginia Slims ads, and more recently, the dairy farmers and milk processors' "Got Milk?" ads in magazines and on billboards that feature all kinds of celebrities with milk mustaches, making it "cool" to drink milk.

How Advertisers Target Specific Audiences

When advertisers produce an ad, they create images and copy intended to appeal to the values, hopes, and desires of a specific audience. How do they know the psychological attributes of a specific audience? Much of the market research on which advertisers rely is based on an influential demographic tool developed by SRI Research called the "VALS" (Values And Lifestyle System).* This system divides consumers into three basic categories with further subdivision:

1. **Needs-driven consumers.** Poor, with little disposable income, these consumers generally spend their money only on basic necessities.
   - *Survivors:* Live on fixed incomes or have no disposable income. Advertising seldom targets this group.
   - *Sustainers:* Have very little disposable income, but often spend what they have impulsively on low-end, mass-market items.
2. **Outer-directed consumers.** These consumers want to identify with certain in-groups, to "keep up with the Joneses," or to surpass them.
   - *Belongers:* Believe in traditional family values and are conforming, nonexperimental, nostalgic, and sentimental. They are typically blue-collar or

---

*Our discussion of VALS is adapted from Harold W. Berkman and Christopher Gibson, *Advertising,* 2nd ed. (New York: Random House, 1987), pp. 134–137.

lower middle class, and they buy products associated with Mom, apple pie, and the American flag.

- *Emulators:* Are ambitious and status conscious. They have a tremendous desire to associate with currently popular in-groups. They are typically young, have at least moderate disposable income, are urban and upwardly mobile, and buy conspicuous items that are considered "in."
- *Achievers:* Have reached the top in a competitive environment. They buy to show off their status and wealth and to reward themselves for their hard climb up the ladder. They have high incomes and buy top-of-the-line luxury items that say "success." They regard themselves as leaders and persons of stature.

3. ***Inner-directed consumers.*** These consumers are individualistic and buy items to suit their own tastes rather than to symbolize their status.

- *I-am-me types:* Are young, independent, and often from affluent backgrounds. They typically buy expensive items associated with their individual interests (such as mountain bikes, stereo equipment, or high-end camping gear), but may spend very little on clothes, cars, or furniture.
- *Experiential types:* Are process-oriented and often reject the values of corporate America in favor of alternative lifestyles. They buy organic foods, make their own bread, do crafts and music, value holistic medicine, and send their children to alternative kindergartens.
- *Socially conscious types:* Believe in simple living and are concerned about the environment and the poor. They emphasize the social responsibility of corporations, take on community service, and actively promote their favorite causes. They have middle to high incomes and are usually very well educated.

No one fits exactly into any one category, and most people exhibit traits of several categories, but advertisers are interested in statistical averages, not individuals. When a company markets an item, it enlists advertising specialists to help target the item to a particular market segment. Budweiser is aimed at belongers, while upscale microbeers are aimed at emulators or achievers. To understand more precisely the fears and values of a target group, researchers can analyze subgroups within each of these VALS segments by focusing specifically on women, men, children, teenagers, young adults, or retirees or on specified ethnic or regional minorities. Researchers also determine what kinds of families and relationships are valued in each of the VALS segments, who in a family initiates demand for a product, and who in a family makes the actual purchasing decisions. Thus, ads aimed at belongers depict traditional families; ads aimed at I-am-me types may depict more ambiguous sexual or family relationships. Advertisements aimed at women can be particularly complex because of women's conflicting social roles in our society. When advertisers target the broader category of gender, they sometimes sweep away VALS distinctions and try to evoke more deeply embedded emotional and psychological responses.

For Writing and Discussion

You own a successful futon factory that has marketed its product primarily to experiential types. Your advertisements have associated futons with holistic health, spiritualism (transcendental meditation, yoga), and organic wholesomeness (all-natural materials, gentle people working in the factory, incense and sitar music in your retail stores, and so forth). You have recently expanded your factory and now produce twice as many futons as you did six months ago. Unfortunately, demand hasn't increased correspondingly. Your market research suggests that if you are going to increase demand for futons, you have to reach other VALS segments.

Working in small groups, develop ideas for a magazine or TV advertisement that might sell futons to one or more of the other target segments in the VALS system. Your instructor can assign a different target segment to each group, or each group can decide for itself which target segment constitutes the likeliest new market for futons.

Groups should then share their ideas with the whole class.

Sample Analysis of an Advertisement

With an understanding of possible photographic effects and the compositional features of ads, you now have all the background knowledge needed to begin doing your own analysis of ads. To illustrate how an analysis of an ad can reveal the ad's persuasive strategies, we show you our analysis of an ad for Coors Light (Figure 11.4) that ran in a variety of women's magazines. First, consider the contrast between the typical beer ads that are aimed at men (showing women in bikinis fulfilling adolescent male sexual fantasies or men on fishing trips or in sports bars, representing male comradeship and bonding) and this Coors Light ad with its "Sam and Me" theme.

Rather than associating beer drinking with a wild party, this ad associates beer drinking with the warm friendship of a man and a woman, with just a hint of potential romance. The ad shows a man and a woman, probably in their early- to mid-twenties, in relaxed conversation; they are sitting casually on a tabletop, with their legs resting on chair seats. The woman is wearing casual pants, a summery cotton top, and informal shoes. Her braided, shoulder-length hair has a healthy, mussed appearance, and one braid comes across the front of her shoulder. She is turned away from the man, leans on her knees, and holds a bottle of Coors Light. Her sparkling eyes are looking up, and she smiles happily, as if reliving a pleasant memory. The man is wearing slacks, a cotton shirt with the sleeves rolled up, and scuffed tennis shoes with white socks. He also has a reminiscing smile on his face, and he leans on the woman's shoulder. The words "Coors Light. Just between friends." appear immediately below the picture next to a Coors Light can.

This ad appeals to women's desire for close friendships and relationships. Everything about the picture signifies long-established closeness and intimacy—

FIGURE 11.4 Beer Ad Aimed at Women

old friends rather than lovers. The way the man leans on the woman shows her strength and independence. Additionally, the way they pose, with the woman slightly forward and sitting up more than the man, results in their taking up equal space in the picture. In many ads featuring male-female couples, and man appears larger and taller than the woman; this picture signifies mutuality and equality.

The words of the ad help interpret the relationship. Sam and the woman have been friends since the first grade, and they are reminiscing about old times. The relationship is thoroughly mutual. Sometimes he brings the Coors Light and sometimes she brings it; sometimes she does the listening and sometimes he does; sometimes she leans on his shoulder and sometimes he leans on hers. Sometimes the ad says, "Sam and me"; sometimes it says, "me and Sam." Even the "bad grammar" of "Sam and me" (rather than "Sam and I") suggests the lazy, relaxed absence of pretense or formality.

These two are reliable, old buddies. But the last three lines of the copy give just a hint of potential romance: "Me and Sam? Together? I've never even thought about it. Okay, so I've thought about it." Whereas beer ads targeting men portray women as sex objects, this ad appeals to many women's desire for relationships and for romance that is rooted in friendship rather than sex.

And why the name "Sam"? Students in our classes have hypothesized that Sam is a "buddy" kind of name rather than a romantic-hero name. Yet it is more modern and more interesting than other buddy names such as "Bob" or "Bill" or "Dave." "A 'Sam,'" said one of our students, "is more mysterious than a 'Bill.'" Whatever associations the name strikes in you, be assured that the admakers spent hours debating possible names until they hit on this one. For an additional example of an ad analysis, see the sample student essay (pp. 320–323).

For Writing and Discussion

1. Examine any of the ads reprinted in this chapter or magazine ads brought to class by students or your instructor, and analyze them in detail, paying particular attention to setting, furnishings, and props; characters, roles, and actions; photographic effects; and words and copy. Prior to discussion, freewrite your own analysis of the chosen ad.

2. An excellent way to learn how to analyze ads is to create your own advertisement. Read the following introduction to a brief article with the headline "Attention Advertisers: Real Men Do Laundry." This article appeared in an issue of *American Demographics,* a magazine that helps advertisers target particular audiences based on demographic analysis of the population.

> Commercials almost never show men doing the laundry, but nearly one-fifth of men do at least seven loads a week. Men don't do as much laundry as women, but the washday gap may be closing. In the dual-career 1990's laundry is going unisex.
>
> Forty-three percent of women wash at least seven loads of laundry a week, compared with 19 percent of men, according to a survey conducted for Lever Brothers Company, manufacturers of Wisk detergent. Men do 29 percent of the 419 million loads of laundry Americans wash each week. Yet virtually all laundry-detergent advertising is aimed at women.

Working in small groups, create an idea for a laundry-detergent ad to be placed in a men's magazine such as *Men's Health, Sports Illustrated, Field and Stream,* or *Esquire.* Draw a rough sketch of your ad that includes the picture, the placement of words, and a rough idea of the content of the words. Pay particular attention to the visual features of your ad—the models, their ages, ethnicity, social status or class, and dress; the setting, such as a self-service laundry or a home laundry room; and other features. When you have designed a possible approach, explain why you think your ad will be successful.

Cultural Perspectives on Advertisements

There isn't space here to examine in depth the numerous cultural issues raised by advertisements, but we can introduce you to a few of them and provide some thought-provoking tasks for exploratory writing and talking. The key issue we want you to think about in this section is how advertisements not only reflect the cultural values and the economic and political structures of the society that produces them but also actively construct and reproduce that society.

For example, look at the 1924 advertisement for the Hoover vacuum cleaner shown in Figure 11.5. This ad appealed to a middle class that was becoming more dependent on household inventions as the use of domestic help became less common. In this ad, a well-dressed wife with carefully-styled hair embraces her well-dressed husband as he returns from a day of work in the business world. Notice that the image and the words reinforce the idea of distinct gender roles while promoting pride in a comfortable, clean, and aesthetically pleasing home. The ad sells more than Hoover vacuum cleaners; it sells a vision of middle class domestic harmony in which the wife's "natural" role is housecleaning.

In its depiction of gender roles, the Hoover ad now strikes us as very old-fashioned. However, cultural critics often argue that contemporary advertisements continue to depict women in culturally subordinate ways. In 1979, the influential sociologist and semiotician* Erving Goffman published a book called *Gender Advertising,* arguing that the way in which women are pictured in advertisements removes them from serious power. In many cases, Goffman's point seems self-evident. Women in advertisements are often depicted in frivolous, childlike, exhibitionistic, sexual, or silly poses that would be considered undignified for a man, such as the "Of Sound Body" Zenith Ad (Figure 11.6). Women in advertisements are often fun to look at or enthralling to "gaze" at, but are seldom portrayed in positions of power. What distinguishes Goffman's work is his analysis of apparently positive portrayals of women in advertisements. He points out tiny details that differentiate the treatment of men from that of women. For example, when men hold umbrellas in an ad, it is usually raining, but women often hold umbrellas for decoration; men grip objects tightly, but women often caress objects or cup them in a gathering in or nurturing way. Female models dance and jump and wiggle in front of the camera (like children playing), whereas male models generally

*A *semiotician* is a person who studies the meanings of signs in a culture. A *sign* is any human-produced artifact or gesture that conveys meaning. It can be anything from a word to a facial expression to the arrangement of silverware at a dinner table.

FIGURE 11.5   Hoover Ad

you darling!

"Give her a Hoover and you give her the Best"

The HOOVER

It BEATS … as it Sweeps   as it Cleans

ANOTHER year has slipped by since you last thought of giving her a Hoover.

But *she* has thought of it many times.

As cleaning days come and go she struggles resolutely with the only "tools" she has in her "workshop," your home.

And they are woefully inadequate, wasteful of time and strength.

As she wields her broom foot by foot across the dusty, dirty rugs her arms rebel and her back seems near to breaking.

Yet she tries to greet you with a smile when you come home at night.

In your heart you pay her tribute. "She's a brave little woman," you say.

But why put her courage to such an unfair test?

Why ask her to bear her burdens patiently when they can so easily be lifted?

The Hoover will save her strength.

The Hoover will speed her work.

The Hoover will safeguard her pride in a clean home.

You cannot afford to deny her these things for the small monthly payments which The Hoover costs.

Don't disappoint her again this Christmas!

Show her that you really *do* care, and throughout her lifetime your thoughtfulness will be ever in her mind.

FIGURE 11.6   Zenith Audio Products Ad

stand or sit in a dignified manner. Even when trying to portray a powerful and independent woman, ads reveal cultural signs that the woman is subordinate.

A decade later, another cultural critic, researcher Jean Kilbourne, made a more explicit argument against the way advertisements negatively construct women. In her films *Still Killing Us Softly* (1987) and *Slim Hopes: Advertising and the Obsession with Thinness* (1995), Kilbourne argues that our culture's fear of powerful women is embodied in advertisements that entrap women in futile pursuit of an impossible, flawless standard of beauty. Advertisements help construct the social values that pressure women (particularly middle-class white women) to stay thin, frail, and little-girlish and thus become perfect objects. In *Slim Hopes,* she claims that basically only one body type is preferred (the waif look or the waif-made-voluptuous-with-reconstructed-breasts look). Further, the dismemberment of women in ads—the focus on individual body parts—both objectifies women and intensifies women's anxious concentration on trying to perfect each part of their bodies. Kilbourne asserts that ads distort women's attitudes toward food through harmful and contradictory messages that encourage binging while equating moral goodness with thinness and control over eating. Ads convert women into lifelong consumers of beauty and diet products while undermining their self-esteem.

To what extent do the criticisms of Goffman or Kilbourne still apply to the most current advertisements? To what extent has advertising made gains in portraying women as strong, independent, intelligent, and equal with men in their potential for professional status? The picture painted by Goffman and Kilbourne is complicated by some new ads—for example, the new genre of physical fitness ads that emphasize women's physical strength and capabilities as well as their sexuality and femininity. Ads for athletic products feature models with beautiful hair and faces and strong, trim, and shapely bodies. These ads strike different balances between female athleticism and sexuality, perhaps creating a more powerful view of women. (See the ad for Adidas "Adrenaline" Figure 11.7.) It is also more common today to find ads picturing women in professional "business executive" roles. For example, how much cultural power is possessed by the woman in the AT&T calling card ad in Figure 11.8?

For Writing and Discussion

To test for yourself the extent to which Goffman and Kilbourne's claims about ads still apply, we invite you to explore this issue in the following sequence of activities, which combine class discussion with invitations for exploratory writing.

1. Examine again the four ads discussed in the previous section: the Hoover ad (Figure 11.5); the "Of Sound Body" Zenith ad (Figure 11.6); the Adidas "Adrenaline" ad (Figure 11.7); and the AT&T Calling Card ad (Figure 11.8). To what extent does each of these ads construct women as lacking in power in the economic, political, and professional structures of our culture? Which ads, if any, treat women as powerful? Using these ads as your evidence, draw some conclusions about how the social roles for women have changed in the last eighty years. Freewrite your responses to the way women are constructed in these ads as preparation for class discussion.

FIGURE 11.7 Adidas "Adrenaline" Ad

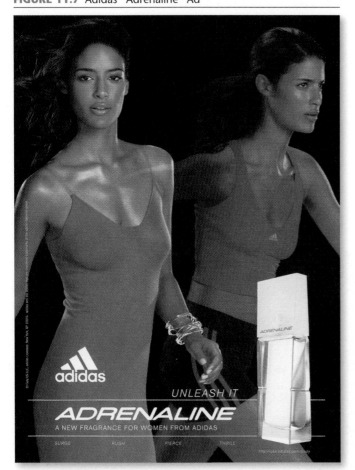

2. Consider again the AT&T Calling Card ad (Figure 11.8). To what extent would you call the woman in this ad an empowered professional? How might Goffman or Kilbourne argue that this ad subtly subordinates women? Try playing the "What if they changed . . . .?" game with this ad. What would be different if this ad featured a man rather than a woman to advertise the calling card? How would the image change? How would the verbal text change?

The "What if they changed . . . ?" game is explained earlier in this chapter on pp. 295–296.

3. Bring to class advertisements for women's clothing, perfumes, or accessories from recent fashion and beauty magazines such as *Glamour, Elle, InStyle,* and *Vogue.* Study the ways that female models are typically posed in these ads. Then have male students assume the postures of the female models. How many of the postures, which look natural for women, seem ludicrous when adopted by men? To what extent are these postures really

(continued)

FIGURE 11.8 AT&T Calling Card Ad

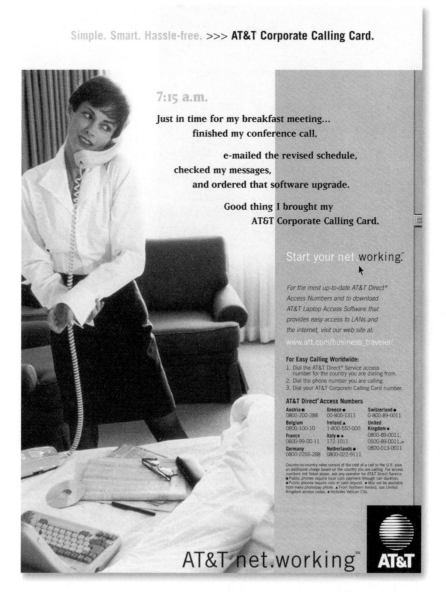

natural for women? To what extent do these postures illustrate Goffman's point that advertisements don't take women seriously?

4. Bring to class some examples of recent advertisements that you think portray women in a particularly positive and empowered way—ads that you think neither Goffman nor Kilbourne could deconstruct to show the subordination of women in our culture. Share your examples with the class and see whether your classmates agree with your assessment of these ads.

READINGS

Our first reading is an excerpt from Paul Messaris's book *Visual Persuasion: The Role of Images in Advertising*. Messaris, a communications professor at the University of Pennsylvania, intended this book for an academic audience (hence his frequent parenthetical references to other scholars). His purpose is to analyze the distinctive features of visual communication and to examine the role of visual images in political campaigns and commercial advertising. In the following excerpt, Messaris explains his position on the ethical responsibility of advertisers. The particular question at issue is whether advertisers are being unethical when they display certain groups of people—in this passage, adolescents and African-Americans—in ways that are stereotypical, unrealistic, or potentially harmful to individuals or society.

Paul Messaris
From Visual Persuasion:
The Role of Images in Advertising

1   As we have seen, the iconicity* of images makes it possible for ads to elicit our attention and emotions by simulating various significant features of our real-world visual experiences. By virtue of their iconicity, visual ads are able to erect before our eyes a mirror world, with whose inhabitants we are invited to identify or to imagine that we are interacting. These acts of identification and imaginary interaction have real-world consequences. Some of the most revealing analyses of advertising have described the ways in which viewers use the characters they see in ads as reference points for their own evolving identities (Barthel, 1988; Ewen, 1988; Ewen & Ewen, 1982). For example, Carol Moog (1990) recalls how, as a young girl, she studied the posture of a woman in a refrigerator commercial to learn how to carry herself as an adult (p. 13). Together with fictional movies and TV programs, ads are a major source of images that young people can use to previsualize their places in the world of sexual and status relationships. It can be argued that advertisers have an ethical responsibility to take these circumstances into account in fashioning the images that they place before the public.

2   What might constitute a violation of this ethical responsibility? Critics of advertising images often focus on the discrepancy between the vision of life offered in ads and the needs or abilities of real people. Drawing on her practice as a psychotherapist, Moog (1990) cites the story of a young lawyer who expressed dissatisfaction with her life because she had not lived up to her potential as a member of "the Pepsi generation"—that is, "beautiful, sexy, happy, young people . . . a generation that didn't slog through law school, work twelve-hour days, or break up with fiancés" (p. 15). Moog presents this

---

Iconicity is an academic term (related to *icon*, meaning "image") referring to the power of images to influence a viewer. When you desire, for example, to meet a stranger in a Parisian café or to ride a horse through the pounding surf because you saw characters do these things in an ad, you experience the *iconic power* of the image.

vignette as a reminder of the fact that "advertisers are not in the business of making people feel better about themselves, they're in the *selling* business" (p. 16). As this statement implies, commercial advertising often does create a vision of a fantasy world that may become a source of dissatisfaction in people's real lives, and this is especially true of ads that use sex or status as part of their appeal. Some people may find this practice objectionable in and of itself, although in my view it would be rather fatuous, as well as somewhat puritanical, to suggest that advertisers should stop purveying the images of "beautiful, sexy, happy young people" that led to Moog's client's distress. However, there is a related trend in advertising that does seem to me to raise especially troublesome ethical issues.

3   In recent years, ads aimed at young people have increasingly sought to appeal to an adolescent sense of frustration and resentment at the constricting demands of adult society. There may be a lingering element of this type of sentiment in the dissatisfaction expressed by Moog's client, but the kind of advertising to which I am referring is quite different from the old, Pepsi-generation style of happy, carefree images. Instead, these more recent ads, for products such as athletic shoes, off-road vehicles, or video games, often make a point of displaying abrasive, belligerent behavior and physical recklessness (cf. Lull, 1995, pp. 73–81). A defender of such ads might argue that they are simply being honest. Adolescents often have good reason to chafe at the standards imposed on them by older people and to recoil from the vision of the future that many of them face. The aggression and recklessness depicted in some of these ads are no doubt authentic expressions of how many young people feel. To put a happy face on those feelings could be considered hypocritical. Nevertheless, with due respect for such views, I would argue that the type of resentment exploited in these ads is unproductive at best, counterproductive at worst. Dissatisfaction that leads to impulsiveness and disregard for other people gains nothing from being expressed openly. In that sense, I would say that the ethics of this genre of advertising are certainly questionable.

4   This is not to say, however, that advertising aimed at young people should necessarily revert to the untroubled imagery of earlier times. It should be possible to portray and address youth honestly without pandering to the irresponsible tendencies that are sometimes associated with adolescence. For instance, despite the criticism that has recently been directed at the advertising of Calvin Klein, it seems to me that there are many Calvin Klein ads that manage to strike this balance quite effectively. In particular, the print ads for cK one fragrance have generated record-breaking sales while presenting a view of youthful sexuality that is remarkably unglamorized (compared to most other ads) and, furthermore, notably inclusive both racially and in terms of sexual orientation. This inclusiveness deserves special mention. The cK one ads are among the few examples of mass-produced imagery in which the mingling of people from different backgrounds appears relatively natural, rather than an artificial (albeit well-meaning) concoction of the media.

5   But, again, this comment should not be interpreted as a blanket endorsement of unvarnished naturalism in all of advertising. In a recent discussion of the portrayal of blacks and whites in the mass media, DeMott (1995) has argued that movies and ads present a phony picture of harmony between the races that serves to obscure the unpleasant truth about race relations in the United States. I do not find this argument persuasive. For one thing, information about racial friction is abundantly available elsewhere in the media. More importantly, though, I think it is a mistake to assume that people always look at advertising images expecting to see the way things really are in society. Almost by definition, the portrayals of the good life presented in ads carry with them the implicit understanding that they are idealizations, not documentary reports (cf. Schudson, 1984). What people look for in such ads is a vision of the way things ought to be. Furthermore, when an ad is produced by a large corporation, people are likely to see this vision as an indicator of socially approved values—even though it also may be understood tacitly that those values do not correspond very closely to current social reality. From this perspective, the kinds of advertisements that DeMott criticizes—depictions of people from different racial and ethnic backgrounds living together in harmony and prosperity—are actually highly desirable. For example, an American Express Gold Card ad (attacked by DeMott) shows elegantly dressed blacks and whites occupying adjacent box seats in an opulent-looking theater or concert hall, while an ad for Chubb Insurance portrays two suburban families, one black, one white, posing together in a setting of obvious wealth. Such ads should be praised, not subjected to carping objections. In my view, they are models of the responsible use of advertising's iconic powers.

Thinking Critically about *Visual Persuasion*

1. Messaris seeks to establish a middle position between two extreme views of advertisers' responsibility to viewers and consumers. How would you describe his view and the extremes he is reacting against?
2. Can you find examples of adolescent-directed ads portraying, in Messaris's words, "abrasive, belligerent behavior and physical recklessness"? What points can you raise in support of or against his censure of this type of ad?
3. Over the last two decades, the number of magazine ads featuring persons of color has increased substantially. Sometimes ads show multiracial groups. At other times, especially in middlebrow magazines such as *Parents' Magazine, Working Mother, Good Housekeeping,* or *Sports Illustrated,* ads now feature models from minority groups, where formerly the models would have been white. Observe closely the ads shown in Figures 11.9 through 11.12. Although we will call Figure 11.12 an "ad," it is actually a photograph of a huge poster placed on the wall of a youth-oriented clothing store in an urban shopping mall. To what extent do these ads present a harmonious multiracial and multicultural society?

FIGURE 11.9 MetLife Ad

If you knew you had a safety net, how high would you climb?
Our advisors can create a personal plan to build your financial freedom. So you can focus on what really matters. Click metlife.com, call 800-MetLife or stop by for more on the range of products in our Protection and Investment Portfolios.
MetLife
Financial Services
have you met life today?

Courtesy of MetLife. PEANUTS © United Feature Syndicate, Inc.

FIGURE 11.10 PINE-SOL® Household Cleaner Ad

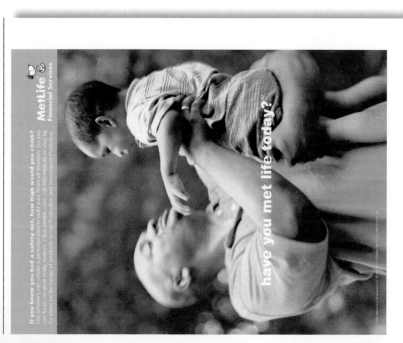

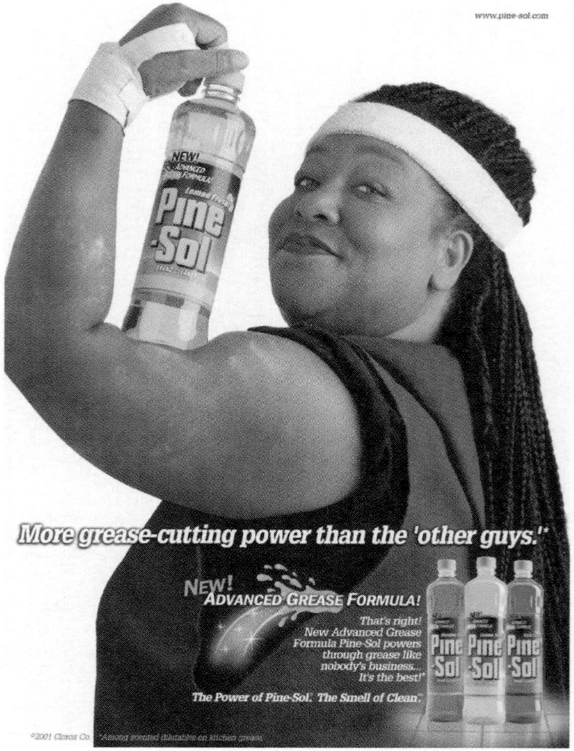

www.pine-sol.com
More grease-cutting power than the 'other guys.'*
NEW! ADVANCED GREASE FORMULA!
That's right! New Advanced Grease Formula Pine-Sol powers through grease like nobody's business... It's the best!"
The Power of Pine-Sol. The Smell of Clean.
©2001 Clorox Co.
Pine-Sol

© 2001 The Clorox Company. Reprinted with permission. PINE-SOL® is a registered trademark of the Clorox Company. Used with permission.

FIGURE 11.12 Wall Poster in Clothing Store

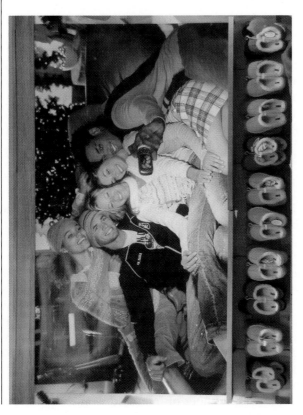

FIGURE 11.11 Vokal by Nelly Ad

Do any of them contain racial or ethnic stereotypes? What vision of social reality, race, and class are these ads constructing?

4. Messaris refers to the argument of Benjamin DeMott that buddy movies featuring pals from different races or "happy harmony" ads showing blacks and whites together create a false sense that America no longer has a race problem. How do you think Messaris and DeMott would analyze the ads in Figures 11.9 through 11.12? Do you think the clothing store poster (Figure 11.12) illustrates DeMott's idea of a "happy harmony" ad? How would you describe the difference in the image of black males in the MetLife ad (Figure 11.9) and the Vokal ad (Figure 11.11)? How would the effect of the MetLife ad differ if the model were dressed like Nelly? Why doesn't Nelly dress like the MetLife model?

5. Messaris distinguishes between ads that include people of different races "naturally" and those that appear "artificial" and "concocted." Do the ads in Figures 11.9 and 11.11 seem to you to be natural or artificially concocted? Why or why not?

6. These ads also raise questions about the intersection of race and gender. We have asked how Messaris and DeMott might analyze these ads. Now ask how Goffman and Kilbourne might analyze them. Imagine the PINE-SOL Household Cleaner ad (Figure 11.10) using a white model rather than a black model (same pose, clothing, and body type with only the skin color changed). Would the ad work? Why or why not? Also consider the clothing store poster (Figure 11.12). The poster image features three women and two men. Why did the poster designers choose that ratio rather than, say, three men and two women or an even number of men and women? Would the effect of the ad be different if the models were placed in a different order? What impression of young people do you think the poster designers were trying to achieve? How is that impression dependent upon the arrangement and posing of the models by gender and race?

The final reading is a student essay written in response to the assignment in this chapter. It contrasts the strategies of two different cigarette ads to make smoking appear socially desirable despite public sentiment to the contrary.

Stephen Bean (Student)
How Cigarette Advertisers Address the Stigma Against Smoking:
A Tale of Two Ads

1   Any smoker can tell you there's a social stigma attached to smoking in this country. With smokers being pushed out of restaurants, airports, and many office buildings, how could anyone not feel like a pariah lighting up? While never associated with the churchgoing crowd, smoking is increasing-

ly viewed as lower class or as a symbol of rebellion. Smoking has significantly decreased among adults while increasing among teenagers and young adults in recent years—a testament to its growing status as an affront to middle- and upper-class values. Cigarette advertisers are sharply tuned into this cultural attitude. They must decide whether to overcome the working-class/rebellious image of smoking in their advertisements or use it to their advantage. The answer to this question lies in what type of people they want an ad to target—the young? the rich? the poor?—and in what values, insecurities, and desires they think this group shares. Two contrasting answers to these questions are apparent in recent magazine ads for Benson & Hedges cigarettes and for Richland cigarettes.

2   The ad for Benson & Hedges consists of a main picture and a small insert picture below the main one. The main picture shows five women (perhaps thirty years old) sitting around, talking, and laughing in the living room of a comfortable and urbane home or upscale apartment. The room is filled with natural light and is tastefully decorated with antique lamps and Persian rugs. The women have opened a bottle of wine, and a couple of glasses have been poured. They are dressed casually but fashionably, ranging from slightly hip to slightly conservative. One woman wears a loose, black, sleeveless dress; another wears grungesque boots with a sweater and skirt. One of the women, apparently the hostess, sits on a sofa a bit apart from the others, smiles with pleasure at the conversation and laughter of her friends, and knits. Two of the women are smoking, and three aren't. No smoke is visible coming from the cigarettes. Underneath the main picture is a small insert photograph of the hostess—the one knitting in the main picture—in a different pose. She is now leaning back in pleasure, apparently after the party, and this time she is smoking a cigarette. Underneath the photos reads the slogan "For people who like to smoke."

3   The ad for Richland cigarettes shows a couple in their late twenties sitting in a diner or perhaps a tavern off the freeway. The remains of their lunch—empty burger and fries baskets, a couple of beer bottles—lie on the table. They seem to be talking leisurely, sharing an after-meal smoke. The man is wearing black jeans and a black T-shirt. The woman is wearing a pinkish skirt and tank top. Learning back with her legs apart she sits in a position that signals sexuality. The slogan reads, "It's all right here." And at the bottom of the ad, "Classic taste. Right price." Outside the window of the diner you can see a freeway sign slightly blurred as if from heated air currents.

4   Whom do these different advertisements target? What about them might people find appealing? Clearly the Benson & Hedges ad is aimed at women, especially upper-middle-class women who wish to appear successful. As the media have noted lately, the social stigma against smoking is strongest among middle- and upper-class adults. My sense of the B&H ad is that it is targeting younger, college-educated women who feel social pressure to quit smoking. To them the ad is saying, "Smoking makes you no less sophisticated; it only shows that you have a fun side too. Be comfortable doing whatever makes you happy."

5   What choices did the advertisers make in constructing this scene to create this message? The living room—with its antique lamps and vases, its Persian rugs and hardcover books, and its wall hanging thrown over what appears to be an old trunk—creates a sense of comfortable, tasteful, upscale living. But figuring out the people in the room is more difficult. Who are these women? What is their story? What brought them together this afternoon? Where did their money come from? Are these professional women with high-paying jobs, or are they the wives of young bankers, attorneys, and stockbrokers? One woman has a strong business look—short hair feathered back, black sleeveless dress—but why is she dressed this way on what is apparently a Saturday afternoon? In contrast, another woman has a more hip, almost grunge look—slightly spiky hair that's long in the back, a loose sweater, a black skirt, and heavy black boots. Only one woman wears a wedding ring. It seems everything about these women resists easy definition or categorization. The most striking image in the ad is the hostess knitting. She looks remarkably domestic, almost motherly, with her knees drawn close, leaning over her knitting and smiling to herself as others laugh out loud. Her presence gives the scene a feeling of safety and old-fashioned values amidst the images of independence. Interestingly, we get a much different image of the hostess in the insert picture placed just above the B&H logo. This picture shows the hostess leaning back pleasurably on the couch and smoking. The image is undeniably sexual. Her arms are back; she's deeply relaxed; the two top buttons of her blouse are open; her hair is slightly mussed; she smokes languidly, taking full pleasure in the cigarette, basking in the party's afterglow.

6   The opposing images in the advertisement (knitting/smoking, conservative/hip, wife/career, safe/independent, domestic/sexual) mean that these women can't easily be defined—as smokers or as anything else. For an ad promoting smoking, the cigarettes themselves take a back seat. In the main picture the cigarettes are hardly noticeable; the two women holding cigarettes do so inconspicuously and there is no visible smoke. The ad doesn't say so much that it is good to smoke, but that it is okay to smoke. Smoking will not make you less sophisticated. If anything, it only shows that you have an element of youth and fun. The slogan, "For people who like to smoke," targets nonsmokers as much as it does smokers—not so much to take up smoking but to be more tolerant of those who choose to smoke. The emphasis is on choice, independence, and acceptance of others' choices. The ad attacks the social stigma against smoking; it eases the conscience of "people who like to smoke."

7   While the B&H ad hopes to remove the stigma attached to smoking, the Richland ad feasts on it. Richland cigarettes aren't for those cultivating the upper-class look. The ad goes for a rebellious, gritty image, for beer drinkers, not wine sippers. While the story of the women in the B&H ad is difficult to figure out, the Richland ad gives us a classic image: a couple on the road who have stopped at a diner or tavern. Here the story is simpler: a man and

woman being cool. They are going down the freeway to the big city. I picture a heavy American cruising car parked out front. Everything about the ad has a gritty, blue-collar feel. They sit at a booth with a Formica tabletop; the walls are bare, green-painted wood. The man is dressed in black with a combed-back, James Dean haircut. The woman wears a pink skirt with a tank top; her shoulder-length hair hasn't been fussed over, and she wears a touch of make-up. Empty baskets and bottles cluttering the table indicate they had a classic American meal—hamburgers, fries, and a beer—eaten for pleasure without politically correct worries about calories, polyunsaturated fats, cruelty to animals, or cancer. While the sexual imagery in the B&H ad is subtle, in the Richland ad it is blatant. The man is leaning forward with his elbows on the table; the woman is leaning back with her legs spread and her skirt pushed up slightly. Her eyes are closed. They smoke leisurely, and the woman holds the cigarette a couple of inches from her expecting lips. The slogan, "It's all right here," is centered beneath the woman's skirt. Smoking, like sex, is about pure pleasure—something to be done slowly. Far from avoiding working-class associations with smoking, this ad aims to reinforce them. The cigarettes are clearly visible, and, unlike the cigarettes in the B&H ad, show rings of rising smoke. This ad promotes living for the moment. The more rebellious, the better.

8   So we see, then, two different ways that cigarette companies address the stigma against smoking. The B&H ad tries to eliminate it by targeting middle-class, college-educated women. It appeals to upscale values, associating cigarette smoking with choice, and showing that "people who like to smoke" can also knit (evoking warm, safe images of domestic life) or lean back in postparty pleasure (evoking a somewhat wilder, more sexual image). In contrast, the Richland ad exploits the stigma. It associates smoking with on-the-road freedom, rebellion, sexuality, and enjoyment of the moment. The smoke visibly rising from the cigarettes in the Richland ad and noticeably absent from the Benson & Hedges ad tells the difference.

Thinking Critically about "How Cigarette Advertisers Address the Stigma Against Smoking"

1. Stephen Bean argues that the Benson & Hedges and the Richland ads use very different appeals to encourage their target audiences to smoke. What are the appeals he cites? Do you agree with Stephen's analysis?
2. Collect a variety of cigarette ads from current magazines, and analyze their various appeals. How do the ads vary according to their intended audiences? Consider ads targeted at men versus women or at audiences from different VALS segments.
3. What do you see as the strengths and weaknesses of Stephen's essay?

Composing Your Essay

Generating and Exploring Ideas

Your first task is to find two ads that sell the same general product to different target audiences or that make appeals to noticeably different value systems. Look for ads that are complex enough to invite detailed analysis. Then, analyze the ads carefully, using the strategies suggested earlier in this chapter. The sample student essay (pp. 320–323) provides an example of the kind of approach you can take.

If you get stuck, try freewriting your responses to the following questions: (a) What attracted your attention to this ad? (b) Whom do you think this ad targets? Why? (c) What photographic techniques, visual devices, and camera angles are used in this ad? (d) What props and furnishings are in this ad, and what values or meanings are attached to them? (e) What are the characters like, what are they doing, and why are they wearing what they are wearing and posed the way they are posed? (f) How do the words of the ad interplay with the picture? (g) How would the ad be less effective if its key features were changed in some way? (h) Overall, to what fears, values, hopes, or dreams is this ad appealing?

Shaping and Drafting

Your essay should be fairly easy to organize at the big-picture level, but each part will require its own organic organization depending on the main points of your analysis. At the big-picture level, you can generally follow a structure like this:

I. Introduction (hooks readers' interest, gives background on how ads vary their appeals, asks the question your paper will address, and ends with initial mapping in the form of a purpose or thesis statement)
II. General description of the two ads
   A. Description of ad 1
   B. Description of ad 2
III. Analysis of the two ads
   A. Analysis of ad 1
   B. Analysis of ad 2
IV. Conclusion (returns to the big picture for a sense of closure; makes final comments about the significance of your analysis or touches in some way on larger issues raised by the analysis)

We recommend that you write your rough draft rapidly, without worrying about gracefulness, correctness, or even getting all your ideas said at once. Many people like to begin with the description of the ads and then write the analysis before writing the introduction and the conclusion. After you have written your draft, put it aside for a while before you begin revising. We recommend that you ask classmates for a peer review of your draft early in the revising process.

Revising

Most experienced writers make global changes in their final drafts when they revise, especially when they are doing analytical writing. The act of writing a rough draft generally leads to the discovery of more ideas. You may also realize that many of your original ideas aren't clearly developed or that the draft feels scattered and unorganized.

GUIDELINES FOR PEER REVIEWS

Instructions for peer reviews are provided in Chapter 17 (pp. 519–520).

For the Writer

Prepare two or three questions you would like your peer reviewer to address while responding to your draft. The questions can focus on some aspect of your draft that you are uncertain about, on one or more sections where you particularly seek help or advice, on some feature that you particularly like about your draft, or on some part you especially wrestled with. Write out your questions and give them to your peer reviewer along with your draft.

For the Reviewer

I. Read the draft at a normal reading speed from beginning to end. As you read, do the following:
   A. Place a wavy line in the margin next to any passages that you find confusing, that contain something that doesn't seem to fit, or that otherwise slow down your reading.
   B. Place a "Good!" in the margin next to any passages where you think the writing is particularly strong or interesting.
II. Read the draft again slowly and answer the following questions by writing brief explanations of your answers.
   A. Introduction:
      1. Is the title appropriate for an academic analysis? Does it suggest the thesis and focus of the paper and pique your interest? How might the title be improved?
      2. What does the writer do to capture your interest, provide needed background, and set up the question to be addressed?
      3. How does the thesis statement, purpose statement, or forecasting statement provide the big picture for both the description and the analysis of the two ads? How might the writer improve the introduction?
   B. Description of the ads:
      1. Does the writer describe the ads in an interesting and vivid manner? How could this description help you "see" the ads more clearly?
      2. In what ways do the ads appeal to different audiences or have different value systems? What makes the ads complex enough to justify an analysis?

C. Analysis of the ads:
1. How does the analysis of the ads shed light on and build on the description of the ads?
2. How many of the following features does the writer discuss? Which could be added to deepen and complicate the analysis?
   a. Setting, props, and furnishings: how they indicate lifestyle and socioeconomic status; appeal to certain values; carry certain cultural associations or meanings; serve as symbols.
   b. Characters, roles, and actions: the story of the ad; power relationships and status of the characters; gender, age, or ethnic roles followed or violated; the significance of clothing and accessories, of hair and facial expressions, and of posing, positioning, and gestures.
   c. Photographic effects: lighting, camera angle, cropping, focus.
   d. Language and wording of the ad's copy: its overt message; feelings, mood, and values communicated through connotations, double entendres, and so forth; visual layout of copy.
3. What portions of the analysis are convincing? Which details of the ads contradict the analysis? Do you disagree with the writer's view of these ads?
4. How could the body of the paper be made clearer, better organized, or easier to follow? Where might the writer better apply the principles of clarity from Chapter 18 (starting with the big picture; putting points before particulars; using transitions; following the old/new contract)?

III. Rhetorical considerations
A. *Purpose, audience,* and *genre:* Your purpose is to write an academic paper analyzing two advertisements for an audience who hasn't seen them. How effectively does this paper describe and analyze these ads for this audience? How effectively does it meet the genre expectations for an academic paper?
B. *Logos, ethos,* and *pathos:* How convincing or effective is the logical or conceptual part of this draft? How does the writer build an *ethos* that readers will find reliable, fair, and authoritative? How does the writer connect this analysis to the interests and values of the audience?

IV. If the writer has prepared questions for you, respond to his or her inquiries.

V. Sum up what you see as the chief strengths and problem areas of this draft:
A. Strengths
B. Problem areas

VI. Read the draft one more time. Place a check mark in the margin wherever you notice problems in grammar, spelling, or mechanics (one check mark per problem).

Analyzing and Synthesizing Ideas

About the Analysis and Synthesis of Ideas

In many of your college courses, you'll be asked to explore connections and contradictions among groups of texts. Distilling main points from more than one text, seeing connections among texts, commenting on meaningful relationships, and showing how the texts have influenced your own thinking on a question are all part of the thinking and writing involved in synthesis.

Synthesis, which is a way of seeing and coming to terms with complexities, is a counterpart to *analysis.* When you analyze something, you break it down into its parts to see the relationships among them. When you synthesize, you take one more step, putting parts together in some new fashion. The cognitive researcher Benjamin Bloom has schematized "synthesis" as the fifth of six levels of thinking processes, ranked in order of complexity and challenge: knowledge, comprehension, application, analysis, *synthesis,* and evaluation. Bloom defined synthesis in these terms: "putting together of constituent elements or parts to form a whole requiring original creative thinking."* Synthesis drives those light-bulb moments when you exclaim, "Ah! Now I see how these ideas are related!"

A second useful and related way to think of synthesis is as a dialectical thinking process. Throughout this text, we have explained that college writing involves posing a significant question that often forces you to encounter clashing or contradictory ideas. Such conflicts intrigued the German philosopher Hegel, who posited that thinking proceeds dialectically when a thesis clashes against an antithesis, leading the thinker to formulate a synthesis encompassing dimensions of both the original thesis and the antithesis. When you write a synthesis essay, your interaction with a group of related texts exemplifies this dialectical process. From your encounter with alternative perspectives on an issue, you emerge with a new, enlarged perspective of your own.

This Hegelian view is also discussed in Chapter 8, pp. 195–197.

Synthesis is an especially important component of research writing, where you use synthesis to carve out your own thinking space on a research question while sifting through the writings of others. Synthesis, then, is the skill of wrestling with ideas from different texts or sources, trying to forge a new whole out of potentially confusing parts. It is the principal way you enter into a conversation on a social, civic, or scholarly issue.

---

*Benjamin Bloom, *Taxonomy of Educational Objectives: Handbook I: Cognitive Domain* (New York: David McKay, 1956).

College synthesis assignments sometimes specify the readings and the questions you are to explore, or they may, as in the case of research assignments, ask you to originate your own questions and find your own readings. Here are examples of synthesis assignments that you might encounter in different disciplines. In these sample assignments, note that the readings and focusing questions are provided in each case.

ENVIRONMENTAL POLITICS COURSE

Texts to Be Analyzed	**Synthesis Questions**
Garrett Hardin's essay on over-population, "The Tragedy of the Commons," from *Science* (1968)	Are there any common assumptions about the world's environment in these readings
Kenneth E. Boulding's essay "Economics of the Coming Spaceship Earth" (1966)	What problems and solutions appear in these readings?
A chapter from Dixie Lee Ray's *Trashing the Planet* (1992)	What direction would you take in proposing a solution?
A chapter from Ron Bailey's *The True State of the Planet* (1995)	

AMERICAN LITERATURE SURVEY COURSE

Texts to Be Analyzed	**Synthesis Questions**
Selections from the *Lowell Offering,* a publication produced in Lowell, Massachusetts, in the 1840s, featuring the writings of young female factory workers	What common questions about changes in women's social roles in the 1800s emerge in these texts?
Historian Gerda Lerner's essay "The Lady and the Mill Girl: Changes in the Status of Women in the Age of Jackson 1800–1840" (1969)	Which text gives you the clearest understanding of the problems with women's changing roles and why?
Herman Melville's short story "The Paradise of Bachelors and the Tartarus of Maids" (1835)	

FILM CRITICISM COURSE

Films to Be Analyzed	**Synthesis Questions**
Drums along the Mohawk (1939)	What similarities and differences do you see in these films' representations of Native Americans?
Fort Apache (1948)	
Dances with Wolves (1990)	How do you explain these differences?
Smoke Signals (1998)	

The assignment for this chapter is modeled after assignments like those just shown and draws on the kinds of readings you will typically be asked to synthesize in your college courses. As an introduction to synthesis thinking, this chapter provides extended examples of student writers who are analyzing and synthesizing readings on the impact of technology. Specifically, the students are asked to address a focusing question that many cultural critics are pondering: *To what extent does technology enrich or dehumanize our lives?* As one contemporary critic puts it, "Does technology liberate or enslave us?"*

Exploring the Analysis and Synthesis of Ideas

In this exercise, we ask you to read two pieces about the value and effects of technology. The first reading, "Young Entrepreneurs' Disdain for Time Off" by John Gallagher, appeared in the Business section of *The Seattle Times,* July 4, 2001. The second, "The Late, Great Outdoors" by Keith Goetzman, is from the September–October 2001 *Utne Reader.* Read these pieces carefully and then do the exercises that follow.

READINGS

John Gallagher
Young Entrepreneurs' Disdain for Time Off

1   A weeklong cruise in the Caribbean this spring left Detroit software executive John Lauer feeling so cut off from his work that he couldn't wait to get to an island.

2   "I'll pull into the port and all of a sudden get a voice-mail alert because they had cellular connectivity and I'd be, like, 'Thank God!'" He recalled, "The only reason I was glad to be on land is because my cell phone was working again."

3   The 26-year-old Lauer typifies the gigabyte lifestyle of young entrepreneurs. It's a life gladly given to stretched workdays and little time off.

4   "I hate to not be at the office," said the sandal- and T-shirt-clad chief executive and founder of Rootlevel, a Web application-service firm based in Detroit. "Fortunately, I'm as connected at home now as I am at work."

5   A compulsive workaholic? Not necessarily. Some experts think working on vacation is growing more common. Lauer's disdain for time off reflects not just a choice of the computer elite but a growing trend for many Americans, for good or for ill.

6   Once conceived of as an extended time of renewal and exploration, vacation today too often means a cramped few days juggling kids at the beach and calls to the office.

*This quotation come from Bernd Herzogenrath, "The Question Concerning Humanity: Obsolete Bodies and (Post)Digital Flesh" in the online journal *Enculturation: A Journal of Rhetoric, Writing, and Culture* 3.1 (Fall 2000). We accessed this article on March 27, 2002 at http://www.uta.edu/huma/enculturation/3_1/herzogenrath/.

7   The New York-based Families and Work Institute reported in May that 26 percent of 1,003 adults surveyed do not take all the vacation to which they are entitled. They blamed the demands of their jobs.

8   Among the managerial class, the toll looks even worse. A 1999 survey of 5,000 executives by the Cleveland-based Management Recruiters International reported that 82 percent said they checked in with their office while on vacation.

9

Vacation Time
Average annual vacation days per employee, by country:

U.S.	13
Japan	25
S. Korea	25
Canada	26
Britain	28
Brazil	34
Germany	35
France	37
Italy	42

Such behavior can take a toll. Some 55 percent of employees who skip some or all of their vacation say they experience feelings of being overworked, vs. 27 percent of those who use all their vacation, the Families and Work Institute study found.

10   Perhaps worst of all, paid vacation isn't even an option for most of the nation's working poor.

11   Eileen Appelbaum, an economist with the Washington, D.C.-based Economic Policy Institute, a think tank that studies poverty issues, said that of the people who make less than $10 an hour—roughly one in five workers—two-thirds either have had no paid vacation for the past five years or had some years with no time off.

12   When the working poor do get paid time off, it's usually one week or less per year.

13   "Paid vacation is definitely a middle-class-or-better benefit," Appelbaum said.

14   Americans clearly are of two minds about working during vacation. Many bemoan the trend. Others, like Lauer, don't seem to care.

15   "I cannot be disconnected," Lauer said. "Going on vacation is horrible. It's absolutely miserable."

16   Today's connectivity encourages working on vacation. Vince Webb, senior vice president of marketing and strategy for Management Recruiters, said the profusion of laptops, cell phones, pagers and other devices makes it too easy to stay plugged in thousands of miles from the office.

17   "You can get sucked in so easily 365 days a year, 24/7," Webb said.

18   And it's only going to get worse. Airline maker Boeing said last month that it's going into business with three major airlines to let fliers access e-mail and the Internet in aircraft cabins.

19   American Airlines, United Airlines and Delta Air Lines—the nation's three largest carriers—are the first three to sign up, but Boeing is also in talks with 30 other airlines. . . .

20   If technology helps the overworked stay plugged in, it can also help would-be vacationers tune out. E-mail programs like Microsoft's Outlook

have an "out-of-office" feature that responds to incoming e-mails with an announcement that the recipient is away.

21   Ron Watson, vice president of human resources for Compuware, the Farmington Hills, Mich.-based software firm, urges employees to use such features to smooth the transition to time off.

22   "At Compuware, we really encourage people to separate themselves when they go on vacation," Watson said. "In order to be effective, they really need to get out and recharge."

23   But even those who know better sometimes get caught up in vacation work. Gary Baker, an Ann Arbor, Mich.-based partner with the Andersen consulting firm and host of the radio show "Internet Adviser," recalls the sideways glances his wife shot him when he made cell-phone calls in between rides at Walt Disney World in Florida.

24   "There's so much going on that you need to stay in touch with," he explained.

25   Baker said he tries to schedule his work time on vacation when it will least disrupt his family. "Your kids are playing in the surf, so you go upstairs and make the call."

26   But like many a New Year's Eve resolution, promising to take more time off doesn't always stick. "We have the same kind of rules that everybody else has," Baker said. "Leave the cell phone at home; take the time off." Yet Baker left unused all but a day and a half of his four weeks of vacation last year.

27   For those truly dedicated to work, vacationing may always be more burden than boon.

28   Describing plans for his wedding, Lauer outlines a three-week honeymoon with Ribiat in Europe this fall. The itinerary includes Britain, France, Spain, Italy and Greece. But then Lauer added, "Once that's done, there's no way we're going to be taking any huge vacations like that until we're old and gray."

29   His voice dropped, and he added softly, "Kind of sad, in a way."

Keith Goetzman
The Late, Great Outdoors

1   In the 2000 Sydney Olympics, whitewater kayaking competitors bucked through an artificial channel surging with machine-pumped water, then rode conveyor belts back upstream without ever getting out of their boats. In Chamonix, France, gateway to the Alps and a mountaineering mecca, ice climbers in the 2001 Ice World Cup ascended not nearby peaks but an elaborate ice-covered structure erected in the middle of town.

2   The artificial outdoors isn't just for world-class competitors, though. At the $130 million Gotcha Glacier sports complex being built in Anaheim, California, everyone will be able to surf faux waves, climb imitation cliffs, "skydive," ski, snowboard, skateboard—and, of course, shop—under one gigantic roof.

3   Gotcha may be just the tip of the glacier when it comes to the future of recreation. Increasingly, the great outdoors are being brought indoors or altered considerably to produce more accessible venues for adventure seekers. Indoor climbing walls are sprouting everywhere, artificial whitewater courses are on the drawing boards in dozens of cities, and several "snow-domes" are being built in Europe and the United States.

4   The phenomenon is generating considerable debate within the outdoor sports world. Some feel that something is lost when the rapids are always just right and the view at the top of the climb is the checkout line. Many of these are conservationists who oppose manipulating or re-creating natural environments. But for the "extreme" sports crowd—whose allies include much of the outdoor gear industry—the more places to play, the better.

5   Witness a recent exchange between paddlers on an Internet message board. "I am opposed to taking a backhoe and cement truck to the river, to supposedly make it more 'fun.' It strikes me as obscene," wrote "dancewater."

6   But "paddleboy" was unapologetic: "Artificial courses are for convenience, not getting in touch with the flow. We don't eat at McDonald's because the burgers taste good. Most 'natural' rivers aren't natural. . . . We paddle what's wet."

7   Similar differences exist among rock climbers, says Lloyd Athearn, deputy director of the American Alpine Club in Golden, Colorado. "For some people, climbing is about achieving the greatest level of technical difficulty they can achieve. There are people who climb at just obscene levels of difficulty, and they may not care at all about the scenery," he explains. "Others prefer being out on a remote peak someplace where they've bushwhacked 10 miles to get to the base of it. To them the inspiration of the environment is as important as the technical difficulties, if not more so."

8   Artificial environments have caught on for various reasons, says Professor Alan Ewert, who teaches outdoor leadership at Indiana University. For some participants, they are simply places to train for "real" outdoor experiences. Others are seeking a nontraditional athletic workout in a controlled, safe setting. And a growing number of people are using climbing walls and the like as social gathering spots. Says Athearn: "As the whole climbing gym scene evolved, there ended up being some people who like that environment, and they don't really climb outside."

9   Proponents of artificial environments, which are usually in metropolitan areas, say it's all about access, convenience, and a good time. "This is a fun sport. Why should we have to drive 200 miles to participate?" says Damon Peters, an avid kayaker and owner of L'eau Vive Paddlesports, a kayak accessory distributor based in Portland, Maine.

10   Backers of artificial environments often point out that they're helping expose urban dwellers to outdoor recreation. Gotcha Glacier's marketing and operations chief, Mike Gerard, told the *Los Angeles Times* he's performing a service. "It costs money to get to the mountains," he said. "Snowboarding is a sport with huge growth potential. We just need to get it to the people. I want to see kids of all ages and ethnic groups have a chance to do this."

11   Ewert says it's not yet clear whether artificial environments are instilling a desire for real wilderness experience in city dwellers. "We hope that's happening, but we're not really sure," he says. What is happening, he believes, is that indoor adventurers are being connected with organizations that can take them to the next step, and they may be more likely to develop an environmental consciousness.

12   And the outdoors may need some help in attracting new enthusiasts. Athearn points to a recent study that attempted to determine why younger people weren't as interested in wilderness experiences as the previous generation. One teen responded, "If I'm in the mountains, I'm out of cell-phone coverage, and I can't do that."

Individual Tasks

1. How would you describe each writer's perspective or angle of vision on technology? In one or two sentences, summarize each writer's main points in these passages.
2. List ideas that these pieces have in common.
3. List any contradictions or differences you see in these pieces.
4. Freewrite your own response to these readings for five minutes, exploring what questions they raise for you or personal experiences that they might remind you of.

Group or Whole-Class Tasks

1. Working in small groups or as a whole class, try to reach consensus answers to questions 1, 2, and 3.
2. Share your individual responses to question 4. What are the major questions and issues raised by your group or the whole class? What different views of technology emerged?

WRITING PROJECT

Write a synthesis essay that meets the following criteria:

- Addresses a focusing question that your instructor provides or that you formulate for yourself
- Summarizes and analyzes the views of at least two writers on this question
- Shows how you have wrestled with different perspectives on the question and have synthesized these ideas to arrive at your own new view of the question

To help you generate ideas for this assignment, your instructor may ask you to write your own exploratory pieces in response to some or all of the chapter's five learning log tasks.

This assignment asks you to take apart, make sense of, assess, and recombine—that is, synthesize—the ideas from two or more readings. In the introduction to your essay, present the focusing question to your readers so that they become interested in it, see its problematic nature, and appreciate its significance. Then present your own thesis that grows out of your analysis and synthesis of your chosen or assigned readings. At appropriate places in your essay, you need to summarize these readings briefly because you should assume that your audience has not read them.

In the body of your paper, you have two main goals: (1) through analysis, show how the pieces you have selected provide different perspectives on the focusing question based on differing values, assumptions, beliefs, or framing of the question; and (2) through synthesis, add your own perspective and independent thinking by making your own connections among the ideas in the readings. In other words, create a new view by combining ideas gathered from readings with your own ideas.

To help you develop ideas for your synthesis essay, we have included five learning log tasks. These tasks will guide you gradually from understanding through analysis to synthesis and will provide thinking that you can use directly in your formal essay. On several occasions you will have an opportunity to share your learning log explorations with classmates and to use them for the basis of discussions that will help you generate more ideas for your formal essay. Your instructor will specify whether you are to complete these learning logs and, if so, how much time to spend on them. If you do the learning log tasks, keep your writing informal and exploratory with an emphasis on idea generation rather than correctness and polish.

Suggested Ideas for Synthesis Questions and Readings

This text provides a number of options from which your instructor can choose. Many instructors will follow our own approach, which is to assign both the readings and the focusing question. Others may assign the readings but invite students to formulate their own focusing questions. Still others may leave both the focusing question and the readings up to the student.

The articles in the "Readings" section of this chapter raise questions about the causes of obesity and possible lifestyle changes needed for better health. But other readings throughout the text can be successfully combined for a synthesis essay. What follows is list of possible focusing questions and readings. In addition, your instructor might assign readings not found in this text.

Further suggestions for combinations of readings can be found in the "Thematic Table of Contents" in the front of the book.

Reading Options for This Assignment	
Focusing Question	**Possible Readings**
What can we do to combat obesity in children and adults and attain better health?	• Ellen Goodman, "The Big Fat Case Against Big Macs," pp. 377–378 • Dale Buss, "Is the Food Industry the Problem or the Solution?" pp. 378–381 • Marilyn Larkin, "Can Cities Be Designed to Fight Obesity?" pp. 381–385
What social attitude should we take toward smoking?	• Florence King, "I'd Rather Smoke Than Kiss," pp. 144–149 • Lyndon Haviland, "A Silence That Kills," pp. 150–153 • Gasp Consultancy, Ltd. "Steps to Stop Smoking," pp. 154–155 • Welcome to Malboro Country," spoof ad, p. 156 • Gina Escamilla, Angie L. Cradock, and Ichiro Kawachi, "Women and Smoking in Hollywood Movies: A Content Analysis," pp. 271–276
What position should we take on the Patriot Act?	• Clay Bennett, "USA PATRIOT ACT," p. 418 • John Ashcroft, "Prepared Remarks of Attorney General Ashcroft at the Federalist Society National Convention," pp. 419–425 • James Bovard, "Surveillance State," pp. 426–432
How can we appreciate, enjoy, and preserve nature?	• Edward Abbey, "The Damnation of a Canyon," pp. 157–161 • Friends of Lake Powell, Home page, p. 161 • Thomas Merton, "A Festival of Rain," p. 18 • Annie Dillard, "Living Like Weasels," pp. 594–597 • Keith Goetzman, "The Late, Great Outdoors," pp. 361–363 • Photographs of the Arctic National Wildlife Refuge, pp. 98–101 • Selected excerpts on automobiles and energy consumption, pp. 12–15

An Explanation of the Student Examples in This Chapter

The student examples in this chapter focus on the technological question "To what extent does technology enrich or dehumanize our lives?" These examples enable you to role-play the same sort of audience stipulated in the assignment—readers who have not read the articles being discussed. You will need to depend, then, on the writers' summaries of these readings. The two student writers, Kara Watterson and Kate MacAulay, are working with the following texts:

- George Ritzer, "The Irrationality of Rationality: Traffic Jams on Those 'Happy Trails.'" This is a chapter from Ritzer's widely discussed book *The McDonaldization of Society,* New Century Edition (Thousand Oaks, CA: Pine Forge Press, 2000).
- Sherry Turkle, "Who Am We?" published in the magazine *Wired* 4.1 (January 1996): 148–52, 194–99.

Understanding Analysis and Synthesis

The Challenge of Synthesizing Ideas

The need to synthesize ideas usually begins when you pose a problematic question that sends you off on an intellectual journey through a group of texts. Your goal is to achieve your own informed view on that question, a view that reflects your intellectual wrestling with the ideas in your sources and in some way integrates ideas from these sources with your own independent thinking.

The most efficient and productive way to handle this multitask challenge is to break it into a series of incremental thinking steps that take you gradually from understanding your chosen texts, to an analysis of them, to a synthesis of their ideas with your own. The learning log tasks in each of the sections that follow show you a series of thinking steps to guide you through this process.

Understanding Your Texts Through Summary Writing

> **Learning Log Task 1:** Write a 200–250-word summary of each of the main texts you will use in your final paper.

As a starting point for grappling with a writer's ideas, writing careful summaries prompts you to read texts with the grain, adopting each text's perspective and walking in each author's shoes. When you summarize a text, you try to achieve an accurate, thorough understanding of it by stating its main ideas in a tightly distilled format.

Instructions on how to write a summary are found on pp. 126–130.

What follows are Kara's summary of the book chapter by Ritzer and Kate's summary of Turkle's article—the two readings they will use in their synthesis essays.

Notice how they use attributive tags to show that they are representing Ritzer's and Turkle's ideas as objectively as they can and that these ideas belong to Ritzer or Turkle, not to them.

Instructions on how to use attributive tags are found on pp. 129 and 652–655.

KARA'S SUMMARY OF RITZER'S CHAPTER

In "The Irrationality of Rationality," the seventh chapter in <u>The McDonaldization of Society</u>, sociologist George Ritzer identifies a major sociological and economic problem: in an effort to find the most efficient way to run a business (what Ritzer calls "rationalizing"), more and more companies are following the franchise model pioneered by McDonald's. Although McDonaldization is efficient and economical for the companies, Ritzer argues it can be irrational, inconvenient, inefficient, and costly for consumers who often stand in long lines at fast-food restaurants and supermarkets. Ritzer also claims that McDonaldized systems cause people to forfeit real fun for manufactured fun and illusion. He cites the example of fake international villages at amusement parks and the fake friendliness of the "scripted interactions" (138) that employees are supposed to have with customers. Ritzer explains that our McDonaldized society has begun focusing more on quantity than quality. He believes that McDonaldized systems are dehumanizing: jobs "don't offer much in the way of satisfaction or stability" (137) and families hardly ever eat together any more, a situation that is contributing to the "disintegration of the family" (141). Ritzer also argues that by franchising everywhere, we are losing cultural distinctions. Whether you are in Japan or the United States, products are beginning to look the same. Finally, Ritzer shows that when companies become rationalized, they limit the possibility of connection between human beings. Citing examples from fast-food restaurants to hospitals, he states that there are many serious drawbacks to "our fast-paced and impersonal society" (140).

KATE'S SUMMARY OF TURKLE'S ARTICLE

In her <u>Wired</u> article "Who Am We?" psychologist and MIT professor Sherry Turkle explores how computers and the Internet are transforming our views of ourselves and the way we interact socially. Turkle believes that the Internet is moving us toward a "decentered" (149) sense of the self. She says that computers used to be thought of as "calculating machines" (149), but they are increasingly now seen as intelligent objects capable of interaction and simulation. She uses children's interactive computer games to illustrate how some people now think of computers as having personalities and psyches, which make them "fitting partners for dialog and relationship" (150). In the second half of her article, she argues that virtual life raises new moral issues. She uses the example of MUDs (multiuser domains), which allow people to create multiple and often simultaneous virtual identities by playing different characters. She presents examples of the relationships of cyber characters—often cyber-sex—that raise the question of whether cyber-sex is an act of real-life infidelity or adultery. Turkle concludes that it is easy for people to lose themselves between the real world and these virtual worlds. Because we have the ability to create better "selves" in the virtual world, it is possible to become addicted to virtual life and be "imprisoned by the screens" (199). According to Turkle, we are moving toward a "postmodernist culture of simulation" (149), and she cautions that it is more important than ever that we are very self-aware.

For Writing and Discussion

Working in small groups or as a whole class, share your summaries of your two chosen or assigned readings. What important main ideas does your group agree must be included in a summary of each text? What points are secondary and can be left out?

Examining the Rhetorical Strategies Used in Your Texts

Explanations of these terms and concepts are found in Chapters 3 and 4.

Learning Log Task 2: Analyze the rhetorical strategies used in each of your texts (for example, the way your texts handle purpose, audience, genre, angle of vision, appeals to *logos*, *ethos*, and *pathos*, and use of evidence).

In order to analyze a text and synthesize its ideas, you need to consider the text rhetorically. To whom is the author writing and why? Do you see how the genre of each text influences some of the author's choices about language and structure? What angle of vision shapes each text and accounts for what is included and excluded? Do you share the values of the author or of his or her intended audience?

Instructions on how to write a rhetorical analysis of a text are found in Chapter 6 on pp. 134–137.

Here is Kara's learning log entry exploring the rhetorical contexts of the Ritzer and Turkle texts:

KARA'S RESPONSE TO LEARNING LOG TASK 2

Although both George Ritzer and Sherry Turkle are scholars, their texts are not really written for scholarly audiences. Both would fall in the category of nonfiction books (articles) written for general audiences and both are written to raise audience awareness of sociological/cultural problems—in this case, the way that technological advances and the fast-food model of business are affecting the quality of life and the way that the Internet is affecting our sense of ourselves and our relationships.

Both Ritzer and Turkle have chosen to write in accessible language so that their ideas can easily be understood by a general audience, and both use many examples to build credibility. Still, because I had no previous personal background with multi-user domains, I found it challenging to imagine some of Turkle's descriptions of the virtual world of MUDs, but I did have previous experience with all of Ritzer's examples so I never felt in over my head while reading his chapters.

Kara defines "rationalization" in the opening sentences of her summary of Ritzer, p. 367.

From Ritzer's angle of vision, McDonaldization has had a damaging and irreversible effect on the quality of contemporary life, and he is trying to prompt people to slow down this destructive process. His approach is quite one-sided, though. He does admit that "we undoubtedly have gained much from the rationalization of society in general" (132), but he does not develop this idea any further. He refuses to make any further concessions to the rationalization he is fighting. Instead of acknowledging contradicting ideas, Ritzer hammers his point strongly with example after example. By the end of the chapter, the reader is left with a glazed-over feeling, not really taking in the information.

    Turkle's angle of vision seems to include curiosity and exploration as well as concern about the way computers are transforming society. She seems to analyze more than argue. She is trying to get across her notion that the Internet lets people adopt many different characters and have multiple selves, for example when they play in MUDs and simulation games. So maybe, in claiming that computers are no longer calculating machines, Turkle, like Ritzer, is only presenting one limited view of her subject, the view that interests her as a psychologist who has written many books and articles on computers, and our changing sense of identity and community.

For Writing and Discussion

Working in small groups or as a whole class, share what each of you discovered in Learning Log Task 2. Try to reach consensus on the most important rhetorical features of each of the texts you are using for your synthesis essay.

Identifying Main Themes and Examining Similarities and Differences in the Ideas in Your Texts

Learning Log Task 3: Identify main issues or themes in your assigned or chosen texts. Then explore the similarities and differences in their ideas.

    This learning log task asks you to identify main issues, ideas, or themes that surface in your texts as preparation for looking for similarities and differences among your texts. This process of thinking—comparison and contrast—will help you clarify your understanding of each reading and promote analysis of the underlying values, assumptions, and ideas of each author. Here are some questions that can guide your learning log writing at this stage of your thinking:

QUESTIONS TO HELP YOU GRAPPLE WITH SIMILARITIES AND DIFFERENCES IN YOUR TEXTS

- What main ideas or themes do you see in each text?
- What similarities and differences do you see in the way the authors choose to frame the issues they are writing about? How do their theses (either implied or stated) differ?
- What are the main similarities and differences in their angles of vision?
- What commonalities and intersections do you see in their ideas? What contradictions and clashes do you see in their ideas?

- What similarities and differences do you see in the authors' underlying values and assumptions?
- What overlap, if any, is there in these authors' examples and uses of terms?
- How would Author A respond to Author B?

Here are excerpts from Kara's and Kate's learning logs, showing their exploratory analyses of Ritzer's and Turkle's texts. Note how they each begin to organize comparisons by points, to make analytical connections among them, and to push themselves to think out exactly where these authors agree and differ.

EXCERPT FROM KARA'S RESPONSE TO LEARNING LOG TASK 3

Both Ritzer and Turkle make strong comments about health problems that may be caused by the particular type of technology they are dealing with. For Ritzer, the dangers that arise from McDonaldization can most easily be seen in fast-food restaurants and their fatty, unhealthy foods: "such meals are the last things many Americans need, suffering as they do from obesity, high cholesterol levels, high blood pressure, and perhaps diabetes" (133). He also considers the high level of stress created by our high-speed society that can cause heart attacks, panic attacks, maybe nervous breakdowns. Turkle, too, is concerned about the effects of technology on people's health, but her focus is people's psyches and minds. One person in her research study who creates different identities on the Internet thinks that "MUDding has ultimately made him feel worse about himself" (196). For Turkle, the Internet can be dangerous for what it can do to a person's psyche.

Both authors agree that technological advances are causing a loss of real human connection. McDonaldization fosters fake contact; employees are given guidelines about how to interact with customers and are programmed with what to say and what not to say: "rule Number 17 for Burger King workers is 'Smiles at all times' " (Ritzer 130). Quick sales, not real customer relations, are the main concern. For Turkle too, this loss of human contact is a dilemma. MUDs are not places where you truly get to know a person; they are places where people are acting out characters. These are not real friends that can aid you when you are feeling ill or down. Also, people are spending vast quantities of time logging on, spending time with a computer screen instead of family and friends. . . .

EXCERPT FROM KATE'S RESPONSE TO LEARNING LOG TASK 3

. . . Last, I think that Turkle and Ritzer have very different attitudes about what they observe and claim is happening to society. Turkle seems to be a little more optimistic than Ritzer. While she sees the changes that advanced technology is causing in society, she seems to think that we, as human beings, have the ability to adjust to the changes facing us and to change ourselves in order to preserve our humanity. In contrast to that view, Ritzer seems to take the position that we are on a downward spiral and McDonaldized systems are destroying us and society as a whole. Ritzer and Turkle would have a really great discussion about all the negative effects that technology and rationality are having on individuals and society, but they would probably largely disagree on society's ability to bounce back and fix itself.

For Writing and Discussion

Working as a whole class or in small groups, share your analyses of similarities and differences in your chosen or assigned texts. Pay close attention to these two overarching questions: How are the texts similar and different? How do each author's assumptions, beliefs, purposes, and values account for these similarities and differences?

Moving Toward Your Own Views

Learning Log Task 4: In light of what you have read and thought about so far, explore your own views on the original focusing question that has guided your probing of the texts.

One of your biggest challenges in writing a synthesis essay is to move beyond analysis to synthesis. A successful synthesis essay incorporates ideas from your texts and yet represents your own independent thinking, showing evidence of the dialectic process. You need to think about how the differing perspectives of Texts A and B have led you to new realizations that will let you enter the conversation of these texts. As you begin to formulate your synthesis views, you will also need to reassert your personal/intellectual investment in the conversation of the texts. You will need to take ownership of the ideas and to emerge with a clearer sense of your own views. You may also want to consider which text—in your mind—makes the most significant contribution to the question you are exploring. You may want to evaluate the texts to determine which has influenced your thinking the most and why. The following questions should help you think of ideas for Learning Log 4:

QUESTIONS TO HELP YOU DEVELOP YOUR OWN VIEWS

- What do I agree with and disagree with in the texts I have analyzed?
- How have these texts changed my perception and understanding of an issue, question, or problem? You might want to use these prompts: "I used to think _____, but now I think _____." "Although these texts have persuaded me that _____, I still have doubts about _____."
- What do I see or think now that I didn't see or think before I read these texts?
- What new, significant questions do these texts raise for me?
- What do I now see as the main controversies?
- What is my current view on the focusing question that connects my texts and that all my texts explore?
- How would I position myself in the conversation of the texts?
- If I find one author's perspective more valid, accurate, interesting, or useful than another's, why is that?

To illustrate this learning log task, we show you excerpts from the explorations of both Kara and Kate.

EXCERPT FROM KARA'S RESPONSE TO LEARNING LOG TASK 4

When I was in Puerto Rico one spring break, I remember how excited my friend and I were to go to a burger place for dinner one night. It was so nice to have American food after days of eating fajitas and enchiladas. At the time, I did not think about how this American restaurant got to Puerto Rico; I was just glad it was there. However, after reading "The Irrationality of Rationality" by George Ritzer, I began to take a closer look at this experience. Both this article and "Who Am We?" have caused me to take a closer look at our society. . . . What is it that causes people to surf the Internet for hours on end, to chat with people they have never met? What is this doing to our culture? Are we losing the distinctions evident when you travel from one region to the next, from one country to another? . . .

EXCERPT FROM KATE'S RESPONSE TO LEARNING LOG TASK 4

Reading the articles by Ritzer and Turkle made me much more aware of a social problem that I didn't really pay attention to before. I didn't realize how much modern technology is changing our human relationships. For example, the other night I was at a family gathering, and some of my cousins began discussing the idea of purchasing a new car. After talking for a short while about how much it would cost and how to get the best deal, one of my cousins had that modern craving for wanting to know the answer immediately. He logged on to the Internet and spent the remainder of the evening looking at cars and prices, and had limited interaction with the family. It made me think about the articles and how things were becoming more immediate and less personal, and how interactions between machines and humans are decreasing the interactions between people. Why speak with another person who might not know the answer to a question or the solution to a problem when you can just log on to the Internet and find the right answer immediately? It makes me wonder what the Internet does not offer. . . .

Taking Your Position in the Conversation: Your Synthesis

Learning Log Task 5: Reread your first four learning logs and consider how your own views on the focusing question have evolved and emerged. Think about the risky, surprising, or new views that you can bring to your readers. In light of your reading and thinking, explore what you want to say in your own voice to show the connections you have made and the new insights you now have.

After you have discovered what you think about the texts you have analyzed—what ideas you accept and reject, what new questions you have formulated, how your ideas have been modified and transformed through your reading experience—you need to find a way to pull your ideas together. Your synthesis view should be the fruit of your intellectual work, a perspective that you have come to after reading the ideas of other writers, pondering them reflectively and keenly. Here are some synthesis questions that can help you articulate the points that you want to develop in your essay:

QUESTIONS TO HELP YOU FORMULATE AND DEVELOP YOUR SYNTHESIS VIEWS

- What discoveries have I made after much thought?
- What are the most important insights I have gotten from these readings?
- What is my intellectual or personal investment with the focusing question at this point?
- Where can I step out on my own, even take a risk, in my thinking about the ideas discussed in these texts?
- What new perspective do I want to share with my readers?

What follows is an excerpt from Kara's learning log. Note how she is beginning to find her stance on the focusing question of whether technology enriches or dehumanizes our lives.

EXCERPT FROM KARA'S RESPONSE TO LEARNING LOG TASK 5

What is technology doing to our relationships with one another? Both Ritzer and Turkle seem to be urging us away from dependency on technology, and these authors have made me aware of my complacence in accepting technology, but still I see value in technology that these writers don't discuss. . . .

I find myself questioning these writers' views. Ritzer seems to believe that families go to McDonald's rather than eat family meals together. He doesn't consider that it is when people are on the road or out already that these restaurants are visited, not when they are sitting at home deciding what is for dinner. Turkle also speaks of the loss of connection that can arise from people constantly at their computers. She raises some very important questions about what technology is doing to our relationships and self-image, but I think she focuses too much on MUDs. How many people actually are doing this MUDding? Also, there are some valid things that come out of relationships on the Internet. I know of several examples of people who have met their future spouses through chat rooms. When I left for college, I was not sure whom I would stay in touch with, but because of the Internet, I am able to stay connected to people I would have drifted away from otherwise.

Also, while we note the dangers of technology, I think we need to remember the benefits as well. I agree that cell phones are overused, but how often have cell phones saved people in emergencies or aided people stranded on the road with car problems? I hope to be a doctor. I have great appreciation for the way that cameras can see inside a patient as surgeons are operating and thus reduce the risk of many surgeries. . . .

For Writing and Discussion

Prior to the start of this task, work individually to write two or three main points that you want to make in the synthesis portion of your final essay. Working in small groups or as a whole class, share your short list of main points. Briefly explain to your group or to the whole class why these points interest you. Take notes on group ideas.

Student Example of a Synthesis Essay

We conclude this section by showing you Kate's final synthesis essay. Note that Kate begins by presenting the focusing question that connects the texts she is analyzing. She then summarizes these texts and presents her mapping thesis statement. She devotes more than half of the body of the essay to a close analysis of the texts before she moves on to present her own independent thinking in the synthesis section of the essay.

TECHNOLOGY'S PERIL AND POTENTIAL

Kate MacAulay (student)

Introduces focusing questions and context

Recently in English class, we have been focusing on the question, What effect is technology having on humanity and the quality of life in the twenty-first century? We have had heated discussions about the use of cell phones, palm pilots, beepers, e-mail, chat rooms, and the Web. As part of my investigation of this question, I read

Introduces the texts to be analyzed

two texts: a chapter from George Ritzer's book The McDonaldization of Society, entitled "The Irrationality of Rationality: Traffic Jams on Those 'Happy Trails,'" and an article published in the magazine Wired entitled "Who Am We?", by Sherry Turkle.

Brief summary of Ritzer's text

In his chapter, Ritzer, a sociology professor, explains how technology has rationalized businesses and many facets of society following the McDonald's model. He argues that modern technology is causing loss of quality products, time, and relationships. In the McDonaldized system, where everything is designed logically for economy and convenience, things have become more artificial, and our relationships have become more superficial. In her article "Who Am We?", Sherry Turkle, a

Brief summary of Turkle's text

psychology professor at MIT, shows how computers and the Internet are transforming our views of ourselves and the way we interact socially. Focusing on computers' capacities for simulation and promoting interaction, Turkle has explored MUDs (multiuser domains), which allow people to create virtual identities. MUDs, Turkle believes, contribute to the formation of postmodern multiple selves and raise new

Thesis statement with analytical points and synthesis points

questions about personal identity and morality. Although both Turkle and Ritzer identify problems in technology's influence and in society's responses to it, Turkle sees more potential and gain where Ritzer sees mostly peril and loss. Both articles made me question how we define our values and morality in this postmodern, technologically advanced world and persuaded me of the need for caution in embracing technology.

Analytical point: compares and contrasts Ritzer's and Turkle's ideas

Although Ritzer and Turkle both see technology as having some negative effects on human relations and the quality of life, they disagree about exactly where the most interesting and serious problems lie. Ritzer believes that the problems caused by technology are not problems within the individual, but problems imposed on the individual by McDonaldized systems. For example, Ritzer claims that fast-food

Analyzes and elaborates on Ritzer's ideas

restaurants encourage us to eat unhealthy food quickly and also contribute to "the disintegration of the family" (141) by taking away family time. He also believes that rationalized systems create illusions of fun, reality, and friendliness. He talks about the "scripted interactions" (138) that employees are supposed to have with customers, where they are told exactly what to say to every customer, making interactions less real. Further, rationalized systems are dehumanizing in the kinds of jobs they create that "don't offer much in the way of satisfaction or stability" (137), benefiting only stockholders, owners, and employers.

In contrast, Turkle responds to technology's threat by focusing inward on technology's effect on the self and on relationships. While she is clearly intrigued by such Internet capabilities as multiuser domains, she acknowledges that this potential for multiple simultaneous identities threatens the wholeness of individuals, possibly damaging our emotional and psychological selves. Her concern is that people become addicted to these games because in the virtual world it is easy to create better "selves," to be what you wish you were. Turkle shows that people can lose themselves between the real world and the virtual world and be "imprisoned by the screens" (199). Although the virtual world is exciting and fun, she notes that "[o]ur experiences there are serious play" (199). She also examines cases of virtual characters who get into relationships with other characters, including cyber-sex relationships. She ponders the issue of cyber-sex immorality and adultery.

Analyzes, contrasts, and elaborates on Turkle's ideas

Despite Turkle and Ritzer's agreement that technology can damage us as a society, they disagree on their overall outlook and on our power to respond positively to technology's influence. I find Ritzer's views almost entirely negative. He believes that we are irreversibly damaged by technological advances because we are completely caught up in the McDonaldized system, with few parts of society left unchanged. Almost all of the family-owned neighborhood restaurants or mom-and-pop grocery stores have been taken over by franchises like Red Robin or Safeway. The costs of these rationalized systems, he says, are "inefficiency, illusions of various types, disenchantment, dehumanization, and homogenization" (124). In this chapter of his book, Ritzer doesn't mention any ways that our lives could be improved by these systems; he gives only examples of the way we are misled and damaged by them.

Analytical point: compares and contrasts Ritzer's and Turkle's ideas

Analyzes and elaborates on Ritzer's ideas

Presents writer's independent thinking

Turkle's approach strikes me as much more positive and balanced than Ritzer's. Optimistically, she explains that MUDs can give people self-knowledge that they can apply to real life: "[t]he anonymity of MUDs gives people the chance to express multiple and often unexplored aspects of the self, to play with their identity and to try out new ones" (152). Turkle sees an opportunity for us to grow as individuals and to learn to use technology in a positive way: "If we can cultivate awareness of what stands behind our screen personae, we are more likely to succeed in using virtual experience for personal transformation" (199). I think Turkle's views are more complex than Ritzer's. She believes that we have to take responsibility for our own habits and psychological responses to technology. She encourages us to be aware of how we interact with technology and believes that we can grow as individuals using this technology.

Analyzes, contrasts, and elaborates on Turkle's ideas

Presents writer's independent thinking

After reading these articles, I have realized how the continuing advancement of technology raises new moral questions. In a McDonaldized system, where everything is designed for convenience, there seem to be many places for morals to be left out of the picture. For example, is it okay for us to exchange real human interaction for convenience and saving time? Is there something wrong with our ethics when interesting and fulfilling jobs are eliminated by machines or replaced by dead-end, low-paying Mcjobs? Turkle too shows us how virtual worlds pose new moral questions for us. In MUDs, people can form virtual relationships, even cyber-sex relationships. The people behind the characters are real people, even if they are acting as someone else. If a married person has a cyber-sex relationship on a MUD, is he or she cheating? If a person commits a virtual assault or other crime that has no real-world, physical effects, should he or she feel guilty or sinful for the intention? Ritzer and Turkle have made me see how important these questions are.

Transition to writer's synthesis. Synthesis point discusses writer's own view

Elaborates on the connections the writer is making

Reading the articles made me strongly believe that we must use this technology in moderation in order to preserve individual qualities and our relationships. From our

Synthesis point discusses writer's view

class discussions, I remember what Scott said about the way that the Internet connects people. He said that people like his uncle, who was severely injured on the job, use the Internet as a way of "getting out" to meet people and socialize. He pointed out how the Microsoft Gaming Zone has brought his uncle into an ongoing backgammon tournament through which he has made friends. Meanwhile his aunt has gotten a lot of pleasure out of playing and problem solving in the world of MUDs.

Synthesis point discusses writer's own view

But my own experience has left me concerned about the danger we face as emotional, social beings in the face of technology. The other night at a family gathering, one of my cousins, after discussing car buying with some of the relatives, got the urge to research new car prices. He left the room, logged onto the Internet, and spent the rest of the evening looking at cars and prices. We saw him only once the whole evening when he came out to get a slice of pie. My cousin's withdrawal from the conversation made me think about Ritzer's and Turkle's concerns that technology decreases real interactions among people.

Transition and final connections

Ritzer and Turkle offer us a warning that technology can be damaging if we don't recognize and overcome its dangers. I would encourage us not to let ourselves become dominated by technology, not to let it take our full attention just because it is there,

Conclusion

and not to overlook the complex moral questions that technology poses. The convenience that technology offers—our e-mail, cell phones, and debit cards—should help us save time that can be spent in nurturing our relationships with other people. The real challenge is to find ways to become even better people because of technology.

Works Cited

Complete citation of articles in MLA format

Ritzer, George. <u>The McDonaldization of Society</u>. Thousand Oaks: Pine Forge, 2000.

Turkle, Sherry. "Who Am We?" <u>Wired</u> Jan. 1996: 148+.

READINGS

The readings in this chapter immerse you in the network of issues related to obesity in industrialized countries, particularly the United States. In the last few years, public speculations have proliferated over the causes of obesity with blame targeting an array of social phenomena: Americans' love of fast food; the seductive and relentless advertising of the food industry; our fondness for watching television, playing video games, surfing the Web, and spending hours at our computers; our lack of physical exercise; corporate promotions of fast food and soft drinks in schools; the stress of our lives; and even low-fat food itself. Public voices have also warned about the serious consequences of the obesity crisis, consequences including higher rates of diseases such as diabetes, shorter lives, and higher insurance costs. For example, the documentary film *Super Size Me* (2004) exposes the dangers of a regular diet of fast food. Lately the controversy has also raged over possible solutions to help children, teens, and adults achieve healthier lives. The readings that follow explore some of these proposals for constructive action. We have framed several focusing questions for synthesis essays on these readings: What is the most promising solution or combination of solutions to the health crisis of obesity? What should we do to help our children avoid obesity and lead healthier lives? To avoid influencing your own analysis of these readings, we omit the discussion questions that typically follow readings in other chapters.

The first reading, by highly reputed syndicated columnist Ellen Goodman, appeared in *The Washington Post* in December 2002. Goodman is known for her insightful delving into complex issues.

Ellen Goodman
The Big Fat Case Against Big Macs

1   I don't believe there's any magical mathematical equation between the speed of the food and the circumference of the waistline. After all, you can gain weight eating slow food as well as fast food. You can bulk up with haute cuisine as well as Big Macs. And you can, alas, trust me on this.

2   So I was inclined to scoff at the Conspiracy Theory of Obesity. This is the idea that McDonald's dunnit. That Burger King and Wendy's and their speed-eating cohorts are responsible for the Incredible Expanding American.

3   Right before Thanksgiving, some lawyers went to court in pursuit of this theory. They filed a class action against McDonald's on behalf of New York children with health problems. These plaintiffs ate at Ronald McDonald's more than at Mom's. One 13-year-old weighed 278 pounds, while a 15-year-old weighed in at 400.

4   I would have called the case frivolous, except my dictionary defines frivolous lawsuits as "of little or no weight." Nevertheless, the story was enough to make me want to cross lawyers off my dinner party list. Who wants to be sued for serving cheesecake?

5   Now I'm not so sure. I think the lawyers have made their point, if not their case.

6   Consider the toy in my hand. It comes with the Happy Meal at my neighborhood McDonald's. The yellow rattle has a safety warning on the plastic wrapper. But the nutritional information for this beginner meal—20 fat grams and 36 sugar grams—is nowhere to be seen. It is stashed under the counter and printed in agate that's off the eye chart.

7   Then there is the Mighty Kids meal, sold with a collection of Disney "Treasure Planet" toys. This newer, bigger, presumably "happier" meal for little kids totals around 1,160 calories. The Burger King version, dubbed the "Big Kids Meal," is marketed with a question for the 4-and-over eater: "Do you want to be a Big Kid?" It cheerfully supplies answers: "You Should." Indeed eat this often enough and you will.

8   A few facts? On any given day, one-quarter of Americans eat at a fast-food restaurant. In any given month, 90 percent of American children between the ages of 3 and 9 eat at a McDonald's.

9   They're not forcing hamburgers down open gullets. But if people have their share of personal responsibility for what they eat, is it really frivolous to expect some responsibility on the part of corporations for what and how they market? If parents are supposed to protect their little kids' health, is it really okay for Big Food to market and advertise in and around and over the heads of parents?

10   In a motion to dismiss the case, the lawyers for McDonald's wrote. "Every responsible person understands what is in products such as hamburgers and fries." They sound more than vaguely like all those tobacco moguls who righteously announced that "everyone knows" smoking is dangerous while they sent Joe Camel out on a recruiting mission.

11   Of course, food and tobacco are not the same, though some of the same lawyers who fought big tobacco have turned their sights to a big fat target. As Dick Daynard, head of Northeastern University's Tobacco Products Liability Project, says, "Nobody needs to smoke cigarettes unless they're hooked, but everyone needs food. And there's no such thing as secondhand eating."

12   But a deep, dark secret of the fast-food industry is that it makes most of its money from the people targeted as, ahem, "heavy users." Like the tobacco companies, says Daynard, "food companies have very sophisticated motivational people on their payroll to figure out how to get kids to use their product."

13   That's fine if there aren't any health problems associated with the product. But if fast food is good for you, how come Mickey D's took out an ad in France telling parents that kids shouldn't eat les hamburgers more than once a week?

14   I don't like to talk about the obesity epidemic; fat isn't exactly contagious. But today 61 percent of adults and 14 percent of adolescents from 12 to 19 are overweight, an increase of 300 percent over three decades.

15   That's not just a Big Mac mistake. Blame it on a sedentary lifestyle. Blame it on portion (out of) control, from candy bars on steroids to the bagels that ate New York. Blame it on schools selling soda pop in the hallway. If we are what we do and what we eat, we're potatoes: couched and fried.

16   I don't think the best lawyers in town can prove that the fast-food industry fattened its customers. But they may prove it fooled its customers. Especially the young ones.

17   Mark my words and label your lunch. This is just the beginning of a big, fat food fight.

Our second reading examines the food industry's response to public criticism and legal attacks like the one mentioned by Ellen Goodman. This piece, by journalist and author Dale Buss, first appeared in the *New York Times* on August 29, 2004.

Dale Buss
Is the Food Industry the Problem or the Solution?

1   Diet trends aren't just for adults anymore. A new obsession of America's food, beverage and restaurant companies is thwarting childhood obesity. With more nutritious products, healthier menus and new activity programs, the companies have begun a big push aimed at the youngest generation.

2   Frito-Lay is offering reduced-fat Doritos in school lunch rooms. Oscar Mayer has added apple sauce and other healthy choices to its Lunchables meal-kit line. Kraft has come out with a sugarless Kool-Aid that is being marketed in magazines like Diabetic Cooking and Diabetes Forecast.

3   Among restaurant chains, Wendy's has slipped orange slices into children's meals, and Denny's has made French fries much harder to find on its menu than new side dishes of fruits and vegetables.

4   And, this fall, Coca-Cola is helping finance a new after-school fitness program. "The big idea is to give kids education, motivation and access to ways to change," said Brock Leach, the chief innovations officer at PepsiCo, which owns Frito-Lay. "The food business can play a very constructive role in that, making these foods available to kids and marketing them in ways that make a healthier lifestyle more attractive."

5   For decades, of course, the industry has been known for serving up sugary or fat-laden products, promoted with ceaseless advertising. And despite all the new, healthier options, that will not change. "If they stop, their competitors are right there and will fill the void," said Dr. Walter Willett, chief of the nutrition department at the Harvard School of Public Health.

6   Critics say these companies are taking a new direction only to escape or mitigate possible court verdicts that could blame the food industry for the fact that about 15 percent of American youth now are plumper than they should be, more than double the proportion of 25 years ago. "There are hordes of lawyers looking at the industry's marketing practices in a way that's never happened before," said Marion Nestle, a nutrition professor at New York University.

7   Food, drink and restaurant executives are quick to place blame on video games, television watching and the recent decline of physical education programs in schools.

8   "Blaming industry is not going to get us any closer to a solution," said Richard Martin, a spokesman for the Grocery Manufacturers of America. "The only way to get there is to work collaboratively, not by pointing fingers."

9   Even more important, according to nutritionists and child psychologists, is the confounding truth that parents—whether distracted, oblivious or both—are ultimately to blame for what their children eat. "Parents were created for that function," said Dan Jaffe, executive vice president for government relations at the Association of National Advertisers, an organization based in Washington whose members include food companies. "I don't know of any little child who jumps in the car and drives to a supermarket and buys their own food."

10   So the industry is trying to shake up both generations. Subway restaurants, for example, have new 30-second commercials, aimed at adults, that highlight the weight-loss success stories of three real children. The $20 million national campaign does not mention Subway products and refers to the chain primarily with shots of the children with Jared Fogle, who lost 250 pounds while eating mostly Subway sandwiches.

11   But there were obstacles along the way for Subway, which is based in Milford, Conn. Critics inside the company found the background choral music too ponderous and reminiscent of political advertising, so the advertising agency Fallon Worldwide changed to a lighter, more inspirational tone. At first, the ads mentioned the actual number of pounds each youngster had shed, but officials of the American Heart Association, which was consulting on the project, balked and suggested that the spots focus more on the fact that the children felt better.

12   Then standards executives at two networks refused at first to broadcast the ads. "They felt as though Jared represented an extreme weight loss and that we shouldn't teach kids that they needed to have an extreme loss like that," said Chris Carroll, senior vice president for marketing at Subway's franchise-marketing group. "I didn't think we should back off, though, because kids' obesity is a real issue. And we didn't." Instead, it added disclaimers that spelled out the complexity of children's weight loss.

13   Innovative Candy Concepts Inc., based in Atlanta, has gone further, replacing its entire main product line, Too Tarts, with a new brand called Too Tarts Smart Choice, which contains only fruit juice as sweeteners and up to 60 percent fewer calories than the original. The company's chief executive, Armand Hammer (not related to the oil company executive of the same name), said he was motivated in part by a twinge of guilt last year at distributing sugar-laden products to his own grandchildren.

14   "For us to make that kind of statement, we thought, was responsible and would be well accepted," said Mr. Hammer, whose company is donating 5 percent of net earnings from the new line to the American Diabetes Association. "And we were hoping that by doing so, we would make sort of a mission statement for the industry."

15   PepsiCo has also changed focus. Some 56 percent of the growth in its North American revenue in the first half of this year came from fare that PepsiCo defines as healthful, like Quaker Oats cereals, Gatorade sports drinks, Aquafina bottled waters and baked and reduced-fat Frito-Lay snacks. The company has started a program called Smart Spot, in which healthier products across all its brands carry a green logo.

16   Yet the way some critics see it, PepsiCo has a lot to change, considering the role that soft drinks and high-calorie salty snacks have played in childhood obesity. And while the practice has declined recently, they also note that some Pepsi bottlers still make big cash payments to win exclusive on-campus vending contracts from school districts that may be short on money.

17   Mr. Leach said Pepsi had embraced the idea that "it's in our interest for kids to be able to make sustainable health choices." Last year, Pepsi introduced 30 reduced-calorie products that are sold at schools, like SoBe Synergy, which is 50 percent fruit juice and has fewer calories than all-juice alternatives. The Quaker Oats division is test-marketing a flavored-milk product called Chillers that is sweetened without sugar and has vitamins and minerals added. Frito-Lay has reformulated its snack-food recipes to

eliminate nearly all trans-fats, which contribute to coronary problems like blocked arteries. And PepsiCo said it had placed 17,000 new Aquafina and Gatorade vending machines in schools last year.

18   Like Coca-Cola, Kraft, McDonald's and others, PepsiCo is also aiming to make children more active. Gatorade, for example, is working with the University of North Carolina on ideas that include simple things like promoting construction of more sidewalks where children can play. And PepsiCo has committed $2 million a year for three years to an in-school program beginning this fall called Balance First, whose goal is to have 2.5 million students eat 100 fewer calories each day and burn off 100 calories more, mainly through walking; several hundred elementary schools around the country have committed to introducing the program through science or health classes.

19   "The idea is to prevent kids from accumulating that excess one or two pounds each year," said James O. Hill, a professor at the health sciences center of the University of Colorado, who developed Balance First. "We can look at the industry as the enemy," he added, "but we're only going to change this problem with kids if we actually engage the private sector in helping."

20   Still, skeptics say all this can be a smokescreen for food, beverage and restaurant companies.

21   Their role first and foremost should be producing and promoting only healthy-as-possible kinds of foods, especially when it comes to children," said Dr. Willett of Harvard.

22   Even with the new products, it remains difficult for the industry to resist the profits offered by the status quo. As part of an effort called Kids Smart Eating that it introduced in June, Ruby Tuesday, a restaurant chain based in Maryville, Tenn., took grilled-cheese sandwiches and macaroni-and-cheese casserole off its new children's menu in favor of entrees like whole-grain tortillas with turkey and cheese.

23   But by mid-August—thanks to popular demand—grilled cheese and mac-and-cheese were back on the menu.

Our third reading, from the September 27, 2003, edition of the British medical journal the *Lancet*, looks beyond the food industry to architecture and city planning as a means to change our lifestyle and improve our health. The author of this piece, Marilynn Larkin, is a well-known journalist and contributing editor to the *Lancet*.

Marilynn Larkin
Can Cities Be Designed to Fight Obesity?

1   In the USA, one in three adults is obese—as are roughly one in seven children and adolescents—and Europeans are not far behind. Even China has seen the prevalence of overweight double in women and triple in men from 1989 to 1997.

2   According to research in the USA, we tend to put on weight gradually. Adults in one study, for example, added about 2 pounds (0.9 kg) a year from age 20 to 40 years. This means they were taking in an excess of only about 100 kcal of energy a day—suggesting that if people could be induced to eat just a little less—or to move around just a little more, it might be possible to prevent obesity. And not much activity would be required, according to a new US fitness campaign called America on the Move, which maintains that Americans could burn off the extra calories by taking only 2000 extra steps a day—about 15–20 min of walking. Sounds easy enough, but the problem, experts say, is that in many modern cities, cut by busy streets and roaring expressways, it can be difficult to find a place to walk.

3   "Many people do not have safe and easy access to activity-friendly environments", says Richard Killingsworth, director of Active Living by Design (http://www.activelivingbydesign.org), a programme of the University of North Carolina's School of Public Health and the Robert Wood Johnson Foundation looking at ways communities can be designed to encourage more physical activity. "In the USA, most communities have a transportation system that is built around the automobile. And so our research asks which elements will draw people outside and entice them to engage in physical activity: Is it sidewalks? Bikeways? Aesthetics? Traffic speed around them? Perception of crime? Weather? We're going to try to influence these variables to improve health outcomes."

4   The philosophy behind the programme, says Killingsworth, "is recognising that physical activity does not necessarily begin and end in the gym or fitness centre; it can be simple things such as gardening, walking instead of driving, and taking stairs instead of the elevator. Incorporating these activities into a daily routine can serve as a gateway to more vigorous activity." To accomplish

this, changes need to be made not just in thinking, but also in physical structures, he says.

5   "The idea is that as communities are built or rebuilt, the design standard is to build to the human scale, instead of to the automotive scale", he explains. An important step in this direction was taken in July, 2003, when the Pedestrian and Cyclists Equity Act was introduced in the US Congress. The bill would funnel US$350 million per year for 6 years to fund active-living strategies—building safe routes to schools, bicycle trails, and community demonstration projects that provide incentives for people to become more physically active.

6   Much of the impetus for such projects comes from a shift in thinking on the part of the US Centers for Disease Control and Prevention (CDC), says Marya Morris, head of the Planning and Designing the Physically Active Community project at the American Planning Association. "The CDC has realised over the past few years that individual interventions simply aren't getting people moving. And it turns out that a lot of the solutions city planners are looking at for solving 'sprawl'—scattered development that increases traffic and destroys open space—are also appropriate for solving issues related to physical activity. This convergence of priorities represents a remarriage of city planning and public health. Planners come at it with the imperative of solving congestion or lack of open-space issues, and health professionals are asking, 'what is it about these same patterns that are making people fat?"

7   For the "remarriage" to work, city planners must recognise the need to partner with advocacy groups and city councils to push the agenda through on a public policy level, says Morris. "Physicians also need to shift away from an individualistic approach and ask what in the environment prevents people from incorporating activity into their daily lives and what changes can they recommend to policy makers to make the changes happen."

8   Demonstration projects in a variety of communities are under way. In New York City, Majora Carter, executive director of the Sustainable South Bronx project, is overseeing a feasibility study for a greenway that would extend along 5 miles of the area's shoreline, creating a public waterfront with cycling and walking paths and recreational activities.

9   The South Bronx, explains Carter, "is among the poorest districts in the USA, with a large minority population and some of the largest concentrations

of waste facilities, diesel trucks, and environmental burdens. Trees, green parks—you name it, and we don't have it. In terms of active living, it's not just the air quality that's dangerous, but also the streets themselves. When people are selling drugs on the street, it's hard to say, 'let's go out and play'."

10   A recent pilot project showed that the South Bronx waterway could be used for something other than waste facilities and industry, by creating a small park that has become a focal point of activity, notes Carter. "People do things because the doctor tells them to", she emphasises, and so her group is partnering with physicians at Montefiore Medical Center's Children's Hospital, as well as local schools, to ensure that young people, in particular, take advantage of the evolving waterfront.

11   At the other end of the spectrum, Helen Thompson, programme and research liaison in the Center for Human Nutrition (University of Colorado Health Sciences Center), is involved with Stapleton, a planned community near Denver being built from the ground up to support active living. Stapleton is located on 4700 acres of land where Denver's old airport used to be. "We're making it a learning lab and model community for health and active living", says Thompson.

12   The community now has about 1000 residents, although eventually there will be 20,000–30,000, plus another 30 000 people working in the area. Design plans call for smaller housing lots but with more parks, and open space and with shops, restaurants, theatres, and workplaces within walking distance of homes and apartments. Even now, with a handful of stores and a

---

Panel 1: UK and Australia already on the move

The UK and Australia are far ahead of the USA and already have several well-developed programmes for promoting fitness-friendly environments. The UK's Walking the Way to Health Initiative (http://www.whi.org.uk), which is a project of the British Heart Foundation and the Countryside Agency, is an example. "We started with the idea of pulling together information about health and the accessibility and availability of the countryside—everything from local green space, parks, and gardens to the wildest and remotest areas that we have in the UK", explains project coordinator Mitch Counsell. Pilot projects in the south of England "showed good returns in terms of people accessing the countryside. In addition, we had a great deal of feedback regarding social interaction benefits; aside from feeling better, people were getting out and meeting other people. One of the byproducts has been improvement in mental wellbeing."

Panel 2. Websites for the projects discussed in this feature

Active Living by Design: http://www.activelivingbydesign.org

American Planning Association: http://www.planning.org/physicallyactive

American on the Move: http://www.americaonthemove.org

National Recreation and Parks Association: http://www.nrpa.org

Walking the Way to Health: http://www.whi.org.uk

Stapleton: http://www.stapletondenver.com

Text of the Pedestrian and Cyclists Equity Act: http://www.house.gov/transportation_democrats/Of_Interest/030612_PACESummary.htm

town centre, "everything's accessible, and it's easy to walk or bike to do what you need to", says Thompson. About 80% of people now working in Stapleton use alternative modes of transportation, she says.

13   Karen Donato, coordinator of the US National Heart, Lung, and Blood Institute (NHLBI)'s Obesity Education Initiative, notes that many communities already have venues that are conducive to physical activity. "Many people aren't even aware of what might be available locally", says Donato, who works with Hearts n' Parks, an initiative of the NHLBI and the National Parks and Recreation Association. The programme recently reported results from written questionnaires given to children and adults in 36 sites ("magnet centers") regarding knowledge, behaviour, and attitudes towards healthy eating and physical activity before and after participating in a Hearts n' Parks programme. Participants improved on almost all indicators.

14   The initiative sets forth certain principles, and communities are free to implement suitable programmes. "Some are quite inventive", says Donato. "The Roswell, New Mexico, site had an alien chase. In Arizona, young people performed in a play that modelled what it feels like to be heavy and carry around a lot of weight, and what happens when they take off the pounds. In Nevada, we worked with the local university to implement a public health curriculum that involved students in a Hearts n' Parks internship." Gathering reliable data for outcomes measures is a challenge, says Donato. "These are nonprofessionals doing before-and-after outcomes studies against enormous odds—older people, for example, are reluctant to fill out anything and often have vision problems; children come in and out of the programme, and so they're not exposed every day." NHLBI ultimately developed scripts to help local health and activity personnel ask the right questions and gather as much reliable information on the effects of the programme as possible.

15   "Now that parks and recreation departments are being geared up to recognising their role in health, there's a receptivity that physicians can take advantage of," notes Donate. "We've seen studies showing that overweight people are not even told by their doctors that they have a problem, and that they need to do something about it. Now physicians can say, go to your park and recreation centre."

References

Anderson, C. L., & Nickols, S. Y. (2001). The essence of our being: A synopsis of the 2001 Commemorative Lecture. Journal of Family and Consumer Sciences, 93, 15–18.

Braet, C., Mervielde, I., & Vandereycken, W. (1997). Psychological aspects of childhood obesity: A controlled study in a clinical and nonclinical sample. Journal of Pediatric Psychology, 22, 59–71.

Bruce, G. M. (1993). Implementing a university campus wellness model. American Association of Occupational Health Nurses Journal, 41, 120–123.

Epstein, L. H. (1996). Family-based behavioural intervention for obese children. International Journal of Obesity and Related Metabolic Disorders, 20, S14–S21.

Composing Your Synthesis Essay

The main project of composing your synthesis essay is to move from the kernels of good ideas that you generated in your learning logs or personal reflection to the fully developed and logically organized discussion of these ideas.

Generating and Exploring Ideas

If you have speculated about, responded to, and explored your texts using the progression of learning logs, you should now have a body of ideas to use in the development of your synthesis essay. Your task in the production of your essay is to sort through, make decisions about, and pursue further both the analysis ideas and the synthesis ideas that you have generated.

   If you did the learning logs, look again at your reflections. For the analysis part of your essay, identify the points in Learning Logs 2 and 3 that strike you as the most interesting, lively, profound, or significant. For the synthesis part of your essay, identify the points in Learning Logs 4 and 5 that you feel most excited about or interested in. In both cases, add new ideas generated by class discussion and further reflection.

Shaping and Drafting

Both focusing and organizing your ideas for a synthesis essay are challenging writing tasks. We offer some suggestions for formulating a thesis that will direct and hold together your essay. There are also several plans you can use for developing your essay.

Analysis section: About two-thirds of your essay should focus on analyzing the texts. This part of the body of your essay should compare and contrast what the texts claim and argue, how they frame the problem you are exploring, how they present different angles of vision, and where they intersect or differ in their perspectives or approaches. The analysis part of your essay should show how you have wallowed in the complexity of the texts. What do the authors of the texts do to make their readers think? How rhetorically effective are these texts? How and how well do the authors' examples and approaches support their theses and advance their views?

Synthesis section: About one-third of your essay should be your synthesis. Where do the texts and their authors leave you in your thinking? What have you discovered or realized after studying these texts? What new perspectives have you gained through the contrast and/or clash of different ideas? How much or how little have these texts changed your views and why?

Writing a Thesis for a Synthesis Essay

It is often difficult to write a one-sentence, high-level thesis statement for a synthesis essay that encompasses all your analysis and synthesis points. In such cases you can write two lower-level thesis statements—one for your analysis section and one for your synthesis section—and simply join them together. What is important is that your thesis forecasts your main analysis and synthesis points and creates a map for your reader. This is the strategy used by Kate at the end of her introduction:

For a full explanation of thesis statements, purpose statements, and mapping statements, see pp. 545–546.

KATE'S THESIS

Although both Turkle and Ritzer identify problems in technology's influence and in society's responses to it, Turkle sees more potential and gain where Ritzer sees mostly peril and loss. Both articles made me question how we define our values and morality in this postmodern, technologically advanced world and persuaded me of the need for caution in embracing technology.

Lower-level thesis for analysis

Lower-level thesis for synthesis

Your thesis statement should be clear, specific, focused, and risky. It should be the product of earnest intellectual work, insights achieved through serious reflection, and your own original connecting of ideas. Avoid noncontestable thesis statements such as "These articles have both good points and bad points." Try to formulate your thesis so that it challenges or surprises your reader.

See pp. 34–37 for a discussion of how to avoid unsurprising, noncontestable thesis statements.

Here are some more examples:

EXAMPLE 1

Whereas Ritzer focuses on the way high-tech society makes us homogeneous and superficial, Turkle focuses on how the Internet unsettles traditional views of the self. Although I agree with Ritzer's argument that McDonaldization is dehumanizing, I think that role-playing in MUDs is actually a healthy way to oppose McDonaldization and expresses human desire to be creative, to develop the self, and to make human connections.

Lower-level thesis for analysis

Lower-level thesis for synthesis

EXAMPLE 2

Ritzer's attack on technological society and Turkle's more optimistic belief that it offers opportunity for growth and discovery have together forced me to consider the superficiality and vulnerability of human relationships in our high-tech society.

Writer chooses high-level, one-sentence thesis rather than two lower-level theses

Possible Organizations for Synthesis Essays

The biggest organizational decision you have to make in writing a synthesis essay is how much to summarize your texts and how to incorporate these summaries into your essay. Your decision should be guided by your audience's familiarity with the texts you are discussing and the complexity of the points you are making.

PLAN 1

- Introductory paragraph that presents the focusing question and hooks the reader

- Summaries of the texts you are examining (unless your instructor posits that readers have already read the texts, in which case you can omit the summaries or reduce them to one or two sentences each)
- A thesis that maps out your main analytical points and your main synthesis points. Your thesis can come at the end of the paragraph(s) with your summaries or in a mini-paragraph of its own.
- Paragraphs discussing and developing your analytical points
- Synthesis section consisting of paragraphs discussing and developing your synthesis points
- Concluding paragraph that reiterates the values and limitations of the texts you have analyzed, pulls together your new insights, and leaves readers thinking about your views

PLAN 2

- Introductory paragraph that presents the focusing question and hooks the reader
- A thesis that maps out your main analytical points and your main synthesis points
- Summary and analysis of the first text
- Summary and analysis of the second text
- Synthesis section that develops several main synthesis points
- Concluding paragraph that reiterates the values and limitations of the texts you have analyzed, pulls together your new insights, and leaves readers thinking about your views

Revising

As you revise your synthesis essay, make sure that you have set up the focusing question effectively. Then work on clarifying and developing your analytical points while striving for an engaging style. Also consider how to make your synthesis views more clearly reflect your wrestling with the texts' ideas. Think about finding the most interesting ways to show how these texts have enlarged and deepened your own views on technology's effect on us. The following Guidelines for Peer Reviews can both help your peer reviewers and direct you as you think of ways to revise your paper.

GUIDELINES FOR PEER REVIEWS

Instructions for peer reviews are provided in Chapter 17 (pp. 519–520).

For the Writer
Prepare two or three questions you would like your peer reviewer to address while responding to your draft. The questions can focus on some aspect of your draft

that you are uncertain about, on one or more sections where you particularly seek help or advice, on some feature that you particularly like about your draft, or on some part you especially wrestled with. Write out your questions and give them to your peer reviewer along with your draft.

For the Reviewer

I. Read the draft at a normal reading speed from beginning to end. As you read, do the following:

   A. Place a wavy line in the margin next to any passages that you find confusing, that contain some idea or word that doesn't seem to fit, or that otherwise slow down your reading.

   B. Place a "Good!" in the margin next to any passages where you think the writing is particularly strong or interesting.

II. Read the draft again slowly and answer the following questions by writing brief explanations of your answers.

   A. Introduction and summaries of the texts:

      1. How could the introduction present the focusing question more powerfully, showing its significance, relevance, and problematic nature?

      2. How could the summaries be expanded or condensed to suit more closely the audience's knowledge of these texts? In other words, does this audience need longer or shorter summaries of the texts in order to understand the writer's analysis and synthesis?

      3. How could the placement of the summaries—in the introductory paragraph or woven into the analysis section of the paper—be improved?

      4. How could the summaries be made more accurate, fair, and clear?

      5. How could the thesis be made more focused, risky, and clear in setting up the writer's analytical and synthesis points?

   B. Analytical section of the essay:

      1. How could the analytical points more clearly compare and contrast the authors' values, assumptions, angles of vision, or rhetorical strategies in addressing the question of the problem of technology?

      2. What further textual evidence could the writer add to develop these analytical points and make them more interesting or comprehensive?

   C. Synthesis section of the essay:

      1. How could the writer's synthesis points more clearly demonstrate the writer's thoughtful interaction with these texts and with the question of technology's influence?

      2. What examples or other specifics could the writer include to develop these synthesis points more effectively?

      3. How could the writer conclude this essay more effectively to leave readers with a new perspective on the texts and on the underlying question?

III. Rhetorical considerations

   A. *Purpose, audience,* and *genre:* Your purpose is to write an academic paper that analyzes two or more texts and synthesizes its ideas. How effectively does this paper summarize and analyze these texts for an audience who hasn't read them? Where does this draft do a good job at synthesizing ideas to show the writer's own original thinking? How effectively does this draft meet the genre expectations for an academic paper?

B. *Logos, ethos,* and *pathos:* How effectively does this draft present and develop its ideas? Where or how does the writer establish credibility as a thoughtful and knowledgeable person? How has the writer connected this analysis and synthesis with the values and interests of the audience?

IV. If the writer has prepared questions for you, respond to his or her inquiries.

V. Sum up what you see as the main strengths and problem areas of the draft:

A. Strengths

B. Problem areas

VI. Read the draft one more time. Place a check mark in the margin wherever you notice problems in grammar, spelling, or mechanics (one check mark per problem).

Writing as a Problem-Solving Process

I rewrite as I write. It is hard to tell what is a first draft because it is not determined by time. In one draft, I might cross out three pages, write two, cross out a fourth, rewrite it, and call it a draft. I am constantly writing and rewriting. I can only conceptualize so much in my first draft—only so much information can be held in my head at one time; my rewriting efforts are a reflection of how much information I can encompass at one time. There are levels and agenda which I have to attend to in each draft.*

> —DESCRIPTION OF REVISION BY AN EXPERIENCED WRITER

I read what I have written and I cross out a word and put another word in; a more decent word or a better word. Then if there is somewhere to use a sentence that I have crossed out, I will put it there.*

> —DESCRIPTION OF REVISION BY AN INEXPERIENCED WRITER

Blot out, correct, insert, refine,
Enlarge, diminish, interline;
Be mindful, when invention fails,
To scratch your head, and bite your nails.

> —JONATHAN SWIFT

In Part One of this text we focused on writing as a problem-solving process in which writers pose and solve both subject-matter problems and rhetorical problems. Part Three shows you how to translate these basic principles into effective strategies for composing and revising your writing along the continuum from closed to open forms. The three self-contained chapters, which can be read in whatever sequence best fits your instructor's course plan, will help you compose and revise the essays you write for the assignments in Part Two.

This chapter explains how experienced writers use multiple drafts to manage the complexities of writing and suggests ways for you to improve your own writing processes. Chapter 18, which takes the form of ten self-contained lessons,

*From Nancy Sommers, "Revision Strategies of Student Writers and Experienced Adult Writers," *College Composition and Communication* 31 (October 1980): 291–300.

focuses on key strategies for composing and revising closed-form prose. Chapter 19 switches from closed to open forms, showing you how, when appropriate, to open your prose by creating surprises of style and structure that engage readers and involve them in the process of completing your text's meaning.

Understanding How Experts Compose and Revise

We begin this chapter with a close look at how experienced writers compose, explaining what they think about when they write and why they often need multiple drafts. Composition theorist Peter Elbow has asserted that "meaning is not what you start out with" but "what you end up with." Thus composing is a discovery process. In the early stages of writing, experienced writers typically discover what they are trying to say, often deepening and complicating their ideas rather than clarifying them. Only in the last drafts will such writers be in sufficient control of their ideas to shape them elegantly for readers.

It's important not to overgeneralize, however, because no two writers compose exactly the same way; moreover, the same writer may use different processes for different kinds of prose. Some writers outline their ideas before they write; others need to write extensively before they can outline. Some write their first drafts very slowly, devoting extensive thought and planning to each emerging paragraph; others write first drafts rapidly, to be sure to get all their ideas on paper, and then rework the material part by part. Some prefer to work independently, without discussing or sharing their ideas; others seek out classmates or colleagues to help them hash out ideas and rehearse their arguments before writing them down. Some seek out the stillness of a library or private room; others do their best writing in noisy cafeterias or coffee shops.

The actual mechanics of composing differ from writer to writer as well. Some writers create first drafts directly at a keyboard, whereas others require the reassuring heft of a pen or pencil. Among writers who begin by planning the structure of their work, some make traditional outlines (perhaps using the flexible outline feature on their word processors), whereas others prefer tree diagrams or flowcharts. Some of those who use word processors revise directly at the computer, whereas others print out a hard copy, revise with pen, and then type the changes into the computer.

Also, writers often vary their composing processes from project to project. A writer might complete one project with a single draft and a quick editing job, but produce a half dozen or more drafts for another project.

What experienced writers do have in common is a willingness to keep revising their work until they feel it is ready to go public. They typically work much harder at drafting and revising than do inexperienced writers, taking more runs at their subject. And experienced writers generally make more substantial alterations in their drafts during revision. (Compare the first two quotations that open this chapter—one from an experienced and one from an inexperienced writer.) An experienced writer will sometimes throw away a first draft and start over; a beginning writer tends to be more satisfied with early drafts and to think of revi-

FIGURE 17.1 Draft Page of Experienced Writer

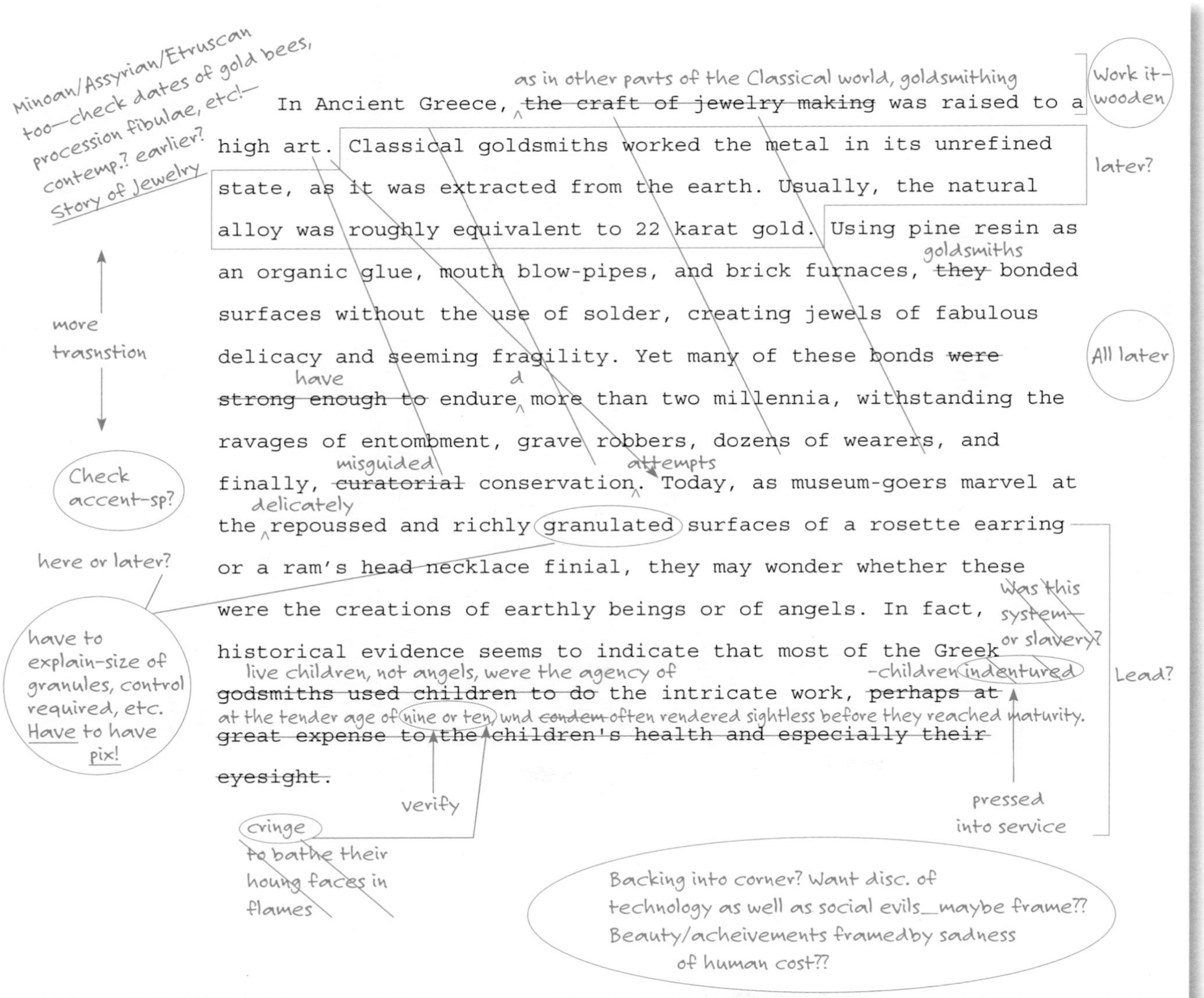

In Ancient Greece, the craft of jewelry making was raised to a high art. Classical goldsmiths worked the metal in its unrefined state, as it was extracted from the earth. Usually, the natural alloy was roughly equivalent to 22 karat gold. Using pine resin as an organic glue, mouth blow-pipes, and brick furnaces, they bonded surfaces without the use of solder, creating jewels of fabulous delicacy and seeming fragility. Yet many of these bonds were strong enough to endure more than two millennia, withstanding the ravages of entombment, grave robbers, dozens of wearers, and finally, curatorial conservation. Today, as museum-goers marvel at the repoussed and richly granulated surfaces of a rosette earring or a ram's head necklace finial, they may wonder whether these were the creations of earthly beings or of angels. In fact, historical evidence seems to indicate that most of the Greek goldsmiths used children to do the intricate work, perhaps at great expense to the children's health and especially their eyesight.

Handwritten annotations:

Minoan/Assyrian/Etruscan too—check dates of etc—
procession fibulae? earlier?
contemp? earlier?
Story of jewelry

as in other parts of the Classical world, goldsmithing

Work it- wooden later?

goldsmiths

All later

have / a / misguided attempts / delicately

move transition

Check accent-sp?

here or later?

have to explain-size of granules, control required, etc. Have to have pix!

cringe / to bathe their hung faces in flames

verify

Was this system— or slavery?
children indentured Lead?

-children often rendered sightless before they reached maturity.

at the tender age of nine or ten, who condem

live children, not angels, were the agency of

pressed into service

Backing into corner? Want disc. of technology as well as social evils...maybe frame?? Beauty/acheivements framed by sadness of human cost??

509

sion as primarily cleaning up errors. Figure 17.1 shows the first page of a first draft for a magazine article written by an experienced writer.

A Working Description of the Writing Process

The writing process we have just described may be considerably different from what you have previously been taught. For many years—before researchers began studying the composing processes of experienced writers—writing teachers typically taught a model something like this:

OLD MODEL OF THE WRITING PROCESS

1. Choose a topic
2. Narrow it
3. Write a thesis
4. Make an outline
5. Write a draft
6. Revise
7. Edit

The major problem with this model is that hardly anyone writes this way. We know of no writers who being by choosing a topic and narrowing it. Rather, as we explained in Part One, writers begin with a sense of a problem or of a conversation that isn't quite satisfactory. Writers identify questions that impel them to add their own voice to a conversation. Nor is the process neatly linear, as the old model implies. Sometimes writers settle on a thesis early in the writing process. But just as frequently they formulate a thesis during an "Aha!" moment of discovery later in the process, perhaps after several drafts. (So *this* is my point! Here is my argument in a nutshell!) Even very late in the process, while checking spelling and punctuation, experienced writers are apt to think of new ideas, thus triggering more revision.

More Accurate View of the Writing Process

Early in the process	• *Writers become aware of a question or problem.* Initially the question may not be well defined, but writers identify something unknown about the topic, feel dissatisfied with someone else's view of it, or wish to add something new or different to the conversation.
	• *Writers explore the problem.* Through research, critical thinking, and exploratory writing and talking, writers search for an effective response to the problem. They consider what different audiences might already know about the problem, what these audiences believe, and how they might be surprised by the writer's view. Writers might take time off from the problem and let ideas cook in the subconscious.

More Accurate View of the Writing Process *continued*

- *Writers begin conceptualizing the paper in terms of purpose, audience, and genre.* As ideas for a paper take shape—through outlining or early drafting—writers try to imagine a purpose for writing in terms of the change they want to bring about in the audience. They also consider the conventions and constraints of their intended genre.

- *Writers complete a first draft.* At some point writers put ideas on paper in a whole or partial draft. Some writers make an informal outline prior to writing. Others discover direction as they write, putting aside concerns about form and coherence until later. One of the major causes of writer's block among less experienced writers is the desire to make the paper perfect the first time. Experienced writers know their first drafts are often messy and unfocused, and they lower their expectations accordingly. Some writers even like to call their first drafts "zero drafts" or "garbage drafts" to emphasize these lower expectations.

Midway through the process

- *Writers begin to revise and reformulate.* The real work of actual composing now begins. Once they have written a first draft, writers can start to see the whole territory. The second draft may be quite different from the first. Some writers actually discard the first draft, reshaping their initial insights into a different structure. Others go slowly through the first draft, adding, deleting, reordering, or completely rewriting passages.

- *Writers increasingly consider the needs and expectations of readers.* As writers clarify their ideas for themselves, they increasingly reorganize for readers. Using knowledge of "reader expectation theory," which we describe in detail in Chapter 18, writers build into their text mapping statements, transitions, and structural cues. They also create unity and coherence by following the "old/new contract" explained in Chapter 18.

- *Writers seek feedback from readers.* Experienced writers regularly ask trusted colleagues to read their drafts and offer feedback. Composition instructors often try to create the same experience for students by organizing peer review workshops.

- *Writers often go through many additional drafts.* It is not unusual for an experienced writer to go through numerous drafts, making both large-scale "global revisions" (different structure, complete rewriting of sections, revised purpose) as well as small-scale "local revisions" (unifying or developing paragraphs, rewriting sentences).

Late in the process

- *Writers edit for style and correctness.* Eventually the writer's sense of purpose and audience stabilizes, and the ideas become increasingly clear, well organized, and developed. At this point writers begin shifting their attention to the craft of writing—getting each word, phrase, sentence, and paragraph just right so that the prose is clear, graceful, and correct.

- *Writers edit for manuscript form and genre considerations.* Writers also edit to meet the genre conventions of document design, citation style, and so forth. The professional appearance of a manuscript creates the audience's first impression of the writer's *ethos*.

We should emphasize again that the writing process is recursive, rather than linear. A writer might be "early in the process" for one part of a draft and "late in the process" for another. Frequently, a writer can also reconceptualize the argument late in the process and seemingly "start over"—but the time has not been wasted since the whole process has led to the writer's new ideas.

For Writing and Discussion

When you write, do you follow a process resembling the one we just described? Have you ever

- had a writing project grow out of your engagement with a problem or question?
- explored ideas by talking with others or by doing exploratory writing?
- made major changes to a draft because you changed your mind or otherwise discovered new ideas?
- revised a draft from a reader's perspective by consciously trying to imagine and respond to a reader's questions, confusions, and other reactions?
- road-tested a draft by trying it out on readers and then revising it as a result of what they told you?

Working in groups or as a whole class, share stories about previous writing experiences that match or do not match the description of experienced writers' processes. To the extent that your present process differs, what strategies of experienced writers might you like to try?

Improving Your Own Writing Processes

The previous section describes the many ways in which experienced writers compose. In this section we'll show you how to use this knowledge to improve your own writing processes. We'll begin with an overview list of expert composing strategies that you can start to practice right away. We'll then explain techniques for exploratory writing followed by some advice on drafting and global revision.

Practice the Composing Strategies of Experienced Writers

One of the best ways to improve your composing processes is to practice strategies used by experienced writers.

- *Use exploratory writing and talking to discover and clarify ideas.* Don't let your first draft be the first time you put your ideas into written words. Use exploratory writing to generate ideas and deepen thinking. (Later in this section we explain the techniques of freewriting, focused freewriting, and idea-mapping.) Also seek out opportunities to talk about your ideas with classmates or friends in order to clarify your own thinking and appreciate alternative points of view. Whenever possible, talk through your draft with a friend; rehearse your argument in conversation as practice for putting it in writing.

- **Schedule your time.** Plan for exploration, drafting, revision, and editing. Don't begin your paper the night before it is due. Give ideas time to ruminate in your mind. Recognize that your ideas will shift, branch out, even turn around as you write. Allow some time off between writing the first draft and beginning revision. Experienced writers build in time for revision.

- **Discover what methods of drafting work best for you.** Some people compose rough drafts directly on the computer; others write longhand. Some make outlines first; others plunge directly into drafting and make outlines later. Some revise extensively on the computer as they are drafting; others plough ahead until they have a complete draft before they start revising. Some people sit at their desk for hours at a time; others need to get up and walk around every couple of minutes. Some people need a quiet room; others work best in a coffee shop. Discover the methods that work best for you.

- **Occasionally revise on double- or triple-spaced hard copy.** Because many experienced writers revise on the screen without going through paper drafts, it is hard to say when one draft ends and another begins. Nevertheless, there are powerful advantages in printing off occasional paper drafts. Research suggests that writers are apt to make more large-scale changes in a draft if they work from hard copy. Because they can see the whole draft at once without having to scroll through a file, they can see more easily how the parts connect to the whole. They can look back at page two while revising page six. We suggest that you occasionally print out a double- or triple-spaced hard copy of your draft and then mark it up aggressively. Cross out text to be changed and write new text in the blank spaces between the lines. Make inserts. Draw arrows. (See again Figure 17.1, which shows how a professional writer marks up a draft.) When your draft gets too messy, type your changes in your computer and begin another round of revision.

- **Exchange drafts with others.** Get other people's reactions to your work in exchange for your reactions to theirs. Experienced writers regularly seek critiques of their drafts from trusted readers. Later in this chapter we explain procedures for peer review of drafts.

- **Save correctness for last.** To revise productively, concentrate first on the big questions: Do I have good ideas in this draft? Am I responding appropriately to the assignment? Are my ideas adequately organized and developed? Save questions about exact wording, grammar, and mechanics for later. These concerns are important, but they cannot be efficiently attended to until after higher-order concerns are met. Your first goal is to create a thoughtful, richly developed draft.

Explore Ideas through Freewriting, Idea-Mapping, and Good Talking

Another way to improve your writing processes is to explore ideas through informal writing and talking. Composition theorists sometimes refer to this stage of writing as *prewriting* or *invention*. When you use exploratory writing, such as writing in a journal or doing regular "thinking pieces," you'll have a record of your thinking that you can draw on later. Moreover, the very act of recording your thoughts on paper—or articulating them to others orally—stimulates more ideas. In this section, we will briefly describe four exploratory strategies that will help you learn to think like an experienced writer: freewriting, focused freewriting, idea-mapping, and dialectic discussion.

Freewriting

Freewriting, also sometimes called *nonstop writing* or *silent, sustained writing,* asks you to record your thinking directly. To freewrite, put pen to paper (or sit at your computer screen, perhaps turning *off* the monitor so that you can't see what you are writing) and write rapidly, *nonstop,* for ten to fifteen minutes at a stretch. Don't worry about grammar, spelling, organization, transitions, or other features of edited writing. The object is to think of as many ideas as possible. Some freewriting looks like stream of consciousness. Some is more organized and focused, although it lacks the logical connections and development that would make it suitable for an audience of strangers.

Many freewriters find that their initial reservoir of ideas runs out in three to five minutes. If this happens, force yourself to keep your fingers moving. If you can't think of anything to say, write, "Relax" over and over (or "This is stupid" or "I'm stuck") until new ideas emerge.

What do you write about? The answer varies according to your situation. Often you will freewrite in response to a question or problem posed by your instructor. Sometimes you will pose your own questions and use freewriting to explore possible answers or simply generate ideas. Here is an example of a student's freewrite in response to the prompt "What puzzles you about homelessness?"

> Let's see, what puzzles me about homelessness? Homeless homeless. Today on my way to work I passed a homeless guy who smiled at me and I smiled back though he smelled bad. What are the reasons he was out on the street? Perhaps an extraordinary string of bad luck. Perhaps he was pushed out onto the street. Not a background of work ethic, no place to go, no way to get someplace to live that could be afforded, alcoholism. To what extent do government assistance, social spending, etc, keep people off the street? What benefits could a person get that stops "the cycle"? How does welfare affect homelessness, drug abuse programs, family planning? To what extent does the individual have control over homelessness? This question of course goes to the depth of the question of how community affects the individual. Relax, relax. What about the signs that I see on the way to work posted on the windows of businesses that read, "please don't give to panhandlers it only promotes

drug abuse etc" a cheap way of getting homeless out of the way of business? Are homeless the natural end of unrestricted capitalism? What about the homeless people who are mentally ill? How can you maintain a living when haunted by paranoia? How do you decide if someone is mentally ill or just laughs at society? If one can't function obviously. How many mentally ill are out on the street? If you are mentally ill and have lost the connections to others who might take care of you I can see how you might end up on the street. What would it take to get treatment? To what extent can mentally ill be treated? When I see a homeless person I want to ask, How do you feel about the rest of society? When you see "us" walk by how do you think of us? Do you possibly care how we avoid you?

Note how this freewrite rambles, moving associatively from one topic or question to the next. Freewrites often have this kind of loose, associative structure. The value of such freewrites is that they help writers discover areas of interest or rudimentary beginnings of ideas. When you read back over one of your freewrites, try to find places that seem worth pursuing. Freewriters call these places "hot spots," "centers of interest," "centers of gravity," or simply "nuggets" or "seeds." The student who wrote the preceding freewrite discovered that he was particularly interested in the cluster of questions beginning "What about the homeless people who are mentally ill?" and he eventually wrote a research paper proposing a public policy for helping the mentally ill homeless. Because we believe this technique is of great value to writers, we suggest that you use it to generate ideas for class discussions and essays.

Focused Freewriting

Freewriting, as we have just described it, can be quick and associational, like brainstorming aloud on paper. Focused freewriting, in contrast, is less associational and aimed more at developing a line of thought. You wrestle with a specific problem or question, trying to think and write your way into its complexity and multiple points of view. Because the writing is still informal, with the emphasis on your ideas and not on making your writing grammatically or stylistically polished, you don't have to worry about spelling, punctuation, grammar, or organizational structure. Your purpose is to deepen and extend your thinking on the problem. Some instructors will create prompts or give you specific questions to ponder, and they may call this kind of exploratory writing "focused freewriting," "learning log responses," "writer's notebook entries," or "thinking pieces." You can see examples of focused freewriting in students' responses to the learning log tasks in Chapter 13.

Examples of these learning log entries are found on pp. 367–373.

Idea Mapping

Another good technique for exploring ideas is *idea mapping,* a more visual method than freewriting. To make an idea map, draw a circle in the center of a page and write down your broad topic area (or a triggering question or your thesis) inside the circle. Then record your ideas on branches and subbranches that extend out from the center circle. As long as you pursue one train of thought, keep recording your ideas on subbranches off the main branch. But as soon as that chain of ideas runs dry, go back and start a new branch.

Often your thoughts will jump back and forth between one branch and another. This technique will help you see them as part of an emerging design rather than as strings of unrelated ideas. Additionally, idea mapping establishes at an early stage a sense of hierarchy in your ideas. If you enter an idea on a subbranch, you can see that you are more fully developing a previous idea. If you return to the hub and start a new branch, you can see that you are beginning a new train of thought.

An idea map usually records more ideas than a freewrite, but the ideas are not as fully developed. Writers who practice both techniques report that they can vary the kinds of ideas they generate depending on which technique they choose. Figure 17.2 shows a student's idea map made while he was exploring issues related to the grading system.

Dialectic Discussion

Another effective way to explore the complexity of a topic is through face-to-face discussions with others, whether in class, over coffee in the student union, or late at night in bull sessions. Not all discussions are productive; some are too superficial and scattered, others too heated. Good ones are *dialectic*—participants with differing views on a topic try to understand each other and resolve their differences by examining contradictions in each person's position. The key to dialectic conversation is careful listening, made possible by an openness to each other's views. A dialectic discussion differs from a talk show shouting match or a pro/con debate in which proponents of opposing positions, their views set in stone, attempt to win the argument. In a dialectic discussion, participants assume that each position has strengths and weaknesses and that even the strongest position contains inconsistencies, which should be exposed and examined. When dialectic conversation works well, participants scrutinize their own positions more critically and deeply, and often alter their views. True dialectic conversation implies growth and change, not a hardening of positions.

For more discussion of dialectic conversation, see the criteria for class discussions in Chapter 4, p. 77; for more discussion on how to work cooperatively with others through dialectic discussion, see Chapter 23 on oral communication.

Draft Purposefully

When you sit down to compose your first draft, write purposefully by thinking of your rhetorical context: What is the question or problem you are addressing? Who is your audience? What change do you want to bring about in your audience's thinking? Sometimes you will know the answers to these questions before you start drafting. At other times, the act of drafting helps you discover ideas. Have confidence that the revising process will help you eventually make your ideas well structured, clear, and surprising to your readers. When writing your first draft, lower your expectations. (We said earlier that many experienced writers think of the first draft as their *zero draft* or *garbage draft*.) For more specific advice on drafting and revising, see Chapters 18 and 19 on composing and revising

FIGURE 17.2 Idea Map on Problems with the Grading System

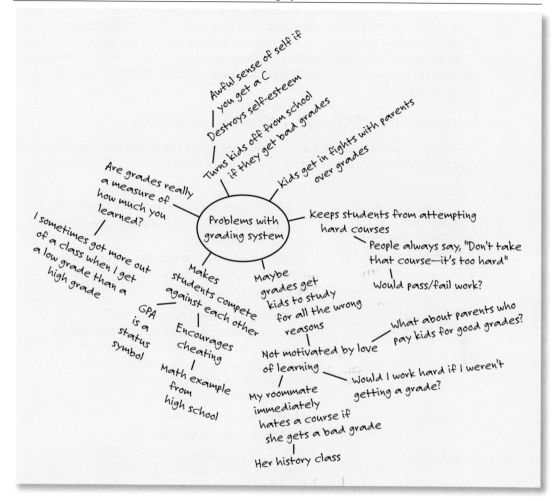

closed-form and open-form prose. If you are writing closed-form prose, pay particular attention at the drafting stage to Chapter 18's advice on planning and visualizing your structure (Lesson 3, pp. 535–541) and on writing introductions (Lesson 4, pp. 542–548). We have found that these lessons particularly help writers get started on a draft.

After Drafting, Revise Globally

As we explained at the start of this chapter, experienced writers revise their drafts much more extensively than do inexperienced writers. Inexperienced writers tend to revise *locally*; experienced writers revise *globally*. By *local revision*, we mean small-scale revisions at the level of the sentence—correcting spelling, finding a different word, perhaps adding a short example. By *global revision*, we mean large-scale revision at the level of ideas and structure—reshaping a whole section, crossing out a series of paragraphs, and rewriting from scratch in the light of new ideas.

To appreciate the significance of both global and local revision, consider the changes that experienced writers typically make in their drafts.

Recognize Kinds of Changes Typically Made in Drafts

We begin by classifying the kinds of changes writers typically make in drafts and explaining their reasons for making each sort of change.

Kinds of Changes	Reasons for Change
Crossing out whole passage and rewriting from scratch	Original passage was unfocused; ideas have changed.
	New sense of purpose or point meant that whole passage needed reshaping.
	Original passage was too confused or jumbled for mere editing.
Cutting and pasting; moving parts around	Original was disorganized.
	Points weren't connected to particulars.
	Conclusion was clearer than introduction; part of conclusion had to be moved to introduction.
	Rewriting introduction led to discovery of more effective plan of development; new forecasting required different order in body.
Deletions	Material not needed or irrelevant.
	Deleted material was good but went off on a tangent.
Additions	Supporting particulars needed to be added: examples, facts, illustrations, statistics evidence (usually added to bodies of paragraphs).
	Points and transitions needed to be supplied (often added to openings of paragraphs).
	New section needed to be added or a brief point expanded.
Recasting of sentences (crossing out and rewriting portions of sentences; combining sentences; rephrasing; starting sentences with a different grammatical structure)	Passage violated old/new contract (see pp. 556–562).
	Passage was wordy or choppy.
	Passage lacked rhythm and voice.
	Grammar was tangled, diction odd, meaning confused.
Editing sentences to correct mistakes	Words were misspelled or mistyped.
	Comma splices, fragments, dangling participles, other grammatical errors were found.

For Writing and Discussion

Choose an important paragraph in the body of a draft you are currently working on. Then write out your answers to these questions about that paragraph.

1. Why is this an important paragraph?
2. What is its main point?
3. Where is that main point stated?

Now—as an exercise only—write the main point at the top of a blank sheet of paper, put away your original draft, and, without looking at the original, write a new paragraph with the sole purpose of developing the point you wrote at the top of the page.

When you are finished, compare your new paragraph to the original. What have you learned that might help you revise your original?

Here are some typical responses of writers who have tried this exercise:

I recognized that my original paragraph was unfocused. I couldn't find a main point.

I recognized that my original paragraph was underdeveloped. I had a main point but not enough particulars supporting it.

I began to see that my draft was scattered and that I had too many short paragraphs.

I recognized that I was making a couple of different points in my original paragraph and that I needed to break it into separate paragraphs.

I recognized that I hadn't stated my main point (or that I had buried it in the middle of the paragraph).

I recognized that there was a big difference in style between my two versions and that I had to choose which version I liked best. (It's not always the "new" version!)

Using Peer Reviews to Stimulate Revision

One of the best ways to become a better reviser is to see your draft from a *reader's* rather than a *writer's* perspective. As a writer, you know what you mean; you are already inside your own head. But you need to see what your draft looks like to someone outside your head.

The best way to learn this skill is to practice reading your classmates' drafts and have them read yours. In this section we offer advice on how to respond candidly to your classmates' drafts and how to participate in peer reviews.

Becoming a Helpful Reader of Classmates' Drafts

When you respond to a writer's draft, learn to make readerly rather than writerly comments; describe your mental experience in trying to understand the draft rather than pointing out problems or errors in the draft. For example, instead of saying, "Your draft is disorganized," say, "I got lost when. . . ." Instead of saying,

"This paragraph needs a topic sentence," say, "I had trouble seeing the point of this paragraph."

When you help a writer with a draft, your goal is both to point out where the draft needs more work and to brainstorm with the writer possible ways to improve the draft. Begin by reading the draft all the way through at a normal reading speed. As you read, take mental notes to help focus your feedback. We suggest that you make wavy lines in the margin next to passages that you find confusing; write "Good!" in the margin where you like something; and write "?" in the margin where you want to ask questions.

After you have read the draft, use the following strategies for making helpful responses:

IF THE IDEAS IN THE DRAFT SEEM THIN OR UNDEVELOPED, OR IF THE DRAFT IS TOO SHORT:

- help the writer brainstorm for more ideas.
- help the writer add more examples, better details, more supporting data or arguments.

IF YOU GET CONFUSED OR LOST:

- have the writer talk through ideas to clear up confusing spots.
- help the writer sharpen the thesis: suggest that the writer view the thesis as the answer to a controversial or problematic question; ask the writer to articulate the question that the thesis answers.
- help the writer create an outline, tree diagram, or flowchart.

See Chapter 18 for a detailed explanation of these revision strategies.

- help the writer clarify the focus by asking him or her to complete these statements about purpose:
  My purpose in this paper is ————————————.
  My purpose in this section (paragraph) is ————————————.
  Before reading my paper, the reader will have this view of my topic: ————————————; after reading my paper, my reader will have this different view of my topic: ————————————.
- show the writer where you got confused or misued in reading the draft ("I started getting lost here because I couldn't see why you were giving me this information" or "I thought you were going to say X, but then you said Y").

IF YOU CAN UNDERSTAND THE SENTENCES BUT CAN'T SEE THE POINT:

- help the writer articulate the meaning by asking "So what?" questions, making the writer bring the point to the surface by stating it directly. ("I can understand what you are saying here but I don't quite understand why you are saying it. I read all these facts, and I say, 'So what?' What do these facts have to do with your thesis?")

IF YOU DISAGREE WITH THE IDEAS OR THINK THE WRITER HAS AVOIDED ALTERNATIVE POINTS OF VIEW:

- play devil's advocate to help the writer deepen and complicate ideas.
- show the writer specific places where you had queries or doubts.

For Writing and Discussion

In the following exercise, we ask you to respond to a student's draft ("Should the University Carpet the Dorm Rooms?" below). The assignment asked students to take a stand on a local campus issue. Imagine that you have exchanged drafts with this student and that your task is to help this student improve the draft.

Read the draft carefully; make wavy lines in the margins where you get confused, write "Good!" for something you like, and write "?" where you want to ask questions.

On your own, complete the following tasks:

1. Identify one specific place in the draft where you got confused. Freewrite a brief explanation for why you got confused. Make readerly rather than writerly comments.
2. Identify one place in the draft where you think the ideas are thin or need more development.
3. Identify one place where you might write "So what?" in the margins. These are places where you understand the sentences but don't see the point the writer is getting at.
4. Identify at least one place where you could play devil's advocate or otherwise object to the writer's ideas. Freewrite your objections.

In groups or as a whole class, share your responses. Then turn to the following tasks:

1. With the instructor serving as a guide, practice explaining to the writer where or how you got confused while reading the draft. Readers often have difficulty explaining their reading experience to a writer. Let several class members role-play being the reader. Practice using language such as "I like the way this draft started because . . . ." "I got confused when . . . ." "I had to back up and reread when . . . ." "I saw your point here, but then I got lost again because . . . ." Writing theorist Peter Elbow calls such language a "movie of your mind."
2. Have several class members role-play being devil's advocates by arguing against the writer's thesis. Where are the ideas thin or weak?

Should the University Carpet the Dorm Rooms?

Tricia, a university student, came home exhausted from her work-study job. She took a blueberry pie from the refrigerator to satisfy her hunger and a tall glass of milk to quench her thirst. While trying to get comfortable on her bed, she tipped her snack over onto the floor. She cleaned the mess, but the blueberry and milk stains on her brand-new carpet could not be removed.

(continued)

Tricia didn't realize how hard it was to clean up stains on a carpet. Luckily this was her own carpet.

A lot of students don't want carpets. Students constantly change rooms. The next person may not want carpet.

Some students say that since they pay to live on campus, the rooms should reflect a comfortable home atmosphere. Carpets will make the dorm more comfortable. The carpet will act as insulation and as a soundproofing system.

Paint stains cannot be removed from carpets. If the university carpets the rooms, the students will lose the privilege they have of painting their rooms any color. This would limit students' self-expression.

The carpets would be an institutional brown or gray. This would be ugly. With tile floors, the students can choose and purchase their own carpets to match their taste. You can't be an individual if you can't decorate your room to fit your personality.

According to Rachel Jones, Assistant Director of Housing Services, the cost will be $300 per room for the carpet and installation. Also the university will have to buy more vacuum cleaners. But will vacuum cleaners be all that is necessary to keep the carpets clean? We'll need shampoo machines too.

What about those stains that won't come off even with a shampoo machine? That's where the student will have to pay damage deposit costs.

There will be many stains on the carpet due to shaving cream fights, food fights, beverage parties, and smoking, all of which can damage the carpets.

Students don't take care of the dorms now. They don't follow the rules of maintaining their rooms. They drill holes into the walls, break mirrors, beds, and closet doors, and leave their food trays all over the floor.

> If the university buys carpets our room rates will skyrocket.
>
> In conclusion, it is a bad idea for the university to buy carpets.

Conducting a Peer Review Workshop

Chapter 23 (pp. 697–705) discusses additional ways to use groups and improve group dynamics.

If you are willing to respond candidly to a classmate's draft—in a readerly rather than a writerly way—you will be a valuable participant in peer review workshops. In a typical workshop, classmates work in groups of two to six to respond to each other's rough drafts and offer suggestions for revisions. These workshops are most helpful when group members have developed sufficient levels of professionalism and trust to exchange candid responses. A frequent problem in peer review workshops is that classmates try so hard to avoid hurting each other's feelings that they provide vague, meaningless feedback. Saying, "Your paper's great. I really liked it. Maybe you could make it flow a little better" is much less helpful than saying, "Your issue about environmental pollution in the Antarctic is well defined in the first paragraph, but I got lost in the second paragraph when you began discussing penguin coloration."

Responsibilities of Peer Reviewers and Writers

Learning to respond conscientiously and carefully to others' work may be the single most important thing you can do to improve your own writing. When you review a classmate's draft, you should prepare as follows:

1. ***Understand how experienced writers revise their drafts.*** Prior to reviewing a classmate's draft, review the material in this chapter. Pay particular attention to pages 519–520, which provide general guidelines about what to look for when reading a draft, and to page 518, which summarizes the kinds of changes writers often make in response to reviews: additions, deletions, reordering, complete refocusing and rewriting, and so forth.
2. ***Understand the assignment and the guidelines for peer reviewers.*** For assignments in Part Two of this text, carefully read both the assignment itself and the Guidelines for Peer Reviews at the end of the chapter in which the assignment appears. These guidelines will help both the writer and you, as peer reviewer, to understand the demands of the assignment and the criteria on which it should be evaluated.
3. ***Understand that you are not acting as a teacher.*** A peer reviewer's role is that of a fresh reader. You can help the writer appreciate what it's like to encounter his or her text for the first time. Your primary responsibility is to articulate your understanding of what the writer's words say to you and to identify places where you get confused, where you need more details, where you have doubts or queries, and so on. Although the specific kinds of evaluations called for in the Guidelines for Peer Reviews will be helpful, you don't need to be an expert offering solutions to every problem.

When you play the role of writer during a workshop session, your responsibilities parallel those of your peer reviewers. You need to provide a legible rough draft, preferably typed and double-spaced, that doesn't baffle the reader with illegible handwriting, crossouts, arrows, and confusing pagination. Your instructor may ask you to bring photocopies of your draft for all group members. During the workshop, your primary responsibility is to *listen*, taking in how others respond to your draft without becoming defensive. Many instructors also ask writers to formulate two or three specific questions about their drafts—questions they particularly want their reviewers to address. These questions might focus on something writers particularly like about their drafts or on specific problem areas or concerns.

Exchanging Drafts

An excellent system for exchanging drafts is to have each writer read his or her draft aloud while group members follow along in their own photocopies. We value reading drafts aloud when time allows. Reading expressively, with appropriate emphasis, helps writers distance themselves from their work and hear it anew. When you read your work silently to yourself, it's all too easy to patch up bits of broken prose in your head or to slide through confusing passages. But if you stumble over a passage while reading aloud, you can place a check mark in the margin to indicate where further attention is needed. Another benefit to reading aloud is perhaps more symbolic than pragmatic: Reading your work to others means that you are claiming responsibility for it, displaying your intention to reach a range of readers other than the teacher. And knowing that you will have to read your work aloud will encourage you to have that work in the best possible shape before bringing it to class.

Types of Peer Review Workshops

After you've read your draft aloud, the next stage of your peer review may take one of several forms, depending on your instructor's preference. We describe here two basic strategies: response-centered workshops, and advice-centered workshops. Additional strategies often build on these approaches.

Response-Centered Workshops

This process-oriented, non-intrusive approach places maximum responsibility on the writer for making decisions about what to change in a draft. After the writer reads the draft aloud, group members follow this procedure:

1. All participants take several minutes to make notes on their copies of the manuscript. We recommend using the wavy line, "Good!", "?" system described in the Guidelines for Peer Reviews.
2. Group members take turns describing to the writer their responses to the piece—where they agreed or disagreed with the writer's ideas, where they got confused, where they wanted more development, and so forth. Group members do not give advice; they simply describe their own personal response to the draft as written.
3. The writer takes notes during each response but does not enter into a discussion. The writer listens without trying to defend the piece or explain what he or she intended.

No one gives the writer explicit advice. Group members simply describe their reactions to the piece and leave it to the writer to make appropriate changes.

Advice-Centered Workshops

In this more product-oriented and directive approach, peer reviewers typically work in pairs. Each writer exchanges drafts with a partner, reviews the draft carefully, and then writes specific advice on how to improve the draft. This method works best when peer reviewers use the Guidelines for Peer Reviews that conclude each chapter in Part Two, either addressing all the questions in the guidelines or focusing on specific questions identified by the instructor.

A variation on this approach, which allows peer reviewers to collaborate in pairs when analyzing a draft, uses the following process:

1. The instructor divides the class into initial groups of four.
2. Each group then divides into pairs; each pair exchanges drafts with the other pair.
3. The members of each pair collaborate to compose jointly written reviews of the two drafts they have received.
4. The drafts and the collaboratively written reviews are then returned to the original writers. If time remains, the two pairs meet to discuss their reviews.

When two students collaborate to review a draft, they often produce more useful and insightful reviews than when working individually. In sharing observations and negotiating their responses, they can write their reviews with more confidence and reduce the chances of idiosyncratic advice.

However, because each pair has received two drafts and has to write two peer reviews, this approach takes more class time. Instructors can speed this process by setting up the groups of four in advance and asking pairs to exchange and read drafts prior to the class meeting. Class time can then be focused on collaborative writing of the reviews.

Responding to Peer Reviews

After you and your classmates have gone over each other's papers and walked each other through the responses, everyone should identify two or three things about his or her draft that particularly need work. Before you leave the session, you should have some notion about how you want to revise your paper.

You may get mixed or contradictory responses from different reviewers. One reviewer may praise a passage that another finds confusing or illogical. Conflicting advice is a frustrating fact of life for all writers, whether students or professionals. Such disagreements reveal how readers cocreate a text with a writer: Each brings to the text a different background, set of values, and way of reading.

It is important to remember that you are in charge of your own writing. If several readers offer the same critique of a passage, then no matter how much you love that passage, you probably need to follow their advice. But when readers disagree, you have to make your own best judgment about whom to heed.

Once you have received advice from others, reread your draft again slowly and then develop a revision plan, allowing yourself time to make sweeping, global changes if needed. You also need to remember that you can never make your draft perfect. Plan when you will bring the process to a close so that you can turn in a finished product on time and get on with your other classes and your life.

Chapter Summary

This chapter has focused on the writing processes of experts, showing how experienced writers use multiple drafts to solve subject-matter and rhetorical problems. We have also offered advice on how to improve your own writing processes. Particularly, beginning college writers need to understand the kinds of changes writers typically make in drafts, to role-play a reader's perspective when they revise, and to practice the revision strategies of experts. Because peer reviewing is a powerful strategy for learning how to revise, we showed you how to make "readerly" rather than "writerly" comments on a rough draft and how to participate productively in peer review workshops.

Composing and Revising Closed-Form Prose

*[Form is] an arousing and fulfillment of desires. A work has form insofar as one
part of it leads a reader to anticipate another part, to be gratified by the sequence.*

—KENNETH BURKE, *RHETORICIAN*

*I think the writer ought to help the reader as much as he can without damaging
what he wants to say; and I don't think it ever hurts the writer to sort of stand back
now and then and look at his stuff as if he were reading it instead of writing it.*

—JAMES JONES, *WRITER*

Chapter 17 explained the composing processes of experienced writers and suggested ways that you can improve your own writing processes. In this chapter we present ten lessons in composing and revising closed-form prose. This chapter is not intended to be read in one sitting, lest you suffer from information overload. To help you learn the material efficiently, we have made each lesson a self-contained unit that can be read comfortably in half an hour or less and discussed in class as part of a day's session. You will benefit most from these lessons if you focus on one lesson at a time and then return to the lessons periodically as you progress through the term. Each lesson's advice will become increasingly meaningful and relevant as you gain experience as a writer.

The first lesson—on reader expectations—is intended as a theoretical overview to the rest of the chapter. The remaining nine lessons can then be assigned and read in any order your instructor desires. You will learn how to convert loose structures into thesis/support structures (Lesson 2); how to plan and visualize your structure (Lesson 3); how to create effective titles and introductions (Lesson 4); how to use topic sentences, transitions, and the old/new contract to guide your readers through the twists and turns of your prose (Lessons 5–7); how to perform several common writer's "moves" for developing your ideas (Lesson 8); how to write good conclusions (Lesson 9); and, finally, how to create effective document design (Lesson 10). Together these lessons will teach you strategies for making your closed-form prose reader-friendly, well structured, clear, and persuasive.

Lesson 1: Understanding Reader Expectations

In this opening lesson, we show you how to think like a reader. Imagine for a moment that your readers have only so much *reader energy*, which they can use either to follow and respond to your ideas (the result you want) or to puzzle over what you are trying to say (the result you don't want).* Skilled readers make predictions about where a text is heading based on clues provided by the writer. When readers get lost, the writer has often failed to give clues about where the text is going or has failed to do what the reader predicted. "Whoa, you lost me on the turn," a reader might say. "How does this passage relate to what you just said?" To write effective closed-form prose, you need to help readers see how each part of your text is related to what came before. (Sometimes with open-form prose, surprise or puzzlement may be the very effect you want to create. But with closed-form prose this kind of puzzlement is fatal.)

In this lesson we explain what readers of closed-form prose need in order to predict where a text is heading. Specifically we show you that readers need three things in a closed-form text:

- They need unity and coherence.
- They need old information before new information.
- They need forecasting and fulfillment.

Let's look at each in turn.

Unity and Coherence

Together the terms *unity* and *coherence* are defining characteristics of closed-form prose. *Unity* refers to the relationship between each part of an essay and the larger whole. *Coherence* refers to the relationship between adjacent sentences, paragraphs, and parts. The following thought exercise will illustrate your own expectations for unity and coherence:

THOUGHT EXERCISE 1

Read the following two passages and try to explain why each fails to satisfy your expectations as a reader:

A. Recent research has given us much deeper—and more surprising—insights into the father's role in childrearing. My family is typical of the east side in that we never had much money. Their tongues became black and hung out of their mouths. The back-to-basics movement got a lot of press, fueled as it was by fears of growing illiteracy and cultural demise.

B. Recent research has given us much deeper—and more surprising—insights into the father's role in childrearing. Childrearing is a complex process that is frequently

---

*For the useful term *reader energy*, we are indebted to George Gopen and Judith Swan, "The Science of Scientific Writing," *American Scientist* 78 (1990): 550–559. In addition, much of our discussion of writing in this chapter is indebted to the work of Joseph Williams, George Gopen, and Gregory Colomb. See especially Gregory G. Colomb and Joseph M. Williams, "Perceiving Structure in Professional Prose: A Multiply Determined Experience," in Lee Odell and Dixie Goswamie (eds.), *Writing in Nonacademic Settings* (New York: The Guilford Press, 1985), pp. 87–128.

investigated by psychologists. Psychologists have also investigated sleep patterns and dreams. When we are dreaming, psychologists have shown, we are often reviewing recent events in our lives.

If you are like most readers, Passage A comically frustrates your expectations because it is a string of random sentences. Because the sentences don't relate either to each other or to a larger point, Passage A is neither unified nor coherent.

Passage B frustrates expectations in a subtler way. If you aren't paying attention, Passage B may seem to make sense because each sentence is linked to the one before it. But the individual sentences don't develop a larger whole: the topics switch from a father's role in childrearing to psychology to sleep patterns to the function of dreams. This passage has coherence without unity.

To fulfill a reader's expectations, then, a closed-form passage must be both unified and coherent:

> C. (*Unified and coherent*) Recent research has given us much deeper—and more surprising—insights into the father's role in childrearing. It shows that in almost all of their interactions with children, fathers do things a little differently from mothers. What fathers do—their special parenting style—is not only highly complementary to what mothers do but is by all indications important in its own right. [The passage continues by showing the special ways that fathers contribute to childrearing.]

This passage makes a unified point—that fathers have an important role in childrearing. Because all the parts relate to that whole (unity) and because the connections from sentence to sentence are clear (coherence), the passage satisfies our expectations: It makes sense.

Because achieving unity and coherence is a major goal in revising closed-form prose, we'll refer frequently to these concepts in later lessons.

Old before New

One dominant way that readers process information and register ideas is by moving from already known (old) information to new information. In a nutshell, this concept means that new material is meaningful to a reader only if it is linked to old material that is already meaningful. To illustrate this concept, consider the arrangement of names and numbers in a telephone directory. Because we read from left to right, we want people's names in the left column and the telephone numbers in the right column. A person's name is the old, familiar information we already know and the number is the new, unknown information that we seek. If the numbers were in the left column and the names in the right, we would have to read backward.

You can see the same old-before-new principle at work in the following thought exercise:

THOUGHT EXERCISE 2

You are a passenger on an airplane flight into Chicago and need to transfer to Flight 29 to Memphis. As you descend into Chicago, the flight attendant announces transfer gates. Which of the following formats is easier for you to process? Why?

Option A	Option B
To Atlanta on Flight 29 Gate C12	Gate C12 Flight 29 to Atlanta
To Dallas on Flight 35 Gate C25	Gate C25 Flight 35 to Dallas
To Memphis on Flight 16 Gate B20	Gate B20 Flight 16 to Memphis

If you are like most readers, you prefer Option A, which puts old information before new. In this case, the old/known information is our destination (cities arranged alphabetically) and perhaps our flight number (To Memphis on Flight 16). The new/unknown information is Gate B20. Option B causes us to expend more energy than does Option A because it forces us to hold the number of each gate in memory until we hear its corresponding city and flight number. Whereas Option A allows us to relax until we hear the word "Memphis," Option B forces us to concentrate intensely on each gate number until we find the meaningful one.

The principle of old before new has great explanatory power for writers. At the level of the whole essay, this principle helps writers establish the main structural frame and ordering principle of their argument. An argument's frame derives from the writer's purpose to change some aspect of the reader's view of the topic. The reader's original view of the topic—what we might call the common, expected, or ordinary view—constitutes old/known/familiar material. The writer's surprising view constitutes the new/unknown/unfamiliar material. The writer's hope is to move readers from their original view to the writer's new and different view. By understanding what constitutes old/familiar information to readers, the writer can determine how much background to provide, how to anticipate readers' objections, and how to structure material by moving from the old to the new. We discuss these matters in more depth in Lesson 4, on writing effective introductions.

At the sentence level, the principle of old before new also helps writers create coherence between adjacent parts and sentences. Most sentences in an essay should contain both an old element and a new element. To create coherence, the writer begins with the old material, which links back to something earlier, and then puts the new material at the end of the sentence. (See the discussion of the old/new contract in Lesson 7.)

Forecasting and Fulfillment

Finally, readers of closed-form prose expect writers to forecast what is coming and then to fulfill those forecasts. To appreciate what we mean by forecasting and fulfillment, try one more thought exercise:

THOUGHT EXERCISE 3

Although the following paragraph describes a simple procedure in easy-to-follow sentences, most readers still scratch their heads in bewilderment. Why? What makes the passage difficult to understand?

The procedure is actually quite simple. First, you arrange things into different groups. Of course, one pile may be sufficient depending on how much there is to do. If you have to go somewhere else due to lack of facilities, that is the next step; otherwise, you are pretty well set. Next you operate the machines according to the instructions. After the procedure is completed, one arranges the materials into different groups again. Then they can be put in their appropriate places. Eventually, they will be used once more and the whole cycle will have to be repeated. However, that is part of life.

Most readers report being puzzled about the paragraph's topic. Because the opening sentence doesn't provide enough context to tell them what to expect, the paragraph makes no forecast that can be fulfilled. Now try rereading the paragraph, but this time substitute the following opening sentence:

> The procedure for washing clothes is actually quite simple.

With the addition of "for washing clothes," the sentence provides a context that allows you to predict and understand what's coming. In the language of cognitive psychologists, this new opening sentence provides a schema for interpretation. A *schema* is the reader's mental picture of a structure for upcoming material. The new opening sentence allows you as reader to say mentally, "This paragraph will describe a procedure for washing clothes and argue that it is simple." When the schema proves accurate, you experience the pleasure of prediction and fulfillment. In the language of rhetorician Kenneth Burke, the reader's experience of form is "an arousing and fulfillment of desires."

What readers expect from a closed-form text, then, is an ability to predict what is coming as well as regular fulfillment of those predictions. Writers forecast what is coming in a variety of ways: by writing effective titles and introductions, by putting points at the beginning of paragraphs, by creating effective transitions and mapping statements, and by using effective headings and subheadings if appropriate for the genre. To meet their readers' needs for predictions and fulfillment, closed-form writers start and end with the big picture. They tell readers where they are going before they start the journey, they refer to this big picture at key transition points, and they refocus on the big picture in their conclusion.

Lesson 2: Converting Loose Structures into Thesis/Support Structures

In Lesson 1 we described readers' expectations for unity and coherence, old information before new, and forecasting and fulfillment. In academic contexts, readers also expect closed-form prose to have a thesis/support structure. As we explained in Chapter 2, most closed-form academic writing—especially writing with the aim of analysis or persuasion—is governed by a contestable or risky thesis statement. Because developing and supporting a thesis is complex work requiring much critical thought, writers sometimes retreat into loose structures that are easier to compose than a thesis-based argument with points and particulars.

In this lesson we help you better understand thesis-based writing by contrasting it with prose that looks like thesis-based writing but isn't. We show you three common ways in which inexperienced writers give the appearance of writing thesis-based prose while actually retreating from the rigors of making and developing an argument. Avoiding the pitfalls of these loose structures can go a long way toward improving your performance on most college writing assignments.

And Then Writing, or Chronological Structure

Chronological structure, often called "narrative," is the most common organizing principle of open-form prose. It may also be used selectively in closed-form prose to support a point. But sometimes the writer begins recounting the details of a story until chronological order takes over, driving out the thesis-based structure of points and particulars.

To a large degree, chronological order is the default mode we fall into when we aren't sure how to organize material. For example, if you were asked to analyze a fictional character, you might slip into a plot summary instead. In much the same way, you might substitute historical chronology ("First A happened, then B happened . . .") for historical analysis ("B happened because A happened . . ."); or you might give a chronological recounting of your research ("First I discovered A, then I discovered B . . .") instead of organizing your material into an argument ("I question A's account of this phenomenon on the grounds of B's recent findings . . .").

The tendency toward loose chronological structure is revealed in the following example from a student's essay on Shakespeare's *The Tempest*. This excerpt is from the introduction of the student's first draft:

> ### PLOT SUMMARY—*AND THEN* WRITING
>
> Prospero cares deeply for his daughter. In the middle of the play Prospero acts like a gruff father and makes Ferdinand carry logs in order to test his love for Miranda and Miranda's love for him. In the end, though, Prospero is a loving father who rejoices in his daughter's marriage to a good man.

Here the student seems simply to retell the play's plot without any apparent thesis. (The body of her rough draft primarily retold the same story in more detail.) However, during an office conference, the instructor discovered that the student regarded her sentence about Prospero's being a loving father as her thesis. In fact, the student had gotten in an argument with a classmate over whether Prospero was a good person or an evil one. The instructor helped her convert her draft into a thesis/support structure:

> ### REVISED INTRODUCTION—THESIS/SUPPORT STRUCTURE
>
> Many persons believe that Prospero is an evil person in the play. They claim that Prospero exhibits a harsh, destructive control over Miranda and also, like Faust, seeks superhuman knowledge through his magic. However, I contend that Prospero is a kind and loving father.

This revised version implies a problem (What kind of father is Prospero?), presents a view that the writer wishes to change (Prospero is harsh and hateful), and asserts a contestable thesis (Prospero is a loving father). The body of her paper can now be converted from plot summary to an argument with reasons and evidence supporting her claim that Prospero is loving.

This student's revision from an *and then* to a thesis/support structure is typical of many writers' experience. Because recounting events chronologically is a natural way to organize, many writers—even very experienced ones—lapse into long stretches of *and then* writing in their rough drafts. However, experienced writers have learned to recognize these *and then* sections in their drafts and to rework this material into a closed-form, thesis-based structure.

All About Writing, or Encyclopedic Structure

Whereas *and then* writing turns essays into stories by organizing details chronologically, *all about* writing turns essays into encyclopedia articles by piling up details in heaps. When *all about* writing organizes these heaps into categories, it can appear to be well organized: "Having told you everything I learned about educational opportunities in Cleveland, I will now tell you everything I learned about the Rock and Roll Hall of Fame." But the categories do not function as points and particulars in support of a thesis. Rather, like the shelving system in a library, they are simply ways of arranging information for convenient retrieval, not a means of building a hierarchical structure.

To illustrate the differences between *all about* writing and thesis-based writing, consider the case of two students choosing to write term papers on the subject of female police officers. One student is asked simply to write "all about" the topic; the other is asked to pose and investigate some problem related to female police officers and to support a thesis addressing that problem. In all likelihood, the first student would produce an initial outline with headings such as the following:

I. History of women in police roles
   A. Female police or soldiers in ancient times
   B. 19th century (Calamity Jane)
   C. 1900s–1960
   D. 1960–present
II. How female police officers are selected and trained
III. A typical day in the life of a female police officer
IV. Achievements and acts of heroism of female police officers
V. What the future holds for female police officers

Such a paper is a data dump that places into categories all the information the writer has uncovered. It is riskless, and, except for occasional new information, surpriseless. In contrast, when a student focuses on a significant question—one that grows out of the writer's own interests and demands engagement—the writing can be quite compelling.

Consider the case of a student, Lynnea, who wrote a research paper entitled "Women Police Officers: Should Size and Strength Be Criteria for Patrol Duty?" Her essay begins with a group of male police officers complaining about being assigned to patrol duty with a new female officer, Connie Jones (not her real name), who is four feet ten inches tall and weighs ninety pounds. Here is the rest of the introduction to Lynnea's essay.

> Connie Jones has just completed police academy training and has been assigned to patrol duty in _____. Because she is so small, she has to have a booster seat in her patrol car and has been given a special gun, since she can barely manage to pull the trigger of a standard police-issue .38 revolver. Although she passed the physical requirements at the academy, which involved speed and endurance running, situps, and monkey bar tests, most of the officers in her department doubt her ability to perform competently as a patrol officer. But nevertheless she is on patrol because men and women receive equal assignments in most of today's police forces. But is this a good policy? Can a person who is significantly smaller and weaker than her peers make an effective patrol officer?

Lynnea examined all the evidence she could find—through library and field research (interviewing police officers) and arrived at the following thesis: "Because concern for public safety overrides all other concerns, police departments should set stringent size and strength requirements for patrol officers, even if these criteria exclude many women." This thesis has plenty of tension because it sets limits on equal rights for women. Because Lynnea considers herself a feminist, it caused her considerable distress to advocate setting these limits and placing public safety ahead of gender equity. The resulting essay is engaging precisely because of the tension it creates and the controversy it engenders.

Engfish Writing, or Structure without Surprise

Unlike the chronological story and the *all about* paper, the *engfish* essay has a thesis.* But the thesis is a riskless truism supported with predictable reasons—often structured as the three body paragraphs in a traditional five-paragraph theme. It is fill-in-the-blank writing: "The food service is bad for three reasons. First, it is bad because the food is not tasty. Blah, blah, blah about tasteless food. Second, it is bad because it is too expensive. Blah, blah, blah about the expense." And so on. The writer is on autopilot and is not contributing to a real conversation about a real question. In some situations, writers use *engfish* intentionally: bureaucrats and politicians may want to avoid saying something risky; students may want to avoid writing about complex matters that they fear they do not fully understand. In the end, using *engfish* is bad not because what you say is *wrong,* but because what you say couldn't *possibly be* wrong. To avoid *engfish,* stay focused on the need to surprise your reader.

---

*The term *engfish* was coined by the textbook writer Ken Macrorie to describe a fishy kind of canned prose that bright but bored students mechanically produce to please their teachers. See Ken Macrorie, *Telling Writing* (Rochelle Park, NJ: Hayden Press, 1970).

For Writing and Discussion

As a class, choose a topic from popular culture such as TV talk shows, tattooing, eating disorders, rock lyrics, or something similar.

1. Working as a whole class or in small groups, give examples of how you might write about this topic in an *and then* way, an *all about* way, and an *engfish* way.
2. Then develop one or more questions about the topic that could lead to thesis/support writing. What contestable theses can your class create?

Lesson 3: Planning and Visualizing Your Structure

As we explained in Lesson 2, closed-form writing supports a contestable thesis through a hierarchical network of points and particulars. One way to visualize this structure is to outline its skeleton, an exercise that makes visually clear that not all points are on equal levels. The highest-level point is an essay's thesis statement, which is usually supported by several main points that are in turn supported by subpoints and sub-subpoints, all of which are supported by their own particulars. In this lesson we show you how to create such a hierarchical structure for your own papers and how to visualize this structure through an outline, tree diagram, or flowchart.

At the outset, we want to emphasize two important points. First, structural diagrams are not rigid molds, but flexible planning devices that evolve as your thinking shifts and changes. The structure of your final draft may be substantially different from your initial scratch outline. In fact, we want to show you how your outlines or diagrams can help you generate more ideas and reshape your structure.

Second, outlines or diagrams organize *meanings,* not topics. Note that in all our examples of outlines, diagrams, and flowcharts, we write *complete sentences* rather than phrases in the high-level slots. We do so because sentences can make a point, which conveys meaning, unlike a phrase, which identifies a topic but doesn't make an assertion about it. Any point—whether a thesis, a main point, or a subpoint—is a contestable assertion that requires its own particulars for support. By using complete sentences rather than phrases in an outline, the writer is forced to articulate the point of each section of the emerging argument.

With this background, we now proceed to a sequence of steps you can take to plan and visualize a structure.

Use Scratch Outlines Early in the Writing Process

Many writers can't make a detailed outline of their arguments until they have written exploratory drafts. At these early stages, writers often make brief scratch outlines that list the main ideas they want to develop initially or they make a list of points that emerged from a freewrite or a very early draft. Here is student writer Christopher Leigh's initial scratch outline for his argument against metal detectors in schools:

We first introduced Christopher's research problem in Chapter 1, p. 9. Christopher's final paper is shown in Chapter 22, pp. 675–686.

Schools should not use metal detectors as a way of reducing violence.

- Media have created a panic.
- Metal detectors are easily defeated.
- Students hate them.
- Should I put in a section on whether they violate rights???
- Poland article shows we should put the money into creating better school atmosphere.

Before Making a Detailed Outline, "Nutshell" Your Argument

As you explore your topic and begin drafting, your ideas will gradually become clearer and more structured. You can accelerate this process through a series of short exercises that will help you "nutshell" your argument (see Figure 18.1).

The six exercises in this figure cause you to look at your argument from different perspectives, helping you clarify the question you are addressing, articulate

FIGURE 18.1 Exercises for Nutshelling Your Argument

Exercise 1	What puzzle or problem initiated your thinking about X?
Exercise 2	*(Paradigm: Many people think X, but I am going to argue Y.)*

Before reading my paper, my readers will think this about my topic:

_____ .

But after reading my paper, my readers will think this new way about my topic:

_____ .

Exercise 3	The purpose of my paper is _____ .
Exercise 4	My paper addresses the following question: _____ .
Exercise 5	My one-sentence summary answer to the above question is this:

_____ .

Exercise 6	A tentative title for my paper is this: _____

_____ .

the kind of change you want to make in your audience's view of your topic, and directly state your purpose, thesis, and tentative title. The authors of this text often use this exercise in one-on-one writing conferences to help students create an initial focus from a swirl of ideas. We recommend that you write out your responses to each exercise as a preliminary step in helping you visualize your structure. Here are Christopher Leigh's responses to these questions:

> Exercise 1: I was initially puzzled by how best to reduce school violence. When I found that many schools were using metal detectors, I wondered whether this was a good approach.
>
> Exercise 2: Before reading my paper, my readers will believe that metal detectors are a good way to reduce school violence. After reading my paper, my readers will realize that there are many problems with metal detectors and will want to put money instead into improving the school environment.
>
> Exercise 3: The purpose of my paper is to argue against metal detectors and to argue for a better school environment.
>
> Exercise 4: Should schools use metal detectors? Are metal detectors a good way to reduce school violence?
>
> Exercise 5: Metal detectors should not be used in schools because there are other, more effective, and less costly alternatives for violence prevention.
>
> Exercise 6: The Case Against Metal Detectors in Schools.

Articulate a Working Thesis and Main Points

Once you have nutshelled your argument, you are ready to visualize a structure containing several sections, parts, or chunks, each of which is headed by a main point and supported with particulars. Try answering these questions:

1. My working thesis statement is:
2. The main sections or chunks needed in my paper are:

Here are Christopher Leigh's answers to these questions:

> 1. Metal detectors should not be used in schools because there is no basis for panic about violence and because there are other, more effective, and less costly alternatives for violence prevention.
> 2. (a) A section on the media's having created a panic; (b) a big section on the arguments against metal detectors; (c) a section on my solution, which is to improve the school atmosphere.

Sketch Your Structure Using an Outline, Tree Diagram, or Flowchart

At this point you can make an initial structural sketch of your argument and use the sketch to plan out the subpoints and particulars necessary to support the main points. We offer you three different ways to visualize your argument: outlines, tree diagrams, and flowcharts. Use whichever strategy best fits your way of thinking and perceiving.

Outlines

The most common way of visualizing structure is the traditional outline, which uses letters and numerals to indicate levels of points, subpoints, and particulars. If you prefer outlines, we recommend that you use the outlining feature of your word processing program, which allows you to move and insert material and change heading levels with great flexibility. What follows is Christopher Leigh's detailed outline of his argument. Note that Chris uses complete sentences rather than phrases for each level.

The importance of complete sentences is explained at the beginning of this lesson, p. 535.

Thesis: Except for schools with severe threats of danger, metal detectors should not be used because there is no basis for panic and because there are other, more effective, and less costly alternatives for violence prevention in schools.

I. Media have created panic over school violence.
  A. School violence is actually quite rare.
  B. Frequency of weapons being brought to school has declined since 1993.
II. There are many strong arguments against use of metal detectors.
  A. Metal detectors may violate student rights.
    1. Quotations from students reveal belief that metal detectors violate their rights.
    2. Court rulings leave gray areas.
  B. Metal detectors are easily defeated.
    1. They can't close off all entrances.
    2. A shooter can always find a way to get guns inside.
  C. Metal detectors are costly.
  D. Metal detectors have bad psychological consequences for students.
    1. Quotations from students show students' dislike of prison atmosphere.
    2. Metal detectors create feeling of distrust and humiliation.
III. A better solution is to use the money spent on metal detectors to provide a better school atmosphere.
  A. Quotation from high school senior Malik Barry-Buchanan shows need to create respect and caring in the schools.
  B. Article by Poland shows need to make schools more personal and to provide more counseling.
    1. Teachers should make efforts to know each student as an individual.
    2. Extracurricular activities should not be cut.
    3. Schools should provide more counseling.
IV. Conclusion

Tree Diagrams

A tree diagram displays a hierarchical structure visually, using horizontal and vertical space instead of letters and numbers. Figure 18.2 shows Christopher's argument as a tree diagram. His thesis is at the top of the tree. His main reasons, written as point sentences, appear as branches beneath his claim. Supporting evidence and arguments are displayed as subbranches beneath each reason.

FIGURE 18.2 Christopher's Tree Diagram

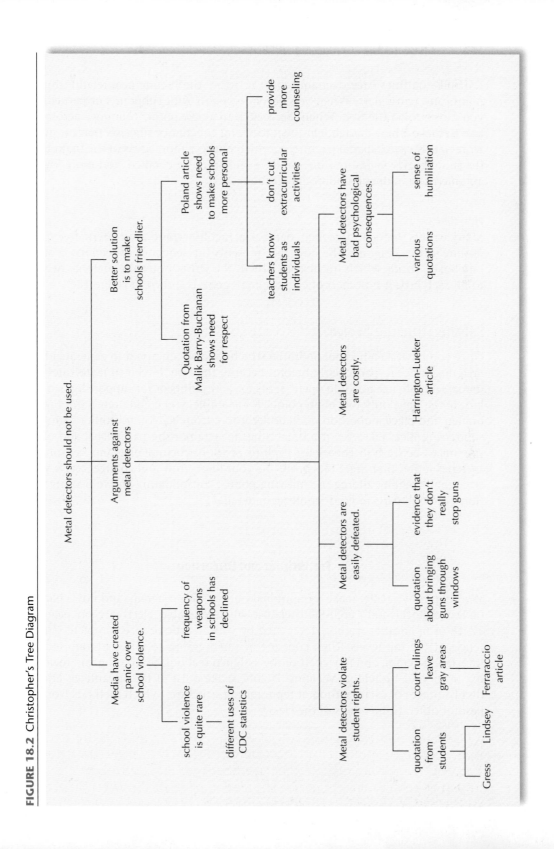

Unlike outlines, tree diagrams allow us to *see* the hierarchical relationship of points and particulars. When you develop a point with subpoints or particulars, you move down the tree. When you switch to a new point, you move across the tree to make a new branch. Our own teaching experience suggests that for many writers, this visual/spatial technique, which engages more areas of the brain than the more purely verbal outline, produces fuller, more detailed, and more logical arguments than does a traditional outline.

Flowcharts

Many writers prefer an informal, hand-sketched flowchart as an alternative to an outline or tree diagram. The flowchart presents the sequence of sections as separate boxes, inside which (or next to which) the writer notes the material needed to fill each box. A flowchart of Christopher's essay is shown in Figure 18.3.

Let the Structure Evolve

Once you have sketched out an initial structural diagram, use it to generate ideas. Tree diagrams are particularly helpful because they invite you to place question marks on branches to "hold open" spots for new points or for supporting particulars. If you have only two main points, for example, you could draw a third main branch and place a question mark under it to encourage you to think of another supporting idea. Likewise, if a branch has few supporting particulars, add question marks beneath it. The trick is to think of your structural diagrams as evolving sketches rather than rigid blueprints. As your ideas grow and change, revise your structural diagram, adding or removing points, consolidating and refocusing sections, moving parts around, or filling in details.

For Writing and Discussion

Working individually, make a traditional outline, tree diagram, and flow chart of David Rockwood's argument against wind-generated electricity on pages 17–18 or of another reading designated by your instructor. Use complete sentences at the top levels. Then convene in small groups to make a group outline, tree diagram, and flowchart of the assigned reading, combining and revising from your individual versions. Finally, make a list of the advantages and disadvantages of each method of representing structure. Which methods work best for different members of the class?

FIGURE 18.3 Christopher's Flowchart

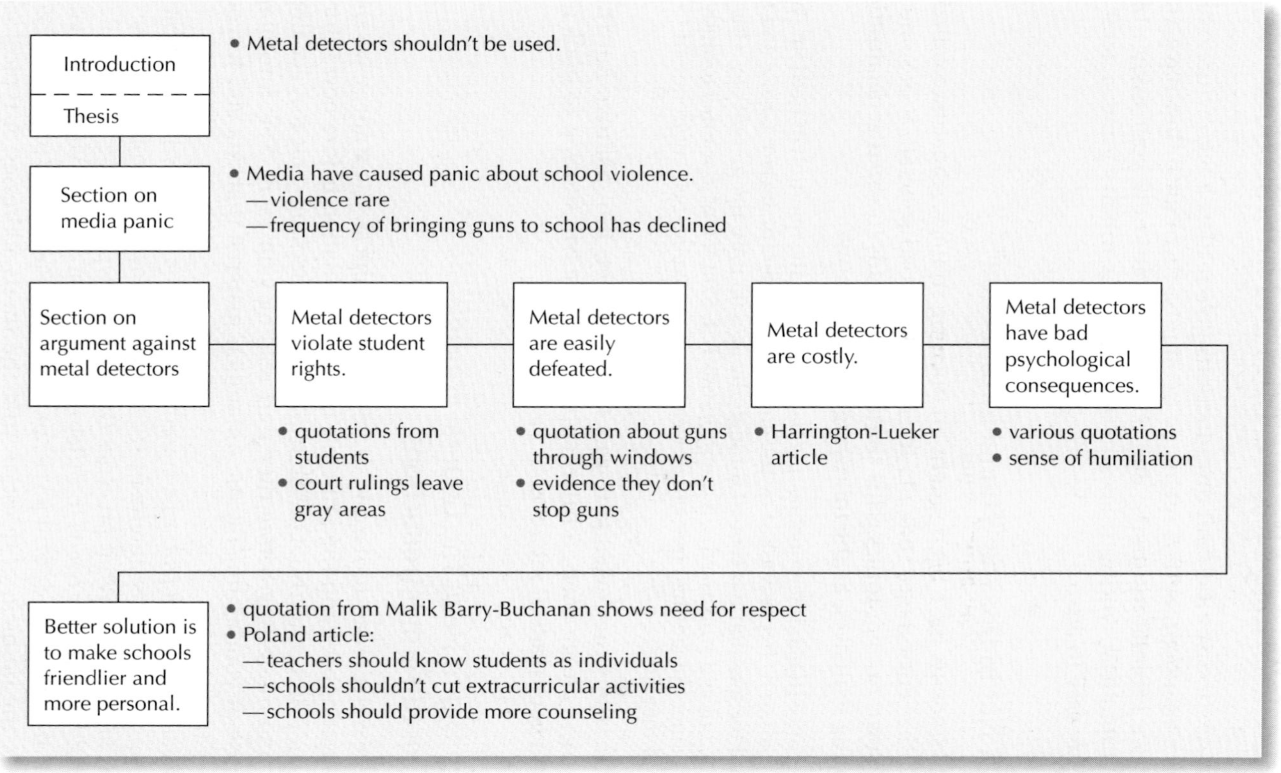

Introduction
- - - - - -
Thesis

• Metal detectors shouldn't be used.

Section on media panic

• Media have caused panic about school violence.
—violence rare
—frequency of bringing guns to school has declined

Section on argument against metal detectors

Metal detectors violate student rights.
• quotations from students
• court rulings leave gray areas

Metal detectors are easily defeated.
• quotation about guns through windows
• evidence they don't stop guns

Metal detectors are costly.
• Harrington-Lueker article

Metal detectors have bad psychological consequences.
• various quotations
• sense of humiliation

Better solution is to make schools friendlier and more personal.

• quotation from Malik Barry-Buchanan shows need for respect
• Poland article:
—teachers should know students as individuals
—schools shouldn't cut extracurricular activities
—schools should provide more counseling

Lesson 4: Writing Effective Titles and Introductions

Because effective titles and introductions give readers a big-picture overview of a paper's argument, writers often can't compose them until they have finished one or more exploratory drafts. But as soon as you know your essay's big picture, you'll find that writing titles and introductions follows some general principles that are easy to learn.

What Not to Do: The "Funnel Introduction"

Some students have been taught an opening strategy, sometimes called the "funnel," that encourages students to start with broad generalizations and then narrow down to their topics. This strategy often leads to vapid generalizations in the opening sentences, as the following example shows:

> Since time immemorial people have pondered the question of freedom. What it means to be free was asked by the great philosophers of ancient Greece and Rome, and the question has echoed through the ages up until the present day. One modern psychologist who asked this question was B. F. Skinner, who wanted to study whether humans had free will or were programmed by their environment to act the way they did. . . .

Here the writer eventually gets to his subject, B. F. Skinner. But the opening sentences are snoozers. A better approach, as we will show, is to hook immediately into your readers' interests.

From Old to New: The General Principle of Closed-Form Introductions

We introduced the principle of old before new in Lesson 1. See pp. 529–530.

Whereas the broad-to-narrow strategy is mechanical, the strategy we show you in this lesson, based on the principle of old information before new information, is dynamic and powerful. Old information is something your readers already know and find interesting before they start reading your essay. New information is the surprise of your argument, the unfamiliar material that you add to your readers' understanding.

Because the writer's thesis statement forecasts the new information the paper will present, a thesis statement for a closed-form essay typically comes *at the end of the introduction.* What precedes the thesis is typically the old, familiar information that the reader needs in order to understand the conversation that the thesis joins. In most closed-form prose, particularly in academic prose, this old information is the problem or question that the thesis addresses. A typical closed-form introduction has the following shape:

See the explanation of a prototypical academic introduction in Chapter 2, pp. 32–34.

PROBLEM
[old information]
↓
THESIS
[new information]

The length and complexity of your introduction is a function of how much your reader already knows and cares about the question or problem your paper addresses. The function of an introduction is to capture the reader's interest in the first few sentences, to identify and explain the question or problem that the essay addresses, to provide any needed background information, and to present the thesis. You can leave out any of the first three elements if the reader is already hooked on your topic and already knows the question you are addressing. For example, in an essay exam you can usually start with your thesis statement because you can assume the instructor already knows the question and finds it interesting.

To illustrate how an effective closed-form introduction takes the reader from the question to the thesis, consider how the following student writer revised his introduction to a paper on Napster.com:

ORIGINAL INTRODUCTION (CONFUSING)

Napster is all about sharing, not stealing, as record companies and some musicians would like us to think. Napster is an online program that was released in October of '99. Napster lets users easily search for and trade mp3s—compressed, high-quality music files that can be produced from a CD. Napster is the leading file sharing community; it allows users to locate and share music. It also provides instant messaging, chat rooms, an outlet for fans to identify new artists, and a forum to communicate their interests.

Thesis statement

Background on Napster

Most readers find this introduction confusing. The writer begins with his thesis statement before the reader is introduced to the question that the thesis addresses. He seems to assume that his reader is already a part of the Napster conversation, and yet in the next sentences, he gives background on Napster. If the reader needs background on Napster, then the reader also needs background on the Napster controversy. In rethinking his assumptions about old-versus-new information for his audience, this writer decides he wants to reach general newspaper readers who may have heard about a lawsuit against Napster and are interested in the issue but aren't sure of what Napster is or how it works. Here is his revised introduction:

REVISED INTRODUCTION (CLEARER)

Several months ago the rock band Metallica filed a lawsuit against Napster.com, an online program that lets users easily search for and trade mp3s—compressed, high-quality music files that can be produced from a CD. Napster.com has been wildly popular among music lovers because it creates a virtual community where users can locate and share music. It also provides instant messaging, chat rooms, an outlet for fans to identify new artists, and a forum to communicate their interests. But big-name bands like Metallica, alarmed at what they see as lost revenues, claim that Napster.com is stealing their royalties. However, Napster is all about sharing, not stealing, as some musicians would like us to think.

Triggers readers' memory of lawsuit

Background on Napster

Clarification of problem (Implied question: Should Napster be shut down?)

Thesis

This revised introduction fills in the old information the reader needs in order to recall and understand the problem; then it presents the thesis.

Typical Elements of a Closed-Form Introduction

Now that you understand the general principle of closed-form introductions, let's look more closely at its four typical features or elements:

An Opening Attention-Grabber.   The first few sentences in an introduction have to capture your reader's interest. If you aren't sure your reader is already interested in your problem, you can begin with an attention-grabber (what journalists call the "hook" or "lead"), which is typically a dramatic vignette, a startling fact or statistic, an arresting quotation, an interesting scene, or something else that taps into your reader's interests. Attention-grabbers are uncommon in academic prose (where you assume your reader will be initially engaged by the problem itself) but frequently used in popular prose. The student writer of the Napster paper initially toyed with the following attention-grabber to begin his essay:

> How many times have you liked one or two songs on a CD but thought the rest of it was garbage? How many times have you burned your own customized CDs by finding your favorite music on Napster.com? Well, that opportunity is about to be lost if Metallica wins its lawsuit against Napster.

He decided not to use this attention-grabber, however, because he wanted to reach audiences who weren't already users of Napster. He decided that these general readers were already interested in the lawsuit and didn't need the extra zing of an attention-grabber.

The brief writing project in Chapter 1 teaches you how to show that a question is problematic and significant. See pp. 24–25.

Explanation of the Question to Be Investigated.   If you assume that your reader already knows about the problem and cares about it, then you need merely to summarize it. This problem or question is the starting point of your argument. Closed-form writers often state the question directly in a single sentence ending with a question mark, but sometimes they imply it, letting the reader formulate it from context. If you aren't sure whether your audience fully understands the question or fully cares about it, then you need to explain it in more detail, showing why it is both problematic and significant.

Background Information.   In order to understand the conversation you are joining, readers sometimes need background information—perhaps a definition of key terms, a summary of events leading up to the problem you're presenting, factual details needed for basic understanding of the problem, and so forth. In scientific papers, this background often includes a review of the preexisting literature on the problem. In the Napster introduction, the writer devotes several sentences to background on Napster.com.

A Preview of the Whole.   The final element of a closed-form introduction sketches the big picture of your essay by giving readers a sense of the whole. This preview is initially new information for your readers (this is why it comes at the end of the introduction). Once stated, however, it becomes old information that readers will use to locate their position in their journey through your argument. By predicting what's coming, this preview initiates the pleasurable process of forecasting/fulfillment that we discussed in Lesson 1. Writers typically forecast the whole by stating their thesis, but they can also use a purpose statement or a blueprint statement to accomplish the same end. These strategies are the subject of the next section.

See this chapter's opening epigraph from rhetorician Kenneth Burke, p. 527.

Forecasting the Whole with a Thesis Statement, Purpose Statement, or Blueprint Statement

The most succinct way to forecast the whole is to state your thesis directly. Student writers often ask how detailed their thesis statements should be and whether it is permissible, sometimes, to delay revealing the thesis until the conclusion—an open-form move that gives papers a more exploratory, mystery-novel feel. It is useful, then, to outline briefly some of your choices as a writer. To illustrate a writer's options for forecasting the whole, we use Christopher Leigh's essay on metal detectors in schools that we discussed in Lesson 3.

To see the choices Christopher Leigh actually made, see his complete essay on pp. 675–686.

Options for Forecasting the Whole

Option	Explanation	Example
Short thesis	State claim without summarizing your supporting argument or forecasting your structure.	Schools should not use metal detectors to reduce school violence.
Detailed thesis	Summarize whole argument; may begin with an *although* clause that summarizes the view you are trying to change.	Although metal detectors may be justified in schools with severe threats of danger, they should generally not be used because there is no basis for panic and because there are other, more effective, and less costly alternatives for violence prevention in schools.
Purpose statement	State your purpose or intention without summarizing the argument. A purpose statement typically begins with a phrase such as "My purpose is to . . ." or "In the following paragraphs I wish to . . .:"	My purpose in this essay is to make a case against using metal detectors in schools.
Blueprint or mapping statement	Describe the structure of your essay by announcing the number of main parts and describing the function or purpose of each one.	First I show that the media have created a false panic about school violence. Next I present four reasons metal detectors have bad consequences. Finally I outline a better approach— making schools friendlier and more personal.

In addition you have at least two other options:

- *Multisentence summary.* In long articles, academic writers often use all three kinds of statements—a purpose statement, a thesis statement, and a blueprint statement. While this sort of extensive forecasting is common in academic and business writing, it occurs less frequently in informal or popular essays. Christopher decided that his paper wasn't complex enough to justify an extensive multisentence overview.
- *Thesis question.* When writers wish to delay their thesis until the middle or the end of their essays, letting their arguments slowly unfold and keeping their stance a mystery, they often end the introduction with a question. This open-form strategy invites readers to join the writer in a mutual search for the answer.

> Although I would prefer having no metal detectors in schools, I am strongly in favor of making schools safer. So the question of whether metal detectors are justified leaves me baffled and puzzled. Should schools use them or not? [This approach would have required a very different structure from the paper Christopher actually wrote.]

Which of these options should a writer choose? There are no firm rules to help you answer this question. How much you forecast in the introduction and where you reveal your thesis is a function of your purpose, audience, and genre. The more you forecast, the clearer your argument is and the easier it is to read quickly. You minimize the demands on readers' time by giving them the gist of your argument in the introduction, making it easier to skim your essay if they don't have time for a thorough reading. The less you forecast, the more demands you make on readers' time: You invite them, in effect, to accompany you through the twists and turns of your own thinking process, and you risk losing them if they become confused, lost, or bored. For these reasons, academic writing is generally closed form and aims at maximum clarity. In many rhetorical contexts, however, more open forms are appropriate.

Chapter 3, pp. 56–57, gives more advice on when to choose closed or open forms.

If you choose a closed-form structure, we can offer some advice on how much to forecast. Readers sometimes feel insulted by too much forecasting, so include only what is needed for clarity. For short papers, readers usually don't need to have the complete supporting argument forecast in the introduction. In longer papers, however, or in especially complex ones, readers appreciate having the whole argument forecast at the outset. Academic writing in particular tends to favor explicit and often detailed forecasting.

Writing Effective Titles

The strategies we have suggested for a closed-form introduction apply equally well to a closed-form title. A good title needs to have something old (a word or phrase that hooks into a reader's existing interests) and something new (a hint of the writer's thesis or purpose). Here is an example of an academic title:

"Style as Politics: A Feminist Approach to the Teaching of Writing" [This title attracts scholars interested either in style or in feminist issues in writing (old); it promises to analyze the political implications of style (new).]

As this example shows, your title should provide a brief but detailed overview of what your paper is about. Academic titles are typically longer and more detailed than are titles in popular magazines. They usually follow one of four conventions:

1. Some titles simply state the question that the essay addresses:

   "Will Patriarchal Management Survive Beyond the Decade?"

2. Some titles state, often in abbreviated form, the essay's thesis:

   "The Writer's Audience Is Always a Fiction"

3. Very often the title is the last part of the essay's purpose statement:

   "The Relationship between Client Expectation of Improvement and Psychotherapy Outcome"

4. Many titles consist of two parts separated by a colon. To the left of the colon the writer presents key words from the essay's issue or problem or a "mystery phrase" that arouses interest; to the right the author places the essay's question, thesis, or summary of purpose:

   "Money and Growth: An Alternative Approach"
   "Deep Play: Notes on a Balinese Cockfight"
   "Fine Cloth, Cut Carefully: Cooperative Learning in British Columbia"

Although such titles might seem overly formal to you, they indicate how much a closed-form writer wishes to preview an article's big picture. Although their titles may be more informal, popular magazines often use these same strategies. Here are some titles from *Redbook* and the business magazine *Forbes*:

   "Is the Coffee Bar Trend About to Peak?" (question)
   "A Man *Can* Take Maternity Leave—And Love It" (abbreviated thesis)
   "Why the Department of Education Shouldn't Take Over the Student Loan Program" (last part of purpose statement)
   "Feed Your Face: Why Your Complexion Needs Vitamins" (two parts linked by colon)

Composing a title for your essay can help you find your focus when you get bogged down in the middle of a draft. Thinking about your title forces you to *nutshell* your ideas by seeing your project's big picture. It causes you to reconsider your purpose and to think about what's old and what's new for your audience.

For Writing and Discussion

Individual task: Choose an essay you are currently working on or have recently completed and examine your title and introduction based on the advice in this lesson. Ask yourself these questions:

- What audience am I imagining? What do I assume are my readers' initial interests that will lead them to read my essay (the old information I must hook into)? What is new in my essay?
- Do I have an attention-grabber? Why or why not?
- Where do I state or imply the question or problem that my essay addresses?
- Do I explain why the question is problematic and significant? Why or why not?
- For my audience to understand the problem, do I provide too much background information, not enough, or just the right amount?
- What strategies do I use to forecast the whole?

Based on your analysis of your present title and introduction, revise as appropriate.

Group task: Working with a partner or in small groups, share the changes you made in your title or introduction and explain why you made the changes.

Lesson 5: Placing Points before Particulars

In our lesson on outlining (Lesson 3), we suggested that you write complete sentences rather than phrases for the high-level slots of the outline in order to articulate the *meaning* or *point* of each section of your argument. In this lesson we show you how to place these points where readers expect them: near the beginning of the sections or paragraphs they govern.

When you place points before particulars, you follow the same principle illustrated in Lesson 1 with the flight attendant announcing the name of the city before the departure gate (the city is the old information, the departure gate the new information). When you first state the point, it is the new information that the next paragraph or section will develop. Once you have stated it, it becomes old information that helps readers understand the meaning of the particulars that follow. If you withhold the point until later, the reader has to keep all the particulars in short-term memory until you finally reveal the point that the particulars are supposed to support or develop.

Place Topic Sentences at the Beginning of Paragraphs

Readers of closed-form prose need to have point sentences (usually called "topic sentences") at the beginnings of paragraphs. However, writers of rough drafts often don't fulfill this need because, as we explained in Chapter 17, drafting is an exploratory process in which writers are often still searching for their points as they compose. Consequently, in their rough drafts writers often omit topic sentences entirely or place them at the ends of paragraphs, or they write topic sentences that misrepresent what the paragraphs actually say. During revision, then, you should check your body paragraphs carefully to be sure you have placed accurate topic sentences near the beginning.

What follow are examples of the kinds of revisions writers typically make. We have annotated the examples to explain the changes the writer has made to make the paragraphs unified and clear to readers. The first example is from a later draft of the essay on dorm room carpets from Chapter 17 (pp. 521–523).

Revision—Topic Sentence First

Another reason for the university not to buy carpets is the cost.
ʌAccording to Rachel Jones, Assistant Director of Housing   *Topic sentence placed first*

Services, the initial purchase and installation of carpeting would

cost $300 per room. Considering the number of rooms in the three

residence halls, carpeting amounts to a substantial investment.

Additionally, once the carpets are installed, the university would

need to maintain them through the purchase of more vacuum cleaners

and shampoo machines. This money would be better spent on other

dorm improvements that would benefit more residents, such as

expanded kitchen facilities and improved recreational space. Thus

carpets would be too expensive.

In the original draft, the writer states the point at the end of the paragraph. In his revision he states the point in an opening topic sentence that links back to the thesis statement, which promises "several reasons" that the university should not buy carpets for the dorms. The words "another reason" thus link the topic sentence to the argument's big picture.

Revise Paragraphs for Unity

In addition to placing topic sentences at the heads of paragraphs, writers often need to revise topic sentences to better match what the paragraph actually says, or revise the paragraph to better match the topic sentence. Paragraphs have unity when all their sentences develop the point stated in the topic sentence. Paragraphs in rough drafts are often not unified because they reflect the writer's shifting, evolving, thinking-while-writing process. Consider the following paragraph from an early draft of an argument against euthanasia by student writer Dao Do. Her peer reviewer labeled it "confusing." What makes it confusing?

We look at more examples from Dao's essay later in this chapter.

<pre>
                   Early Draft—Confusing

     First, euthanasia is wrong because no one has the right to
take the life of another person. Some people say that euthanasia
or suicide will end suffering and pain. But what proofs do they
have for such a claim? Death is still mysterious to us; therefore,
we do not know whether death will end suffering and pain or not.
What seems to be the real claim is that death to those with
illnesses will end <u>our</u> pain. Such pain involves worrying over
them, paying their medical bills, and giving up so much of our
time. Their deaths end our pain rather than theirs. And for that
reason, euthanasia is a selfish act, for the outcome of euthanasia
benefits us, the nonsufferers, more. Once the sufferers pass away,
we can go back to our normal lives.
</pre>

The paragraph opens with an apparent topic sentence: "Euthanasia is wrong because no one has the right to take the life of another person." But the rest of the paragraph doesn't focus on that point. Instead, it focuses on how euthanasia benefits the survivors more than the sick person. Dao had two choices: to revise the paragraph to fit the topic sentence or to revise the topic sentence to fit the paragraph. Here is her revision, which includes a different topic sentence and an additional sentence midparagraph to keep particulars focused on the opening point. Dao unifies this paragraph by keeping all its parts focused on her main point: "Euthanasia . . . benefits the survivors more than the sick person."

Revision for Unity

First, euthanasia is wrong because it benefits the survivors more than the sick person.

ˌFirst, euthanasia is wrong because no one has the right to

take the life of another person. Some people say that euthanasia

the sick person's ◄─────────────────────────

or suicide will end ˌsuffering and pain. But what proofs do they

have for such a claim? Death is still mysterious to us;

therefore, we do not know whether death will end suffering and

Moreover, modern pain killers can relieve most most of the pain a sick person has to endure. ◄─────────

pain or not. ˌWhat seems to be the real claim is that death to

those with illnesses will end <u>our</u> pain. Such pain involves

worrying over them, paying their medical bills, and giving up so

much of our time. Their deaths end our pain rather than theirs.

And for that reason, euthanasia is a selfish act, for the outcome

of euthanasia benefits us, the nonsufferers, more. Once the

sufferers pass away, we can go back to our normal lives.

Revised topic sentence better forecasts focus of paragraph

Keeps focus on "sick person"

Concludes subpoint about sick person

Supports subpoint about how euthanasia benefits survivors

A paragraph may lack unity for a variety of reasons. It may shift to a new direction in the middle, or one or two sentences may simply be irrelevant to the point. The key is to make sure that all the sentences in the paragraph fulfill the reader's expectations based on the topic sentence.

Add Particulars to Support Points

Just as writers of rough drafts often omit point sentences from paragraphs, they also sometimes leave out the particulars needed to support a point. In such cases, the writer needs to add particulars such as facts, statistics, quotations, research summaries, examples, or further subpoints. Consider how adding additional particulars to the following draft paragraph strengthens student writer Tiffany Linder's argument opposing the logging of old-growth forests.

DRAFT PARAGRAPH: PARTICULARS MISSING

One reason that it is not necessary to log old-growth forests is that the timber industry can supply the world's lumber needs without doing so. For example, we have plenty of new-growth forest from which timber can be taken (Sagoff 89). We could also reduce the amount of trees used for paper products by using other materials besides wood for paper pulp. In light of the fact that we have plenty of trees and ways of reducing our wood demands, there is no need to harvest old-growth forests.

REVISED PARAGRAPH: PARTICULARS ADDED

Added particulars support subpoint that we have plenty of new-growth forest

One reason that it is not necessary to log old-growth forests is that the timber industry can supply the world's lumber needs without doing so. For example, we have plenty of new-growth forest from which timber can be taken as a result of major reforestation efforts all over the United States (Sagoff 89). In the Northwest, for instance, Oregon law requires every acre of timber harvested to be replanted. According to Robert Sedjo, a forestry expert, the world's demand for industrial wood could be met by a widely implemented tree farming system (Sagoff 90). We could

Added particulars support second subpoint that wood alternatives are available

also reduce the amount of trees used for paper products by using a promising new innovation called Kenaf, a fast-growing annual herb which is fifteen feet tall and is native to Africa. It has been used for making rope for many years, but recently it was found to work just as well for paper pulp. In light of the fact that we have plenty of trees and ways of reducing our wood demands, there is no need to harvest old-growth forests.

For Writing and Discussion

Individual Task: Bring to class a draft-in-progress for a closed-form essay. Pick out several paragraphs in the body of your essay and analyze them for "points-first" structure. For each paragraph, ask the following questions:

- Does my paragraph have a topic sentence near the beginning?
- If so, does my topic sentence accurately forecast what the paragraph says?
- Does my topic sentence link to my thesis statement or to a higher-order point that my paragraph develops?
- Does my paragraph have enough particulars to develop and support my topic sentence?

Group Task: Then exchange your draft with a partner and do a similar analysis of your partner's selected paragraphs. Discuss your analyses of each other's paragraphs and then help each other plan appropriate revision strategies. If time permits, revise your paragraphs and show your results to your partner. [Note: Sometimes you can revise simply by adding a topic sentence to a paragraph, rewording a topic sentence, or making other kinds of local revisions. At other times, you may need to cross out whole paragraphs and start over, rewriting from scratch after you rethink your ideas.]

Lesson 6: Signaling Relationships with Transitions

As we have explained in previous lessons, when readers read closed-form prose, they expect each new sentence, paragraph, and section to link clearly to what they have already read. They need a well-marked trail with signposts signaling the twists and turns along the way. They also need resting spots at major junctions where they can review where they've been and survey what's coming. In this lesson, we show you how transition words as well as summary and forecasting passages can keep your readers securely on the trail.

Use Common Transition Words to Signal Relationships

Transitions are like signposts that signal where the road is turning and limit the possible directions that an unfolding argument might take. Consider how the use of "therefore" and "nevertheless" limits the range of possibilities in the following examples:

> While on vacation, Suzie caught the chicken pox. Therefore, _____.
> While on vacation, Suzie caught the chicken pox. Nevertheless, _____.

"Therefore" signals to the reader that what follows is a consequence. Most readers will imagine a sentence similar to this one:

> Therefore, she spent her vacation lying in bed itching, feverish, and miserable.

In contrast, "nevertheless" signals an unexpected or denied consequence, so the reader might anticipate a sentence such as this:

> Nevertheless, she enjoyed her two weeks off, thanks to a couple of bottles of calamine lotion, some good books, and a big easy chair overlooking the ocean.

Here is a list of the most common transition words and phrases and what they signal to the reader:*

Words or Phrases	What They Signal
first, second, third, next, finally, earlier, later, meanwhile, afterward	*sequence*—First we went to dinner; then we went to the movies.
that is, in other words, to put it another way,—(dash), :(colon)	*restatement*—He's so hypocritical that you can't trust a word he says. To put it another way, he's a complete phony.
rather, instead	*replacement*—We shouldn't use the money to buy opera tickets; rather, we should use it for a nice gift.
for example, for instance, a case in point	*example*—Mr. Carlysle is very generous. For example, he gave the janitors a special holiday gift.

---

*Although all the words on the list serve as transitions or connectives, grammatically they are not all equivalent, nor are they all punctuated the same way.

Words or Phrases	What They Signal
because, since, for	*reason*—Taxes on cigarettes are unfair because they place a higher tax burden on the working class.
therefore, hence, so, consequently, thus, then, as a result, accordingly, as a consequence	*consequences*—I failed to turn in the essay; therefore I flunked the course.
still, nevertheless	*denied consequence*—The teacher always seemed grumpy in class; nevertheless, I really enjoyed the course.
although, even though, granted that (*with* still)	*concession*—Even though the teacher was always grumpy, I still enjoyed the course.
in comparison, likewise, similarly	*similarity*—Teaching engineering takes a lot of patience. Likewise, so does teaching accounting.
however, in contrast, conversely, on the other hand, but	*contrast*—I disliked my old backpack immensely; however, I really like this new one.
in addition, also, too, moreover, furthermore	*addition*—Today's cars are much safer than those of ten years ago. In addition, they get better gas mileage.
in brief, in sum, in conclusion, finally, to sum up, to conclude	*conclusion or summary*—In sum, the plan presented by Mary is the best choice.

For Writing and Discussion

This exercise is designed to show you how transition words govern relationships between ideas. Working in groups or on your own, finish each of the following statements using ideas of your own invention. Make sure what you add fits the logic of the transition word.

1. Writing is difficult; therefore _____.
2. Writing is difficult; however, _____.
3. Writing is difficult because _____.
4. Writing is difficult. For example, _____.
5. Writing is difficult. To put it another way, _____.
6. Writing is difficult. Likewise, _____.
7. Although writing is difficult, _____.
8. _____. In sum, writing is difficult.

In the following paragraph, various kinds of linking devices have been omitted. Fill in the blanks with words or phrases that would make the paragraph coherent. Clues are provided in brackets.

> Writing an essay is a difficult process for most people. _____ [contrast] the process can be made easier if you learn to practice three simple techniques. _____ [sequence] learn the technique of nonstop writing. When you are first trying to think of ideas for an essay, put your pen to your paper and write nonstop for ten or fifteen minutes without letting your pen leave the paper. Stay loose and free. Let your pen follow the waves of thought. Don't worry about grammar or spelling. _____ [concession] this technique won't work for everyone, it helps many people get a good cache of ideas to draw on. A _____ [sequence] technique is to write your rough draft rapidly without worrying about being perfect. Too many writers try to get their drafts right the first time. _____ [contrast] by learning to live with imperfection, you will save yourself headaches and a wastepaper basket full of crumpled paper. Think of your first rough draft as a path hacked out of the jungle—as part of an exploration, not as a completed highway. As a _____ [sequence] technique, try printing out a triple-spaced copy to allow space for revision. Many beginning writers don't leave enough space to revise. _____ [consequence] these writers never get in the habit of crossing out chunks of their rough draft and writing revisions in the blank spaces. After you have revised your rough draft until it is too messy to work from anymore, you can _____ [sequence] enter your changes into your word processor and print out a fresh draft, again setting your text on triple-space. The resulting blank space invites you to revise.

Write Major Transitions between Parts

In long closed-form pieces, writers often put *resting places* between major parts—transitional passages that allow readers to shift their attention momentarily away from the matter at hand to a sense of where they've been and where they're going. Often such passages sum up the preceding major section, refer back to the essay's thesis statement or opening blueprint plan, and then preview the next major section. Here are three typical examples:

> So far I have looked at a number of techniques that can help people identify debilitating assumptions that block their self-growth. In the next section, I examine ways to question and overcome these assumptions.

> Now that the difficulty of the problem is fully apparent, our next step is to examine some of the solutions that have been proposed.

> These, then, are the major theories explaining why Hamlet delays. But let's see what happens to Hamlet if we ask the question in a slightly different way. In this next section, we shift our critical focus, looking not at Hamlet's actions, but at his language.

Signal Transitions with Headings and Subheadings

In many genres, particularly scientific and technical reports, government documents, business proposals, textbooks, and long articles in magazines or scholarly journals, writers conventionally break up long stretches of text with headings and subheadings. Headings are often set in different type sizes and fonts and mark transition points between major parts and subparts of the argument. We discuss headings in detail in Lesson 10 on document design.

Lesson 7: Binding Sentences Together by Following the Old/New Contract

In the previous lesson we showed you how to mark the reader's trail with transitions. In this lesson we show you how to build a smooth trail without potholes or washed-out bridges.

An Explanation of the Old/New Contract

A powerful way to prevent gaps is to follow the old/new contract—a writing strategy derived from the principle of old before new that we explained and illustrated in Lesson 1. Simply put, the old/new contract asks writers to begin sentences with something old—something that links to what has gone before—and then to end sentences with new information.

To understand the old/new contract more fully, try the following thought exercise. We'll show you two passages, both of which explain the old/new contract. One of them, however, follows the principle it describes; the other violates it.

THOUGHT EXERCISE

Which of these passages follows the old/new contract?

VERSION 1

The old/new contract is another principle for writing clear closed-form prose. Beginning your sentences with something old—something that links to what has gone before—and then ending your sentences with new information that advances the argument is what the old/new contract asks writers to do. An effect called *coherence,* which is closely related to *unity,* is created by following this principle. Whereas the clear relationship between the topic sentence and the body of the paragraph and between the parts and the whole is what *unity* refers to, the clear relationship between one sentence and the next is what *coherence* relates to.

VERSION 2

Another principle for writing clear closed-form prose is the old/new contract. The old/new contract asks writers to begin sentences with something old—something that links to what has gone before—and then to end sentences with new information that advances the argument. Following this principle creates an effect called *coherence,* which is closely related to unity. Whereas *unity* refers to the clear relationship between the body of a paragraph and its topic sentence and between the parts and the whole, *coherence* refers to the clear relationship between one sentence and the next, between part and part.

If you are like most readers, you have to concentrate much harder to understand Version 1 than Version 2 because it violates the old-before-new way that our minds normally process information. When a writer doesn't begin a sentence with old material, readers have to hold the new material in suspension until they have figured out how it connects to what has gone before. They can stay on the trail, but they have to keep jumping over the potholes between sentences.

To follow the old/new contract, place old information near the beginning of sentences in what we call the *topic position* and new information that advances the argument in the predicate or *stress position* at the end of the sentence. We associate topics with the beginnings of sentences simply because in the standard English sentence, the topic (or subject) comes before the predicate—hence the notion of a "contract" by which we agree not to fool or frustrate our readers by breaking with the "normal" order of things. The contract says that the old, backward-linking material comes at the beginning of the sentence and that the new, argument-advancing material comes at the end.

For Writing and Discussion

What follow are two more passages, one of which obeys the old/new contract while the other violates it. Working in small groups or as a whole class, reach consensus on which of these passages follows the old/new contract. Explain your reasoning by showing how the beginning of each sentence links to something old.

PASSAGE A

Play is an often-overlooked dimension of fathering. From the time a child is born until its adolescence, fathers emphasize caretaking less than play. Egalitarian feminists may be troubled by this, and spending more time in caretaking may be wise for fathers. There seems to be unusual significance in the father's style of play. Physical excitement and stimulation are likely to be part of it. With older children more physical games and teamwork that require the competitive testing of physical and mental skills are also what it involves. Resemblance to an apprenticeship or teaching relationship is also a characteristic of fathers' play: Come on, let me show you how.

PASSAGE B

An often-overlooked dimension of fathering is play. From their children's birth through adolescence, fathers tend to emphasize play more than caretaking. This may be troubling to egalitarian feminists, and it would indeed be wise for

(*continued*)

most fathers to spend more time in caretaking. Yet the fathers' style of play seems to have unusual significance. It is likely to be both physically stimulating and exciting. With older children it involves more physical games and teamwork that require the competitive testing of physical and mental skills. It frequently resembles an apprenticeship or teaching relationship: Come on, let me show you how.

How to Make Links to the "Old"

To understand how to link to "old information," you need to understand more fully what we mean by "old" or "familiar." In the context of sentence-level coherence, we mean everything in the text that the reader has read so far. Any upcoming sentence is new information, but once the reader has read it, it becomes old information. For example, when a reader is halfway through a text, everything previously read—the title, the introduction, half the body—is old information to which you can link to meet your readers' expectations for unity and coherence.

In making these backward links, writers have three targets:

1. They can link to a key word or concept in the immediately preceding sentence (creating coherence).
2. They can link to a key word or concept in a preceding point sentence (creating unity).
3. They can link to a preceding forecasting statement about structure (helping readers map their location in the text).

Writers have a number of textual strategies for making these links. In Figure 18.4 our annotations show how a professional writer links to old information within the first five or six words of each sentence. What follows is a compendium of these strategies:

- *Repeat a key word.* The most common way to open with something old is to repeat a key word from the preceding sentence or an earlier point sentence. In our example, note the number of sentences that open with "father," "father's," or "fathering." Note also the frequent repetitions of "play."
- *Use a pronoun to substitute for a key word.* In our example, the second sentence opens with the pronouns "it," referring to "research," and "their," referring to "fathers." The last three sentences open with the pronoun "It," referring to "father's style of play."
- *Summarize, rephrase, or restate earlier concepts.* Writers can link to a preceding sentence by using a word or phrase that summarizes or restates a key concept. In the second sentence, "interactions with children" restates the concept of childrearing. Similarly, the phrase "an often-overlooked dimension" refers to a concept implied in the preceding paragraph—that recent

FIGURE 18.4 How a Professional Writer Follows the Old/New Contract

Refers to "fathers" in previous sentence

Transition tells us new paragraph will be an example of previous concept

Refers to fathers

New information that becomes topic of this paragraph

Repeats words "father" and "play" from the topic sentence of the paragraph

Recent research has given us much deeper—and more surprising—insights into the father's role in childrearing. It shows that in almost all of their interactions with children, fathers do things a little differently from mothers. What fathers do—their special parenting style—is not only highly complementary to what mothers do but is by all indications important in its own right.

For example, an often-overlooked dimension of fathering is play. From their children's birth through adolescence, fathers tend to emphasize play more than caretaking. This may be troubling to egalitarian feminists, and it would indeed be wise for most fathers to spend more time in caretaking.

Yet the fathers' style of play seems to have unusual significance. It is likely to be both physically stimulating and exciting. With older children it involves more physical games and teamwork that require the competitive testing of physical and mental skills. It frequently resembles an apprenticeship or teaching relationship: Come on, let me show you how.

Refers to "research" in previous sentence

Rephrases idea of "childrearing"

Repeats "fathers" from previous sentence

Rephrases concept in previous paragraph

Pronoun sums up previous concept

"It" refers to fathers' style of play

David Popenoe, "Where's Papa?" from *Life Without Father: Compelling New Evidence that Fatherhood and Marriage Are Indispensable for the Good of Children and Society.*

research reveals something significant and not widely known about a father's role in childrearing. An "often-overlooked dimension" sums up this idea. Finally, note that the pronoun "this" in the second paragraph sums up the main concept of the previous two sentences. (But see our warning on page 560 about the overuse of "this" as a pronoun.)

- *Use a transition word.* Writers can also use transition words such as *first . . . , second . . . , third . . .* or *therefore* or *however* to cue the reader about the logical relationship between an upcoming sentence and the preceding ones. Note how the second paragraph opens with "For example," indicating that the upcoming paragraph will illustrate the concept identified in the preceding paragraph.

These strategies give you a powerful way to check and revise your prose. Comb your drafts for gaps between sentences where you have violated the old/new contract. If the opening of a new sentence doesn't refer back to an earlier word, phrase, or concept, your readers could derail, so use what you have learned to repair the tracks.

For Writing and Discussion

Individual Task: Bring to class a draft-in-progress for a closed-form essay. On a selected page, examine the opening of each sentence. Place a vertical slash in front of any sentence that doesn't contain near the beginning some backward-looking element that links to old, familiar material. Then revise these sentences to follow the old/new contract.

Group Task: Working with a partner, share the changes you each made on your drafts. Then on each other's pages, work together to identify the kinds of links made at the beginning of each sentence. (For example, does the opening of a sentence repeat a key word, use a pronoun to substitute for a key word, rephrase or restate an earlier concept, or use a transition word?)

As we discussed in Lesson 1, the principle of old before new has great explanatory power in helping writers understand their choices when they compose. In this last section, we give you some further insights into the old/new contract.

Avoid Ambiguous Use of "This" to Fulfill the Old/New Contract

Some writers try to fulfill the old/new contract by frequent use of the pronoun *this* to sum up a preceding concept. Occasionally such usage is effective, as in our example passage on fathers' style of play when the writer says: "*This* may be troubling to egalitarian feminists." But frequent use of *this* as a pronoun creates lazy and often ambiguous prose. Consider how our example passage might read if many of the explicit links were replaced by *this:*

LAZY USE OF *THIS* AS PRONOUN

Recent research has given us much deeper—and more surprising—insights into **this.** It shows that in doing **this,** fathers do things a little differently from mothers. **This** is not only highly complementary to what mothers do but is by all indications important in its own right.

For example, an often-overlooked dimension of **this** is play.

Perhaps this passage helps you see why we refer to *this* (used by itself as a pronoun) as "the lazy person's all-purpose noun-slot filler."*

---

*It's acceptable to use *this* as an adjective, as in "this usage"; we refer only to *this* used by itself as a pronoun.

How the Old/New Contract Modifies the Rule "Avoid Weak Repetition"

Many students have been warned against repetition of the same word (or *weak repetition,* as your teacher may have called it). Consequently, you may not be aware that repetition of key words is a vital aspect of unity and coherence. The repeated words create what linguists call "lexical strings" that keep a passage focused on a particular point. Note in our passage about the importance of fathers' style of play the frequent repetitions of the words *father* and *play.* What if the writer worried about repeating *father* too much and reached for his thesaurus?

UNNECESSARY ATTEMPT TO AVOID REPETITION

Recent research has given us much deeper—and more surprising—insights into the **male parent's** role in childrearing. It shows that in almost all of their interactions with children, **patriarchs** do things a little differently from mothers. What **sires** do. . . .

For example, an often-overlooked dimension of **male gender parenting** is. . . .

You get the picture. Keep your reader on familiar ground through repetition of key words.

How the Old/New Contract Modifies the Rule "Prefer Active over Passive Voice"

Another rule that you may have learned is to use the active voice rather than the passive voice. In the active voice the doer of the action is in the subject slot of the sentence, and the receiver is in the direct object slot, as in the following examples:

The dog caught the Frisbee.
The women wrote letters of complaint to the boss.
The landlord raised the rent.

In the passive voice the receiver of the action becomes the subject and the doer of the action either becomes the object of the preposition *by* or disappears from the sentence:

The Frisbee was caught by the dog.
Letters of complaint were written (by the women) to the boss.
The rent was raised (by the landlord).

Other things being equal, the active voice is indeed preferable to the passive because it is more direct and forceful. But in some cases, other things *aren't* equal, and the passive voice is preferable. *What the old/new contract asks you to consider is whether the doer or the receiver represents the old information in a sentence.* Consider the difference between the following passages:

| Second Sentence, Active Voice | My great-grandfather was a skilled cabinetmaker. He made this dining room table near the turn of the century. |
| Second Sentence, Passive Voice | I am pleased that you stopped to admire our dining room table. It was made by my great-grandfather near the turn of the century. |

In the first passage, the opening sentence is about *my great-grandfather.* To begin the second sentence with old information ("He," referring to "great-grandfather"), the writer uses the active voice. The opening sentence of the second passage is about the *dining room table.* To begin the second sentence with old information ("It," referring to "table"), the writer must use the passive voice, since the table is the receiver of the action. In both cases, the sentences are structured to begin with old information.

Lesson 8: Learning Four Expert Moves for Organizing and Developing Ideas

In this lesson we show you that writers of closed-form prose often employ a conventional set of moves to organize parts of an essay. In using the term *moves,* we are making an analogy with the "set moves" or "set plays" in such sports as basketball, volleyball, and soccer. For example, a common set move in basketball is the "pick," in which an offensive player without the ball stands motionless in order to block the path of a defensive player who is guarding the dribbler. Similarly, certain organizational patterns in writing occur frequently enough to act as set plays for writers. These patterns set up expectations in the reader's mind about the shape of an upcoming stretch of prose, anything from a few sentences to a paragraph to a large block of paragraphs. As you will see, these moves also stimulate the invention of ideas. Next, we describe four of the most powerful set plays.*

The *For Example* Move

An earlier example of Dao's paragraphs is on p. 551.

Perhaps the most common set play occurs when a writer makes an assertion and then illustrates it with one or more examples, often signaling the move explicitly with transitions such as *for example, for instance,* or *a case in point is. . . .* Here is how student writer Dao Do used the *for example* move to support her third reason for opposing euthanasia:

---

*You might find it helpful to follow the set plays we used to write this section. This last sentence is the opening move of a play we call "division into parallel parts." It sets up the expectation that we will develop four set plays in order. Watch for the way we chunk them and signal transitions between them.

FOR EXAMPLE MOVE

My third objection to euthanasia is that it fails to see the value in suffering. ◄—————— *Topic sentence*
Suffering is a part of life. We see the value of suffering only if we look deeply within — *Transition signaling*
our suffering. For example, I never thought my crippled uncle from Vietnam was a   *the move*
blessing to my grandmother until I talked to her. My mother's little brother was
born prematurely. As a result of oxygen and nutrition deficiency, he was born crippled. His tiny arms and legs were twisted around his body, preventing him from any
normal movements such as walking, picking up things, and lying down. He could
only sit. Therefore, his world was very limited, for it consisted of his own room and
the garden viewed through his window. Because of his disabilities, my grandmother   *Extended example*
had to wash him, feed him, and watch him constantly. It was hard, but she man-   *supporting point*
aged to care for him for forty-three years. He passed away after the death of my
grandfather in 1982. Bringing this situation out of Vietnam and into Western society shows the difference between Vietnamese and Western views. In the West, my
uncle might have been euthanized as a baby. Supporters of euthanasia would have
said he wouldn't have any quality of life and that he would have been a great burden. But he was not a burden on my grandmother. She enjoyed taking care of him,
and he was always her company after her other children got married and moved
away. Neither one of them saw his defect as meaningless suffering because it
brought them closer together.

This passage uses a single, extended example to support a point. You could also
use several shorter examples or other kinds of illustrating evidence such as facts
or statistics. In all cases the *for example* move creates a pattern of expectation and
fulfillment. This pattern drives the invention of ideas in one of two ways: It urges
the writer either to find examples to develop a generalization or to formulate a
generalization that shows the point of an example.

For Writing and Discussion

Working individually or in groups, develop a plan for supporting one or more
of the following generalizations using the *for example* move:

1. Another objection to state sales taxes is that they are so annoying.
2. Although assertiveness training has definite benefits, it can sometimes get
   you into real trouble.
3. Sometimes effective leaders are indecisive.

The *Summary/However* Move

This move occurs whenever a writer sums up another person's viewpoint in order
to qualify or contradict it or to introduce an opposing view. Typically, writers use
transition words such as *but, however, in contrast,* or *on the other hand* between the
parts of this move. This move is particularly common in academic writing, which

often contrasts the writer's new view with prevailing views. Here is how Dao uses a *summary/however* move in the introduction of her essay opposing euthanasia:

SUMMARY/HOWEVER **MOVE**

Issue over which there is disagreement

Summary of opposing viewpoint

Transition to writer's viewpoint

Statement of writer's view

Should euthanasia be legalized? My classmate Martha and her family think it should be. Martha's aunt was blind from diabetes. For three years she was constantly in and out of the hospital, but then her kidneys shut down and she became a victim of life support. After three months of suffering, she finally gave up. Martha believes this three-month period was unnecessary, for her aunt didn't have to go through all of that suffering. If euthanasia were legalized, her family would have put her to sleep the minute her condition worsened. Then, she wouldn't have had to feel pain, and she would have died in peace and with dignity. However, despite Martha's strong argument for legalizing euthanasia, I find it wrong.

The first sentence of this introduction poses the question that the essay addresses. The main body of the paragraph summarizes Martha's opposing view on euthanasia, and the final sentence, introduced by the transition "However," presents Dao's thesis.

For Writing and Discussion

For this exercise, assume that you favor development of wind-generated electricity. Use the *summary/however* move to acknowledge the view of civil engineer David Rockwood, whose letter opposing wind-generated electricity you read in Chapter 1 (pp. 17–18). Assume that you are writing the opening paragraph of your own essay. Follow the pattern of Dao's introduction: (a) begin with a one-sentence issue or question; (b) summarize Rockwood's view in approximately one hundred words; and (c) state your own view, using *however* or *in contrast* as a transition. Write out your paragraph on your own, or work in groups to write a consensus paragraph. Then share and critique your paragraphs.

The *Division-into-Parallel-Parts* Move

Among the most frequently encountered and powerful of the set plays is the *division-into-parallel-parts* move. To initiate the move, a writer begins with an umbrella sentence that forecasts the structure and creates a framework. (For example, "Freud's theory differs from Jung's in three essential ways" or "The decline of the U.S. space program can be attributed to several factors.") Typical overview sentences either specify the number of parts that follow by using phrases such as "two ways," "three differences," or "five kinds," or they leave the number unspecified, using words such as *several, a few,* or *many.* Alternatively, the writer may ask a rhetorical question that implies the framework: "What are some main differences, then, between Freud's theory and Jung's? One difference is. . . ."

To signal transitions from one part to the next, writers use two kinds of signposts in tandem. The first is a series of transition words or bullets to introduce each of the parallel parts. Here are typical series of transition words:

> First . . . Second . . . Third . . . Finally . . .
> First . . . Another . . . Still another . . . Finally . . .
> One . . . In addition . . . Furthermore . . . Also

The second kind of signpost, usually used in conjunction with transitions, is an echolike repetition of the same grammatical structure to begin each parallel part.

> I learned several things from this course. First, *I learned that* [development]. Second, *I learned that* [development]. Finally, *I learned that* [development].

The division-into-parallel parts move can be used within a single paragraph, or it can control larger stretches of text in which a dozen or more paragraphs may work together to complete a parallel series of parts. (For example, you are currently in the third part of a parallel series introduced by the mapping sentence on page 562: "Next we describe four of the most powerful set plays." Here is an example of a student paragraph organized by the division-into-parallel-parts move.

DIVISION-INTO-PARALLEL-PARTS MOVE

In this paper I will argue that political solutions to homelessness must take into account four categories of homeless people. A first category is persons who are out of work and seek new jobs. Persons in this category may have been recently laid off, unable to meet their rental payments, and forced temporarily to live out of a car or van. They might quickly leave the ranks of the homeless if they can find new jobs. A second category includes the physically disabled or mentally ill. Providing housing for these persons addresses only part of their problems since they also need medical care and medication. For many, finding or keeping a job might be impossible. A third category is the street alcoholic or drug addict. These persons need addiction treatment as well as clothing and shelter and will not become productive citizens until they become sober or drug free. The final category includes those who, like the old railroad "hobo," choose homelessness as a way of life.

Mapping statement forecasts "move"

Transition to first parallel part

Transition to second parallel part

Transition to third parallel part

Final transition completes "move"

Instead of transition words, writers can also use bullets followed by indented text:

USE OF BULLETS TO SIGNAL PARALLEL PARTS

The Wolf Recovery Program is rigidly opposed by a vociferous group of ranchers who pose three main objections to increasing wolf populations:

- They perceive wolves as a threat to livestock. [development]
- They fear the wolves will attack humans. [development]
- They believe ranchers will not be compensated by the government for their loss of profits. [development]

For Writing and Discussion

Working individually or in small groups, use the *division-into-parallel-parts* move to create, organize, and develop ideas to support one or more of the following point sentences.

1. To study for an exam effectively, a student should follow these (specify a number) steps.
2. Why do U.S. schoolchildren lag so far behind European and Asian children on standardized tests of mathematics and science? One possible cause is . . . (continue).
3. Constant dieting is unhealthy for several reasons.

The *Comparison/Contrast* Move

A common variation on the *division-into-parallel-parts* move is the *comparison/contrast* move. To compare or contrast two items, you must first decide on the points of comparison (or contrast). If you are contrasting the political views of two presidential candidates, you might choose to focus on four points of comparison: differences in their foreign policy, differences in economic policy, differences in social policy, and differences in judicial philosophy. You then have two choices for organizing the parts: the *side-by-side pattern,* in which you discuss all of candidate A's views and then all of candidate B's views; or the *back-and-forth pattern,* in which you discuss foreign policy, contrasting A's views with B's views, then move on to economic policy, then social policy, and then judicial philosophy. Here is how these two patterns would appear on a tree diagram:

Side-by-Side Pattern

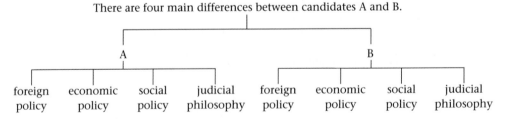

Back-and-Forth Pattern

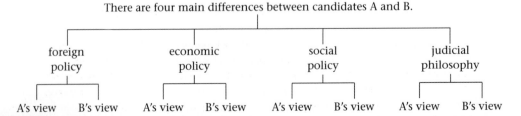

There are no cut-and-dried rules that dictate when to use the *side-by-side pattern* or the *back-and-forth pattern.* However, for lengthy comparisons, the *back-and-forth pattern* is often more effective because the reader doesn't have to store great amounts of information in memory. The *side-by-side pattern* requires readers to remember all the material about A when they get to B, and it is sometimes difficult to keep all the points of comparison clearly in mind.

For Writing and Discussion

Working individually or in groups, create tree diagrams for stretches of text based on one or more of the following point sentences, all of which call for the *comparison/contrast* move. Make at least one diagram follow the *back-and-forth pattern* and at least one diagram follow the *side-by-side pattern.*

1. To understand U.S. politics, an outsider needs to appreciate some basic differences between Republicans and Democrats.
2. Although they are obviously different on the surface, there are many similarities between the Boy Scouts and a street gang.
3. There are several important differences between closed-form and open-form writing.

Lesson 9: Writing Effective Conclusions

Conclusions can best be understood as complements to introductions. In both the introduction and the conclusion, writers are concerned with the essay as a whole more than with any given part. In a conclusion, the writer attempts to bring a sense of completeness and closure to the profusion of points and particulars laid out in the body of the essay. The writer is particularly concerned with helping the reader move from the parts back to the big picture and to understand the importance or significance of the essay.

If you are having trouble figuring out how to conclude an essay, consider the following guide questions, which are designed to stimulate thought about how to conclude and to help you determine which model best suits your situation.

1. How long and complex is your essay? Is it long enough or complex enough that readers might benefit from a summary of your main points?
2. What's the most important point (or points) you want your readers to remember about your essay? How long ago in the essay did you state that point? Would it be useful to restate that point as succinctly and powerfully as possible?
3. Do you know of an actual instance, illustration, or example of your main point that would give it added weight?
4. What larger principle stands behind your main point? Or what must your audience accept as true in order to accept your main point? How would you defend that assumption if someone were to call it into question?

5. Why is your main point significant? Why are the ideas in your paper important and worth your audience's consideration? What larger issues does your topic relate to or touch on? Could you show how your topic relates to a larger and more significant topic? What might that topic be?

6. If your audience accepts your thesis, where do you go next? What is the next issue or question to be examined? What further research is needed? Conversely, do you have any major reservations, unexpressed doubts, or "All bets are off if X is the case" provisos you'd like to admit? What do you *not* know about your topic that reduces your certainty in your thesis?

7. How much antagonism or skepticism toward your position do you anticipate? If it's a great deal, would it be feasible to delay your thesis, solution, or proposal until the very end of the paper?

Because many writers find conclusions challenging to write, we offer the following six possible models:

The *Simple Summary* Conclusion

The most common, though often not the most effective, kind of conclusion is a simple summary, in which the writer recaps what has just been said. This approach is useful in a long or complex essay or in an instructional text that focuses on concepts to be learned. We use *summary* conclusions for most of the chapters in this text. In a short, easy-to-follow essay, however, a *summary* conclusion can be dull and may even annoy readers who are expecting something more significant, but a brief summary followed by a more artful concluding strategy can often be effective.

The *Larger Significance* Conclusion

A particularly effective concluding strategy is to draw the reader's attention to the *larger significance* of your argument. In our discussion of academic problems (see Chapter 1), we explained that a good academic question needs to be significant (worth pursuing). Although readers need to be convinced from the outset that the problem investigated in your paper is significant, the conclusion is a good place to elaborate on that significance by showing how your argument now leads to additional benefits for the reader. For example, you might explain how your proposed solution to a question leads to potential understanding of a larger, more significant question or brings practical benefits to individuals or society. If you posed a question about values or about the interpretation of a confusing text or phenomenon, you might show how your argument could be applied to related questions or to related texts or phenomena. Your goal in writing this kind of conclusion is to show how your answer to the question posed in your paper has larger applications or significance.

The *Proposal* Conclusion

Another option, often used in analyses and arguments, is the *proposal* conclusion, which calls for action. A *proposal* conclusion states the action that the writer believes needs to be taken and briefly demonstrates the advantages of this action over alternative actions or describes its beneficial consequences. If your paper analyzes the negative consequences of shifting from a graduated to a flat-rate income tax, your conclusion may recommend an action such as modifying or opposing the flat tax. A slight variation is the *call-for-future-study* conclusion, which indicates what else needs to be known or resolved before a proposal can be offered. Such conclusions are especially common in scientific writing.

The *Scenic or Anecdotal* Conclusion

Popular writers often use a *scenic* or *anecdotal* conclusion, in which a scene or brief story illustrates the theme's significance without stating it explicitly. A paper opposing the current trend against involuntary hospitalization of the homeless mentally ill might end by describing a former mental patient, now an itinerant homeless person, collecting bottles in a park. Such scenes can help the reader experience directly the emotional significance of the topic analyzed in the body of the paper.

The *Hook and Return* Conclusion

A related variety of conclusion is the *hook and return,* in which the ending of the essay returns to something introduced in the opening hook or lead. If the lead of your essay is a vivid illustration of a problem—perhaps a scene or an anecdote— then your conclusion might return to the same scene or story, but with some variation to illustrate the significance of the essay. This sense of return can give your essay a strong feeling of unity.

The *Delayed-Thesis* Conclusion

This type of conclusion delays the thesis until the end of the essay. Rather than stating the thesis, the introduction merely states the problem, giving the body of the essay an open, exploratory, "let's think through this together" feel. Typically, the body of the paper examines alternative solutions or approaches to the problem and leaves the writer's own answer—the thesis—unstated until the end. This approach is especially effective when writing about highly complex or divisive issues on which you want to avoid taking a stand until all sides have been fairly presented.

For Writing and Discussion

Choose a paper you have just written and write an alternative conclusion using one of the strategies discussed in this lesson. Then share your original and revised conclusions in groups. Have group members discuss which one they consider most effective and why.

Lesson 10: Using Document Design Effectively

Throughout this text, we have suggested that choices about document design are linked to the writer's rhetorical context of purpose, audience, and genre. In Chapter 3, we examined four visual components of document design: fonts (size and style of type), spacing on the page, color, and images or graphics (pp. 62–65). In this chapter, we ask you to consider how document design can play an important role in the effectiveness of closed-form prose. Our advice is eminently practical: Good document design serves the whole communication, enhancing the writer's ethos and the impact of the writer's message.

Match Your Document Design to the Genre Expectations of Your Audience

In Chapter 3 (pp. 54–55), we explained how different genres of writing have their own conventions for approaching subject matter, structure, and style. These conventions function as agreements with readers that a particular kind of writing will meet certain reader expectations, including expectations for the way a document will look.

The closed-form genres you are likely to be assigned in college include academic research papers, experimental/scientific reports, various civic genres (letters to the editor, op-ed pieces, proposals), and various academic or workplace genres inside your major. In this textbook, we have included student examples of several different closed-form genres, each with a different "look" or appearance:

- MLA style research paper (pp. 675–686)
- APA style experimental report (pp. 277–289)
- Practical proposal with headings (pp. 487–491)
- Desk-top published informational piece designed to look like a magazine article (p. 230)
- Advocacy poster and Web page (pp. 483 and 484)

In addition, the text includes many professional examples exhibiting different document designs, including a variety of Web sites (see especially Chapter 21). A common principle of document design for closed-form genres is to keep the design functional—not decorative—with an emphasis on what you are communicating. In academic papers, follow the design specifications provided by appropriate disciplinary style manuals. In writing for workplace or popular genres, find successful examples to use as models. (Many businesses or corporations produce in-house style manuals for their documents.) Familiarizing yourself in advance with the specific document design requirements of a genre can help you throughout the invention, drafting, and revising stages of your writing by letting you envision the structure and appearance of your final document.

Consider Document Design an Important Part of Your *Ethos*

The appearance of your document also communicates your professional *ethos*. As you prepare your final document, ask yourself these questions: Does the appearance of my document reveal my professionalism? Does it convey that I am responsible, serious, and credible? Does it show that I am knowledgeable about this genre? Does my document design show consideration for my audience's time and appreciation of their background and expectations?

Use Document Design Components for Clarity and Emphasis

You can often increase the clarity and persuasiveness of documents through effective use of headings, graphics, or other visuals.

Headings and subheadings can add clarity to your documents by providing readers with a mental frame for processing your ideas. Some genres, such as the experimental report, employ standard headings. In other genres, writers often create their own headings, especially in papers more than six pages long. These headings show readers at a glance not only the structure of the paper but also a capsule of the argument. For example, here are the headings used by one of our students in an argument that coastal Indian tribes should not be allowed to hunt whales. (For first-level heads, she typed the words flush-left, bold-face, and all-caps; for second level heads she used flush-left, bold-face, and title-case.)

See page 250 for an explanation of the headings in an APA experimental report.

ILLUSTRATION OF HEADINGS IN STUDENT PAPER OPPOSING TRIBAL WHALING

THE NATIVE PERSPECTIVE: WHALING AS A CULTURAL TRADITION
> *[The paper's first section summarized the tribal perspective that a resumption of whaling would revive cultural traditions.]*

CULTURAL WHALING AS A STEP TOWARD COMMERCIAL WHALING
> *[In this section the writer argued that allowing any cultural whaling promotes increases commercial whaling.]*

THE HARM OF COMMERCIAL WHALING
> *[This heading marked the start of a long section providing three main arguments against commercial whaling.]*

Increase in the Demand for Whale Meat
> *[This subsection provided evidence that whale meat will grow in popularity, increasing demand.]*

Difficulty in Sustaining Whale Stocks
> *[This subsection showed that commercial whaling will lead toward gradual extinction of whales.]*

Decrease in Biodiversity
> *[This subsection showed the harm of losing biodiversity.]*

INTRINSIC VALUE OF WHALES
> *[In her final main section, the writer argued for the intrinsic value of whales.]*

As you can see, these headings give readers an immediate overview of the structure and content of the paper.

When creating heads, develop and follow the same font style for each level of head and make all the heads at each level grammatically parallel. (All the headings in the previous example are noun phrases.)

Like headings, graphics and images can enhance clarity and emphasize ideas by creating a visually interesting contrast to the written text, by focusing the readers' attention on the points you are making, and by giving your points presence and impact. Graphics and images should contribute to your intended rhetorical effect rather than show off the bells and whistles of your computer's graphics program. To avoid decorative and distracting use of graphics, ask yourself these main questions: What point or story do I want this graph or image to emphasize? What does this graphic add to my written text?

For discussion of visual rhetoric see Chapter 3, pp. 85–88, and all of Chapter 11. For strategies for creating effective graphics, see Chapter 10, pp. 261–266.

Use Design Components to Highlight and Reinforce—But Not Replace—Transitions, Points, and Key Explanations in the Text Itself

See Chapter 10, pp. 264–265 on independent redundancy of text and graphics.

Graphics and design elements should enhance a written text but never replace your verbal explanations of the same points. While headings and subheadings can guide readers through a document and direct them to particular points, you need to repeat the point, key explanation, or transition in the text itself. Your text should make complete sense with headings and graphics removed.

For Writing and Discussion

Consider the following writing scenario.

Spencer works in a drug rehabilitation center as an aide. He has become convinced that the United States should decriminalize possession of drugs, empty prisons of those convicted of victimless drug offenses, and divert money currently being spent on the "War on Drugs" into rehabilitation programs. Spencer wants to write a paper influencing readers to legalize drugs and focus on rehabilitation rather than punishment.

What document design features can you imagine Spencer using for each of the following genres and implied rhetorical contexts?

1. An academic research paper in a sociology class
2. A desktop-published article for a Web site (to be downloadable in pdf format)
3. A one-page newspaper advertisement (purchased space)
4. A newspaper op-ed column?

Working in groups or as a whole class, arrive at possible answers to the questions just posed. How do differences in genres and rhetorical contexts lead to different decisions about document design?

Composing and Revising Open-Form Prose

Good writing is supposed to evoke sensation in the reader—not the fact that it's raining, but the feel of being rained upon.

—E. L. DOCTOROW, *NOVELIST*

Much of this book focuses on closed-form prose where "good writing" means having a surprising thesis supported with effective points and particulars arranged hierarchically into unified and coherent paragraphs. But there are many kinds of good writing, and we probably all share the desire at times to write in ways other than tightly argued, thesis-governed, closed-form prose. In our epigraph, novelist E. L. Doctorow suggests another way to think of "good writing": Writing that evokes sensations, that triggers in the reader's imagination the very feel of the rain.

In this chapter, we shift our attention from closed- to open-form writing. Open-form prose differs from closed-form prose in its basic features, in the challenges and options it presents writers, in the demands it places on its readers, and in the mental and emotional pleasures it creates. Open-form writing, of the kind we discuss here, is often called *literary nonfiction* because it uses literary techniques and strategies such as story, plot, characterization, setting, and theme.

Of course, it should be remembered that writing exists on a continuum from closed to open forms and that many features of open-form prose can appear in primarily closed-form texts. In fact, many of the example essays in this book combine elements of both open and closed styles. At the extremes of the continuum, closed- and open-form writing are markedly different, but the styles can be blended in pleasing combinations.

As we have discussed throughout this text, writing at the closed end of the spectrum seeks to be efficient and reader-friendly. By forecasting what's coming, placing points first, using clear transitions, and putting old information before new, closed-form writers place maximum emphasis on delivering clear ideas that readers can grasp quickly. In contrast, open-form writers, by violating or simply stretching those same conventions, set up a different kind of relationship with readers. They often provide more pleasure in reading, but just as often demand more patience and tolerance of ambiguity. They are likely to take readers backstage to share the process of their thinking. They often cast themselves in the role

Chapter 7 on autobiographical narrative discusses plot, characterization, setting, and theme.

For essays that blend open and closed elements, see Cheryl Carp's "Behind Stone Walls" (pp. 231–232), Florence King's "I'd Rather Smoke than Kiss" (pp. 144–149), or Edward Abbey's "The Damnation of a Canyon" (pp. 157–161).

of narrators or characters reporting their quest for understanding and all the coincidences, disappointments, puzzling advice, and confusion they experienced along the way. In this process of sharing, they make readers codiscoverers of ideas and insights.

Open-form prose is also characterized by its emphasis on an aesthetic use of language—that is, language used to please and entertain. Without the benefit of a thesis or points appearing first to convey meaning, open-form prose depends on the very specificity of words, the ability of words to create mental pictures, to appeal to readers' senses and emotions, and to conjure up memories.

Our goal in this chapter is to give you some practical lessons on how to write effective open-form prose. But we need to acknowledge at the outset that, whereas closed-form prose is governed by a few widely accepted conventions, one of the main features of open-form prose is its freedom to play with conventions in a bewildering variety of ways. Consequently, our discussion of open-form writing seeks more to introduce you to guiding principles rather than to treat open-form writing exhaustively.

Lesson 1: Make Your Narrative a Story, Not an *and Then* Chronology

We have said that open-form prose is narrative based and uses the strategies of a story. In this first lesson we want you to think more deeply about the concept of a story—particularly how a story differs from an *and then* chronology. Both a story and an *and then* chronology depict events happening in time. But there are important differences between them. At the start of this lesson, we'd like you to try your own hand at articulating the differences between a story and an *and then* chronology. Read the following example of a student's autobiographical narrative and then respond to the questions that follow.

And then writing is also discussed in Chapter 18, pp. 532–533.

READINGS

Patrick Klein (student)
Berkeley Blues

1   It was a cold night. That is nothing new in San Francisco, but something made this night particularly frigid. It was early February and the whole city, including the Berkeley section where we were staying, was still held tight in the firm grip of winter. It had also rained that afternoon and the air, having been cleared by the storm, was cold and sharp. It hurt the back of your throat when you inhaled and turned into mist when you exhaled. As the six of us hurriedly walked in a huddled mass, the water that was lying in puddles on the dimly lit sidewalk jumped out of our way as we slammed our dress shoes down into its dregs. We silently decided on our destination and

slipped into the grungy, closet-like pizza joint. We took the only seats the place had and as we pulled them into a circle, we all breathed a sigh of relief.

2 This was our first night at Berkeley. We were there for a debate tournament to be held the next day at the university. On this night, however, we were six high school sophomores in search of food. So, dressed in our suits and ties (we were required to wear them) and heavy coats, we ventured out of the university and entered the city of Berkeley.

3 Berkeley is an interesting place. Many might have romantic notions of a bunch of shaggy intellectuals discussing French existentialism while sipping cappuccino, but while this might have been the case a few decades ago, the reality is that Berkeley is a ghetto. The place is filled with grungy closet shops while newspapers cover the sidewalks and the people lying on them. The university is divided from this ghetto by a two-lane street.

4 As the six of us crossed the two-lane street that fateful night, my thoughts drifted to my own neighborhood, which up until that moment had been the extent of my world.

5 McCormick Ranch, Arizona, is a sheltered place. To a certain extent it's mostly white, with little crime and few domestic problems. Everybody has a pool, at least two cars, and a beautiful desert sunset every night. I had everything I ever wanted. It seemed very gentle and dreamlike compared to the harsh slum we found ourselves in.

6 When we made it into the pizza place and moved the chairs into a protective circle around a square table, anxiety about our "hostile" environment was quickly swept away with hot, greasy pizza. We ate until we were content and were trying to decide how to divide the few remaining pieces among ourselves when it happened.

7 The pizza place was separated from the rest of humanity by a large window. Our table was directly in front of that window and two feet from the door. People had been passing the window and probably remarking on the six well-dressed kids inside, but we paid them no mind and they all walked by without incident. Still, our hearts were seized with terror every time a human being would pass that window, and we hoped with all that we could muster that every one of them would continue on. We were almost right.

8 On this night, when six young yuppie kids from an upper middle-class world decided to risk it and go eat pizza in a ghetto, he walked by. He didn't look any different from others we'd seen that night. Black. Dirty. Tired. Cold. His clothes consisted of a grimy, newspaper-stained jacket, a T-shirt with who-knows-how-old dirt on it, flimsy pants with holes at the knees, and tattered excuses for shoes. He was not quite up to par with our Gucci loafers and Armani jackets.

9 He shuffled past the window and glanced in. We didn't notice. He stopped. We noticed. Twelve eyes glanced up as casually as they could and six hearts stopped beating for a second. Yep, still there. All eyes went back to the floor, except for two. Those eyes belonged to Chad, and in some act of defiance, his eyes met the poor man's eyes and glared.

10   The man opened the door. "We're all going to die," I thought. "All my hopes and dreams are going to end here, in a stupid pizza place, at the hands of a crazy black bum."

11   He took something out of his pocket.

12   It was shiny.

13   I couldn't look.

14   A knife.

15   No. It was a flask. He took a swig from it, and, still propping the door open with his sagging frame, spoke the most jolting, burning words I've ever heard.

16   "I love you," he said. "All of you." He glanced at Chad, "Even you." He stepped back and said, "I know what you think of me, but I still love you." I will probably never forget those words or how he said them with a steady, steely voice.

17   Then he left. That was it. Gone. It took about five minutes for anyone to talk. When the talking started, we exchanged jokes and responded with empty, devastating laughter.

18   We soon left the shop. It had grown colder outside and we quickly returned to our climate-controlled hotel room. We had just eaten a filling meal and paid for it with our own money. We were all about fifteen. The man we had encountered was probably in his fifties. He had no roof, no money, or food. It seemed strange that I owned more than an adult, but in truth, he had more than I. He was able to love us when we ostracized him and thought stereotypically about him.

19   I remember later trying to rationalize my sickening behavior by thinking that there is nothing wrong with being and acting afraid in a strange environment. I tried to use my age as an excuse. Nothing worked. I was guilty of fearing a fellow human being because of his color and my preset notions of bums.

20   To this day I still think about what difference, if any, it would have made if we had given him our leftover pizza. It might have eased my conscience. It was a very cold night and we had made it colder.

For Writing and Discussion

Individual task: Now that you have read "Berkeley Blues," read the following autobiographical narrative entitled "The Stolen Watch," which was submitted by a student as a draft for an assignment on narrative writing.

The Stolen Watch

Last fall and winter I was living in Spokane with my brother, who during this time had a platonic girlfriend come over from Seattle and stay for a weekend. Her name was Karen, and we became interested in each other and I went over to see her at the first of the year. She then invited me to, supposedly, the biggest party of the year, called the Aristocrats' Ball. I said sure and made my way back to Seattle in February. It started out bad on Friday, the day my brother and I left Spokane. We left town an hour late, but what's new. Then my brother had to stop along the way and pick up some parts; we stayed there for an hour trying to find this guy. It all started out bad because we arrived in Seattle and I forgot to call Karen. We were staying at her brother's house and after we brought all our things in, we decided to go to a few bars. Later that night we ran into Karen in one of the bars, and needless to say she was not happy with me. When I got up the next morning I knew I should have stayed in Spokane, because I felt bad vibes. Karen made it over about an hour before the party. By the time we reached the party, which drove me crazy, she wound up with another guy, so her friends and I decided to go to a few bars. The next morning when I was packing, I could not find my watch and decided that someone had to have taken it. We decided that it had to have been the goon that Karen had wound up with the night before, because she was at her brother's house with him before she went home. So how was I going to get my watch back?

We decided the direct and honest approach to the problem would work out the best. We got in contact and confronted him. This turned out to be quite a chore. It turned out that he was visiting some of his family during that weekend and lived in Little Harbor, California. It turned out that Karen knew his half brother and got some information on him, which was not pretty. He had just been released by the army and was trained in a special forces unit, in the field of Martial Arts. He was a trained killer! This information did not help matters at all,

(continued)

but the next bit of information was just as bad if not worse. Believe it or not, he was up on charges of attempted murder and breaking and entering. In a way, it turned out lucky for me, because he was in enough trouble with the police and did not need any more. Karen got in contact with him and threatened him that I would bring him up on charges if he did not return the watch. His mother decided that he was in enough trouble and sent me the watch. I was astounded, it was still working and looked fine. The moral of the story is don't drive 400 miles to see a girl you hardly know, and whatever you do, don't leave your valuables out in the open.

> **Group task:** Share your responses to the following questions:
>
> 1. How does your experience of reading "Berkeley Blues" differ from your experience of reading "The Stolen Watch"? Try to articulate the different ways you reacted to the two pieces while in the process of reading them.
> 2. Based on the differences between these two pieces, how would you define a "story"? Begin by brainstorming all the ways that the two pieces differ. Then try to identify the essential differences that make one a "story" and the other an *and then* chronology.

Now that you have tried to define a story for yourselves, we would like to explain our own four criteria for a story: depiction of events through time, connectedness, tension, and resolution. If we combine these criteria into a sentence, it would read like this: A story depicts events that are connected causally or thematically to create a sense of tension that is resolved through action, insight, or understanding. These four criteria occurring together turn a chronology into a story.

Depiction of Events Through Time

The essence of storytelling is the depiction of events through time. Whereas thesis-based writing descends from problem to thesis to supporting reasons and evidence, stories unfold linearly, temporally, from event to event. You may start in the middle of the action and then jump backward and forward, but you always encounter some sequence of events happening in time. This temporal focus creates a sense of "onceness." Things that happen at a point in time happen only once, as the classic fairy-tale opening "Once upon a time" suggests. When you compose and revise a narrative, you want to try to capture the "onceness" of that experience. As the essayist E. B. White once advised a young writer, "Don't write about Man but about a man."

Consider how Val Plumwood, a professor of women's studies and author of the book *Feminism and the Mastery of Nature,* depicts the events leading up to a disturbing encounter with a crocodile. (Later in the story, the reader sees how this encounter shapes her understanding of humans' place in the food chain and the need for a respectful, rather than a dominating, attitude toward other animals.)

> In the early wet season, Kakadu's paper-bark wetlands are especially stunning, as the water lilies weave white, pink, and blue patterns of dreamlike beauty over the shining thunderclouds reflected in their still waters. Yesterday, the water lilies and the wonderful bird life had enticed me into a joyous afternoon's idyll as I ventured onto the East Alligator Lagoon for the first time in a canoe lent by the park service. "You can play about on the backwaters," the ranger had said, "but don't go onto the main river channel. The current's too swift, and if you get into trouble, there are the crocodiles. Lots of them along the river!" I followed his advice and glutted myself on the magical beauty and bird life of the lily lagoons, untroubled by crocodiles.
>
> Today, I wanted to repeat the experience despite the drizzle beginning to fall as I neared the canoe launch site. I set off on a day trip in search of an Aboriginal rock art site across the lagoon and up a side channel. The drizzle turned to a warm rain within a few hours, and the magic was lost. The birds were invisible, the water lilies were sparser, and the lagoon seemed even a little menacing. I noticed now how low the 14-foot canoe sat in the water, just a few inches of fiberglass between me and the great saurians, close relatives of the ancient dinosaurs. . . .
>
> After hours of searching the maze of shallow channels in the swamp, I had not found the clear channel leading to the rock art site, as shown on the ranger's sketch map. When I pulled my canoe over in driving rain to a rock outcrop for a hasty, sodden lunch, I experienced the unfamiliar sensation of being watched. Having never been one for timidity, in philosophy or in life, I decided, rather than return defeated to my sticky trailer, to explore a clear, deep channel closer to the river I had traveled the previous day.
>
> The rain and wind grew more severe, and several times I pulled over to tip water from the canoe. The channel soon developed steep mud banks and snags. Farther on, the channel opened up and was eventually blocked by a large sandy bar. I pushed the canoe toward the bank, looking around carefully before getting out of the shallow and pulling the canoe up. I would be safe from crocodiles in the canoe—I had been told—but swimming and standing or wading at the water's edge were dangerous. Edges are one of the crocodile's favorite food-capturing places. I saw nothing, but the feeling of unease that had been with me all day intensified.

In this example of literary nonfiction, Plumwood persuades readers to appreciate the beauties of the exotic Australian rain forest as well as its dangers. Note how her method includes the depicting of events that happen once in time—her wondrous first day of exploration, the ranger's warning to stay away from the main river, her second day's unsuccessful search by canoe for a site of Aboriginal rock art, and then her emerging discovery that in the increasing intensity of the rainstorm, she had reached the junction with the main river. Plumwood's powerful narrative becomes the basis for a profound concluding reflection on what she calls humans' "ecological identity."

Connectedness

The events of a story must also be connected, not merely spatially or sequentially, but causally or thematically. When discussing "The Stolen Watch" in the previous exercise, you might have asked yourselves, "What does all that stuff about forgetting to call Karen and stopping for parts, etc., have to do with the stolen watch? Is this story about the watch or about confronting a potential killer?" If so, you instinctively understood the concept of connectedness. Stories are more than just chronicles of events. Novelist E. M. Forster offered the simplest definition of a story when he rejected "The king dies and then the queen died," but accepted "The king died and then the queen died . . . of grief." The words "of grief" connect the two events to each other in a causal relationship, converting a series of events into a patterned, meaningfully related sequence of events. Now examine this passage to see the connections the writer establishes between the scenes.

THEMATIC AND CAUSAL CONNECTEDNESS

I have been so totally erased from nature lately, like a blackboard before school starts, that yesterday when I was in the Japanese section of San Francisco, Japantown, I saw the sidewalk littered with chocolate wrappers.

There were hundreds of them. Who in the hell has been eating all these chocolates? I thought. A convention of Japanese chocolate eaters must have passed this way.

Then I noticed some plum trees on the street. Then I noticed that it was autumn. Then I noticed that the leaves were falling as they will and as they must every year. Where had I gone wrong?

—Richard Brautigan, "Leaves"

Brautigan's narrative becomes a story only when you realize that the "chocolate wrappers" are really plum leaves; the two images are connected by the writer's changed perception, which illuminates the thematic question raised at the beginning and end: Why has he become "so totally erased from nature"? As you write, connect the elements of your narrative causally and thematically.

Tension or Conflict

The third criterion for a story—tension or conflict—creates the anticipation and potential significance that keep the reader reading. In whodunit stories, the tension follows from attempts to identify the murderer or to prevent the murderer from doing in yet another victim. In many comic works, the tension is generated by confusion or misunderstanding that drives a wedge between people who would normally be close. Tension always involves contraries, such as those between one belief and another, between opposing values, between the individual and the environment or the social order, between where I am now and where I want to be or used to be. In the following passage, see how the contraries create dramatic tension that engages readers.

DRAMATIC TENSIONS

Straddling the top of the world, one foot in China and the other in Nepal, I cleared the ice from my oxygen mask, hunched a shoulder against the wind, and stared absently down at the vastness of Tibet. I understood on some dim, detached level that the sweep of earth beneath my feet was a spectacular sight. I'd been fantasizing about this moment, and the release of emotion that would accompany it, for many months. But now that I was finally here, actually standing on the summit of Mount Everest, I just couldn't summon the energy to care.

It was early in the afternoon of May 10, 1996. I hadn't slept in fifty-seven hours. The only food I'd been able to force down over the preceding three days was a bowl of ramen soup and a handful of peanut M&M's. Weeks of violent coughing had left me with two separated ribs that made ordinary breathing an excruciating trial. At 29,028 feet up in the troposphere, so little oxygen was reaching my brain that my mental capacity was that of a slow child. Under the circumstances, I was incapable of feeling much of anything except cold and tired.

—Jon Krakauer, *Into Thin Air*

Notice how this passage presents several contraries or conflicts: the opposition between the narrator's expectation of what it would be like to stand on the top of Mount Everest and the actuality once he's there; and the opposition between the physical strength and stamina of the climber and the extreme danger of climbing this mountain. The reader wonders how Krakauer reached the summit with no sleep, almost no food, and a violent and agonizing cough; more important, the reader wonders why he kept on climbing. We can ask this important query of any narrative: What conflicts and tensions are prompting readers' ongoing questions and holding their interest?

Resolution, Recognition, or Retrospective Interpretation

The final criterion for a story is the resolution or retrospective interpretation of events. The resolution may be stated explicitly or implied. Fables typically sum up the story's significance with an explicit moral at the end. In contrast, the interpretation of events in poetry is almost always implicit. Note how the following haiku collapses events and resolution.

RESOLUTION

A strange old man
stops me,
Looking out of my deep mirror.

—Hitomaro, *One Hundred Poems from the Japanese*

In this tiny story, two things happen simultaneously. The narrator is stopped by a "strange old man" and the narrator looks into a mirror. The narrator's *recognition* is that he is that same old man. This recognition—"That's me in the mirror; when I wasn't looking, I grew old!"—in turn ties the singular event of the story back to more universal concerns and the reader's world.

The typical direction of a story, from singular event(s) to general conclusion, reverses the usual points-first direction of closed-form essays. Stories force readers to read inductively, gathering information and looking for a pattern that's confirmed or unconfirmed by the story's resolution. This resolution is the point *toward* which readers read. It often drives home the significance of the narrative.

Typically, a reader's satisfaction or dissatisfaction with a story hinges on how well the resolution manages to explain or justify the events that precede it. Writers need to ask: How does my resolution grow out of my narrative and fit with the resolution the reader has been forming?

For Writing and Discussion

1. Working as a whole class or in small groups, return to Patrick Klein's essay "Berkeley Blues" and explain how it qualifies as a story rather than an *and then* chronology. How does it meet all four of the criteria: depiction of events through time, connectedness, tension, and resolution?

2. Consider again "The Stolen Watch." It seems to meet the criterion of "depiction of events through time," but it is weak in connectedness, tension, and resolution. How could the writer revise the chronology to make it a story? Brainstorm several different ways that this potentially exciting early draft could be rewritten.

3. If you are working on your own open-form narrative, exchange drafts with a classmate. Discuss each others' drafts in light of this lesson's focus on story. To what extent do your drafts exhibit the features of a story rather than of an *and then* chronology? Working together, develop revision plans that might increase the story elements in your narratives.

Lesson 2: Write Low on the Scale of Abstraction

In Chapter 3 we introduced the concept of "scale of abstraction," in which words can be arranged from the very abstract (living creatures, clothing) down to the very specific (our dog Charley, a Rhodesian Ridgeback with floppy ears; my hippie Birkenstocks with the saltwater stains; see pp. 60–61). In this lesson we show why and how open-form writers stay low on the scale of abstraction through their use of concrete words, revelatory words, and memory-soaked words.

Concrete Words Evoke Images and Sensations

To appreciate the impact of specific, concrete language, look again at the opening sentence of Val Plumwood's narrative about her encounter with crocodiles (p. 579):

> In the early wet season, Kakadu's paper-bark wetlands are especially stunning, as the water lilies weave white, pink, and blue patterns of dreamlike beauty over the shining thunderclouds reflected in their still waters.

Here is how that same passage might sound if rewritten a level higher on the scale of abstraction:

For further discussion of specific, sensory words, see Chapter 5, pp. 112–113, on *show* words versus *tell* words.

> In the early wet season the Kakadu landscape is especially stunning as the water plants weave their colorful patterns of dreamlike beauty over the clouds reflected in the water's surface.

This is still quite a nice sentence. But something is lost when you say "landscape" rather than "paper-bark wetlands," "clouds" rather than "thunderclouds," or "colorful" rather than "white, pink, and blue." The lower you write on the scale of abstraction, the more you tap into your readers' storehouse of particular memories and images.

The power of concrete words has been analyzed by writer John McPhee in a widely quoted and cited interview. When asked why he wrote the sentence "Old white oaks are rare because they had a tendency to become bowsprits, barrel staves, and queen-post trusses" instead of a more generic sentence such as, "Old white oaks are rare because they were used as lumber," he responded in a way that reveals his love of the particular:

> There isn't much life in [the alternative version of the sentence]. If you can find a specific, firm, and correct image, it's always going to be better than a generality, and hence I tend, for example, to put in trade names and company names and, in an instance like this, the names of wood products instead of a general term like "lumber." You'd say "Sony" instead of "tape recorder" if the context made it clear you meant to say tape recorder. It's not because you're on the take from Sony, it's because the image, at least to this writer or reader, strikes a clearer note.

Some readers might complain that the particulars "bowsprits, barrel staves, and queen-post trusses" don't help readers' understanding, as do particulars in closed-form prose, but instead give most readers a moment's pause. Today most barrel staves and bowsprits are made of metal, not oak, and few contemporary readers encounter them on a regular basis no matter what they're made of. Furthermore, few readers at any time could readily identify "queen-post trusses," a technical term from the building trade. Instead of smoothly completing the reader's understanding of a point, McPhee's particulars tend to arrest and even sidetrack, sending the reader in pursuit of a dictionary.

But if McPhee's examples momentarily puzzle, it's the sort of puzzlement that can lead to greater understanding. Precisely because they are exotic terms, these words arouse the reader's curiosity and imagination. "Exotic language is of value," says McPhee. "A queen-post truss is great just because of the sound of the words and what they call to mind. The 'queen,' the 'truss'—the ramifications in everything."

For McPhee, the fact that these words trip up the reader is a point in their favor. If McPhee had said that old white oaks are rare these days because they became parts of "ships, barrels, and roofs," no one would blink or notice. If you were to visualize the items, you'd probably call up some ready-made pictures that leave little trace in your mind. You also wouldn't hear the sounds of the words. (In this regard, notice McPhee's emphasis on images sounding "a clearer note.") Your forward progress toward the point would be unimpeded, but what would be lost? A new glimpse into a lost time when oak trees were used to make exotic items that today exist mostly in old books and memories.

Another quality also recommends words that readers trip over, words such as *bowsprit, barrel stave,* and *queen-post truss:* their power to persuade the reader to believe in the world being described. Tripping over things, whether they're made of steel or words, forces the reader to acknowledge their independence, the reality of a world outside the reader's own head. For this reason, writers of formula fiction—

thrillers, westerns, romances, and the like—will load their texts with lots of little details and bits of technical information from the time and place they describe. Because their stories are otherwise implausible (e.g., the description of the Evil Empire's doomsday machine), they need all the help they can get from their details (the size of the toggle bolts used to keep the machine in place while it's blasting out intergalactic death rays) to convince readers that the story is real.

Using Revelatory Words and Memory-Soaked Words

As we have seen, concrete language, low on the scale of abstraction, can evoke imaginative experiences for readers. Two particularly powerful kinds of concrete language are revelatory words and memory-soaked words. By *revelatory* words we mean specific details that reveal the social status, lifestyle, beliefs, and values of people. According to writer Tom Wolfe, carefully chosen details can reveal a person's *status life*—"the entire pattern of behavior and possessions through which people express their position in the world or what they think it is or hope it to be." Wolfe favors writing that records "everyday gestures, habits, manners, customs, styles of furniture, clothing, decoration, styles of traveling, eating, keeping house, modes of behaving toward children, servants, superiors, inferiors, peers, plus the various looks, glances, poses, styles of walking and other symbolic details that might exist within a scene." Thus subtle differences in a person's status life might be revealed in details about fast food (a Big Mac versus a Subway turkey wrap), body piercing (pierced ears versus pierced tongue), a watch (a Timex versus a Taghauer) or music (Kenny Chesney versus Busta Rhymes). In "Berkeley Blues," Patrick Klein and his classmates are economically revealed as upper-middle-class people by their attire—"Armani jackets" and "Gucci loafers."

Another way to create powerful concrete language is through *memory-soaked* words. Such words trigger a whole complex of ideas, emotions, and sensations in readers who share memories from a particular era. People who grew up in the 1950s, for example, might have deep associations with 45-rpm records, the Ed Sullivan show, or the words "duck tail" or "tail fins." For Vietnam veterans, Nancy Sinatra's "These Boots Were Made for Walking" or the whirr of helicopter blades might evoke strong memories. Persons growing up in the 1970s or 1980s might remember "Cookie Monster," "Pez guns," or 8-track tapes. In recent years, our students have come up with these memory-soaked words from their own childhoods: American Girl dolls, Power Rangers, Ghostbuster action figures, Super Nintendo, and Uno (card game).

For Writing and Discussion

1. Working in small groups or as a whole class, try your own hand at using revelatory words to reveal status life. Create a list of specific details that you might associate with each of the following: junior high girls at a slumber party; friends at a tailgate party before a football game; the kitchen of

an upscale urban apartment of a two-profession couple who subscribe to *Gourmet* magazine; the kitchen of a middle-class, middle America family with three kids and a collection of *Good Housekeeping* magazines; the kitchen of an apartment shared by college students. (If you are describing kitchens, for example, consider the different *status life* signaled by ketchup versus stone ground mustard or by an iceberg lettuce salad with ranch dressing versus an almond mandarin salad.)

2. Also try your hand at finding memory-soaked words. Make a list of specific words and names associated with your childhood that you now rarely hear or see. Share your list with others in your group and identify the items that have the strongest associations.

3. If you are working on your own open-form narrative, exchange drafts with a classmate and, working together, find specific examples where each of you have successfully used concrete, revelatory, or memory-soaked words. Then find passages that could be profitably revised by moving down a level on the scale of abstraction or by adding concrete details that follow the advice in this lesson.

Lesson 3: Disrupt Your Reader's Desire for Direction and Clarity

The epigraph to Chapter 18 by the philosopher Kenneth Burke speaks about form as "an arousing and fulfillment of desires." In closed-form prose, we can easily see this process at work: The writer previews what he or she is going to say, arousing the reader's desire to see the general outline fleshed out with specifics, and then fulfills that desire speedily through a presentation of pertinent points and particulars.

In more open-form prose, the fulfillment of desire follows a less straightforward path. Writers offer fewer overviews and clues, leaving readers less sure of where they're headed; or writers mention an idea and then put it aside for a while as they pursue some other point whose relevance may seem tenuous. Rather than establish the direction or point of their prose, writers suspend that direction, waiting until later in the prose to show how the ideas are meaningfully related. In other words, the period of arousal is longer and more drawn out; the fulfillment of desire is delayed until the end, when the reader finally sees how the pieces fit together.

Open-form prose gives you the opportunity to overlay your narrative core with other patterns of ideas—to move associatively from idea to idea, to weave a complex pattern of meaning in which the complete picture emerges later. Often the way you achieve these surprising twists and turns of structure and meaning is by playing with the conventions of closed-form prose. For example, in the autobiographical narrative "Berkeley Blues," Patrick Klein breaks the cardinal closed-form rule that pronouns should refer only to previously stated antecedents; he introduces the stranger only as *he* and gradually reveals that person's identity. This violation creates an aura of mystery and suspense. Here in this lesson we describe some of your open-form options for surprising your readers and delaying their fulfillment of desires.

Disrupting Predictions and Making Odd Juxtapositions

Open-form writers frequently violate the principle of forecasting and mapping that we stressed in Chapter 18. Consider the following introduction to an essay:

PASSAGE WITH DISRUPTED PREDICTIONS AND ODD JUXTAPOSITIONS

Whose bones?
What feathers?

     I suppose their little bones have years ago been lost among the stones and winds of those high glacial pastures. I suppose their feathers blew eventually into the piles of tumbleweed beneath the straggling cattle fences and rotted there in the mountain snows, along with dead steers and all the other things that drift to an end in the corners of the wire. I do not quite know why I should be thinking of birds over the *New York Times* at breakfast, particularly the birds of my youth half a continent away. It is a funny thing what the brain will do with memories and how it will treasure them and finally bring them into odd juxtapositions with other things, as though it wanted to make a design, or get some meaning out of them, whether you want it or not, or even see it.

Birds? What birds?
What do birds have to do with how the brain works? Where is this writer going?

—Loren Eisley, "The Bird and the Machine"

Note the sequence of ideas from bones to birds to breakfast over *The New York Times* to comments about the workings of the brain. In fact, in this essay it takes Eisley six full paragraphs in which he discusses mechanical inventions to return to the birds with the line: ". . . or those birds, I'll never forget those birds. . . ."

Throughout these paragraphs, what drives the reader forward is curiosity to discover the connections between the parts and to understand the meaning of the essay's title "The Bird and the Machine." Actually, Eisley's comment about the brain's "odd juxtapositions" of memories with "other things, as though it wanted to make a design, or get some meaning out of them" could be a description of this open-form technique we've called "disrupting predictions and making odd juxtapositions." Open-form writers can choose when "odd juxtapositions" are an appropriate strategy for inviting the reader to accompany the discovering, reflecting writer on a journey toward meaning.

Leaving Gaps

An important convention of closed-form prose is the old/new contract, which specifies that the opening of every sentence should link in some way to what has gone before. Open-form prose often violates this convention, leaving *gaps* in the text, forcing the reader to puzzle over the connection between one part and the next.

The following passage clearly violates the old/new contract. This example recounts the writer's thoughts after startling a weasel in the woods and exchanging glances with it.

PASSAGE WITH INTENTIONAL GAPS

Gap caused by unexplained or unpredicted shift from weasel to philosophic musing

     What goes on in [a weasel's brain] the rest of the time? What does a weasel think about? He won't say. His journal is tracks in clay, a spray of feathers, mouse blood and bone: uncollected, unconnected, loose-leaf, and blown.

I would like to learn, or remember, how to live. I come to Hollins Pond not so much to learn how to live as, frankly, to forget about it.

—Annie Dillard, "Living Like Weasels"

Dillard suddenly switches, without transition, from musing about the mental life of a weasel to asserting that she would like to learn how to live. What is the connection between her encounter with the weasel and her own search for how to live? Dillard's open-form techniques leave these gaps for readers to ponder and fill in, inviting us to participate in the process of arriving at meaning. Just as open-form writers can deliberately avoid predicting or mapping statements, they also have the liberty to leave gaps in a text when it suits their purpose.

For Writing and Discussion

If you are currently working on an open-form narrative, exchange drafts with a classmate. Discuss in what way the strategies explained in this lesson might be appropriate for your purposes. Where might you currently "explain too much" and benefit by juxtaposing scenes without explanatory filler? Where might you use other strategies from this lesson?

Lesson 4: Tap the Power of Figurative Language

Open-form writers often use figurative language in situations in which closed-form writers would use literal language. In this brief lesson, we show you some of the power of figurative language.

When journalist Nicholas Tomalin describes a captured Vietnamese prisoner as young and slight, the reader understands him in a literal way, but when, a moment later, he compares the prisoner to "a tiny, fine-boned wild animal," the reader understands him in a different way; the reader understands not only what the subject looks like—his general physical attributes—but how that particular boy appears in that moment to those around him—fierce, frightened, trapped.

Metaphors abound when literal words fail. When writers encounter eccentric people or are overwhelmed by the strangeness of their experiences, they use *figurative language*—imaginative comparisons—to explain their situation and their reactions to it. Figurative language—similes, metaphors, and personifications—enables the writer to describe an unfamiliar thing in terms of different, more familiar things. The surprise of yoking two very unlike things evokes from the reader a perception, insight, or emotional experience that could not otherwise be communicated. The originality and vividness of the imaginative comparison frequently resonates with meaning for readers and sticks in their minds long afterward.

In the following passage, Isak Dinesen describes an experience that most of us have not had—seeing iguanas in the jungle and shooting one. After reading this passage, however, we have a striking picture in our minds of what she saw and a strong understanding of what she felt and realized.

PASSAGE USING FIGURATIVE LANGUAGE

In the Reserve I have sometimes come upon the Iguana, the big lizards, as they were sunning themselves upon a flat stone in a riverbed. They are not pretty in shape, but nothing can be imagined more beautiful than their coloring. They shine like a heap of precious stones or like a pane cut out of an old church window. When, as you approach, they swish away, there is a flash of azure, green and purple over the stones, the color seems to be standing behind them in the air, like a comet's luminous tail.

Similes heaped up

Simile

Once I shot an Iguana. I thought that I should be able to make some pretty things from his skin. A strange thing happened then, that I have never afterwards forgotten. As I went up to him, where he was lying dead upon his stone, and actually while I was walking a few steps, he faded and grew pale, all color died out of him as in one long sigh, and by the time that I touched him he was gray and dull like a lump of concrete. It was the live impetuous blood pulsating within the animal, which had radiated out all that glow and splendor. Now that the flame was put out, and the soul had flown, the Iguana was as dead as a sandbag.

Metaphor of dying applied to color

Simile

Metaphor

Simile

—Isak Dinesen, "The Iguana"

The figurative language in this passage enables readers to share Dinesen's experience. It also compacts a large amount of information into sharp, memorable images.

For Writing and Discussion

1. Figurative language can fall flat when it takes the form of clichés ("I stood transfixed like a bump on a log") or mixed metaphors ("Exposed like a caterpillar on a leaf, he wolfed down his lunch before taking flight"). But when used effectively, figurative language adds powerfully compressed and meaningful images to a passage. Working individually or in small groups, find examples of figurative language in one or more of the example essays in this chapter or in Chapter 7 (pp. 176–185). See if you can reach consensus on what makes a particular instance of figurative language effective or ineffective. As an initial example, consider this passage from the student essay "Masks" (pp. 181–183): "She was so elusive, like a beautiful perfume you smell but can't name, like the whisper that wakes you from a dream and turns out to belong to the dream."

2. If you are currently working on an open-form narrative, exchange drafts with a classmate. See if you can find instances of figurative language in your current drafts and analyze their effectiveness. Perhaps you can also discover places where figurative language could be profitably added to the text.

Lesson 5: Expand Your Repertoire of Styles

In Chapter 3, we introduced you to the concept of style, which is a combination of sentence structure, word choice, and rhythm that allows writers to vary their emphasis and tone in a variety of ways. In this lesson, we show you how to expand your repertoire of styles through a classic method of teaching in which you try to imitate other writers' styles. This rhetorical practice—called "creative imitation"—has a long history beginning with the rhetoricians of classical Greece and Rome. When you do creative imitation, you examine a passage from an expert stylist and try to emulate it. You substitute your own subject matter, but you try to imitate the exact grammatical structures, lengths and rhythms of the sentences, and the tones of the original passage. The long-range effect of creative imitation is to expand your stylistic choices; the more immediate effect is to increase your skill at analyzing a writer's style. Most practitioners find that creative imitation encourages surprising insights into their own subject matter (when seen through the lens of the original writer's style) as well as a new under- See pp. 57–59 for a discussion of style. standing of how a particular piece of writing creates its special effects.

You begin a creative imitation by asking questions such as these: What is distinctive about the sentences in this passage of writing? How do choices about sentence length and complexity, kinds of words, figures of speech, and so forth create a writer's voice? After close examination of the passage, you then think of your own subject matter that could be appropriately adapted to this writer's style.

To help you understand creative imitation, we provide the following example. In this passage, the writer, Victoria Register-Freeman, is exploring how relations between young men and women today threaten to undo some of the twentieth century's progress toward gender equality. In the section of her article that precedes this passage, Register-Freeman explains how she, as a single mother, taught her boys to cook, sew, do laundry, and "carry their weight domestically." But then, as she explains in this passage, teenage girls undid her attempts at creating gender equality:

REGISTER-FREEMAN PASSAGE

Then came puberty and hunkhood. Over the last few years, the boys' domestic skills have atrophied because handmaidens have appeared en masse. The damsels have driven by, beeped, phoned and faxed. Some appeared so frequently outside the front door they began to remind me of the suction-footed Garfields spread-eagled on car windows. While the girls varied according to height, hair color and basic body type, they shared one characteristic. They were ever eager to help the guys out.

—Victoria Register-Freeman, "My Turn: Hunks and Handmaidens"

Register-Freeman's voice projects the image of a concerned mother and feminist social critic. Her tone includes a range of attitudes: serious, personal, factual, ironic, frustrated. Note how this passage begins and ends with short, clipped sentences. The second sentence states a problem that the next three sentences develop with various kinds of details. The third sentence includes a series of colorful verbs; the fourth uses a metaphor (the ever-present girls compared to Garfields on car windows). The fifth sentence builds to the point in the sixth sentence, which is delivered bluntly and simply.

Here is one writer's attempt at a creative imitation:

CREATIVE IMITATION OF REGISTER-FREEMAN

Then came prosperity and popularity. Over the last ten years, Seattle's special charms have faded because expansion has occurred too rapidly. Traffic has multiplied, thickened, amplified, and slowed. Traffic jams appeared so often on the freeways and arterials they began to remind me of ants swarming over spilled syrup. While the congestion varied according to time, seasons, and weather conditions, it had one dominant effect. It increasingly threatened to spoil the city's beauty.

For Writing and Discussion

1. Do your own creative imitation of the passage from Register-Freeman.
2. Choose one or both of the following passages for creative imitation. Begin by jotting down all the specific observations you can make about the stylistic features of the passage. Then choose a topic that matches the topic of the original in its degree of lightness or seriousness and its depth. Explore your topic by presenting it using the sentence structures and kinds of words used in the original. Try to imitate the original phrase by phrase and sentence by sentence. You may find it helpful to use a dictionary and thesaurus.

   a. Africa is mystic; it is wild; it is a sweltering inferno; it is a photographer's paradise, a hunter's Valhalla, an escapist's Utopia. It is what you will, and it withstands all interpretations. It is the last vestige of a dead world or the cradle of a shiny new one. To a lot of people, as to myself, it is just "home." It is all of these things but one thing—it is never dull.
      —Beryl Markham, "Flying Elsewhere," *West with the Night*

   b. The disease was bubonic plague, present in two forms: one that infected the bloodstream, causing the buboes and internal bleeding, and was spread by contact; and a second, more virulent pneumonic type that infected the lungs and was spread by respiratory infection. The presence of both at once caused the high mortality and speed of contagion. So lethal was the disease that cases were known of persons going to bed well and dying before they woke, of doctors catching the illness at bedside and dying before the patient.

      —Barbara Tuchman, "This Is the End of the World," *A Distant Mirror*

Lesson 6: Use Open-Form Elements to Create "Voice" in Closed-Form Prose

So far we have been talking about features of open-form prose in its purer forms. Sometimes, however, writers wish simply to loosen basically closed-form prose by combining it with some features of open-form prose. If, for example, an academic wanted to share new developments in a field with a popular audience, he or she would be well-advised to leaven his or her prose with some elements of open-form writing. In this final lesson, we offer several pieces of advice for loosening up closed-form prose.

Introducing Some Humor

Humor is rare in tightly closed prose because humor is nonfunctional—it doesn't *have* to be there for a writer to make a point—and closed-form prose values efficiency, getting what you have to say said in the most economical fashion.

Humor is closely related to one of the mainsprings of open-form style, surprise. Humor typically depends on sudden twists and abrupt changes in direction. In physical comedy, pratfalls are funny in direct proportion to the audience's inability to see them coming. In verbal humor, the less clearly the audience sees the punch line coming, the more it makes the audience laugh.

Humor is particularly valuable in that it can make imposing subjects more manageable for readers. Just as humor can deflate pretensions and bring down the high and the mighty in an instant, it can make difficult and foreign subjects less anxiety producing. Formal, abstract language can put readers off, estranging them from the subject; humor has the power to "de-strange" a subject, to allow the audience to look at it long enough to understand it. Many popular books on science and many of the best instructional books on car repair, cooking, money management, and others of life's drearier necessities use a humorous style to help their phobic readers get on with life.

To appreciate the effect of humor, consider the following passages from two different instructional books on how to operate the database program Paradox. The first passage, from *Windows in 21 Days,* uses a clear, humor-free, closed-form style.

> In this book, you learn by following detailed step-by-step exercises based on real-world problems in database application design. Every exercise leads you further into the power of "Paradox for Windows" as you develop the components of an automated application. This section does the following: explains the assumptions and conventions used in this book; lists the hardware and software requirements and setup needed to run Paradox for Windows and use this book efficiently; and offers some suggestions for strategies to get the most from this book. The step-by-step exercises make it easy.

Now note the different effect produced by the following passage from one of the hugely popular *For Dummies* books:

> Welcome to *Paradox for Windows for Dummies,* a book that's not afraid to ask the tough questions like "When's lunch?" and "Who finished the cookie dough ice cream?" If you're more interested in food (or Australian Wombats, for that matter) than you are in Paradox for Windows, this book is for you. If you're more interested in Paradox for Windows, please get some professional help before going out into society again.
>
> My goal is to help you get things done despite the fact that you're using Paradox. Whether you're at home, in your office, or at home in your office (or even if you just *feel* like you live at work) *Paradox for Windows for Dummies* is your all-in-one guidebook through the treacherous, frustrating, and appallingly technical world of the relational database.

For Writing and Discussion

1. Which of these two instructional books would you prefer to read?
2. The second passage says that the world of relational databases is "treacherous, frustrating, and appallingly technical," whereas the first stresses that the "step-by-step exercises [in the book] make it easy." Why do you suppose the humorous passage stresses the difficulty of databases whereas the humorless passage stresses the ease of a step-by-step approach? Is it good strategy for the humorous writer to stress the difficulty of Paradox?
3. Under what rhetorical circumstances are humorous instructions better than strictly serious instructions? When is a strictly serious approach better?

Using Techniques from Popular Magazines

Writers who publish regularly for popular audiences develop a vigorous, easy-reading style that differs from the style of much academic writing. The effect of this difference is illustrated by the results of a famous research study conducted by Michael Graves and Wayne Slater at the University of Michigan. For this study, teams of writers revised passages from a high school history textbook.* One team consisted of linguists and technical writers trained in producing closed-form texts using the strategies discussed in Chapter 18 (forecasting structure, putting points first, following the old/new contract, using transitions). A second team consisted of two *Time-Life* book editors.

Whereas the linguists aimed at making the passages clearer, the *Time-Life* writers were more concerned with making them livelier. The result? One hundred eleventh-grade students found the *Time-Life* editors' version both more comprehensible and more memorable. Lack of clarity wasn't the problem with the original textbook; unbearable dryness was the problem. According to the researchers, the *Time-Life* editors did not limit themselves

> to making the passages lucid, well-organized, coherent, and easy to read. Their revisions went beyond such matters and were intended to make the texts interesting, exciting, vivid, rich in human drama, and filled with colorful language.

To see how they achieved this effect, let's look at their revision. Here is a passage about the Vietnam War taken from the original history text:

ORIGINAL HISTORY TEXT

> The most serious threat to world peace developed in Southeast Asia. Communist guerrillas threatened the independence of the countries carved out of French Indo-China by the Geneva conference of 1954. In South Vietnam, Communist guerrillas (the Viet Cong) were aided by forces from Communist North Vietnam in a struggle to overthrow the American-supported government. . . .

---

*The study involved three teams, but for purposes of simplification we limit our discussion to two.

Shortly after the election of 1964, Communist gains prompted President Johnson to alter his policy concerning Vietnam. American military forces in Vietnam were increased from about 20,000 men in 1964 to more than 500,000 by 1968. Even so, North Vietnamese troops and supplies continued to pour into South Vietnam.

Here is the *Time-Life* editors' revision:

HISTORY PRESENTED IN POPULAR MAGAZINE STYLE

In the early 1960's the greatest threat to world peace was just a small splotch of color on Kennedy's map, one of the fledgling nations sculpted out of French Indo-China by the Geneva peacemakers of 1954. It was a country so tiny and remote that most Americans had never uttered its name: South Vietnam. . . .

Aided by Communist North Vietnam, the Viet Cong guerrillas were eroding the ground beneath South Vietnam's American-backed government. Village by village, road by road, these jungle-wise rebels were waging a war of ambush and mining: They darted out of tunnels to head off patrols, buried exploding booby traps beneath the mud floors of huts, and hid razor-sharp bamboo sticks in holes. . . .

No sooner had Johnson won the election than Communist gains prompted Johnson to go back on his campaign promise. The number of American soldiers in Vietnam skyrocketed from 20,000 in 1964 to more than 500,000 by 1968. But in spite of GI patrols, leech-infested jungles, swarms of buzzing insects, and flash floods that made men cling to trees to escape being washed away—North Vietnamese troops streamed southward without letup along the Ho Chi Minh Trail.

What can this revision teach you about envigorating closed-form prose? What specifically are the editors doing here?

First, notice how far the level of abstraction drops in the revision. The original is barren of sensory words; the revision is alive with them ("South Vietnam" becomes a "small splotch of color on Kennedy's map"; "a struggle to overthrow the American-supported government" becomes "[They] buried exploding booby traps beneath the mud floors of huts, and hid razor-sharp bamboo sticks in holes").

Second, notice how much more dramatic the revision is. Actual scenes, including a vision of men clinging to trees to escape being washed away by flash floods, replace a chronological account of the war's general progress. According to the editors, such scenes, or "nuggets"—vivid events that encapsulate complex processes or principles—are the lifeblood of *Time-Life* prose.

Finally, notice how the revision tends to delay critical information for dramatic effect, moving information you would normally expect to find early on into a later position. In the first paragraph, the *Time-Life* writers talk about "the greatest threat to world peace" in the early 1960s for five lines before revealing the identity of that threat—South Vietnam.

For Writing and Discussion

Here is a passage from a student argument opposing women's serving on submarines. Working individually or in small groups, enliven this passage by using some of the techniques of the *Time-Life* writers.

(continued)

Not only would it be very expensive to refit submarines for women personnel, but having women on submarines would hurt the morale of the sailors. In order for a crew to work effectively, they must have good morale or their discontent begins to show through in their performance. This is especially crucial on submarines, where if any problem occurs, it affects the safety of the whole ship. Women would hurt morale by creating sexual tension. Sexual tension can take many forms. One form is couples' working and living in a close space with all of the crew. When a problem occurs within the relationship, it could affect the morale of those directly involved and in the workplace. This would create an environment that is not conducive to good productivity. Tension would also occur if one of the women became pregnant or if there were complaints of sexual harassment. It would be easier to deal with these problems on a surface ship, but in the small confines of a submarine these problems would cause more trouble.

READING

To conclude this chapter, we present a famous short example of open-form prose—Annie Dillard's "Living Like Weasels." The exercises that follow the reading will help you review the lessons in this chapter.

Annie Dillard
Living Like Weasels

1   A weasel is wild. Who knows what he thinks? He sleeps in his underground den, his tail draped over his nose. Sometimes he lives in his den for two days without leaving. Outside, he stalks rabbits, mice, muskrats, and birds, killing more bodies than he can eat warm, and often dragging the carcasses home. Obedient to instinct, he bites his prey at the neck, either splitting the jugular vein at the throat or crunching the brain at the base of the skull, and he does not let go. One naturalist refused to kill a weasel who was socketed into his hand deeply as a rattlesnake. The man could in no way pry the tiny weasel off, and he had to walk half a mile to water, the weasel dangling from his palm, and soak him off like a stubborn label.

2   And once, says Ernest Thompson Seton—once, a man shot an eagle out of the sky. He examined the eagle and found the dry skull of a weasel fixed by the jaws to his throat. The supposition is that the eagle had pounced on the weasel and the weasel swiveled and bit as instinct taught him, tooth to neck, and nearly won. I would like to have seen that eagle from the air a few weeks or months before he was shot: was the whole weasel still attached to his feathered throat, a fur pendant? Or did the eagle eat what he could reach, gutting the living weasel with his talons before his breast, bending his beak, cleaning the beautiful airborne bones?

3   I have been reading about weasels because I saw one last week. I startled a weasel who startled me, and we exchanged a long glance.

4   Twenty minutes from my house, through the woods by the quarry and across the highway, is Hollins Pond, a remarkable piece of shallowness, where I like to go at sunset and sit on a tree trunk. Hollins Pond is also called Murray's Pond; it covers two acres of bottomland near Tinker Creek with six inches of water and six thousand lily pads. In winter, brown-and-white steers stand in the middle of it, merely dampening their hooves; from the distant shore they look like miracle itself, complete with miracle's nonchalance. Now, in summer, the steers are gone. The water lilies have blossomed and spread to a green horizontal plane that is terra firma to plodding blackbirds, and tremulous ceiling to black leeches, crayfish, and carp.

5   This is, mind you, suburbia. It is a five-minute walk in three directions to rows of houses, though none is visible here. There's a 55 mph highway at one end of the pond, and a nesting pair of wood ducks at the other. Under every bush is a muskrat hole or a beer can. The far end is an alternating series of fields and woods, fields and woods, threaded everywhere with motorcycle tracks—in whose bare clay wild turtles lay eggs.

6   So. I had crossed the highway, stepped over two low barbed-wire fences, and traced the motorcycle path in all gratitude through the wild rose and poison ivy of the pond's shoreline up into high grassy fields. Then I cut down through the woods to the mossy fallen tree where I sit. This tree is excellent. It makes a dry, upholstered bench at the upper, marshy end of the pond, a plush jetty raised from the thorny shore between a shallow blue body of water and a deep blue body of sky.

7   The sun had just set. I was relaxed on the tree trunk, ensconced in the lap of lichen, watching the lily pads at my feet tremble and part dreamily over the thrusting path of a carp. A yellow bird appeared to my right and flew behind me. It caught my eye. I swiveled around—and the next instant, inexplicably, I was looking down at a weasel, who was looking up at me.

8   Weasel! I'd never seen one wild before. He was ten inches long, thin as a curve, a muscled ribbon, brown as fruitwood, soft-furred, alert. His face was fierce, small and pointed as a lizard's; he would have made a good arrowhead. There was just a dot of chin, maybe two brown hairs' worth, and then the pure white fur began that spread down his underside. He had two black eyes I didn't see, any more than you see a window.

9   The weasel was stunned into stillness as he was emerging from beneath an enormous shaggy wild rose bush four feet away. I was stunned into stillness twisted backward on the tree trunk. Our eyes locked, and someone threw away the key.

10   Our look was as if two lovers, or deadly enemies, met unexpectedly on an overgrown path when each had been thinking of something else: a clearing blow to the gut. It was also a bright blow to the brain, or a sudden beating of brains, with all the charge and intimate grate of rubbed balloons. It emptied our lungs. It felled the forest, moved the fields, and drained the pond; the world dismantled and tumbled into that black hole of eyes. If you and I looked at each other that way, our skulls would split and drop to our shoulders. But we don't. We keep our skulls. So.

11   He disappeared. This was only last week, and already I don't remember what shattered the enchantment. I think I blinked, I think I retrieved my brain from the weasel's brain, and tried to memorize what I was seeing, and the weasel felt the yank of separation, the careening splashdown into real life and the urgent current of instinct. He vanished under the wild rose. I waited motionless, my mind suddenly full of data and my spirit with pleadings, but he didn't return.

12   Please do not tell me about "approach-avoidance conflicts." I tell you I've been in that weasel's brain for sixty seconds, and he was in mine. Brains are private places, muttering through unique and secret tapes—but the weasel and I both plugged into another tape simultaneously, for a sweet and shocking time. Can I help it if it was a blank?

13   What goes on in his brain the rest of the time? What does a weasel think about? He won't say. His journal is tracks in clay, a spray of feathers, mouse blood and bone: uncollected, unconnected, loose-leaf, and blown.

14   I would like to learn, or remember, how to live. I come to Hollins Pond not so much to learn how to live as, frankly, to forget about it. That is, I don't think I can learn from a wild animal how to live in particular—shall I suck warm blood, hold my tail high, walk with my footprints precisely over the prints of my hands?—but I might learn something of mindlessness, something of the purity of living in the physical senses and the dignity of living without bias or motive. The weasel lives in necessity and we live in choice, hating necessity and dying at the last ignobly in its talons. I would like to live as I should, as the weasel lives as he should. And I suspect that for me the way is like the weasel's: open to time and death painlessly, noticing everything, remembering nothing, choosing the given with a fierce and pointed will.

15   I missed my chance. I should have gone for the throat. I should have lunged for that streak of white under the weasel's chin and held on, held on through mud and into the wild rose, held on for a dearer life. We could live under the wild rose wild as weasels, mute and uncomprehending. I could very calmly go wild. I could live two days in the den, curled, leaning on mouse fur, sniffing bird bones, blinking, licking, breathing musk, my hair tangled in the roots of grasses. Down is a good place to go, where the mind is single. Down is out, out of your ever-loving mind and back to your careless senses. I remember muteness as a prolonged and giddy fast, where every moment is a feast of utterance received. Time and events are merely poured, unremarked, and ingested directly, like blood pulsed into my gut through a jugular vein. Could two live that way? Could two live under the wild rose, and explore by the pond, so that the smooth mind of each is as everywhere present to the other, and as received and as unchallenged, as falling snow?

16   We could, you know. We can live any way we want. People take vows of poverty, chastity, and obedience—even of silence—by choice. The thing is

to stalk your calling in a certain skilled and supple way, to locate the most tender and live spot and plug into that pulse. This is yielding, not fighting. A weasel doesn't "attack" anything; a weasel lives as he's meant to, yielding at every moment to the perfect freedom of single necessity.

17   I think it would be well, and proper, and obedient, and pure, to grasp your one necessity and not let it go, to dangle from it limp wherever it takes you. Then even death, where you're going no matter how you live, cannot you part. Seize it and let it seize you up aloft even, till your eyes burn out and drop; let your musky flesh fall off in shreds, and let your very bones unhinge and scatter, loosened over fields, over fields and woods, lightly, thoughtless, from any height at all, from as high as eagles.

For Writing and Discussion

Working in small groups or as a whole class, use the questions that follow to guide your close examination of Dillard's structural and stylistic choices.

1. How does Dillard's essay meet the criteria for a story—events depicted in time, connectedness, tension, and resolution? What final resolution or interpretation does Dillard offer?
2. Find ten examples of Dillard's use of specific words and concrete language. Try rewording some of these examples at a higher level of abstraction and then compare Dillard's "low on the scale" version with your "higher on the scale" version.
3. Choose three consecutive paragraphs in this essay and examine how Dillard employs gaps between sentences to stimulate readers to think actively about the questions she is raising. Try tracking her ideas from sentence to sentence in these paragraphs. Where does she disrupt readers' expectations by violating conventions of closed-form prose?
4. Find ten examples of figurative language and explain how these are particularly effective in holding the reader's interest and portraying the intensity or meaning of her experience.
5. Suppose that you were going to do a stylistic imitation of one of Dillard's passages. Choose a passage that you think is particularly interesting stylistically and explain why you have chosen it.
6. Imagine the entry on "weasels" in an encyclopedia. How could you use some of Dillard's strategies to make a typical closed-form encyclopedia article more lively?

Using, Citing, and Documenting Sources

The previous chapter focused on the first five of seven research skills listed at the end of Chapter 20 (see pp. 605–606). In Chapter 21, you learned how to conduct an argument in your own voice, how to use appropriate search engines to find different kinds of research sources, and how to read and evaluate those sources using the skills of rhetorical reading emphasized throughout this text. We also examined the special problems of evaluating Web sources.

In this chapter we turn to the final two skills on our list: how to incorporate sources into your writing and how to cite and document them properly.

Skill 6: Use Sources Purposefully Through Clearly Attributed Summary, Paraphrase, or Quotation

One of the essential skills you need as a researcher is the ability to incorporate research sources purposefully into your prose. This section shows you how to do so. Specifically we show you how to use sources for your own purposes and how to weave them gracefully into your prose through effective summary, paraphrase, and quotation. We also show you how to shape your readers' response to these sources through rhetorically effective attributive tags. Finally, we show you how to recognize and scrupulously avoid plagiarism.

Using Sources for Your Own Purposes

In Chapter 21, we explained how you should remain aware of your research goals when you take notes and evaluate sources. To use sources purposefully, you need to understand why you are using any given source and how it functions in your argument. Keep in mind the following reasons for using research sources:

See Table 21.4, "Note Taking According to Purpose" on p. 627.

- To provide direct evidence, such as facts, information, statistics, and other data, in support of your reasons and points
- To provide indirect evidence through testimony of experts
- To show conflicting or puzzling data that you will analyze or interpret
- To show your understanding of alternative views

- To provide big-picture overviews and background
- To convey your general knowledge, credibility, and authority

The most typical way that inexperienced researchers use sources is through block quotations—a method that often seems amateurish because it simply reproduces a source without foregrounding the writer's voice and purpose.

To illustrate the difference between reproducing a source and using a source purposefully, we show you the hypothetical case of three writers using the same article for different purposes. Read carefully the following short article about violence in the Old West. Then proceed to the examples of three writers who use this article for their own different purposes.

READING

Roger D. McGrath
The Myth of Violence in the Old West

1   It is commonly assumed that violence is part of our frontier heritage. But the historical record shows that frontier violence was very different from violence today. Robbery and burglary, two of our most common crimes, were of no great significance in the frontier towns of the Old West, and rape was seemingly nonexistent.

2   Bodie, one of the principal towns on the trans-Sierra frontier, illustrates the point. Nestled high in the mountains of eastern California, Bodie, which boomed in the late 1870s and early 1880s, ranked among the most notorious frontier towns of the Old West. It was, as one prospector put it, the last of the old-time mining camps.

3   Like the trans-Sierra frontier in general, Bodie was indisputably violent and lawless, yet most people were not affected. Fistfights and gunfights among willing combatants—gamblers, miners, and the like—were regular events, and stagecoach holdups were not unusual. But the old, the young, the weak, and the female—so often the victims of crime today—were generally not harmed.

4   Robbery was more often aimed at stagecoaches than at individuals. Highwaymen usually took only the express box and left the passengers alone. There were eleven stagecoach robberies in Bodie between 1878 and 1882, and in only two instances were passengers robbed. (In one instance, the highwaymen later apologized for their conduct.)

5   There were only ten robberies and three attempted robberies of individuals in Bodie during its boom years, and in nearly every case the circumstances were the same: the victim had spent the evening in a gambling den, saloon, or brothel; he had revealed that he had on his person a significant sum of money; and he was staggering home drunk when the attack occurred.

6   Bodie's total of twenty-one robberies—eleven of stages and ten of individuals—over a five-year period converts to a rate of eighty-four robberies per 100,000 inhabitants per year. On this scale—the same scale used by the FBI to index crime—New York City's robbery rate in 1980 was 1,140, Miami's was 995, and Los Angeles's was 628. The rate for the United States as a whole was 243. Thus Bodie's robbery rate was significantly below the national average in 1980.

7   Perhaps the greatest deterrent to crime in Bodie was the fact that so many people were armed. Armed guards prevented bank robberies and holdups of stagecoaches carrying shipments of bullion, and armed homeowners and merchants discouraged burglary. Between 1878 and 1882, there were only thirty-two burglaries—seventeen of homes and fifteen of businesses—in Bodie. At least a half-dozen burglaries were thwarted by the presence of armed citizens. The newspapers regularly advocated shooting burglars on sight, and several burglars were, in fact, shot at.

8   Using the FBI scale, Bodie's burglary rate for those five years was 128. Miami's rate in 1980 was 3,282, New York's was 2,661, and Los Angeles's was 2,602. The rate of the United States as a whole was 1,668, thirteen times that of Bodie.

9   Bodie's law enforcement institutions were certainly not responsible for these low rates. Rarely were robbers or burglars arrested, and even less often were they convicted. Moreover, many law enforcement officers operated on both sides of the law.

10   It was the armed citizens themselves who were the most potent—though not the only—deterrent to larcenous crime. Another was the threat of vigilantism. Highwaymen, for example, understood that while they could take the express box from a stagecoach without arousing the citizens, they risked inciting the entire populace to action if they robbed the passengers.

11   There is considerable evidence that women in Bodie were rarely the victims of crime. Between 1878 and 1882 only one woman, a prostitute, was robbed, and there were no reported cases of rape. (There is no evidence that rapes occurred but were not reported.)

12   Finally, juvenile crime, which accounts for a significant portion of the violent crime in the United States today, was limited in Bodie to pranks and malicious mischief.

13   If robbery, burglary, crimes against women, and juvenile crime were relatively rare on the trans-Sierra frontier, homicide was not: thirty-one Bodieites were shot, stabbed, or beaten to death during the boom years, for a homicide rate of 116. No U.S. city today comes close to this rate. In 1980, Miami led the nation with a homicide rate of 32.7; Las Vegas was a distant second at 23.4. A half-dozen cities had rates of zero. The rate for the United States as a whole in that year was a mere 10.2.

14   Several factors contributed to Bodie's high homicide rate. A majority of the town's residents were young, adventurous, single males who adhered to a code of conduct that frequently required them to fight even if, or perhaps especially

15   if, it could mean death. Courage was admired above all else. Alcohol also played a major role in fostering the settlement of disputes by violence.

15   If the men's code of conduct and their consumption of alcohol made fighting inevitable, their sidearms often made it fatal. While the carrying of guns probably reduced the incidence of robbery and burglary, it undoubtedly increased the number of homicides.

16   For the most part, the citizens of Bodie were not troubled by the great number of killings; nor were they troubled that only one man was ever convicted of murder. They accepted the killings and the lack of convictions because most of those killed had been willing combatants.

17   Thus the violence and lawlessness of the trans-Sierra frontier bear little relation to the violence and lawlessness that pervade American society today. If Bodie is at all representative of frontier towns, there is little justification for blaming contemporary American violence on our frontier heritage.

There is no one right way to use this article in your research paper. What you use depends on your research question and your purpose in using the source. Sometimes you will summarize a source's whole argument; sometimes you will summarize only a part; at other times you will use an isolated fact or statistic from the source or quote a sentence or two as testimonial evidence. In what follows we show how three hypothetical writers, addressing three different research questions, use this source in different ways.

Writer 1: Summary for an Analytical Paper on Causes of Violence

For an explanation of the numbers in parentheses, see the discussion of MLA in-text documentation on pp. 661–662.

The first hypothetical writer is analyzing the causes of violence in contemporary U.S. society. She wants to reject one possible cause—that contemporary violence grows out of our violent past. To make this point in her argument, she summarizes McGrath's article.

Many people believe that violence is part of our Wild West heritage. But Roger McGrath, in his article "The Myth of Violence in the Old West," shows that frontier violence was very different from contemporary violence. He explains that in a typical frontier town, violence involved gunslingers who were "willing combatants," whereas today's typical victims—"the old, the young, the weak, and the female"— were unaffected by crime (644). Because the presence of an armed populace deterred robbery and burglary, theft was much less common in the Old West than today. On the other hand, McGrath explains, killings were fueled by guns, alcohol, and a code of conduct that invited fighting, so murders were much more frequent than in any U.S. city today (645). Thus, according to McGrath, there is little resemblance between violence on the frontier and violence in today's cities, so we cannot blame current violence on our tumultuous frontier past.

In this passage the author summarizes McGrath's argument in order to refute the violent frontier theory about the causes of contemporary violence. Presumably, this author will proceed to other causes of violence and will not return again to McGrath.

Writer 2: Partial Summary for a Persuasive Paper in Support of Gun Control

In our next case, the hypothetical writer uses McGrath's article in an argument supporting gun control. He wants to refute the popular anti–gun control argument that law-abiding citizens need to be armed to protect themselves against crime.

> Opponents of gun control often argue that guns benefit society by providing protection against intruders. But such protection is deadly, as Roger McGrath shows in his study of violence in the frontier town of Bodie, California. Although guns reduced theft, as seen in the low rate of theft in the well-armed town of Bodie, the presence of guns also led to a homicide rate far above that of the most violent city in the U.S. today. The homicide rate in the frontier town of Bodie, California, for example, was 116 per 100,000, compared to the current national average of 10.2 per 100,000 (645). True, Bodie citizens reduced the theft rate by being heavily armed, but at a cost of a homicide rate more than ten times the current national average. To protect our consumer goods at the cost of so much human life is counter to the values of most Americans.

McGrath's article contains data that could be used on either side of the gun control debate. This writer acknowledges the evidence showing that gun possession reduces theft and then works that potentially damaging information into an argument for gun control. How might you use the McGrath article to oppose gun control?

Writer 3: Partial Summary for an Analytical Paper on Shifting Definitions of Crime

Looking at another facet of McGrath's article, the last hypothetical writer summarizes part of McGrath's article to support her thesis that a community's definition of crime is constantly shifting.

> Our notion of criminal activity shifts over time. For example, only a short time ago on the American frontier, murder was often ignored by law enforcement. Roger McGrath, in his discussion of violence in the frontier town of Bodie, California, during the 1870s and 1880s, showed that the townspeople accepted homicides as long as both the murderer and the victim were "willing combatants" who freely participated in gunfights (646). These young males who were the "willing combatants" in Bodie share many characteristics with modern gang members in that they were encouraged to fight by a "code of conduct": "A majority of the town's residents were young, adventurous, single males who adhered to a code of conduct that frequently required them to fight even if . . . it could mean death" (645–646). Today's gang members also follow a code of conduct that requires violence—often in the form of vengeance. Although joining a gang certainly makes youths "willing combatants," that status doesn't prevent prosecution in court. Today's "willing combatants" are criminals, but yesterday's "willing combatants" were not.

This writer uses McGrath's article to make a point completely different from McGrath's. But by extending and applying information from McGrath's article to a new context, the writer gathers fuel for her own argument about shifting definitions of the word *criminal*.

For Writing and Discussion

Each of the hypothetical writers uses McGrath's article for a different purpose. Working individually or in groups, answer the following questions. Be ready to elaborate on and defend your answers.

1. What are the differences in the ways the writers use the original article? How are these differences related to differences in each writer's purpose?
2. What differences would you expect to find in the research notes each writer took on the McGrath article?
3. What makes each writer's paragraph different from a purposeless listing of random information?

Working Sources into Your Own Prose

As a research writer, you need to incorporate sources gracefully into your own prose so that your paper's focus stays on your own argument. In this section we examine some of the techniques that the three hypothetical writers used to adapt the McGrath article to their own purposes: summarizing a source's argument, paraphrasing a relevant portion of a source, or quoting the source directly. Let's look at each of these options.

Summarizing

See Chapter 6, pp. 126–130, for detailed advice on summary writing.

Writing a summary of a source's argument (either of the whole argument or of a relevant section) is an appropriate strategy when the source represents an opposing or alternative view or when it supports or advances one of your own points. Summaries can be as short as a single sentence or as long as a paragraph. Writer 1's summary of the McGrath article is a good example of a graceful summary.

Paraphrasing

We explain how to cite sources later in this chapter; see pp. 658–693.

Unlike a summary, which is a condensation of a source's whole argument, a paraphrase translates a short passage from a source's words into the writer's own words. You should paraphrase when you are using brief, specific information from a source and don't want to interrupt the flow of your own voice with a quotation. Of course, you must still acknowledge the source through a citation.

When you paraphrase, be careful to avoid the original writer's grammatical structure and syntax. If you mirror the original sentence structure while replacing some words with synonyms, you are plagiarizing rather than paraphrasing. Here is an acceptable paraphrase of a short passage from the McGrath article:

ORIGINAL

There is considerable evidence that women in Bodie were rarely the victims of crime. Between 1878 and 1882 only one woman, a prostitute, was robbed, and there were no reported cases of rape. (There is no evidence that rapes occurred but were not reported.)

PARAPHRASE

According to McGrath, women in Bodie seldom suffered at the hands of criminals. Between 1878 and 1882, the only female robbery victim in Bodie was a prostitute. Also rape seemed nonexistent, with no reported cases and no evidence that unreported cases occurred (645).

Note that to avoid plagiarism, the writer has changed the sentence structure substantially. However, the writer still acknowledges the original source with the phrase "According to McGrath" and provides the page number.

Quoting Directly

Occasionally, you will want to quote an author's words directly. Avoid quoting too much because the effect, from your reader's perspective, is a collage of quotations rather than an argument. Quote only when doing so strengthens your argument. Here are some occasions when a direct quotation is appropriate:

- When the quotation comes from a respected authority and, in a pithy way, supports one of your points. (Your use of the quotation is like expert testimony in a trial.)
- When you are summarizing an opposing or alternative view and want to use brief quotations to show that you have listened carefully and accurately.
- When you want to give readers the flavor of a source's voice, particularly if the language is striking or memorable.
- When you want to analyze the writer's choice of words or metaphors. (You would first quote the passage and then begin your analysis.)

When you quote, you must be meticulous in copying the passage *exactly*, including punctuation. When the quoted material takes up more than four lines in your paper, use the following block quotation method:

EXAMPLE OF A BLOCK QUOTATION

McGrath describes the people most affected by violence in the frontier town of Bodie:

> Fistfights and gunfights among willing combatants—gamblers, miners, and the like—were regular events, and stagecoach holdups were not unusual. But the old, the young, the weak, and the female—so often the victims of crime today—were generally not harmed. (644)

EXPLANATION*

- The block quotation is indented one inch.
- There are *no quotation marks*. The block indentation itself signals a quotation.

---

*This and subsequent examples follow the guidelines of the MLA (Modern Language Association) style. We explain this style in detail in the last half of this chapter (Skill 7), where we also explain APA (American Psychological Association) style.

- The number in parentheses indicates the page number where the quotation is found in the original source. Note that in block quotations the parentheses come after the closing period.
- Block quotations are usually introduced with a colon.

If the quoted passage is fewer than four typed lines in your own text, insert it directly into your paragraph using quotation marks. How you punctuate depends on whether the inserted quotation is a complete sentence or part of a sentence.

EXAMPLE OF AN INSERTED QUOTATION WHEN THE QUOTATION IS A COMPLETE SENTENCE

According to McGrath, "It was the armed citizens themselves who were the most potent—though not the only—deterrent to larcenous crime" (645).

EXPLANATION

- The page number in parentheses is inserted *after* the quotation mark but *before* the closing period.
- Because the quotation is a complete sentence, it starts with a capital letter and is separated from the introductory phrase by a comma.

Often you won't want to quote a complete sentence but instead work brief words and phrases from your source into your own grammatical structure.

EXAMPLE OF AN INSERTED QUOTATION WHEN THE QUOTATION IS NOT A COMPLETE SENTENCE

McGrath contrasts frontier violence to crime today, pointing out that today's typical crime victims are "the old, the young, the weak, and the female" and showing that these groups were not molested in Bodie (644).

EXPLANATION

- Because the quoted material is not a complete sentence, it is worked into the grammar of the writer's own sentence.
- No comma introduces the quotation; commas should be used only to fit the grammar of the writer's own sentence.
- The number in parentheses is the page number where the quotation is found in the original source. Note that it comes wherever the borrowed idea ends.

Modifying Quotations to Fit Your Grammatical Structure

Occasionally the grammar of a desired quotation doesn't match the grammatical structure of your own sentence, or the meaning of a quoted word will not be clear because the passage has been removed from its original context. In these cases, use brackets to modify the quotation's grammar or to add a clarifying explanation: Change the quotation, placing your changes in brackets to indicate that the bracketed material is not part of the original wording. You should also use brackets to show a change in capitalization.

ORIGINAL PASSAGE

The newspapers regularly advocated shooting burglars on sight, and several burglars were, in fact, shot at.

QUOTATION MODIFIED TO FIT THE GRAMMAR OF THE WRITER'S SENTENCE

In Bodie, an armed citizenry successfully eliminated burglaries, aided by newspapers "regularly advocat[ing] shooting burglars on sight" (McGrath 645).

ORIGINAL PASSAGE

Highwaymen, for example, understood that while they could take the express box from a stagecoach without arousing the citizens, they risked inciting the entire populace to action if they robbed the passengers.

USE OF BRACKETS TO CHANGE THE CAPITALIZATION AND EXPLAIN MISSING REFERENTS

Public sentiment influenced what laws were likely to be broken. According to McGrath, "[W]hile they [highwaymen] could take the express box from a stagecoach without arousing the citizens, they risked inciting the entire populace to action if they robbed the passengers" (645).

Perhaps the most frequent modification writers make is omitting portions of a quotation. To indicate an omission in a quotation in MLA style, use three spaced periods, called an *ellipsis*. Placement of the ellipsis depends on where the omitted material occurs. In the middle of a sentence, each of the periods should be preceded and followed by an additional space.

ORIGINAL PASSAGE

Finally, juvenile crime, which accounts for a significant portion of the violent crime in the United States today, was limited in Bodie to pranks and malicious mischief.

USING ELLIPSES TO INDICATE OMISSION

"Finally, juvenile crime . . . was limited in Bodie to pranks and malicious mischief" (McGrath 645).

When your ellipsis comes at the boundary between sentences, use an additional period to mark the end of the sentence. Do not leave an extra space before the sentence-ending period. When a parenthetical page number must follow the ellipsis, insert it before the final (fourth) period in the sequence.

| **Original** | Bodie's law enforcement institutions were certainly not responsible for these low rates. Rarely were robbers or burglars arrested, and even less often were they convicted. Moreover, many law enforcement officers operated on both sides of the law. |

Omitting Sentence within Quotation	According to McGrath, "Bodie's law enforcement institutions were certainly not responsible for these low rates. . . . Moreover, many law enforcement officers operated on both sides of the law" (645).
Omitting End of Quoted Sentence	According to McGrath, "Bodie's law enforcement institutions were certainly not responsible for these low rates. Rarely were robbers or burglars arrested. . . . Moreover, many law enforcement officers operated on both sides of the law" (645).
Placing Parenthetical Citation after Ellipsis	According to McGrath, "Bodie's law enforcement institutions were certainly not responsible for these low rates. Rarely were robbers or burglars arrested . . ." (645).

Quotations within Quotations

Occasionally a passage that you wish to quote will already contain quotation marks. If you use block indentation, keep the quotation marks exactly as they are in the original. If you set the passage within your own quotation marks, however, change the original double marks (") into single marks (') to indicate the quotation within the quotation. The same procedure works whether the quotation marks are used for quoted words or for a title.

ORIGINAL PASSAGE: ROBERT HEILBRONER QUOTING WILLIAM JAMES

And finally, we tend to stereotype because it helps us make sense out of a highly confusing world, a world which William James once described as "one great, blooming, buzzing confusion."

QUOTED PASSAGE: WRITER QUOTING HEILBRONER

Robert Heilbroner explains why people tend to create stereotypes: "And finally, we tend to stereotype because it helps us make sense out of a highly confusing world, a world which William James once described as 'one great, blooming, buzzing confusion' " (22).

Creating Rhetorically Effective Attributive Tags

As we have shown in this section, whenever you use sources in your writing, you need to distinguish your source's words and ideas from your own. The most precise way of doing so is to use strategically placed attributive tags—short phrases like "according to McGrath," "McGrath says," "in McGrath's view," and so on. As we show in a moment, attributive tags can have a powerful rhetorical effect by letting you create the angle of vision from which you want your readers to view a source.

Using Attributive Tags to Separate Your Ideas from Your Source's
The previous examples of citing, summarizing, paraphrasing, and quoting use attributive tags to signal which ideas are the writer's and which are taken from another source. Here, for example, are excerpts from Writer 1's summary of McGrath, in which we have highlighted the attributive tags with boldfaced font. (The complete summary appears on p. 646.)

USE OF ATTRIBUTIVE TAGS

Many people believe that violence is part of our Wild West heritage. But **Roger McGrath, in his article "The Myth of Violence in the Old West,"** shows that frontier violence was very different from contemporary violence. **He explains** that . . . . On the other hand, **McGrath explains,** killings were fueled . . . . Thus, **according to McGrath,** there is little resemblance between violence on the frontier and violence in today's cities. . . .

Using Parenthetical Citations without Attributive Tags and the Resulting Ambiguities
You can also indicate borrowed material by inserting the source author's name and appropriate page number in a parenthetical citation at the end of the borrowed material:

(McGrath 645)

However, this approach—which is common in some academic writing, particularly in the social sciences—can introduce two kinds of ambiguity. First, it does not clearly mark where the borrowed material begins or how far it extends. Second, it tends to imply that the borrowed material is a "fact" as opposed to an author's argument filtered through that author's angle of vision. Note these ambiguities in the following passage, where parenthetical citations are used without attributive tags:

AMBIGUOUS ATTRIBUTION

There are many arguments in favor of preserving old-growth forests. First, it is simply unnecessary to log these forests to supply the world's lumber. We have plenty of new-growth forest from which lumber can be taken (Sagoff 89–90). Recently there have been major reforestation efforts all over the United States, and it is common practice now for loggers to replant every tree that is harvested. These new-growth forests, combined with extensive planting of tree farms, provide more than enough wood for the world's needs. Tree farms alone can supply the world's demand for industrial lumber (Sedjo 90).

When confronted with this passage, skeptical readers might ask, "Who are Sagoff and Sedjo? I've never heard of them." It is also difficult to tell how much of the passage is the writer's own argument and how much is borrowed from Sagoff and Sedjo. Is this whole passage a paraphrase? Finally, the writer tends to treat Sagoff's and Sedjo's assertions as uncontested facts rather than as professional opinions. Compare the preceding version with this one, in which attributive tags are added:

CLEAR ATTRIBUTION

There are many arguments in favor of preserving old-growth forests. First, it is simply unnecessary to log these forests to supply the world's lumber. **According to environmentalist Carl Sagoff**, we have plenty of new-growth forest from which lumber can be taken (89–90). Recently there have been major reforestation efforts all over the United States, and it is common practice now for loggers to replant every tree that is harvested. These new-growth forests, combined with extensive planting of tree farms, provide more than enough wood for the world's needs. **According to forestry expert Robert Sedjo**, tree farms alone can supply the world's demand for industrial lumber (90).

We can now see that most of the paragraph is the writer's own argument, into which she has inserted the expert testimony of Sagoff and Sedjo, whose views are treated not as indisputable facts but as the opinions of authorities in this field.

Using Attributive Tags to Create Context and Shape Reader Response

When you introduce a source for the first time, you can use the attributive tag not only to introduce the source but also to shape your readers' attitudes toward the source. In the previous example, the writer wants readers to respect Sagoff and Sedjo, so she identifies Sagoff as an "environmentalist" and Sedjo as a "forestry expert." If the writer favored logging old-growth forests and supported the logging industry's desire to create more jobs, she might have used different tags: "Carl Sagoff, an outspoken advocate for spotted owls over people," or "Robert Sedjo, a forester with limited knowledge of world lumber markets."

When you compose an initial tag, you can add to it any combination of the following kinds of information, depending on your purpose, your audience's values, and your sense of what the audience already knows or doesn't know about the source:

Add to Attributive Tag	Example
Author's credentials or relevant specialty (enhances credibility)	Civil engineer David Rockwood, a noted authority on stream flow in rivers
Author's lack of credentials (decreases credibility)	City Council member Dilbert Weasel, a local politician with no expertise in international affairs
Author's political or social views	Left-wing columnist Alexander Cockburn [has negative feeling]; Alexander Cockburn, a longtime champion of labor [has positive feeling]
Title of source if it provides context	In her book *Fasting Girls: The History of Anorexia Nervosa,* Joan Jacobs Brumberg shows that [establishes credentials for comments on eating disorders]

Add to Attributive Tag	Example
Publisher of source if it adds prestige or otherwise shapes audience response	Dr. Carl Patrona, in an article published in the prestigious *New England Journal of Medicine*
Historical or cultural information about a source that provides context or background	In his 1960s book popularizing the hippie movement, Charles Reich claims that
Indication of source's purpose or angle of vision	Feminist author Naomi Wolfe, writing a blistering attack on the beauty industry, argues that

Our point here is that you can use attributive tags rhetorically to help your readers understand the significance and context of a source when you first introduce it and to guide your readers' attitudes toward the source.

For Writing and Discussion

What follow are four different ways that a writer can use the same passage from a source to support a point about the greenhouse effect. Working in groups or as a whole class, rank the four methods from "most effective" to "least effective." Assume that you are writing a researched argument addressed to your college classmates.

1. *Quotation without attributive tag*
   The greenhouse effect will have a devastating effect on the earth's environment: "Potential impacts include increased mortality and illness due to heat stress and worsened air pollution, as in the 1995 Chicago heat wave that killed hundreds of people. . . . Infants, children and other vulnerable populations—especially in already-stressed regions of the world—would likely suffer disproportionately from these impacts" (Hall 19).

2. *Quotation with attributive tag*
   The greenhouse effect will have a devastating effect on the earth's environment. David C. Hall, president of Physicians for Social Responsibility, claims the following: "Potential impacts include increased mortality and illness due to heat stress and worsened air pollution, as in the 1995 Chicago heat wave that killed hundreds of people. . . . Infants, children and other vulnerable populations—especially in already-stressed regions of the world—would likely suffer disproportionately from these impacts" (19).

3. *Paraphrase without attributive tag*
   The greenhouse effect will have a devastating effect on the earth's environment. One of the most frightening effects is the threat of diseases

(continued)

stemming from increased air pollution and heat stress. Infants and children would be most at risk (Hall 19).

4. *Paraphrase with attributive tag*

The greenhouse effect will have a devastating effect on the earth's environment. One of the most frightening effects, according to David C. Hall, president of Physicians for Social Responsibility, is the threat of diseases stemming from increased air pollution and heat stress. Infants and children would be most at risk (19).

Avoiding Plagiarism

Before we proceed to the nuts and bolts of documenting sources, we'd like you to understand the ethical issue of plagiarism. As you know from writing your own papers, developing ideas and putting them into words is hard work. *Plagiarism* occurs whenever you take someone else's work and pass it off as your own. Plagiarism has two forms: borrowing another person's ideas without giving credit through proper citation and borrowing another writer's language without giving credit through quotation marks or block indentation.

The second kind of plagiarism is far more common than the first, perhaps because inexperienced writers don't appreciate how much they need to change the wording of a source to make the writing their own. It is not enough just to change the order of phrases in a sentence or to replace a few words with synonyms. In the following example, compare the satisfactory paraphrase of a passage from McGrath's piece with a plagiarized version.

Original	There is considerable evidence that women in Bodie were rarely the victims of crime. Between 1878 and 1882 only one woman, a prostitute, was robbed, and there were no reported cases of rape. (There is no evidence that rapes occurred but were not reported.)
Acceptable Paraphrase	According to McGrath, women in Bodie rarely suffered at the hands of criminals (645). Between 1878 and 1882, the only female robbery victim in Bodie was a prostitute. Also rape seemed nonexistent, with no reported cases and no evidence that unreported cases occurred.
Plagiarism	According to McGrath, there is much evidence that women in Bodie were seldom crime victims (645). Between 1878 and 1882 only one woman, a prostitute, was robbed, and there were no reported rapes. There is no evidence that unreported cases of rape occurred (645).

For Writing and Discussion

The writer of the plagiarized passage perhaps assumed that the accurate citation of McGrath is all that is needed to avoid plagiarism. Yet this writer is guilty of plagiarism. Why? How has the writer attempted to change the wording of the original? Why aren't these changes enough?

The best way to avoid plagiarism is to be especially careful at the note-taking stage. If you copy from your source, copy exactly, word for word, and put quotation marks around the copied material or otherwise indicate that it is not your own wording. If you paraphrase or summarize material, be sure that you don't borrow any of the original wording. Also be sure to change the grammatical structure of the original. Lazy note taking, in which you follow the arrangement and grammatical structure of the original passage and merely substitute occasional synonyms, leads directly to plagiarism.

Also remember that you cannot borrow another writer's ideas without citing them. If you summarize or paraphrase another writer's thinking about a subject, you should indicate in your notes that the ideas are not your own and be sure to record all the information you need for a citation. If you do exploratory reflection to accompany your notes, then the distinction between other writers' ideas and your own should be easy to recognize when it's time to incorporate the source material into your paper.

For Writing and Discussion

The following exercise asks you to apply all the research and writing skills that you have learned in this part of the chapter. After reading Edward Abbey's article "The Damnation of a Canyon" (pp. 157–161), imagine that you are going to use Abbey's article in an essay of your own. Working individually or in small groups, write an appropriate passage for each of the following scenarios. You will need to decide how much you will quote from Abbey's article and how you will use attributive tags to create a context and to shape your readers' responses to your source.

Scenario 1 You are a supporter of dams and wish to write an article supporting the Glen Canyon Dam and opposing Abbey's article. Write a one-paragraph summary of Abbey's views to include in your own essay.

Scenario 2 You are doing research on the ecological effects of dams and want to use Abbey's article as one source. For your essay, write a paragraph, citing Abbey's article, on how building the Glen Canyon Dam changed the river's ecology.

(*continued*)

Scenario 3 You are investigating the socioeconomic status of people who use Lake Powell for recreation. You particularly want to investigate Abbey's claim that the lake is used only by the wealthy. For your essay, write a short passage that reports Abbey's view of the socioeconomic status of the lake's recreational users.

Skill 7: Cite and Document Sources Effectively According to Appropriate Conventions

In this final section we focus on the nuts and bolts of documentation that is appropriate for your purpose, audience, and genre. As we have explained, proper documentation not only helps other researchers locate your sources but also contributes substantially to your own *ethos* as a writer. Specifically, this section helps you understand the general logic of parenthetical citation systems, the MLA and APA methods for in-text citations, the MLA and APA methods for documenting sources in a "Works Cited" and "References" list, respectively, and the MLA and APA styles for formatting academic papers.* As you use one or both of these methods in papers for various classes, your familiarity with the type of information expected in citations will make it easier to follow the formatting details in the models we provide as well as in other systems your professors may expect you to use.

Understanding the Logic of Parenthetical Citation Systems

An example of a research paper written in MLA style is Christopher Leigh's paper on pp. 675–686. An example of a research paper written in APA style is Brittany Tinker et al.'s on pp. 277–289.

Not too many years ago, most academic disciplines used footnotes or endnotes to document sources. Today, however, both the MLA (Modern Language Association) system, used primarily in the humanities, and the APA (American Psychological Association) system, used primarily in the social sciences, use parenthetical citations instead of footnotes or endnotes. Before we examine the details of MLA and APA styles, we want to explain the logic of parenthetical citation systems.

Connecting the Body of the Paper to the Bibliography
In both the MLA and APA systems, the writer places a complete bibliography at the end of the paper. In the MLA system this bibliography is called "Works Cited." In the APA system it is called "References." The bibliography is arranged alphabetically by author or by title (if an author is not named). The key to the systems' logic is this:

---

*Our discussion of MLA style is based on Joseph Gibaldi, *MLA Handbook for Writers of Research Papers,* 6th ed. (New York: Modern Language Association of America, 2003). Our discussion of APA style is based on the *Publication Manual of the American Psychological Association,* 5th ed. (Washington, D.C.: American Psychological Association, 2001).

- Every source in the bibliography must be mentioned in the body of the paper.
- Conversely, every source mentioned in the body of the paper must be listed in the bibliography.
- There must be a one-to-one correspondence between the first word in each bibliographic entry (usually, but not always, an author's last name)* and the name used to identify the source in the body of the paper.

Suppose a reader sees this phrase in your paper: "According to Debra Goldstein . . . ." The reader should be able to turn to your bibliography and find an alphabetized entry beginning with "Goldstein, Debra." Similarly, suppose that in looking over your bibliography, your reader sees an article by "Guillen, Manuel." This means that the name "Guillen" has to occur in your paper in one of two ways:

- As an attributive tag: "Economics professor Manuel Guillen argues that. . . ."
- As a parenthetical citation, probably following a quotation: ". . . changes in fiscal policy" (Guillen 49).

Because this one-to-one correspondence is so important, let's illustrate it with some complete examples using the MLA formatting style:

If the body of your paper has this:	Then the "Works Cited" list must have this:
According to linguist Deborah Tannen, political debate in America leaves out the complex middle ground where most solutions must be developed. [author cited in an attributive tag]	Tannen, Deborah. <u>The Argument Culture: Moving From Debate to Dialogue</u>. New York: Random, 1998.
In the 1980s, cigarette advertising revealed a noticeable pattern of racial stereotyping (Pollay, Lee, and Carter-Whitney). [authors cited in parentheses]	Pollay, Richard W., Jung S. Lee, and David Carter-Whitney. "Separate, but Not Equal: Racial Segmentation in Cigarette Advertising." <u>Journal of Advertising</u> 21.1 (1992): 45–57.
In its award-winning Web site, the National Men's Resource Center offers advice to parents whose teenagers want to get a nose stud or other form of body piercing ("Ouch!"). [shortened title used to identify source in "Works Cited" list]	"Ouch! Body Piercing." <u>Menstuff</u>. 1 Feb. 2001. National Men's Resource Center. 17 July 2004 <http://www.menstuff.org/issues/byissue/fathersgeneral.html#bodypiercing>.

*Sometimes a source won't have a named author. In such cases your parenthetical citation should identify the source by title, shortened for efficiency, and your bibliographic entry should begin with those title words (for example, "Guidelines for School Safety" could be shortened to "Guidelines" as long as no other sources begin with that title). To cite a source from a Web site identified by a corporation or group's name (for example, "Centers for Disease Control"), you have the choice of beginning the entry with the title of the document you are citing or with the corporate author, whichever you think will make more sense in your text and will help readers find the source more easily.

Citation Problems with Downloaded Sources

Now that you understand the concept of connecting the body of your text to your bibliography, you need to understand some special citation problems associated with sources downloaded from a licensed database or the Web. It is easy to cite a print source that you read in its original form (books, articles from the actual magazine or journal) because these sources can be retrieved in the same paper format from library to library all over the world. Both the MLA and APA systems have a basic format for citing books and articles. Although you'll encounter variations on the basic formats—more than one author, a revised edition, a translation, and so forth—in general, you simply find a bibliographic model that matches your source and plug the information into the correct slots.

The case is more difficult when you download an article from a licensed database or the Web. First of all, scholarly organizations usually expect researchers to find the original print version rather than use the downloaded version. But for college students, it is often difficult to locate the original print source if their libraries don't have it. There are three main problems with relying on downloaded articles: (1) you can't be sure the electronic article is a completely accurate version of the print article; (2) the downloaded version often doesn't reproduce the visual images that appear in the print version and that may be important; (3) the downloaded version usually doesn't reproduce the page numbering of the original source, so there is no clear way to cite pages.* Because downloaded versions are unstable, you must include in your bibliographic entry all the publication information about the original print version of the article *plus* information about the electronic source.

You will encounter the most difficulty when citing Web sources, where material often is ephemeral. (There are important exceptions. For example, totally electronic, peer-reviewed scholarly journals are now being published online. The publisher archives all accepted articles, making them stable and electronically available to future scholars.) In general, though, you can't be sure that material available today from the Web will still be available tomorrow, not to mention twenty or more years from now. Another problem with Web sources, as we saw in Chapter 21, is that it is often hard to determine publication dates and authorship of material. Also, as with licensed database sources, page numbers are usually impossible to specify for Web sites. Sometimes the only certain thing you'll know about a Web site is the URL in your computer's location window and the date you accessed the site. At the very minimum, you have to include this information in the citation.

From this point on, we separate our discussions of the MLA and APA systems. We begin with the MLA system because it is the one most commonly used in writing courses. We then explain the APA system.

---

*Databases are increasingly offering some sources in .pdf format, which reproduces the original look of the article. In these cases, images are usually reproduced, and the original page formatting is maintained.

Understanding the MLA Method of In-Text Citation

To cite sources in your text using the MLA system, place the author's last name and the page reference in parentheses immediately after the material being cited. If an attributive tag already identifies the author, give only the page number in parentheses. Once you have cited the author and it is clear that the same author's material is being used, you need cite only the page references in parentheses. The following examples show parenthetical documentation with and without an attributive tag. Note that the citation precedes the period. If you are citing a quotation, the parenthetical citation follows the quotation mark but precedes the final period.

> The Spanish tried to reduce the status of Filipina women who had been able to do business, get divorced, and sometimes become village chiefs (Karnow 41).
>
> According to Karnow, the Spanish tried to reduce the status of Filipina women who had been able to do business, get divorced, and sometimes become village chiefs (41).
>
> "And, to this day," Karnow continues, "women play a decisive role in Filipino families" (41).

A reader who wishes to look up the source will find the bibliographic information in the Works Cited section by looking for the entry under "Karnow." If more than one work by Karnow was used in the paper, the writer would include in the in-text citation an abbreviated title of the book or article following Karnow's name.

> (Karnow, "In Our Image" 41)

Citing from an Indirect Source

Occasionally you may wish to use a quotation that you have seen cited in one of your sources. You read Jones, who has a nice quotation from Smith, and you want to use Smith's quotation. What do you do? Whenever possible, find the quotation in its original source and cite that source. But if the original source is not available, cite the source indirectly by using the term "qtd. in" and list only the indirect source in your "Works Cited" list. In the following example, the writer wishes to quote a Buddhist monk, Thich Nhat Hanh, who has written a book entitled *Living Buddha, Living Christ.* However, the writer is unable to locate the actual book and instead has to quote from a review of the book by newspaper critic Lee Moriwaki. Here is how he would make the in-text citation:

> A Buddhist monk, Thich Nhat Hanh, stresses the importance of inner peace: "If we can learn ways to touch the peace, joy, and happiness that are already there, we will become healthy and strong, and a resource for others" (qtd. in Moriwaki C4).

The "Works Cited" list will have an entry for "Moriwaki" but not for "Thich Nhat Hanh."

Citing Page Numbers for Downloaded Material

As we discussed earlier, unless the downloaded materials you are citing are available in .pdf format, it is very difficult to provide accurate page numbers for parenthetical citations. If you are working with text or HTML files, do not use the page numbers on a printout because they will not be consistent from printer to printer. However, you can be confident in citing page numbers when a downloaded article indicates the source's original page breaks or has numbered paragraphs. Cite paragraphs with the abbreviation *par.* or *pars.*—for example, (Jones, pars. 22–24). In the typical case of the absence of reliable page numbers for the original material, MLA says to omit page references from the parenthetical citation. When researchers locate the source through the database or via its URL, they can use a software search function to pinpoint a specific quotation or passage.

Documenting Sources in a "Works Cited" List (MLA)

To see what citations look like when typed in a manuscript, see Christopher Leigh's Works Cited list on pp. 685–686. The MLA example citations on pp. 663–673 show the correct elements, sequence, and punctuation, but not typing formats.

In the MLA system, you place a complete bibliography, titled "Works Cited," at the end of the paper. The list includes all the sources that you mention in your paper. However, it does not include works you read but did not use. Entries in the Works Cited list are arranged alphabetically by author, or by title if there is no author.

Here are some general formatting guidelines for a works cited list:

- Begin the list on a new sheet of paper with the words "Works Cited" centered one inch from the top of the page.
- Sources are listed alphabetically, the first line flush with the left margin and succeeding lines indented one-half inch, known as a "hanging indentation."
- MLA formatting style uses abbreviations for months of the year (except for May, June, and July) and for publishers' names (for example, Random House is shortened to "Random" and "University Press" is shortened to "UP"). For a complete list of abbreviations, consult the sixth edition of the *MLA Handbook for Writers of Research Papers.*
- Author entries include the name as it appears in the article by-line or on the book's title page.
- MLA style recommends underlining rather than italicizing book titles and names of journals and magazines (because underlines stand out better on the page). Do not underline any punctuation marks following an underlined title.

Here is a typical example of a work, in this case a book, cited in MLA form.

> Karnow, Stanley. <u>In Our Image: America's Empire in the Philippines</u>. New York: Random, 1989.

Two or More Listings for One Author

When two or more works by one author are cited, the works are listed alphabetically by title. For the second and all additional entries, type three hyphens and a period in place of the author's name.

Dombrowski, Daniel A. <u>Babies and Beasts: The Argument from Marginal Cases</u>. Urbana: U of Illinois P, 1997.

---. <u>The Philosophy of Vegetarianism</u>. Amherst: U of Massachusetts P, 1984.

The remaining pages in this section show examples of MLA formats for different kinds of sources, provide explanations as needed, and give examples of the most frequently encountered variations and source types.

MLA Citation Models

Books

General Format for Books

Author. <u>Title</u>. City of publication: Publisher, year of publication.

One author

Brumberg, Joan J. <u>The Body Project: An Intimate History of American Girls</u>. New York: Vintage, 1997.

Two or more authors

Dombrowski, Daniel A., and Robert J. Deltete. <u>A Brief, Liberal, Catholic Defense of Abortion</u>. Urbana: U of Illinois P, 2000.

Belenky, Mary, et al. <u>Women's Ways of Knowing: The Development of Self, Voice, and Mind</u>. New York: Basic, 1986.

If there are four or more authors, you have the choice of listing all the authors in the order in which they appear on the title page or using "et al." (meaning "and others") to replace all but the first author. Make the same decision for the works cited entry and the parenthetical citation so they match.

Second, later, or revised edition

Montagu, Ashley. <u>Touching: The Human Significance of the Skin</u>. 3rd ed. New York: Perennial, 1986.

In place of "3rd ed.," you can include abbreviations for other kinds of editions: "Rev. ed." (for "Revised edition") or "Abr. ed." (for "Abridged edition").

Republished book (for example, a paperback published after the original hardback edition or a modern edition of an older work)

Hill, Christopher. <u>The World Turned Upside Down: Radical Ideas During the English Revolution</u>. 1972. London: Penguin, 1991.

Wollstonecraft, Mary. <u>The Vindication of the Rights of Woman, with Strictures on Political and Moral Subjects</u>. 1792. Rutland: Tuttle, 1995.

The date immediately following the title is the original publication date of the work.

Multivolume work

Churchill, Winston S. <u>A History of the English-Speaking Peoples</u>. 4 vols. New York: Dodd, 1956–58.

Churchill, Winston S. <u>The Great Democracies</u>. New York: Dodd, 1957. Vol. 4 of <u>A History of the English-Speaking Peoples</u>. 4 vols. 1956–58.

Use the first method when you cite the whole work; use the second method when you cite one specific volume of the work.

Article in familiar reference work

"Mau Mau." <u>The New Encyclopedia Britannica</u>. 15th ed. 2002.

Article in less familiar reference work

Ling, Trevor O. "Buddhism in Burma." <u>Dictionary of Comparative Religion</u>. Ed. S. G. F. Brandon. New York: Scribner's, 1970.

Translation

De Beauvoir, Simone. <u>The Second Sex</u>. 1949. Trans. H. M. Parshley. New York: Bantam, 1961.

Corporate author (a commission, committee, or other group)

American Red Cross. <u>Standard First Aid</u>. St. Louis: Mosby Lifeline, 1993.

No author listed

<u>The New Yorker Cartoon Album: 1975–1985</u>. New York: Penguin, 1987.

Edited Anthologies

An edited anthology looks like a regular book but has an editor rather than an author, and the contents are separate articles written by individual scholars. Anthology editors might also produce collections of short stories, poems, art-work, cartoons, or other kinds of documents. When you refer to the whole book, you cite the editor. When you refer to an individual work within the anthology, you cite the author of that work.

Citing the editor

O'Connell, David F., and Charles N. Alexander, eds. <u>Self Recovery: Treating Addictions Using Transcendental Meditation and Maharishi Ayur-Veda</u>. New York: Haworth, 1994.

Citing an individual article

Royer, Ann. "The Role of the Transcendental Meditation Technique in Promoting Smoking Cessation: A Longitudinal Study." <u>Self Recovery: Treating Addictions Using Transcendental Meditation and Maharishi Ayur-Veda</u>. Eds. David F. O'Connell and Charles N. Alexander. New York: Haworth, 1994. 221–39.

When you cite an individual article, the inclusive page numbers for the article come at the end of the citation.

Articles in Scholarly Journals Accessed in Print

The differences between a scholarly journal and a magazine are explained on page 615. When citing scholarly journals, you need to determine how the journal numbers its pages. Typically, separate issues of a journal are published four times per year. The library then binds the four separate issues into one "annual volume." Some journals restart the page numbering with each issue, which means that during the year there would be four instances of, say, page 31. Other journals number the pages consecutively throughout the year. In such a case, the fall issue might begin with page 253 rather than page 1. When pages are numbered sequentially throughout the year, you need to include only the volume number in the volume slot (for example, "25"). When page numbering starts over with each issue, you need to include in the volume slot both the volume and the issue number, separated by a period (for example, "25.3").

General Format for Scholarly Journals

Author. "Article Title." <u>Journal Title</u> volume number.issue number (year): page numbers.

Scholarly journal that numbers pages continuously

Barton, Ellen L. "Evidentials, Argumentation, and Epistemological Stance." <u>College English</u> 55 (1993): 745–69.

Scholarly journal that restarts page numbering with each issue

Pollay, Richard W., Jung S. Lee, and David Carter-Whitney. "Separate, but Not Equal: Racial Segmentation in Cigarette Advertising." <u>Journal of Advertising</u> 21.1 (1992): 45–57.

Articles in Magazines and Newspapers Accessed in Print

Magazine and newspaper articles are easy to cite. If no author is identified, begin the entry with the title or headline. Distinguish between news stories and editorials by putting the word "Editorial" after the title. If a magazine comes out weekly or biweekly, include the complete date (27 Sept. 1998). If it comes out monthly, then state the month only (Sept. 1998).

General Format for Magazines and Newspapers

Author. "Article Title." <u>Magazine Title</u> [day] Month year: page numbers.

   Note: If the article continues in another part of the magazine or newspaper, add "+" to the number of the first page to indicate the nonsequential pages.

Magazine article with named author

Snyder, Rachel L. "A Daughter of Cambodia Remembers: Loung Ung's Journey." <u>Ms.</u> Aug.—Sept. 2001: 62–67.

Hall, Stephen S. "Prescription for Profit." <u>New York Times Magazine</u> 11 Mar. 2001: 40+.

Magazine article without named author

"Daddy, Daddy." <u>New Republic</u> 30 July 2001: 2–13.

Review of book, film, or performance

Schwarz, Benjamin. "A Bit of Bunting: A New History of the British Empire Elevates Expediency to Principle." Rev. of <u>Ornamentalism: How the British Saw Their Empire</u>, by David Cannadine. <u>Atlantic Monthly</u> Nov. 2001: 126–35.

Kaufman, Stanley. "Polishing a Gem." Rev. of <u>The Blue Angel</u>, dir. Josef von Sternberg. <u>New Republic</u> 30 July 2001: 28–29.

Lahr, John. "Nobody's Darling: Fascism and the Drama of Human Connection in <u>Ashes to Ashes</u>." Rev. of <u>Ashes to Ashes</u>, by Harold Pinter. The Roundabout Theater Co. Gramercy Theater, New York. <u>New Yorker</u> 22 Feb. 1999: 182–83.

Follow this general model: Name of reviewer. "Title of Review." Rev. of <u>book, film, or play</u>, by Author/Playwright [for films, use name of director preceded by "dir."; for play, add production data as in last example]. <u>Periodical Title</u> [day] month year: inclusive pages. Include company and theater information only for live performances.

Newspaper article

Henriques, Diana B. "Hero's Fall Teaches Wall Street a Lesson." <u>Seattle Times</u> 27 Sept. 1998: A1+.

Page numbers in newspapers are typically indicated by a section letter or number as well as a page number. Include these designations exactly as they appear in the source. The "+" indicates that the article is completed on one or more pages later in the newspaper.

Newspaper editorial

"Dr. Frankenstein on the Hill." Editorial. <u>New York Times</u> 18 May 2002: A22.

Letter to the editor of a magazine or newspaper

Tomsovic, Kevin. Letter. <u>New Yorker</u> 13 July 1998: 7.

Print Articles or Books Downloaded from a Database

Because of the difficulty in determining original page numbers for downloaded articles, citations in this category must begin with complete print information, followed by the electronic information.

General Format for Material from Licensed Databases

Author. "Title." <u>Periodical Name</u> Print publication data including date and volume/issue numbers: pagination. <u>Database</u>. Database company (if different). Library information. Date of access <URL of the database service's home page, if known>.

Note that there is no punctuation between the date of access and the URL; the intended effect is a statement that on that date, the material was found at that location or via that service.

Print article retrieved from licensed database

Lanza, Robert P., Betsy L. Dresser, and Philip Damiani. "Cloning Noah's Ark." <u>Scientific American</u> Nov. 2000: 84- . <u>Academic Search Elite</u>. EBSCO. Alexandria (Va.) Lib. 14 Sept. 2003 <http://www.epnet.com/>.

Watanabe, Myrna. "Zoos Act as Sentinels for Infectious Diseases." <u>Bioscience</u> 53 (2003): 792. <u>ProQuest</u>. Raynor Lib., Marquette U. 26 July 2004 <http://www.il.proquest.com/proquest/>.

Follow the formats for print magazines or scholarly journals, as relevant. When the database text provides only the starting page number of a multipage article, insert a hyphen and a space after the number, before the period. Providing only one number (as in the Watanabe citation above) indicates that the article has only one page.

Broadcast transcript retrieved from licensed database

Conan, Neal. "Arab Media." <u>Talk of the Nation</u>. With Shibley Telhami. 4 May 2004. Transcript. <u>LexisNexis</u>. Reed Elsevier. Raynor Lib., Marquette U. 31 July 2004 <http://www.lexisnexis.com/>.

The label "Transcript" after the broadcast date shows that a print copy was used.

Reference material retrieved from licensed database

"Cicada." <u>Encyclopaedia Britannica</u>. 2004. Encyclopaedia Britannica Online. Raynor Lib., Marquette U. 31 July 2004 <http://0search.eb.com.libus.csd.mu.edu:80/ eb/article?eu=84788>.

This example uses the MLA citation provided at the end of the Britannica article. The URL is unique to the database license for the academic library through which we accessed it.

"Toni Morrison." <u>American Decades 1990–1999</u>. Ed. Tandy McConnell. Detroit: Gale Group, Inc., 2001. <u>Biography Resource Center</u>. Seattle Public Lib. 14 Sept. 2003 <http://www.galegroup.com/BiographyRC/>.

For MLA-approved alternatives to providing URLs, see p. 670.

Because the URL for the Toni Morrison article was long and unwieldy, we inserted the URL for the Biography Resource Center's home page, which we found quickly via a Google search.

Papers and monographs from an information service

Information services such as ERIC (Educational Resources Information Center) or NTIS (National Technical Information Service) provide material to your library on microfiche or online with indexes on CD-ROM or online. Much of the material from these services has not been published in major journals or magazines. Frequently they are typescripts of conference papers or other scholarly work disseminated on microfiche. Cite microfiche copies as you would cite print materials, adding an identifying phrase instead of publication information, and then an accession number at the end.

Coll, Richard K., Sara Tofield, Brent Vyle, and Rachel Bolstad. "Free-Choice Learning at a Metropolitan Zoo." Paper presented at the Annual Meeting of the National Association for Research in Science Teaching, Philadelphia, PA, 23–26 Mar. 2003. ERIC ED 477832.

For electronic versions, follow the format for periodical articles from a licensed database, adding the database information after the descriptive phrase and the accession number.

Coll, Richard K., Sara Tofield, Brent Vyle, and Rachel Bolstad. "Free-Choice Learning at a Metropolitan Zoo." Paper presented at the Annual Meeting of the National Association for Research in Science Teaching, Philadelphia, PA, 23–26 Mar. 2003. ERIC ED 477832. <u>Ovid</u>. Raynor Lib., Marquette U. 26 July 2004 <www.ovid.com>.

E-book

Hanley, Wayne. <u>The Genesis of Napoleonic Propaganda, 1796–1799</u>. Columbia UP, 2002. <u>Gutenberg-e</u>. 31 July 2004 <http://www.gutenberg-e.org>.

Machiavelli, Niccolo. <u>Prince</u>. [1513.] <u>Bibliomania</u>. 31 July 2004 <http://www.bibliomania.com>.

Information about the original print version, including a translator if relevant and available, should be provided. Use brackets for adding information not provided in the source.

Web and Internet Sources

Because Web and Internet sources vary widely in design and in the ways they approach content, creating citations for them can sometimes be a puzzling process. To help you create useful, accurate citations, we provide a general format followed by some general principles you can apply when creating Web citations; we then devote the rest of this section to model citations for types of sources that students frequently use.

General Format for Web Sources

Author of the page or document, if available. "Title of page or document." <u>Title of the overall site, usually taken from the home page</u>. Date of publication online or last update of the site, if available. Total range of paragraphs or pages, if they are numbered within the site itself (as in a .pdf document). Name of site sponsor, if available and not already stated in the Web site title. Date you accessed the site <URL of the specific document>.

Note that the main divisions are separated by periods except that no punctuation is used between the date of access and the URL.

Here is an illustration that contains nearly all of the elements listed above:

Smith, Anne-Marie. "Advances in Understanding International Peacemaking." <u>United States Institute of Peace</u>. 2000. 76 pp. 25 May 2004 <http://www.usip.org/pubs/summaries/advances.pdf>.

This citation indicates a seventy-six-page .pdf document by Anne-Marie Smith titled "Advances in Understanding International Peacemaking" and published in 2000. It was posted on the Web site of the United States Institute of Peace, which uses its name as the title of the site. The researcher accessed this document on 25 May 2004 at the URL given.

The next example shows a citation for which not all the information elements were available:

"Nuclear Power Plant Accidents." <u>Infoplease</u>. Pearson Education. 21 Sept. 2004
     <http://www.infoplease.com/ipa/A0001457.html>.

This citation begins with the article title because there is no named author. We
learned by clicking on the "About" link that the Web site <u>Infoplease</u> is sponsored
by Pearson Education. There is no entry for the date of the article because none
was provided; also, there is no entry for number of pages because the site doesn't
indicate page breaks. The researcher accessed the site on 21 Sept. 2004 at the
URL given.

General Principles for Web Sources

As with print sources, the fundamental rule is to give your readers enough
details to find the source you used. Since Web sites are frequently updated,
altered, or dropped, it is important to provide the date that you accessed the
material. In light of this variability, MLA advises that you print or download
your Web and Internet sources so that you can ensure your ability to verify the
material later. Here are a few additional useful principles for using the formats
we provide:

- Always include the date on which you retrieved the material.
- Always include either a URL or, if the URL is too long or unwieldy, an alternative means of finding the source (see p. 670 for how to cite a search page
  or give path designations).
- Provide the title of the overall Web site. These are usually available at the
  top of your browser page on the site's home page. Also identify the name of
  the organization sponsoring the site (often available through an "About us"
  link) to see if it is different from the Web site title. For example, the Web site
  shown on page 599 is titled <u>Women Against Gun Control</u>, which is also the
  name of the sponsoring organization; a citation for this site would include
  only the Web site title (underlined). In contrast, the Web site of the National
  Men's Resource Center is entitled <u>Menstuff</u>. A citation for that site would
  include both names (the title underlined, the sponsor not underlined).
- If you wish to cite an entire Web site rather than a specific page or document, you need to provide only the title of the Web site, the sponsoring
  organization if different from the title, the date of latest update, the date
  you accessed the Web site, and the URL.
- When you wish to cite a specific section or document within a Web site,
  you need to provide the section or document's title and, if available, its
  author. (As with print sources, if an author is not named, the citation starts
  with the title of the section or document.)
- When you are citing a specific document or section, include the date on
  which it was written, published, or posted to the site. If these are unavailable, omit this element of the citation.
- When citing a specific document, include its length in pages or paragraphs
  if these are indicated in the document itself. For example, .pdf documents
  show page numbers from paper publication, and some other documents
  indicate pagination from a print source. However, in most cases, you will
  not be able to provide the number of pages or paragraphs because they

won't be specified. Do not include data about number of pages based on printouts because different computers and printers will process pages in different ways.

- Some sites provide model citations for use in a research paper. These may not be in MLA style, so be sure to convert them to MLA format.

Alternatives to providing a URL

In MLA style, the preferred way to show Web location is to copy the source's URL directly into the citation. In some cases, however, this is difficult if not impossible. Some URLs are so long that they are unwieldy and prone to transcription errors, and some Web sites seek to simplify access by using just a primary URL with internal links that do not appear in the URL window. MLA suggests the following three alternatives to providing specific URLs:

1. Provide the URL of the site's search page (if available).

   Gidley, Cheryl. "The Best of Both Worlds." *Philanthropy News Digest* 2004. The
       Foundation Center. 15 Aug. 2004 <http://fdncenter.org/pnd/archives/
       index.jhtml>.

   (This URL takes you immediately to the site's search box. Enter "Gidley" in the search box to locate the source.)
2. Provide the URL of the site's home page.
3. Indicate the sequence of links a reader can follow from the site home page.

   "Myths and Realities about Antibiotic Resistance." *Union of Concerned Scientists.*
       <http://www.ucsusa.org>. Path: Food and Environment; Antibiotic
       Resistance; FAQs.

   (This citation tells the user to start at the UCSUSA home page, click on "Food and Environment," then "Antibiotic Resistance," and finally "FAQs.")

Entire Web site

BlogPulse. Intelliseek. 24 July 2004 <http://www.blogpulse.com/>.

William Faulkner on the Web. Ed. John B. Padgett. 26 Mar. 2004. U of Mississippi. 25
    June 2004 <http://www.mcsr.olemiss.edu/~egjbp/faulkner/faulkner.html>.

Agatucci, Cora. Culture and Literature of Africa. Course home page. Humanities
    Department, Central Oregon Community College. 31 July 2004
    <http://web.cocc.edu/cagatucci/classes/hum211/>.

African Studies Program. Home page. School of Advanced International Study, Johns
    Hopkins U. 31 July 2004 <http://www.sais-jhu.edu/programs/africa/index.html>.

Sharpe, William F. Home page. May 2004. 31 July 2004
    <http://www.stanford.edu/~wfsharpe/>.

These examples show typical variations in the way to cite an entire Web site. The easiest case is the first, where you provide the site's title, its sponsoring organization, your date of access, and the URL. (If a "last updated" date is available for the entire site, it should be included, but BlogPulse dates and time-stamps individual entries, not the overall site.) The second citation adds the name of the site's editor and the date the site was last updated. The next two examples add the term "Home page" (not underlined) to signal the site's relation to a university course or program, and the final example refers to a personal home page that doesn't have a separate title.

Documents within a Web site

Marks, John. "Overview: Letter from the President." <u>Search for Common Ground</u>. 25 June 2004 <http://www.sfcg.org>. Path: About SFCG; Overview.

Bailey, Ronald. "The Impact of Science on Public Policy. Testimony before House Subcommittee on Energy and Mineral Resources. 108th Congress." <u>Reason Public Policy Institute</u>. 4 Feb. 2004. 10 pp. 18 Sept. 2004 <http://www.rppi.org/impact.pdf>.

The first example uses the "path method" rather than a URL to indicate Web access. The second includes data about the length of the document, available from a quick check of the .pdf document.

Article from a newspaper or newswire site

Thevenot, Brian. "Once in a Blue Moon." <u>Times Picayune</u> [New Orleans] 31 July 2004. 31 July 2004 <http://www.nola.com/news/t-p/frontpage/index.ssf?/base/ news-1/1091264442208250.xml>.

"Great Lakes: Rwanda backed dissident troops in DRC-UN panel." <u>IRIN News.org</u>. 21 July 2004. 31 July 2004 <http://www.irinnews.org/advsearch.asp>.

Broadcast transcript from a Web site

Michels, Spencer, and Margaret Warner. "The Politics of 9/11." <u>Online NewsHour</u>. 28 July 2004. Transcript: background and discussion. PBS. 31 July 2004 <http://www.pbs.org/newshour/bb/terrorism/july-dec04/9-11_7-28.html>.

Article from a scholarly e-journal

Welch, John R., and Ramon Riley. "Reclaiming Land and Spirit in the Western Apache Homeland." <u>American Indian Quarterly</u> 25 (2001): 5–14. 19 Dec. 2001 <http://muse.jhu.edu/journals/american_indian_quarterly/v025/25.1welch.pdf>.

E-mail

Daffinrud, Sue. "Scoring Guide for Class Participation." E-mail to the author. 12 Dec. 2001.

Use the subject line as the title of the e-mail.

Online posting to a Listserv, bulletin board, newsgroup, or blog*

CalEnergyGuy. "Energy Crisis Impacts on the Economy: Changes since 2001." Blog posting. 27 July 2004. California Energy Blog. 1 Aug. 2004 <http://calenergy.blogspot.com/2004_07_01_calenergy_archive.html>.

Follow the format for citing an e-mail, using the appropriate label before the date of posting. After the posting date, add these elements: name of the forum, your

---

*Forums for blog entries are not listed in the *MLA Handbook,* so we have interpolated a format based on the formats given for other types of Internet forums.

date of access, a URL for—in order of preference—an archived version of the post, the forum home page, or the posting itself. It may be helpful to insert the name of a sponsoring organization, if available, after the name of the forum.

Miscellaneous Sources

Television or radio program

"Lie Like a Rug." <u>NYPD Blue</u>. Dir. Steven Bochco and David Milch. ABC. KOMO, Seattle. 6 Nov. 2001.

For a program with episodes, begin with the episode name in quotation marks followed by the program name, underlined. If the program is part of a series (such as Masterpiece Theatre), add the series name without quotation marks or underlining after the program title.

Film or video recording

<u>Shakespeare in Love</u>. Dir. John Madden. Perf. Joseph Fiennes and Gwyneth Paltrow. Screenplay by Marc Norman and Tom Stoppard. Universal Miramax, 1998.

A minimal citation begins with the name of the film, underlined, and includes the name of the film company or the distributor and distribution date. Most citations also include the name of the director and may include the names of major performers and writers.

<u>Shakespeare in Love</u>. Dir. John Madden. Perf. Joseph Fiennes and Gwyneth Paltrow. Screenplay by Marc Norman and Tom Stoppard. 1998. Videocassette. Universal Miramax, 1999.

Cite the original film data. Then cite the recording medium (videocassette, laser disc, or DVD), name of recording company, and date of the videocassette or disc.

Sound recording

Dylan, Bob. "Rainy Day Woman." <u>Bob Dylan MTV Unplugged</u>. Columbia, 1995.

For sound recordings begin the entry with what your paper emphasizes—for example, the artist's name, composer's name, or conductor's name—and adjust the elements accordingly.

Cartoon or advertisement

Trudeau, Garry. "Doonesbury." Comic strip. <u>Seattle Times</u> 19 Nov. 2001: B4.

Banana Republic. Advertisement. <u>Details</u> Oct. 2001: 37.

Interview

Castellucci, Marion. Personal interview. 7 Oct. 2001.

Lecture, speech, or conference presentation

Sharples, Mike. "Authors of the Future." Conference of European Teachers of Academic Writing. U of Groningen. Groningen, Neth. 20 June 2001.

Government publications

Government publications are often difficult to cite because there are so many varieties. In general, follow these guidelines:

- Usually cite as author the government agency that produced the document. Begin with the highest level and then branch down to the specific agency:

> United States. Dept. of Justice. FBI
>
> Idaho. Dept. of Motor Vehicles

- Follow this with the title of the document, underlined.
- If a specific person is clearly identified as the author, you may begin the citation with that person's name, or you may list the author (preceded by the word "By") after the title of the document.
- Follow standard procedures for citing publication information for print sources or retrieval information for Web sources.

> United States. Dept. of Justice. FBI. <u>The School Shooter: A Threat Assessment</u>
> <u>Perspective</u>. By Mary O'Toole. 2000. 16 Aug. 2001
> <http://www.fbi.gov/publications/school/school2.pdf>.

The in-text citation would be: (United States). If you have more than one U.S. government document, continue to narrow down the in-text citation: (United States. Dept. of Justice. FBI. <u>School Shooter</u>). Had this document been published in print rather than online, you would list the standard publishing information found on the title page. Typically the press would be the GPO (Government Printing Office).

Formatting an Academic Paper in MLA Style

An example research paper in MLA style is shown on pages 675–686. Here are the distinctive formatting features of MLA papers:

- Double-space throughout including block quotations and the Works Cited list.
- Use one-inch margins top and bottom, left and right. Indent one-half inch or five spaces from the left margin at the beginning of each paragraph.
- Number pages consecutively throughout the manuscript including the Works Cited list, which begins on a new page. Page numbers go in the upper right-hand corner, flush with the right margin, and one-half inch from the top of the page. The page number should be preceded by your last name. The text begins one inch from the top of the page.
- Do *not* create a separate title page. Type your name, professor's name, course number, and date in the upper left-hand corner of your paper (all double-spaced), beginning one inch from the top of the page; then double-space and type your title, centered, without underlining or any distinctive

fonts (capitalize the first word and important words only); then double-space and begin your text.

- Start a new page for the Works Cited list. Type "Works Cited" centered, one inch from the top of the page in the same font as the rest of the paper; do not enclose it in quotation marks. Use hanging indentation of five spaces or one-half inch for each entry longer than one line. Format entries according to the instructions on page 662.

Student Example of an MLA-Style Research Paper

As an illustration of a student research paper written in MLA style, we present Christopher Leigh's paper on metal detectors in schools. Christopher's process in producing this paper has been discussed in various places throughout the text.

Leigh 1

Christopher Leigh

Professor Grosshans

English 110

September 1, 2001

    The Case Against Metal Detectors in Public Schools

     One of the most watched news stories of the last
decade took place on April 20, 1999, when two students
walked into their suburban Colorado high school and
shot twelve students and one teacher before shooting
themselves. The brutal slayings sent shock waves around
the country, leaving everyone asking the same
questions. What drove them to commit such a horrible
crime? What can we do to prevent something like this
from happening again?

     Panic over school safety has caused school boards
from coast to coast to take action. Though their use is
far from widespread, many schools are installing metal
detectors to keep guns and knives out of school.
Unfortunately, such measures do not address the causes
of violence and are simply an ill-considered quick fix
that may do more harm than good. Except for schools
with very severe threats of danger, metal detectors
should not be used because there is no basis for panic
and because there are other more effective and less
costly alternatives for violence prevention in schools.

     An important point to realize about school violence
is that the media have created a public outcry over

Leigh 2

school safety when in fact violent incidents are
extremely rare. The media have taken uncommon incidents
like the one at Columbine High and, according to school
psychologist Tony Del Prete, "overanalyze[d] and
sensationalize[d] them to the point of hysteria" (375).

Statistics and studies regarding school violence
are astonishingly conflicting and reported in
sensationalized ways. For example, one study conducted
by the Centers for Disease Control and Prevention
(United States) reports percentages of youths who
carried a gun or weapon to school from 1993 to 1999
(Table 1).

Table 22.1

Percentage of Youths Carrying Weapon or Gun to School,
1993–1999

	1993	1995	1997	1999
Carried a weapon	11.8%	9.8%	8.5%	6.9%
Carried a gun	7.9%	7.6%	5.9%	4.9%

Source: United States. Dept. of Health and Human
Services. Centers for Disease Control and Prevention.

These numbers can be cited in a frightening way ("In
1993 nearly 8 percent of teenagers reported carrying a
gun to school"). But it is also possible to display
these numbers in a graph (see Figure 1 and report them
in a more comforting way: "As shown in Figure 1,

Leigh 3

between 1993 and 1999 the number of students who
carried a gun to school has dropped 38 percent from 7.9
percent to 4.9 percent." Proponents of metal detectors
generally cite the figures in the most alarming way. For
example, advocates of metal detectors claim that
100,000 students carry guns to school each day (Wilson
and Zirkel 32), but they fail to note that these
statistics are based on data before 1993. Since 1993,
violence incidents in schools have declined steadily
each year, and youth homicide has dropped by over 50
percent (Barr 44). Of course it is true that weapons
and violence are undeniably present in schools. But the
percentage of schools in which violence is a recurring
problem is perceived to be exponentially larger than it
actually is. As a result, metal detectors have been
installed in schools that have had no problems with
weapons and violence simply to appease a panicked and
irrational public.

Figure 1. Percentage of Students Carrying a Gun or Other Weapon (1993–1999)

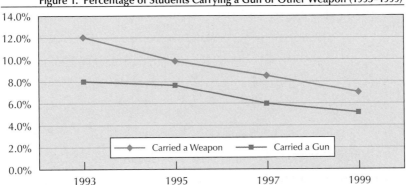

Leigh 4

Although metal detectors may seem like a quick and
tangible way to fight violence in schools, there are
many strong arguments against them based on students'
rights, the ease of defeating metal detectors, the
cost, and the psychological consequences that the
devices have on the school environment.

Many students believe that metal detectors violate
their rights. According to Arizona student Jon Gress,
the use of metal detectors

> invades the student's personal space,
>
> permitting anyone to see into their bags and
>
> purses. And if the detector went off, they
>
> would be required to subject their bags and
>
> body to a more thorough search. This act alone
>
> seems to infringe on the Fourth Amendment
>
> right of unwarranted search and seizure.

Another student, Lindsey, in a message posted on the
juvenile.net message board, says,

> [L]earning in such a threatening environment is
>
> not good for the students. . . . Does anyone
>
> else believe [besides me] that [use of metal
>
> detectors] disrupts the 'good' students and is
>
> [a] violation against student's rights . . . ?

So far the few court cases involving metal
detectors have ruled in favor of the schools, saying
that the benefit of public safety outweighs the right to
privacy. According to Michael Ferraraccio, the Supreme

Leigh 5

Court has said metal detectors in schools are legal.
However, he says, the Supreme Court decision "seemed to
indicate that generally some level of individualized
suspicion is necessary for a search to be reasonable
under the Fourth Amendment" (215). Although this case
does not address generalized metal detector searches,
legal experts believe that minimally invasive
"administrative" searches will be permitted by the
courts (Stefkovich and O'Brien 155). Judges liken them
to searches used in airports where people are searched
for weapons without reasonable suspicion. But I think
there is a key distinction between the two situations.
People are not required to travel through airports and
may walk away from a search, but students are required
by law to attend school and do not have the option of
refusing a search. Despite court rulings so far, many
students will continue to believe their constitutional
rights are being violated.

Besides possibly violating students' rights, metal
detectors have another serious problem: they can be
easily defeated. As <u>American School Board Journal</u>
contributor Donna Harrington-Lueker points out, schools
have many entrances that can't be locked due to fire
codes, windows that can be opened, "and legions of
youngsters arriving en masse at the same time each day"
(26). As she forcefully puts it, a "permanent, full
time metal detector at the front door isn't going to

Leigh 6

stop a youngster from passing a gun to a buddy through the side window" (26).

Also, metal detectors are often used only at the beginning of the day and sometimes not every day, which creates a false sense of security. In 1992, a student in a New York school was shot and killed on a day when the metal detectors were not in use (Yarbrough 586). Other shootings have taken place in schools despite the use of metal detectors. In Los Angeles, ten shooting incidents occurred after the school district began using metal detectors in schools, and not a single gun was confiscated through the searches (Stecklow A1). Similar conditions exist in a Washington, D.C., school district, which left one security guard "convinced that the [metal] detectors were useless" (Stecklow A6). Dennis Cunningham, a spokesman for a metal detector manufacturer, notes that the devices are a " 'Band Aid' solution that 'an innovative student' could foil 'very easily' " (qtd. in Stecklow A1). Some students interviewed note that "anyone could sneak in a knife . . . or a gun" (Stecklow A6). Even organizations that strongly advocate metal detectors, such as the National School Safety and Security Services, warn on their Web site that metal detectors are "not a panacea for solving safety concerns." Yet schools continue to use the devices despite the compelling evidence that indicates that they are not working.

Leigh 7

Another major concern surrounding the use of metal
detectors is cost. Airport-style units cost anywhere
between four and ten thousand dollars (Harrington-
Lueker 27). Handheld units are cheaper and therefore
considerably more common, but they are much more time
consuming and much less effective. Personnel are also
required to operate the machinery, and large schools
will often require upwards of fifteen officers to conduct
the searches. According to Harrington-Lueker, it is not
unusual for school districts to spend several million
dollars to implement a comprehensive metal detector
system in their schools (27). Parents and citizens
argue that the safety of our children shouldn't carry a
price tag, but when metal detectors prove ineffective,
alternatives need to be investigated.

Perhaps the most harmful effect of metal detectors
is their psychological impact on students subjected to
daily searches. Student essays posted on the Web, along
with dozens of postings on electronic message boards,
show students' dismay at being subjected to metal
detectors. "Guards, cameras, scanners, and metal
detectors every day take over our schools," a
Philadelphia high school senior complained to Venture
Lee. Another student, using the nickname "ummm" on a
message board, says:

> It's not actually walking through the metal
> detectors that I'm against. . . . . It's much

Leigh 8

more the principle of the thing. These damn

things, and the people the school board has

hired to run them, cost so much freaking money

that could be used for useful things. Metal

detectors will not stop a shooting in [this

high school]. If someone wanted to kill people

then they could just as well shoot people in

the damn line to get through them.

Metal detectors not only reinforce the feeling that

schools are unsafe, but they also instill a sense of

humiliation in students and, as a result, a feeling of

distrust between students and school administrators.

These feelings of distrust and susceptibility erode the

atmosphere of learning that is so important to a

student's education, and schools begin to feel more

like prisons than schools.

   If metal detectors are an inappropriate means to

curb violence in our schools, what is a better

approach? If we look again at student postings on the

Web, we see a consistently recurring suggestion:

friendlier schools, personal relationships, and better

counseling. As one student told Lee, "City kids get

metal detectors, suburban kids get counselors." Atlanta

high school senior Malik Barry-Buchanan was asked how

the school environment can be changed "so people don't

feel the need to bring a weapon to school." Here is his

answer:

Leigh 9

Well, for starters, we need to find ways for
students to respect each other, have teachers
go through training to encourage them to make
even the smallest attempt at getting in touch
with the students, and have school
administrators look at students as
independent, free-thinking young adults and
not 5-year-old rug rats.

In order to combat the problem of school violence
head-on, it is essential to provide students with
better counseling and to work towards improving the
overall school environment. Scott Poland, the president
of the National Association of School Psychologists,
writes that administrators need to do more to
personalize schools and provide better counseling
services to students who may be troubled (45). He
writes that most counselors are already overworked and
are required to do things such as scheduling that take
away from their attention to the students. Poland also
emphasizes that it is important for teachers to form
strong relationships with each and every student. He
suggests that teachers set aside a small amount of time
each day to interact with students, and discourages
schools from cutting extracurricular programs that may
help students feel connected to the school (46).

In my opinion, Poland's article offers the most
encouraging and perhaps the best advice for the

Leigh 10

prevention of school violence. Teachers might complain that they do not have the time to spend getting to know every student. But getting to know each student should be part of the job requirement. If teachers know their students on a personal level, they will be able to sense when a student is in trouble, reach out to that student, and create an atmosphere of care and trust rather than suspicion and surveillance.

Violence does undoubtedly exist in schools, but the percentage of schools where the level of violence justifies metal detectors is extremely small. The problem of school violence is simply a reflection of the high level of violence in American society in general, and the problem is not the schools, but society as a whole. Metal detectors may deter some students from bringing weapons to school, but they can't prevent violence and they create an atmosphere of fear and suspicion rather than trust and community. The key to preventing school violence is to focus on improving students' relationships with teachers and, more importantly, themselves, rather than treat them like potential criminals.

Leigh 11

Works Cited

Barr, Bob. "Liberal Media Adored Gun-Control Marchers."

    <u>Insight on the News</u> 5 June 2000: 44- . <u>ProQuest</u>.

    Lemieux Lib., Seattle U. 15 Aug. 2001

    <http://proquest.umi.com>.

Barry-Buchanan, Malik. "More Rules + More Security =

    Feelings of Safety." <u>Alternet.org</u> 16 Aug. 2001

    <http://alternet.org/print.html?StoryID=9623>.

Del Prete, Tony. "Unsafe Schools: Perception or

    Reality?" <u>Professional School Counseling</u> 3 (2000):

    375-76.

Ferraraccio, Michael. "Metal Detectors in the Public

    Schools: Fourth Amendment Concerns." <u>Journal of Law

    and Education</u> 28 (1999): 209-29.

Gress, Jon. "School Violence: How to Stop the Crime of

    Today's Youth." <u>Gecko--The Student Server</u> 5 May

    2000. 16 Aug. 2001 <http://gecko.gc.maricopa.edu/

    ~jtgress/argue2.htm>.

Harrington-Lueker, Donna. "Metal Detectors." <u>American

    School Board Journal</u> 179.5 (1992): 26-27.

Lee, Venture. "Detectors Alarm Some Students." <u>Said &

    Done</u>. Urban Journalism Workshop. Summer 2000. 16

    Aug. 2001 <http://ujw.philly.com/

    2000/detector.htm>.

Lindsey. "Re: School Security." Online posting. 23 Oct.

    1999. Juvenile Information Network. 16 Aug. 2001

    <http://www.juvenilenet.org/messages/27.html>.

Leigh 12

National School Safety and Security Services. "School

Security Equipment and Technology." 23 Aug. 2001

<http://www.schoolsecurity.org/

resources/security-equipment.html>.

Poland, Scott. "The Fourth R--Relationships." American

School Board Journal 187.3 (2000): 45-46.

Stecklow, Steve. "Metal Detectors Find a Growing

Market, But Not Many Guns." Wall Street Journal 7

Sept. 1993: A1+.

Stefkovich, Jacqueline, and G. M. O'Brien. "Students'

Fourth Amendment Rights and School Safety."

Education and Urban Society 29 (1997): 149-59.

Ummm. "Alright." Online posting. 27 May 2000. ezboard.

16 Aug. 2001 <http://pub6.ezboard.com/

fmastermanschool.showMessage?topicID=99.topic>.

United States. Dept. of Health and Human Services. Centers

for Disease Control and Prevention. "Youth Risk

Behavior Trends from CDC's 1991, 1993, 1995, 1997,

and 1999 Youth Risk Behavior Surveys." Adolescent and

School Health 6 Aug. 2001. 11 Aug. 2001

<http://www.cdc.gov/nccdphp/dash/yrbs/trend.htm>.

Wilson, Joseph M., and Perry Zirkel. "When Guns Come to

School." American School Board Journal 181.1

(1994): 32-34.

Yarbrough, Jonathan W. "Are Metal Detectors the Answer

to Handguns in Public Schools?" Journal of Law and

Education 22 (1993): 584-87.

Understanding APA Style and Formatting

In many respects, the APA style and the MLA style are similar and the basic logic is the same. In the APA system, the list where readers can find full bibliographic information is titled "References"; as in MLA format, it includes only the sources cited in the body of the paper. Pay careful attention to possibly unfamiliar punctuation and format details in the models we present in this section. The most distinguishing features of APA style are highlighted in the following list:

- APA style emphasizes dates of books and articles and de-emphasizes the names of authors. Therefore the date of publication appears in parenthetical citations and is the second item mentioned in each entry in the "References" list.

  For an example of a student paper in APA style, see the experimental report by Brittany Tinker, Trevor Tsuchikawa, and Tatiana Whizar on pp. 277–289.

- Only published or retrievable documents are included in the "References" list. Personal correspondence, e-mail messages, interviews, and lectures or speeches are referenced only through in-text citations.
- APA style uses fewer abbreviations and spells out the complete names of university presses. It uses an ampersand (&) instead of the word *and* for items in a series in both the reference list and in-text citations.
- APA style uses italics rather than underlining for titles and capitalizes only the first word of titles and subtitles of books and articles. It doesn't place titles of articles in quotation marks.
- APA style uses only an initial for authors' or editors' first names in citations.
- APA style calls for every page of a periodical article to be listed in a reference, even when the pages are not continuous.
- APA style streamlines the presentation of information about electronic documents into sentence-like statements at the end of a citation, requiring inclusion of a URL for Web documents but not for databases.
- For electronic documents without page numbers, APA suggests citing material by heading labels if they are available, and permits the writer to count paragraphs within a section. Paragraphs are cited with a ¶ symbol before the number. A parenthetical citation might then read: (Elrod, 2005, Introduction section, ¶ 7).
- APA style has a distinctive format for title pages and frequently includes an "Abstract" of the paper immediately following the title page.
- Page numbers are placed at the top right-hand margin and are preceded by a "running head" (a short version of the title).
- APA uses block indentation for quotations when they are longer than forty words. Quotations shorter than forty words are worked into your own text using quotation marks as in other systems.

APA Formatting for In-Text Citations

When you make an in-text citation in APA style, you place inside the parentheses the author's last name and the year of the source as well as the page number if a particular passage or table is cited. The elements in the citation are separated by commas, and a "p." or "pp." precedes the page number(s). If a source has more than one author, use an ampersand (&) to join their names. When the author is mentioned in an attributive tag, include only the date (and page if applicable) in the parenthetical citation. The following examples show parenthetical documentation with and without attributive tags according to APA style:

> The Spanish tried to reduce the status of women who had been able to do business, get divorced, and sometimes become village chiefs (Karnow, 1989, p. 41).
>
> According to Karnow (1989), the Spanish tried to reduce the status of women who had been able to do business, get divorced, and sometimes become village chiefs (p. 41).

Citing from an Indirect Source

Ideally, if you want to use a quotation or data cited by one of your sources, you should track down the original source. When this isn't possible, APA style calls for using the phrase "as cited in" within the parenthetical reference. Only the indirect source would appear in the list of references. Here is an example:

> Morrison's data from the 1980s provides multiple examples of the phenomenon (as cited in Stephanbach, 2004, p. 828).

Documenting Sources in a "References" List (APA)

The APA "References" list at the end of a paper presents entries alphabetically in a hanging indentation format like that of MLA style. A typical entry would look like this:

Smith, R. (1995). *Body image in Western cultures, 1750–present.* London: Bonanza Press.

Two or more listings for one author

If you cite more than one item for an author, repeat the author's name each time and arrange the items in chronological order, beginning with the earliest. In cases where two works by an author appeared in the same year, arrange them in the list alphabetically by title, and then add a lowercase "a" or "b" (etc.) after the date so that you can distinguish between them in the in-text citations. As illustration, the following parenthetical citations refer to the hypothetical book and article cited in the sample entries that follow them:

(Smith, 1999a)

(Smith, 1999b)

Smith, R. (1999a). *Body image in non-Western cultures.* London: Bonanza Press.

Smith, R. (1999b). Eating disorders reconsidered. *Journal of Appetite Studies, 45,* 295–300.

APA Citation Models

Books

One author

Brumberg, J. J. (1997). *The body project: An intimate history of American girls.* New York: Vintage.

Two or more authors

Dombrowski, D. A., & Deltete, R. J. (2000). *A brief, liberal, Catholic defense of abortion.* Urbana: University of Illinois Press.

Belenky, M., Clinchy, B. M., Goldberger, N. R., & Tarule, J. M. (1986). *Women's ways of knowing: The development of self, voice, and mind.* New York: Basic Books.

APA style uses "et al." only for books with more than six authors.

Second, later, or revised edition

Montagu, A. (1986). *Touching: The human significance of the skin* (3rd ed.). New York: Perennial Press.

The number of the edition goes in parentheses. One could also say "Rev. ed." for "Revised edition."

Republished book (for example, a paperback published after the original hardback edition or a modern edition of an older work)

Hill, C. (1991). *The world turned upside down: Radical ideas during the English revolution.* London: Penguin. (Original work published 1972)

The in-text citation should read: (Hill, 1972/1991).

Wollstonecraft, M. (1995). *The vindication of the rights of woman, with strictures on political and moral subjects.* Rutland, VT: Tuttle. (Original work published 1792)

The in-text citation should read: (Wollstonecraft, 1792/1995).

Multivolume work

Churchill, W. S. (1956–1958). *A history of the English-speaking peoples* (Vols. 1–4). New York: Dodd, Mead.

Citation for all the volumes together. The in-text citation should read: (Churchill, 1956–1958).

Churchill, W. S. (1957). *A history of the English-speaking peoples: Vol. 4. The great democracies.* New York: Dodd, Mead.

Citation for a specific volume. The in-text citation should read: (Churchill, 1957).

Article in reference work

Ling, T. O. (1970). Buddhism in Burma. In S. G. F. Brandon (Ed.), *Dictionary of comparative religion.* New York: Scribner's.

Translation

De Beauvoir, S. (1961). *The second sex* (H. M. Parshley, Trans.). New York: Bantam Books. (Original work published 1949)

The in-text citation should read: (De Beauvoir, 1949/1961).

Corporate author (a commission, committee, or other group)

American Red Cross. (1993). *Standard first aid.* St. Louis, MO: Mosby Lifeline.

Anonymous author

The New Yorker cartoon album: 1975–1985. (1987). New York: Penguin Books.

The in-text citation may be a shortened version of the title such as: (*New Yorker,* 1987).

Edited Anthologies

Citing the editor

O'Connell, D. F., & Alexander, C. N. (Eds.). (1994). *Self recovery: Treating addictions using transcendental meditation and Maharishi Ayur-Veda.* New York: Haworth Press.

Citing an individual article

Royer, A. (1994). The role of the transcendental meditation technique in promoting smoking cessation: A longitudinal study. In D. F. O'Connell & C. N. Alexander (Eds.), *Self recovery: Treating addictions using transcendental meditation and Maharishi Ayur-Veda* (pp. 221–239). New York: Haworth Press.

The pattern is as follows: Author of article. (Year of publication). Title of article. In Name of editor (Ed.), *Title of anthology* (pp. inclusive page numbers of article). Place of publication: Name of press.

Articles in Scholarly Journals Accessed in Print

Scholarly journal that numbers pages continuously

Barton, E. L. (1993). Evidentials, argumentation, and epistemological stance. *College English, 55,* 745–769.

The pattern is as follows: Author. (Year of publication). Article title. *Name of Journal, volume number,* inclusive page numbers. Note that the volume number is italicized along with the title of the journal.

Scholarly journal that restarts page numbering with each issue

Pollay, R. W., Lee, J. S., & Carter-Whitney, D. (1992). Separate, but not equal: Racial segmentation in cigarette advertising. *Journal of Advertising, 21*(1), 45–57.

The citation includes the issue number in parentheses as well as the volume number. Note that the issue number and the parentheses are *not* italicized.

Articles in Magazines and Newspapers Accessed in Print

Magazine article with named author

Snyder, R. L. (2001, August—September). A daughter of Cambodia remembers: Loung Ung's journey. *Ms., 12,* 62–67.

Hall, S. S. (2001, March 11). Prescription for profit. *New York Times Magazine,* 40–45, 59, 91–92, 100.

The pattern is as follows: Author. (Year, Month [Day]). Title of article. *Name of Magazine, volume number [if stated in magazine],* inclusive pages. If page numbers are discontinuous, identify every page, separating numbers with a comma.

Magazine article without named author

Daddy, daddy. (2001, July 30). *New Republic, 225,* 12–13.

Review of book or film

Schwarz, B. (2001, November). A bit of bunting: A new history of the British empire elevates expediency to principle [Review of the book *Ornamentalism: How the British saw their empire*]. *Atlantic Monthly, 288,* 126–135.

Kaufman, S. (2001, July 30). Polishing a gem [Review of the motion picture *The blue angel*]. *New Republic, 225,* 28–29.

Newspaper article

Henriques, D. B. (1998, September 27). Hero's fall teaches Wall Street a lesson. *Seattle Times,* pp. A1, A24.

Newspaper editorial

Dr. Frankenstein on the hill [Editorial]. (2002, May 18). *The New York Times,* p. A22.

Letter to the editor of a magazine or newspaper

Tomsovic, K. (1998, July 13). Culture clash [Letter to the editor]. *The New Yorker,* p. 7.

Print Articles or Books Downloaded from a Database

Print article downloaded from licensed database

Watanabe, M. (2003). Zoos act as sentinels for infectious diseases. *Bioscience, 53,* 792. Retrieved July 26, 2004, from ProQuest database.

Note the commas before and after the year in the retrieval statement.

Broadcast transcript retrieved from licensed database

Conan, N. (Anchor), & Telhami, S. (Guest). (2004, May 4). Arab media [Radio transcript]. *Talk of the nation.* Retrieved July 31, 2004, from LexisNexis database.

Reference material retrieved from licensed database

Cicada. (2004). *Encyclopaedia Britannica.* Retrieved July 31, 2004, from Britannica Online database.

The *Publication Manual of the American Psychological Association,* 5th ed., has no model format for an online reference database, so we followed the manual's advice to adapt the format of similar items.

Papers and monographs from an information service

Information services such as ERIC (Educational Resources Information Center) or NTIS (National Technical Information Service) provide material to your library on microfiche or online, offering indexes on CD-ROM or online. Much of the material from these services has not been published in major journals or magazines. Frequently they are typescripts of conference papers or other scholarly work disseminated on microfiche.

Coll, R. K., Tofield, S., Vyle, B., & Bolstad, R. (2003, March). *Free-choice learning at a metropolitan zoo.* Paper presented at the annual meeting of the National Association for Research in Science Teaching, Philadelphia, PA. (ERIC Document Reproduction Service No. ED477832)

If you retrieve the document online, add a retrieval statement indicating the name of the database and the date retrieved, as in the preceding examples.

Web and Internet Sources

Documents within a Web site

Provide corporate authors when a document does not list an individual author. Use "n.d." if no publication date is provided.

Marks, J. (n.d.). Overview: Letter from the president. Retrieved June 25, 2004, from the Search for Common Ground Web site: http://www.sfcg.org/sfcg/sfcg_overview.html

United States Institute of Peace. (2000). Advances in understanding international peacemaking. Retrieved May 25, 2004, from http://www.usip.org/pubs/summaries/adv_intl.html

Article from a newspaper site

Thevenot, B. (2004, July 31). Once in a blue moon. *Times Picayune* [New Orleans]. Retrieved July 31, 2004, from http://www.nola.com/t-p/

Broadcast transcript from a Web site

Michels, S. (Correspondent), & Warner, M. (Anchor). (2004, July 28). The politics of 9/11 [Television transcript]. *Newshour with Jim Lehrer.* Retrieved July 31, 2004, from the Online Newshour Website: http://www.pbs.org/newshour/bb/terrorism/july-dec04/9-11_7-28.html

Because the APA *Manual* doesn't have a model for broadcast transcripts, we modified the format for television broadcasts by adding identifying labels.

Article from a scholarly E-journal

Welch, J. R., & Riley, R. (2001). Reclaiming land and spirit in the western Apache homeland. *American Indian Quarterly, 25,* 5–14. Retrieved December 19, 2001, from http://muse.jhu.edu/journals/american_indian_quarterly/v025/25.1welch.pdf

E-book

Hoffman, F. W. (1981). *The literature of rock: 1954–1978.* Retrieved December 19, 2001, from http://www.netlibrary.com/ebook_info.asl?product_id=24355

The *Publication Manual of the American Psychological Association,* 5th ed., has no example of an E-book. We followed the manual's advice about how to proceed when an unusual case arises.

E-mail, interviews, and personal correspondence

APA guidelines limit the "References" list to published or retrievable information. Cite personal correspondence in the body of your text, but not in the References list: "Daffinrud (personal communication, December 12, 2001) claims that. . . ."

Online posting to a Listserv, bulletin board, newsgroup, or blog

CalEnergyGuy. (2004, July 27). Energy crisis impacts on the economy: Changes since
 2001 [Blog posting]. Retrieved August 1, 2004, from the Web site of the California
 Energy Blog: http://calenergy.blogspot.com/2004_07_01_calenergy_archive.html

We have again followed the APA's advice to interpolate a format from similar models.

Miscellaneous Sources

Television program

Bochco, S., & Milch, D. (Directors). (2001, November 6). Lie like a rug [Television series
 episode]. In *NYPD blue*. New York: American Broadcasting Company.

Film

Madden, J. (Director). (1998). *Shakespeare in love* [Motion picture]. United States:
 Universal Miramax.

Sound recording

Dwarf Music. (1966). Rainy day woman [Recorded by B. Dylan]. On *Bob Dylan MTV
 unplugged* [CD]. New York: Columbia. (1995)

Follow this format: Writer of song or copyright holder. (Date of copyright). Title of song [Recorded by artist if different from writer]. On *Title of album* [Medium such as CD, record, or cassette]. Location: Label. (Date of album if different from date of song)

Unpublished paper presented at a meeting

Sharples, M. (2001, June 20). *Authors of the future*. Keynote address presented at
 Conference of European Teachers of Academic Writing, Groningen, the
 Netherlands.

Government publications

O'Toole, M. (2000). *The school shooter: A threat assessment perspective*. Washington, DC:
 U.S. Federal Bureau of Investigation. Retrieved August 16, 2001, from
 http://www.fbi.gov/publications/school/school2.pdf

Student Example of an APA-Style Paper

An example of a paper in APA style is shown on pages 277–289.

Index